王泉　编著

Learn English from World Culture

这里是非洲

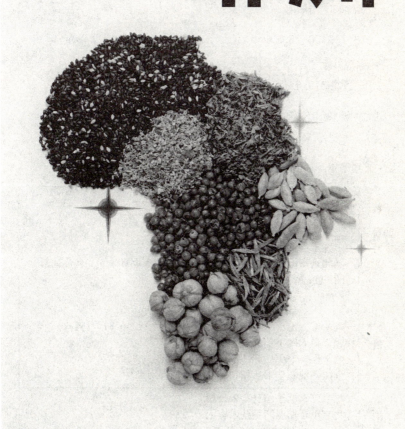

中国水利水电出版社
www.waterpub.com.cn

内容提要

　　文化大餐，至尊阅读——阅读可以升华人格情操，其更本质、更核心的意义在于培养学习者的兴趣，而兴趣才是一切学习者学习的动力、成功的源泉。

　　"我是英语文化书"系列正是这样一套让人感觉妙趣横生、受益匪浅的英语读物。本套丛书包括《每天读点世界文化：这里是非洲》《每天读点世界文化：这里是美国》《每天读点世界文化：这里是英国》《每天读点世界文化：这里是欧洲》《每天读点世界文化：这里是加拿大》等。本书是一本浓缩世界文化精髓的知识储备书，旨在让读者在品味国外文化魅力的过程中，熟悉英语的逻辑思维和文化背景，从而适应深入沟通和交流的需要，使英语学习事半功倍。

图书在版编目（ＣＩＰ）数据

　　每天读点世界文化　这里是非洲 / 王泉编著. -- 北京：中国水利水电出版社，2014.12
　　（我是英语文化书）
　　ISBN 978-7-5170-2588-7

　　Ⅰ. ①每… Ⅱ. ①王… Ⅲ. ①英语－语言读物②文化史－非洲 Ⅳ. ①H319.4：K

　　中国版本图书馆CIP数据核字(2014)第229323号

策划编辑：陈艳蕊　责任编辑：邓建梅　封面设计：潘国文

书　　名	我是英语文化书 **每天读点世界文化：这里是非洲**	
作　　者	王泉　编著	
出版发行	中国水利水电出版社 　（北京市海淀区玉渊潭南路 1 号 D 座　100038） 网　址：www.waterpub.com.cn E-mail: mchannel@263.net（万水） 　　　　　sales@waterpub.com.cn 电　话：（010）68367658（发行部）、82562819（万水）	
经　　售	北京科水图书销售中心（零售） 电　话：（010）88383994、63202643、68545874 全国各地新华书店和相关出版物销售网点	
排　　版	北京万水电子信息有限公司	
印　　刷	北京正合鼎业印刷技术有限公司	
规　　格	170mm×240mm　16 开本　19.5 印张　415 千字	
版　　次	2014 年 12 月第 1 版　2014 年 12 月第 1 次印刷	
印　　数	0001—5000 册	
定　　价	39.90 元	

前　言

"Think globally, act multiculturally!" ——打造适应国际竞争、充满自信、勇于进取的你!

初学英语时,每个月都感觉得到自己的进步,每个学期都切实掌握了新的内容。然而进入大学、特别是进入社会后,英语学习久了反而不易再有很大的突破,买再多的单词书、语法书来看也只能帮助我们通过考试,而对提高我们实际的英语应用水平起不到什么作用。更糟糕的是,我们对英语的热情,也渐渐被这种挫败和迷茫磨灭。产生如此结果的原因主要有以下三个:缺乏英语的语感,没有英语的语言环境,不熟悉英语的思维逻辑和文化背景。而这三个原因中最重要的就是"对英语思维逻辑和文化背景的不熟悉"。语言是思维的工具,也是思维的轨迹。不同的语言承载着不同的文化,不同文化背景的人其思维习惯和思维特点也必然存在着差异,而思维方式的差异也造成了文化和语言的差异。

若想精通一门语言,没有对其文化背景的深入了解,恐怕永远难登"大雅之堂"。文化背景的不同,会导致不同国家的人对同一个词、同一句话展开的联想也不尽相同,由此也就会产生这样那样的误解。例如"老"与"old",中国人历来有"尊老敬老"的传统美德,在我们看来,长者不仅是智慧的化身,也是威望的象征,"姜还是老的辣"正是对这一点最好的体现。然而西方国家却极少有人愿意用"old"来形容自己,在他们看来,"old"不仅表示年龄老,更表示能力不济。类似的还有,与刚上完课的教师在走廊上相遇,中国人可能互相会说"早上好,辛苦您了"等问候,但如果你对欧美教师说"Good morning, you must be tired after the class.",他们会觉得你是怀疑其能力不济,连上一堂课都会觉得累。这就是中西文化背景和思维意识的差异。因此,与外国友人的交流中不仅要注意表达的准确性,还要注意中西文化间的差异。在全球化、国际化的大趋势下,英语学习者如果仍停留在日常生活的层次上,必将难以适应深入沟通和交流的需要。

阅读可以升华人格情操,增长知识,提高语言文化的综合素质,其更本质、更核心的意义在于培养学习者的兴趣,而兴趣才是一切学习者的学习动力、成功源泉。"我是英语文化书"系列丛书正是这样一套让人感觉妙趣横生、受益匪浅的英语读物。本套丛书分为《每天读点世界文化:这里是非洲》《每天读点世界文化:这里是英国》《每天读点世界文化:这里是美国》《每天读点世界文化:这里是澳洲》《每天读点世界文化:这里是加拿大》等书,书中为读者奉上原汁原味的人文阅读精华,让读者在学习英语的同时,又能品味西方文化的独特魅力。

编者

2014年11月

编委

董立新	王　迪	袁　丹	武　超	徐永生	胡玲玲
范　超	王　莹	王　慧	张　静	彭亚平	武　雯
朱诗晴	徐　晨	沈楠忻	常　成	张晓菲	刘晓芳
许　文	周　芬	华　巧	曾　莹	徐　焱	宋晓冬
胡　庆	李月英				

目录
Contents

每天读点世界文化
Africa

第六章　　你不可不到的非洲城市 ……………………… 149

第七章　　你不可不知的非洲动植物 ……………………… 175

广阔的非洲大地绚丽多彩，极具自然之美。它东临印度洋，西接大西洋，上承地中海与欧洲相望，东北以红海和著名的苏伊士运河与亚洲相邻；地形以高原为主；属热带雨林和热带草原气候。非洲南北跨越了72个纬度，最长达8100公里；东西约跨69个经度，最大宽度7500公里。赤道横贯非洲大陆中部，将其一分为二。非洲是世界第二大洲，面积达3020万平方公里，人口约5.53亿。

本章里，编者将呈现给你10处不得不说的非洲自然景观。有人说非洲因自然、原始而美丽。其实，美不美，任评说。

第一章

你不可不知的非洲自然景观

01 世界最长河——尼罗河

The Nile is famous as the longest river in the world. The river got its name from the Greek word "Neilos", which means valley. The Nile floods the lands in Egypt, leaving behind black **sediment**. That's why the ancient Egyptians named the river "Ar", meaning black.

The Nile River is actually 6,695 kilometers (4,184 miles) long. With such a long length, the Nile River is **speculated** to be the longest river in the world. The Amazon River runs a very close second, although it has been difficult to determine which is actually longer. While the Nile River is often associated with Egypt, it actually touches Ethiopia, Zaire, Kenya, Uganda, Tanzania, Rwanda, Burundi and Sudan, as well as Egypt. It's only recent that the first known **navigation** team successfully followed the river from beginning to its end.

The Nile River has played an extremely important role in the civilization, life and history of the Egyptian nation. One of the most well known river Nile facts is the river's ability to produce extremely fertile soil, which made it easy for cities and civilizations to spring up alongside the banks of the Nile. The fertile soil is contributed by the annual spring floods, when the Nile River overflows onto the banks. Much of the Egyptian nation consists of dry desert land. Throughout most of the year, very little rain falls on Egyptian deserts. This has remained true for thousands of years. The abundant Nile River provided much needed irrigation, even in ancient times. This waterway also provided a source of drinking water, and source of irrigation for farming as well as papyrus reeds that could be used for a variety of purposes such as paper and building materials.

The Nile Crocodile has been a major component of the Egyptian culture and way of life since the first

尼罗河有"世界最长河"之称，其名称来源于希腊语"Neilos"，意思为"山谷"。尼罗河经常泛滥淹没埃及的土地，留下黑色的沉积物。古埃及人因此将它命名为"Ar"，意思为"黑色"。

尼罗河实际长约6695公里（4184英里）。正因如此之长，它被看作是世界最长河。亚马逊河紧随其后，是世界第二长河，实际上很难决定到底哪条河更长一些。人们经常将尼罗河与埃及联系起来，事实上，它除了埃及之外，还流经埃塞俄比亚、扎伊尔、肯尼亚、乌干达、坦桑尼亚、卢旺达、布隆迪和苏丹。第一个航海队从头到尾沿此河流进行航行也是近几年的事。

尼罗河在埃及人的文明、生活和历史中扮演着非常重要的角色。其中最为人所熟知的就是尼罗河可以形成十分肥沃的土壤，这为尼罗河两岸城市和文明的兴起提供了条件。每年春天尼罗河泛滥，淹没河岸两旁的土地，就形成了肥沃的土壤。而埃及大部分土地都是干旱的沙漠，这些地方几千年来终年少雨。即使是在古代，充沛的尼罗河水也提供了必要的灌溉水源。同时，它还为人们提供了饮用水，为农业和纸莎草提供了灌溉用水。纸莎草有很多用途，可用来造纸和生产建筑材料。

自从第一批埃及人在尼罗河两岸肥沃的土地上定居以来，尼

Egyptians settled along the fertile banks of the Nile. Most Nile Crocodiles are approximately 4 meters in length, although some have been reported as longer. The animals make their nests along the banks of the Nile River, where the female may lay up to 60 eggs at one time. About three months later the babies are born and are taken to the water by their mother. They will remain with her for at least two years before reaching maturity.

Not only is the Nile River one of the main rivers of Egypt, but many would in fact; say it is the primary river of Egypt. The Nile River has certainly played a critical role in the history of this mysterious nation.

Today, **exotic** and **sophisticated** cities like Cairo grace the banks of the Nile River, as they have for thousands of years. Individuals interested in experiencing the Nile up close and personal can journey along the famous river aboard riverboats and **cruise**s that **depart** from **numerous** cities along the bank.

罗鳄就成为了埃及文明和生活方式的重要组成部分。大部分尼罗鳄长约4米，据报道，有些尼罗鳄甚至更长。 这种生物栖息在尼罗河两岸，雌性尼罗鳄一次可产卵60枚。大约三个月后，小鳄鱼就会孵化出来，由母亲带至水中。在完全长大之前，它们至少会有两年的时间留在母亲身边。

尼罗河是埃及的主要河流之一，埃及境内还有很多其他河流，但尼罗河是埃及最主要的河流。毫无疑问，尼罗河在这个神秘国度的历史长河中起到了非常重要的作用。

今天，像开罗一样繁华的大都市使尼罗河两岸绚丽夺目，几千年来都是这样。尼罗河两岸的城市周围停泊着许多巡航船，想要近距离亲身体验尼罗河的人可以乘坐这些船只尽情欣赏沿岸美景。

词汇 VOCABULARY

sediment：沉积物	sophisticated：复杂的
speculate：推断、推测	cruise：巡洋舰
navigation：航海	depart：离开
exotic：别致的、漂亮的	numerous：大量的

背景知识 PROFILE

壮观的卫星地球照片

美国宇航局网站上一个将不同的卫星及各类太空任务拍摄的地球图片收集到一起的栏目——"地球天文台"评选出了10张最壮观的卫星地球照片。其中就有尼罗河沉积平原。苏丹南部的喀土穆是白尼罗河和蓝尼罗河汇合之处，在此处的阿尔戈齐拉州形成了壮观的沉积平原。

02 非洲屋脊——乞力马扎罗山

Mount Kilimanjaro lies on the border of Tanzania and Kenya, just south of the Equator. To the west lies the Great African **Rift** Valley, created by tremendous **tectonic** forces which also gave birth to a string of other volcanoes. One of these, Mount Kenya, was originally much higher than Mount Kilimanjaro.

The three **summit**s of Mount Kilimanjaro, Shira, Kibo and Mawenzi are all of very recent origin. Shira and Mawenzi both have suffered considerable **erosion** and only **jagged** peaks remain. Kibo, the central, youngest and highest peak has survived as an almost perfect cone.

Although East Africa and nearby Olduvai Gorge is thought to be the **cradle** of mankind it is unlikely that early man would have been attracted to the steep and cold slopes of Kilimanjaro at a time when it was probably very active and dangerous. A Wachagga legend talks of Mawenzi receiving fire for its pipe from his younger brother Kibo. The Wachagga who live on the fertile volcanic soils around the base of the mountain probably only came to the area about 300 years ago thus this legend suggests very recent activity. Another of their legends talks of demons and evil spirits living on the mountain and guarding **immense** treasures. Stories are told of a king who decided to go to the top, few of his party survived and those who did had damaged arms and legs.

Arab and Chinese traders and historians make mention of a giant mountain lying inland from Mombasa or Zanzibar but few early traders ventured into the interior of the continent. Slave traders passed below it and sometimes **raid**ed the villages of the Wachagga but it was not till the middle of the 19th century that a more serious interest was taken in the

乞力马扎罗山坐落于坦桑尼亚和肯尼亚边境，正好位于赤道南部。西部是由地壳运动的巨大力量而形成的东非大裂谷。同时，地壳运动还形成了其他火山。其中之一就是肯尼亚山，最初它比乞力马扎罗山还要高得多。

乞力马扎罗山的三个顶峰分别是希拉、基博和马温西，它们都是近代才形成的。希拉峰和马温西峰都经过了较大程度的侵蚀，只剩下参差不齐的峰顶了。位于中央的基博峰年代最新，也最高，几乎完美地保留了最初的圆锥形。

尽管东非及其附近的奥杜威峡谷被认为是人类文明的摇篮，但早期的人类恐怕不可能将陡峭寒冷的乞力马扎罗山归于此类，因为那时它很可能还在活动，非常危险。当地瓦恰人的一个传说中提到马温西峰正在从它的弟弟基博峰那里取火点烟。瓦恰人居住在山峰底部肥沃的土地上，他们来到这里也仅仅只有大约三百年的时间，因此这个传说表明这座山在近代曾经活动过。还有一个传说是关于住在山上守护大量宝物的妖魔鬼怪的。此外，很多故事讲到了有一个国王决心到达山顶，结果整个队伍几乎无一生还，而那些回来的人不是断了手臂就是断了腿。

阿拉伯和中国商人以及历史学家们都曾经提到在蒙巴萨和桑给巴尔地区有一个巨大的山脉，但是早期的商人中几乎没有人敢冒险到达大陆内部。奴隶贩子曾从山下经过，有时甚

mountain and attempts were made to scale it.

In 1848 Johann Rebmann a missionary from Gerlingen in Germany while crossing the plains of Tsavo saw Mount Kilimanjaro. His guide talked of the cold, and of tales how a group of **porter**s were sent up the mountain to bring back the silver or other treasures from the summit. They came back only with water. Rebmann's report stimulated great interest in Germany and in the following years several expeditions were organised; first by Baron von Decken then later by Dr. Hans Meyer who finally stood on the highest point on the 5th of October 1889.

Mount Kilimanjaro, the highest mountain in Africa, now attracts many thousands of walkers each year. On the 1st of January 2000 over 1000 people reached the summit to see the sun rise over a new **Millennium**.

至突袭瓦恰人的村庄。但直到19世纪中期，人们才开始对这座山脉着实产生了兴趣，并试图进行攀登。

1848年，一位名叫约翰·雷布曼来自德国盖林根的传教士经过察沃平原时，看到了乞力马扎罗山。他的向导给他讲述了这里的寒冷以及一群搬运工曾被派往山上从山顶取回银子及其他珠宝，结果却只带回来水的故事。雷德曼的报告引起了德国人的强烈兴趣，在接下来的几年中，先后有几个探险队被组织起来，第一个是由戴肯男爵组织的，之后是由汉斯·迈尔博士组织的。迈尔于1889年10月5日首次登上最高峰。

乞力马扎罗山是非洲的最高峰，每年都吸引着成千上万的游客。2000年1月1日，有1000多人爬到顶峰迎接千禧年的日出。

背景知识 PROFILE

乞力马扎罗的雪

艺术作品

《乞力马扎罗的雪》是海明威的一部中篇小说，也是其最优秀的文学作品之一。后被改编成电影。

故事通过睡梦中和醒时的两股意识流，相互交叉，相互转化；充分地描写了"死"，并采用了象征手法进一步深化了死亡。

海明威的创作态度十分严肃，一贯反复地修改自己的作品。他喜爱马克·吐温，并深受其影响。文体清秀、流畅明亮，这也是他语言艺术的风格。然而，最突出反映他创作特色的，还是作品中大多数人物都有颇带孤独感的内心独白，即长篇的心理描写，实际上也就是后来发展称为"意识流"的手法。从思想意义上看，他的人物或多或少地存在着悲观主义色彩，反映了他世界观的局限。

电影《乞力马扎罗的雪》是根据海明威作品改编的，是由格里高利·派克(Gregory Peck)、苏珊·海华德(Susan Hayward)、艾娃·加德纳(Ava Gardner)主演。本片曾获最佳摄影金像奖及年度十大卖座影片提名。

现实

乞力马扎罗山有两个主峰，一个叫乌呼鲁，另一个叫马文济，两峰之间有一个10多公里长的马鞍形的山脊相连。根据气候的山地垂直分布规律，乞力马扎罗山的基本气候由山脚向上至山顶，分别是热带雨林气候至冰原气候。风景包括赤道至两极的基本植被。

近年来，海拔5896米的非洲第一高峰——乞力马扎罗山山顶积雪融化、冰川消融现象非常严重，在过去的80年内冰川已经萎缩了80%以上。有环境专家指出，乞力马扎罗雪顶可能将在10年内彻底融化消失，届时乞力马扎罗山独有的"赤道雪山"奇观将与人类告别。

03 惊异而神奇——东非大裂谷

Stretching for over 3,600 miles (5,950 km) across the African continent, from the Dead Sea in Southwest Asia to Mozambique in Southeast Africa, the Great Rift Valley is truly an amazing natural attraction. The Great Rift Valley is a result of tectonic activty in the earth's **crust** and was created due to drifting and separation of the African and Arabian tectonic plates around 35 million years ago. Its width widely varies according to changing location, ranging between 31km and 100 km. The Great Rift Valley is home to spectacular **glacier**s, volcanoes, depressions and lakes, offering some of the most breathtaking scenery on the earth. The Great

东非大裂谷从亚洲西南部的死海一直延伸至非洲东南部的莫桑比克，全长3600英里（5950千米），直跨非洲大陆，是一处令人叹为观止的自然景观。东非大裂谷是地壳运动的结果，由3500万年前非洲板块和阿拉伯板块的飘移和分离造成的。裂谷宽度由于所在位置不同变化幅度很大，在31千米到100千米之间。东非大裂谷内有很多冰川、火山、洼地和湖泊，形成了世界上最壮观的景色。东非大裂谷还因其独特的生态系统而闻

Rift Valley is also renowned for its unique ecosystem, having some of the finest wildlife parks in Africa. The Great Rift Valley in Africa also offers excellent conditions for hiking, **trekking**, rock climbing, mountain biking and much more. So whether you're an adventure seeker, a wildlife enthusiast or nature lover, the Great Rift Valley in Africa is truly a destination to be in, at least once in your life.

Though one can find breathtaking scenery all along the Great Rift Valley, it's at its scenic best in Kenya. Near the famous Nakuru Lake its width is around 45 km, where you can see both walls of this astonishing **fissure** on the planet earth. Among must-see attractions in the Great Rift Valley in Kenya include the Lake Naivasha, Lake Elementeita, Lake Baringo, all known for their scenic beauty as well as rich and diverse **avifauna**, including **flamingoes**. Other major tourist attractions in the valley are the Mount Longonot National Park, Lake Nakuru National Park, Hell's Gate National Park, Lake Bogoria National Park and the renowned Samburu Game **Reserve**. The wildlife in the Great Rift Valley region is unique and varied that include the endangered Colobus Monkey, Black Rhinos, Grevy's Zebras, **Reticulated** Giraffe, Zebra Mouse, and Lesser Kudu Antelopes. Lions, Elephants, Leopards, Giraffes, Gazelles, Hippos, Antelopes, Monkeys, Buffalos, and Impalas are also commonly found in the region. Thousands of adventure seekers and nature lovers travel to the Great African Rift Valley from all over the world every year.

名于世，它拥有非洲最好的野生动物公园。此外，东非大裂谷还为徒步旅行、长途旅行、攀岩、山地自行车运动以及其他运动提供了绝佳条件。所以，无论你是热衷冒险、热爱野生动物还是热爱自然，东非大裂谷都确实是一个好去处，至少值得你在一生中去一次。

人们可以沿着东非大裂谷发现很多美丽壮观的景色，然而最好的景点位于肯尼亚境内。在纳库鲁湖附近，裂谷的宽度约45千米，在这里可以看到地球裂缝的两壁。肯尼亚境内的东非大裂谷有几处不得不看的地方，包括奈瓦沙湖、艾尔曼提亚湖和巴林戈湖，这些地方都因其独特的自然美景以及丰富多样的鸟类而闻名，其中还有火烈鸟。其他主要的旅游景点有隆格诺特火山国家公园、纳库鲁湖国家公园、海耳的盖特国家公园、波咯尼亚湖国家公园以及著名的撒布尔日动物保护区。在东非大裂谷生存的野生动物非常独特而且品种繁多，包括濒危的疣猴、黑犀牛、细纹斑马、网纹长颈鹿、斑马鼠等。狮子、大象、豹子、长颈鹿、瞪羚、河马、羚羊、猴子、水牛以及黑斑羚都是这个地区常见的动物。每年都有成千上万的冒险家和自然爱好者来到东非大裂谷参观游览。

词汇 VOCABULARY

crust：地壳	avifauna：鸟类
glacier：冰川	flamingo：火烈鸟
trekking：长途跋涉	reserve：保留用地、保护区
fissure：裂缝	reticulated：网状的

东非大裂谷的前生与后世

东非大裂谷下陷开始于渐新世，主要断裂运动发生在中新世，大幅度错动时期从上新世一直延续到第四纪。北段形成红海，使阿拉伯半岛与非洲大陆分离；马达加斯加岛在几条活动裂谷扩张作用下，也与非洲大陆分裂开。

这条裂谷带位于非洲东部，南起赞比西河口一带，向北经希雷河谷至马拉维湖（尼亚萨湖）北部分为东西两支。东支裂谷带是主裂谷，沿维多利亚湖东侧，向北经坦桑尼亚、肯尼亚中部，穿过埃塞俄比亚高原入红海，再由红海向西北方向延伸抵约旦谷地，全长近6000千米。西支裂谷带大致沿维多利亚湖西侧由南向北穿过坦噶尼喀湖、基伍湖等一串湖泊，向北逐渐消失，规模比较小，全长1700多公里。

裂谷底部是一片开阔的原野，20多个狭长的湖泊如一串串晶莹的蓝宝石，散落住谷底。中部的纳瓦沙湖和纳库鲁湖是鸟类等动物的栖息之地，也是肯尼亚重要的游览区和野生动物保护区，其中的纳瓦沙湖湖面海拔1900米，是裂谷内最高的湖。南部马加迪湖产天然碱，是肯尼亚的重要矿产资源。北部图尔卡纳湖，是人类发祥地之一，曾在此发现过260万年前古人类头盖骨化石。

草原是裂谷带的重要景观。这里草原不仅面积大，而且集成了非洲大部分特征性动物资源。马塞马拉和塞伦盖蒂两个国家公园则是草原的典型代表。它虽分属肯尼亚和坦桑尼亚，但却连成一体。

2006年，来自英国、法国、意大利和美国的考察队经过分析和研究，预言一个新的大陆将会在100万年间形成，东非大裂谷将会比现在长10倍，东非的好望角将从非洲大陆上分离出去。

04 风暴角——好望角

The Cape of Good Hope is a formation of land along the south coast of Africa. Rounding it by ship has come to represent the **transition** from the Atlantic Ocean to the Indian Ocean in the east, as Cape Horn at the southern end of South America does so between the Atlantic Ocean and Pacific Ocean in the west.

There is some confusion as to the identity of the first nonnative peoples to round the Cape of Good Hope. A fifth-century B.C. Greek historian, Herodotus, made the claim of an expedition by the **Phoenician**s, **sponsor**ed by Necho II of Egypt, in about 600–597 B.C. A 15th-century **cartographer**, Fra Mauro, gave credit to the Chinese for accomplishing the feat in 1420.

The first European known to have sailed around the southern extent of Africa is Portuguese Bartolomeu Dias. Hoping to find a **sea-lane** around Africa to the Spice Islands (Moluccas) in the Indian Ocean, he embarked on his voyage in 1487. After encountering unfavorable winds along Africa's south coast, he sailed southward and, when the winds shifted, continued eastward. He made landfall at Mossel Bay. By checking his navigational measurements, he realized that he had passed the southern tip of the continent. He continued up the coast as far as the Great Fish River. On the return trip to Portugal, in the summer of 1488, he set up a PADRÃO (pillar) at the place that is now known as the Cape of Good Hope. Sources vary as to whether he gave it that name, or named it CaboTormentoso, for "Cape of Storms," after the weather he encountered there, and that King John II of Portugal renamed it Cabo da BõaEsperança, or "Cape of Good Hope." In 1497, Vasco da Gama, also sailing for Portugal, rounded the Cape of Good Hope and continued on to India, establishing a new trade route between Europe and Asia. From that time, such journeys

好望角是位于非洲南部海岸的一处地形。就像是南美的合恩角标志着大西洋和其西面的太平洋的分界一样，乘船绕过好望角就意味着从大西洋到达了东面的印度洋。

对于到底是哪些外国人最先绕过好望角这一问题还存在许多疑问。公元前5世纪的希腊历史学家希罗多德曾称在约公元前600-597年，一个由埃及法老尼科二世资助的腓尼基人舰队最先绕过好望角。而15世纪的制图师弗拉·毛罗则将这一殊荣归于中国人，认为他们在1420年完成了这项创举。

已知的最早绕过非洲南部的欧洲人是葡萄牙人巴尔托洛梅乌·迪亚士。他于1487年开始航行，试图在印度洋上找到通往香料之岛（摩鹿加群岛）的海上航线。他在非洲南部时由于风向不利，只好向南航行，风向改变之后才得以继续向东，之后在莫贝尔湾登陆。检查自己的航海仪器后，他发现自己已经经过了非洲大陆的最南端。之后他继续沿海岸前行，直到大鱼河。在回葡萄牙的旅途中，即1488年夏，他在那个地方立了一根柱子，这个地方就是今天的好望角。对于他遭遇风暴之后是否将那个地方命名为"风暴角"，或"好望角"，或者是否是葡萄牙国王约翰二世将它重新命名为"好望角"，人们的说法不一。1497年，瓦斯科·达·伽马也在回到葡

became routine.

The Cape of Good Hope is referred to in general usage as the southern tip of Africa. Yet, the southernmost point on the African continent is actually located at Cape Agulhas, 34 degrees and 52 minutes south latitude, some 40 miles southeast of the Cape of Good Hope. Moreover, on the **projection** of land referred to as the Cape of Good Hope, there are actually two points equally to the south, about a mile apart with a stretch of water between them. Although the Cape of Good Hope is located in the most temperate zone of the African continent, it is not easy to navigate its waters. The winds in the region circulate fiercely from the west, much like the winds around Cape Horn, and the weather is unpredictable and the seas often rough. The surrounding land is **inhospitable**. It was not until the mid-16th century that **settlement**s were established to **reprovision** ships sailing past on their way to other **destination**s. The modern city of Cape Town, South Africa, is situated to the north of the Cape of Good Hope.

萄牙的旅途中绕过好望角到达印度，从此建立了一条欧亚之间的新的贸易航线。从那时起，这个航线开始固定起来。

从普遍意义上来讲，好望角指的就是非洲最南端。然而非洲最南点实际上是厄加勒斯角，位于南纬34°52′，在好望角东南方向约40英里处。此外，事实上在那块被叫做好望角的突出的土地上，有两点位置相同，都是最南端，它们相距1英里，中间由一片海水隔开。尽管好望角处于非洲大陆最温暖的地方，但想要在这里的水面上航行却不是一件容易的事。这里的风刮得非常猛烈，就像是合恩角那里的风一样，不断循环从西面吹来，天气复杂多变，海水波涛汹涌。周围的土地上也比较荒凉。直到16世纪中期，这里才开始建立殖民点，为过往船只提供补给。南非的现代化都市开普敦就坐落在好望角以南。

背景知识 PROFILE

好望角的补充知识

好望角　最尖端的点称为Cape Point，有标明经纬度的标志牌供游客拍照留念。

迪亚士角　Diaz Point在好望角东面，是拍摄好望角全貌的最佳角度。

老灯塔　位于迪亚士角最高点，是好望角的标志性景观。

新灯塔　由于老灯塔位置太高，海上的大雾经常导致船只根本看不到老灯塔的灯光，于是在老灯塔前端山腰间又修建了一座小灯塔。只有在观景阶梯上才能找到它的位置。

好望角巨浪的生成：除了与大气环流特征有关外，还与当地海况及地理环境有着密切关系。好望角正处在盛行西风带上，西风风力很强，这样的气象条件是形成好望角巨浪的外部原因。南半球是一个陆地小而水域辽阔的半球，自古就有"水半球"之称；好望角接近南纬40度，而南纬40度至南极圈是一个围绕地球一周的大水圈，广阔的海区无疑是好望角巨浪生成的另一个原因。此外，在辽阔的海域，海流突然遇到好望角陆地的侧向阻挡作用，也是巨浪形成的重要原因。因此，西方国家常把南半球的盛行西风带称为"咆哮西风带"，而把好望角的航线比作"鬼门关"。

生态资源　好望角又是一个植物宝库，这里拥有全世界最古老、完全处于原生态的灌木层，有从来没有受过人类干扰的原始植物群，拥有研究植物进化不可多得的原始条件。

达尔文在《物种起源》里曾经描述：在许多情形下，我们对于花园和菜园里栽培悠久的植物，已无法辨认其野生原种。我们大多数的植物改进到或改变到现今于人类有用的标准需要数百年或数千年，因此我们就能理解为什么无论澳大利亚、好望角或未开化人所居住的地方，都不能向我们提供一种值得栽培的植物。

而拥有如此丰富物种的这些地区，并非由于奇异的偶然而没有任何有用植物的原种，只是因为该地植物还没有经过连续选择而得到改进……1836年6月3日，达尔文专程来到好望角，考察这里的植物资源及物种进化情况，并拜访了居住在这儿进行天文研究的约翰·赫歇尔，因为正是赫歇尔，作为一个天文学家，在进行深入的天文研究的同时，早已敏感地意识到了物种进化问题。

人们钟情好望角，关注好望角，同时也为好望角的未来担忧。尽管人们为好望角提供了最严格的保护——这里除观光游览车以外，任何汽车禁止入内；这里的一草一木一砂一石都是自然遗产，哪怕带走一段枯树枝、一枚小石子都是违法的。但人们同时也看到，好望角的自然生态环境是如此脆弱，有时又不得不经受人类不经意的折腾。

两年前，一位从万里以外赶来观光的欧洲人就曾不慎在这里引起了一场火灾，大面积的原生灌木林被付之一炬，时间已经过去几年了，仍未恢复。甚至，几天前又刚刚听到一个令人瞠目结舌的消息，在最近召开的一次国际会议上，专家们经过研究论证后明确指出，随着南极大陆冰山融化，海平面上涨，温室效应加剧，十年之后，好望角将变成一片荒漠。

05 自然美的震撼——维多利亚瀑布

Victoria Falls are a spectacular sight of **awe-inspiring** beauty and **grandeur** on the Zambezi River, bordering Zambia and Zimbabwe. Described by the Kololo tribe living in the area in the 1800's as "Mosi-oa-Tunya"—"the Smoke that thunders". In more modern terms it is known as "the greatest known curtain of falling water".

Columns of spray can be seen from miles away as 546 million cubic meters of water per minute **plummet** over the edge (at the height of the flood season) over a width of nearly two kilometers into a deep gorge over 100 meters below.

The wide **basalt** cliff, over which the falls thunder, transforms the Zambezi from a wide placid river to a ferocious torrent cutting through a series of dramatic gorges.

Facing the Falls is another sheer wall of basalt**,** rising to the same height and capped by **mist-soaked** rain forest. A path along the edge of the forest provides the visitor who is prepared to **brave** the tremendous spray with an **unparalleled** series of views of the Falls.

One special **vantage** point is across the Knife edge bridge, where visitors can have the finest view of the Eastern Cataract and the Main Falls as well as the Boiling Pot where the river turns and heads down the Batoka Gorge.

The Victoria Falls Bridge was **commissioned** by Cecil John Rhodes in 1900, although he never visited the falls and died before construction began, he expressed his wish that the "railway should cross the Zambezi just below the Victoria Falls. I should like to have the spray of the falls over the carriages."

维多利亚瀑布位于赞比西河中游，赞比亚和津巴布韦接壤处，气魄宏大，令人生畏，简直就是人间奇景。19世纪时当地卡洛洛族居民称之为"莫西奥图尼亚"，意即"声若雷鸣的雨雾"。在现代，这个名字则意味着"世界已知的最大瀑布"。

这里的水以5.46亿立方米/分的速度（雨季时）从陡崖上垂直跌入100多米深的谷底，宽度将近2千米，溅起的水柱在几十英里之外都能看到。

广阔的赞比西河在流抵瀑布之前，舒缓地流动在宽浅的河床上，然后突然从玄武岩陡崖上跌下，瞬间变成湍急的水流，从深邃的峡谷中怒涌而过。

瀑布对面的玄武岩峭壁与瀑布高度相同，上面雨林丛生，笼罩在一层薄雾之下。雨林周围有一条小路，大胆的游人可以沿着这条小路亲身体验溅起的巨大水花，欣赏维多利亚瀑布各种绝无仅有的美丽景观。

另外一处特别有利的地势是刀刃桥，游客们可以在这里欣赏到东瀑布和主瀑布的最佳景色；还可以欣赏"沸腾锅"，河水在这里回转形成巨大的漩涡，然后沿着巴托卡峡谷向下流出。

维多利亚瀑布桥由塞西尔·约翰·罗德斯于1900年委任建造，然而他自己却从来没有亲眼看到过维多利亚瀑布，在这座桥开始建设之前就已过世。他曾说，希望这座桥会"在维多利亚瀑布下横跨赞比西河。河水溅起的水花会落在桥上来往的马车上。"

站在这座桥上，既能欣赏到美丽的峡谷，又能看到另一侧壮观的大瀑布。从

The bridge affords a magnificent view both down the gorge on the one side and through to the falls on the other. The immense depth of the gorge can be fully appreciated from this perspective and combined with the sea green river below, the shiny black rock face and **lush** green **foliage**, the 360 degree view from the bridge is breathtaking. You can also throw yourself off this bridge on a bunji rope if you dare.

这个角度可以切身领略美丽深邃的峡谷和下方海绿色的河水、闪闪发光的黑色岩石以及郁郁葱葱的绿色植被。这座桥上周围360度都是美丽惊人的景色。如果你有足够的胆量，还可以去蹦极，体验一下从这座桥上跳下的感觉。

词汇 VOCABULARY

awe-inspiring：令人生畏的、令人惊叹的	brave：勇敢地从事或面对
grandeur：伟大、壮丽	unparalleled：无可比拟的、独一无二的
column：水柱	vantage：优势、有利地位
plummet：垂直落下、骤降	commission：委任、委托
basalt：玄武岩	lush：繁密的、茂盛的
mist-soaked：烟雾弥漫的	foliage：叶子（总称）

背景知识 PROFILE

世界七大自然景观

美国人洛厄尔·托马斯漫游世界时，发现了许多令人兴奋和神往的奇景，他经过反复挑选，提出了"世界七大自然界奇观"：

1、美国科罗拉多大峡谷

美国大峡谷是一个举世闻名的自然奇观，位于西部亚利桑那州西北部的凯巴布高原上，总面积2724.7平方公里。由于科罗拉多河穿流其中，故又名科罗拉多大峡谷，它被联合国教科文组织选为受保护的天然遗产之一。

大峡谷是科罗拉多河的杰作。这条河发源于科罗拉多州的落基山，洪流奔泻，经犹他州、亚利桑那州，由加利福尼亚州的加利福尼亚湾入海。全长2320公里。"科罗拉多"，在西班牙语中，意为"红河"，这是由于河中夹带大量泥沙，河水常为红色。

科罗拉多河的长期冲刷，不舍昼夜地向前奔

流，有时开山劈道，有时让路回流，在主流与支流的上游就已刻凿出黑峡谷、峡谷地、格伦峡谷，布鲁斯峡谷等19个峡谷，而最后流经亚利桑那州多岩的凯巴布高原时，更出现惊人之笔，形成了这个大峡谷奇观，而成为这条水系所有峡谷中的"峡谷之王"。

科罗拉多大峡谷的形状极不规则，大致呈东西走向，总长349公里，蜿蜒曲折，像一条桀骜不驯的巨蟒，匍伏于凯巴布高原之上。它的宽度在6公里至25公里之间，峡谷两岸北高南低，平均谷深1600米，谷底宽度762米。科罗拉多河在谷底汹涌向前，形成两山壁立，一水中流的壮观，其雄伟的地貌，浩瀚的气魄，慑人的神态，奇特的景色，世无其匹。1903年美国总统西奥多·罗斯福来此游览时，曾感叹地说："大峡谷使我充满了敬畏，它无可比拟，无法形容，在这辽阔的世界上，绝无仅有。"

2、非洲维多利亚大瀑布

维多利亚瀑布是世界上最大的瀑布之一，位于构成赞比亚和津巴布韦之间国界的赞比西河上，赞比西河上游缓慢地流经宽浅的谷地，维多利亚大瀑布以1708米的宽度成为世界上跨度最大的瀑布。维多利亚瀑布成形于一条深邃的岩石断裂谷正好横切赞比西河，断裂谷由1.5亿年以前的地壳运动所引起。

关于大瀑布，还有一个动人传说：据说在瀑布的深潭下面，每天都有一群如花般美丽的姑娘，日夜不停地敲着非洲的金鼓，金鼓发出的咚咚声，变成了瀑布震天的轰鸣；姑娘们身上穿的五彩衣裳的光芒被瀑布反射到了天上，被太阳变成了美丽的七色彩虹。姑娘们舞蹈溅起的千姿百态的水花变成了漫天的云雾。

3、美国黄石公园

黄石国家公园（Yellowstone）位于美国（The United States of America）西部北落基山和中落基山之间的熔岩高原上，绝大部分在怀俄明州的西北部。海拔2134米—2438米，面积8956平方公里。

黄石河、黄石湖纵贯其中，有峡谷、瀑布、温泉以及间歇喷泉等，景色秀丽，引人入胜。其中尤以每小时喷水一次的"老实泉"最著名。园内森林茂密，还牧养了一些残存的野生动物如美洲野牛等，供人观赏。园内设有历史古迹博物馆。

自从1872年黄石公园创办以来，已有六千多万人来此观光。游人来自五湖四海，形形色色，所获得的感受自然也就丰富多彩，各不相同：有赏心悦目的赞美，有敬畏或惊诧的

感叹，有肃然起敬的沉思，有惊险恐惧的刺激，有对大自然威力和宁静的领悟，还有悲喜交加的经历……

黄石公园是世界上最原始最古老的国家公园。根据1872年3月1日的美国国会法案，黄石公园"为了人民的利益被批准成为公众的公园及娱乐场所"，同时也是"为了使她所有的树木，矿石的沉积物，自然奇观和风景，以及其他景物都保持现有的自然状态而免于破坏"。

最初吸引人们的兴趣并使黄石成为国家公园的显著特征是地质方面的地热现象，这里拥有比世界上其他所有地方都多的间歇泉和温泉、彩色的黄石河大峡谷、化石森林，以及黄石湖。

4、美国肯塔基州地下洞——猛玛洞穴

猛玛洞穴国家公园位于美国西部肯塔基州中部的山区，是世界上最大的由石灰石构成的天然洞穴群和地下长廊。这个地下洞穴是几百万年以前水流经过灰岩沉积区时，溶蚀岩石形成的底下暗河通道。目前已探明的地下洞穴通道根据分布的高度不同分为五层，全长306公里。洞穴、山洞、岩洞和廊道组成这个宽阔的地下综合体。

林立的石笋和多姿的石钟乳遍布洞中，洞内景象壮观，有两个湖，三条河和八处瀑布。洞里还有一条20～60英尺宽，5～20英尺深的回音河。洞中还有地下暗河通过。洞穴已发现生活着200种以上的动物，有印第安那蝙蝠和肯塔基洞鱼等。肯塔基洞鱼是一种奇特的盲眼淡水鱼。珍稀的动物如盲鱼、无色蜘蛛显示了动物对绝对黑暗和封闭环境的适应，此外洞穴中还生长着67种藻类、27种菌类和7种苔藓类植物。洞内是奇珍异景，神鬼莫测。洞外是花团锦簇、燕语莺吟。将近30英里长的格林河和诺林河蜿蜒流过公园，河里生活着各种各样的鱼类，其中的5种是世界上绝无仅有的。还有3种属于洞穴鱼类，70多种的淡水贻贝中包括3种濒临灭绝的品种生活在河边的泥沙和卵石中。

5、世界最深的湖——贝加尔湖

贝加尔湖湖型狭长弯曲，宛如一弯新月，所以又有"月亮湖"之称。它长636千米，平均宽48千米，最宽79.4千米，面积3.15万平方千米，平均深度744米，最深点1642米，湖面海拔456米。贝加尔湖湖水澄澈清冽，且稳定透明（透明度达40.8m），为世界第二。其总蓄水量23600立方千米，相当于北美洲五大湖蓄水量的总和，约占地表不冻淡水资源总量的1/5。假设贝加尔湖是世界上唯一的水源，其水量也够50亿人用半个世纪。贝加尔湖容积巨大的秘密在于深度。如果在这个湖底最深点把世界上4幢最高的建筑物一幢一幢地叠起来，第4幢屋顶上的电视天线杆仍然在湖面以下58米，如果我们把高大的泰山放入湖中的最深处，山顶距水面还有100米。

贝加尔湖上最大的岛屿是奥利洪达岛（长71.7千米，最宽15千米，面积约为730平方千米）。

贝加尔湖大量的温水海湾和异域风情的奥利洪达岛吸引大量游客到这里来旅游参观。再加上这里相对适宜的气候、美丽的风景、大量的自然和考古古迹、不同种类的生物群、清新的空气、原生态环境以及独特的休闲资源使得贝加尔湖拥有超高的旅游休闲潜力。奥

利洪达岛是6世纪~10世纪古文化的最大文化中心，被认为是萨满教的宗教中心。这里的民族传统、习俗以及独特的民族特征都被完整地保存了下来。

6、阿拉斯加冰河湾

冰河湾国家公园位于美国阿拉斯加，距旧纽西50英里，占地330万公顷，围绕在陡峭的群山中，只能乘船或飞机到达。那里有无数的冰山、各类鲸鱼和爱斯基摩人的皮划舟。冰河湾游人在那里居住在帐篷中或在乡村田舍中。根据碑文的记载，冰河湾国家公园最引人入胜的景观之一就是巨大海湾中活动着的冰河。谬尔（Muir Glacier）是第一个仔细研究冰河的科学家，他从1879年起几次来到这里，为这里美丽多姿的冰河所征服。自谬尔探险时代之后，冰河沿海湾向北移动了很远，这种现象在北半球其他地方也曾被发现。

7、世界最高峰——珠穆朗玛峰

珠穆朗玛峰(Jo-mo glang-ma)，简称珠峰，又意译作圣母峰，位于中华人民共和国和尼泊尔交界的喜马拉雅山脉之上，终年积雪，是亚洲乃至世界第一高峰。藏语"珠穆朗玛jo-mo glang-ma ri"就是"大地之母"的意思。藏语Jo-mo"珠穆"是女神的之意，glang-ma"朗玛"应该理解成母象（在藏语里，glang-ma有两种意思：高山柳和母象）。神话说珠穆朗玛峰是长寿五天女（tshe-ring mched lnga）所居住的宫室。不过还有一种英文说法在中学课本里面多次出现，即Mount Qomolangma或Qomolangma Mount。西方普遍称这山峰作额菲尔士峰或艾佛勒斯峰(Mount Everest)，是纪念英国人占领尼泊尔之时，负责测量喜马拉雅山脉的印度测量局局长乔治·额菲尔士(George Everest)。

06 驴友们的天堂——塞舌尔岛

Located in the **azure** waters of the Indian ocean, just over 2 hours flight from Mauritius, 2 ½ hours from Reunion island, 4 hours flight from Dubai and Johannesburg and 6 hours from Singapore, are the **exotic** islands of the Seychelles. Stretching from four to ten degrees south of the equator, and made up of over 100 islands, the Seychelles lies outside the **cyclone** belt, keeping the country safe from tropical storms, and resulting in year-round sunshine, with temperatures ranging from 25ºC to 32ºC.

These spectacular tropical islands are a mix of towering **granite** rocks, lush tropical forests,

塞舌尔岛是蔚蓝色印度洋上的璀璨明珠，充满异域风情。它离毛里求斯只有两个多小时的航程，离留尼汪岛有两个半小时，离迪拜和约翰内斯堡四个小时，离新加坡六个小时。塞舌尔岛由一百多个岛屿组成，位于南纬4º~6º，因为在热带气旋地区之外，使得这个国家远离热带风暴，一年四季阳光明媚，气温维持在25℃~32℃之间。

这些风光旖旎的热带岛屿，布满了巨大的花岗岩，郁郁葱葱的热带雨林，四周被未开发过的环礁包围，遍

unexplored **atoll**s **fringe**d by **teem**ing coral reefs and some of the world's most spectacular beaches.

Island hopping is a great way to discover the different islands of the Seychelles. Another great way to enjoy the Seychelles is to combine it with other exotic destinations.

Whatever time of year you plan your visit you're sure to have the opportunity to bask in warm **equatorial** sunshine. November to January are warmer months and can mean higher rainfall. Seychelles weather patterns are **predominantly** influenced by the two main trade winds which **shift** twice a year. During the months of May to October the south-east trade wind blows, leading to relatively cooler, drier and windier conditions, peaking in July and August.

The wind shifts in November into a pre-north west condition, when the temperature warms up and winds remain very light. The north-west trade winds occur from December to March, causing a slightly wetter season coupled with higher temperatures. The changing trade winds mean it is very important to consider where you stay when choosing a holiday in the Seychelles.

布珊瑚礁，拥有世界著名的海滩。

跳岛游是欣赏塞舌尔岛不同岛屿景色的不错选择。还可以将跳岛游结合其他的目的地一起游玩，欣赏塞舌尔岛的美丽景色。

一年四季，无论你计划什么时候去塞舌尔岛，都可以置身于温暖的赤道阳光中。每年的十一月到次年一月温度较高，降雨量也更大。塞舌尔岛的天气主要受两股信风影响，信风风向每年转换两次。五月到十月东南信风吹来，使天气相对凉爽一些，而七月和八月则是最干燥最多风的季节。

风向在十一月份开始变成偏西北风，气温回暖，风力较小。西北信风出现在每年的十二月到次年三月，此时气候更加湿润，温度也更高。信风交替意味着在塞舌尔岛度假时选择酒店就非常重要了。

词汇 VOCABULARY

azure：天蓝色的	fringe：以某物为边界
exotic：非本地的、外来的	teem：充满、多产
cyclone：气旋	equatorial：赤道的
granite：花岗岩	predominantly：主要地
atoll：环状珊瑚岛、环礁	shift：转变

背景知识 PROFILE

塞舌尔旅游温馨小贴士

地理 塞舌尔共和国群岛位于非洲东面印度洋上，由115个岛屿组成，最大的是马埃岛。

签证 无须签证，但必须提供有效护照、往返或续航机票以及住宿证明（如旅馆预订单）等。

航班 广州出发前往塞舌尔，可搭乘阿联酋航空从迪拜转机，也可搭乘肯尼亚航空从内罗毕转机。飞行时间十二三个小时。

消费 VISA、万事达和美国运通的信用卡在塞舌尔都可以使用。

货币 卢比(SCR)为塞舌尔的法定货币，1美元可兑换5.5卢比。

时差 塞舌尔比格林威治时间早4小时，晚于北京时间4小时。

国宝 海椰果。海椰树雌雄异株，公树和母树总是并排生长。公树高耸挺拔，最高可达100多英尺，一般要比母树高出20多英尺。公树像雄武的卫士，终日守卫在果实累累的母树身旁。海椰果也有雌雄之分，雌性果圆而大，貌似女性臀部，而雄性果实则如同男性的重要器官，长度可达1米多。这里又被称为"人类的伊甸园"。

07 非洲最大湖——维多利亚湖

Lake Victoria, also referred to as Victoria Nyanza, is the main **reservoir** of the Nile River and is also the largest lake in Africa. It is located in Tanzania and Uganda with a small part extending into Kenya. Lake Victoria occupies an area of approximately 26,800 square miles (69,480 sq. km) and is the second-largest freshwater lake in the world, the only larger one being Lake Superior in North America. From north to south, Lake Victoria is 210 miles (337 km) long and from east to west it is 150 miles (240 km) wide, with over 2,000 miles (3,220 km) of coastline. The lake is situated between the Western and Eastern Rift Valleys along the great plateau. It is 3,720 feet above sea level (1,134 m) and reaches a depth of 270 feet (82 m). Within the lake, one can find many **archipelago**s as well as numerous **reef**s just below the surface. Lake Victoria is known for its abundance of fish, which are exported by local fisherman. There are over 200 species of fish, which all make a major contribution to the economy.

维多利亚湖是尼罗河的主要蓄水池，也是非洲最大湖泊。该湖大部分在坦桑尼亚和乌干达两国境内，一小部分属于肯尼亚。维多利亚湖面积约达26800平方英里（69480平方千米），是世界上第二大淡水湖。世界最大湖是北美的苏必尔湖。维多利亚湖南北长210英里（337千米），东西宽150英里（240千米），湖岸线长逾2000英里（3220千米），该湖位于东、西裂谷大台地之间，海拔3720英尺（1134米），深270英尺（82米）。湖中多岛群和暗礁，暗礁通常就在清澈的水面下。维多利亚湖里鱼类丰富，远近闻名，当地渔民以捕鱼为生。湖内鱼类达200种以上，捕鱼业有效地拉动了当地经济发展。该湖位于维多利亚盆地内，该盆地面积约92240平方英里（238900平方

The lake lies within the Victoria basin, which covers an area of 92,240 square miles (238,900 sq. km).

Lake Victoria is bordered to the south by 300-ft (90 m) high **precipice**s that are backed by the **papyrus** and ambatch **swamp**s that form the delta of the Kagera River. The lake drains water into the Kavirondo Gulf through a narrow channel. The gulf is roughly 16 miles (25 km) wide and extends for at least 40 miles to Kisumu, Kenya. One of the largest and most important contributors to Lake Victoria is the Kagera River, which runs into the western side of the lake. One other source is the Katonga River, which is situated north of the Kagera. There are several other inlets, but the lake's only outlet is the Victoria Nile to the north.

The majority of the people **inhabit**ing this area are Bantu-speaking. Several million people live within 50 miles (80 km) of the Lake Victoria region, which is one of the most densely populated areas in Africa. There are several cities that are built right on or very close to the northern coast of Victoria. Kampala and Entebbe benefit highly from the easy access to the water for fishing. In the northwestern corner of the lake, there is the Sese archipelago which is a chain of 62 islands contained within Lake Victoria. One of the largest islands, Ukerewe, rises over 650 feet (200 m) above the surface of the lake and is **densely** populated.

千米）。

维多利亚湖南部是300英尺（90米）高的悬崖，之后退化为纸莎草与安巴奇树沼泽区，属卡盖拉河三角洲。该湖有一条狭长的水道通卡韦朗多湾，该湾平均宽约16英里（25公里），向东延伸40英里（64公里）到肯亚基苏木。卡盖拉河是注入该湖的最大也是最重要的河流，注入湖的西侧。另一条从西侧注入维多利亚湖的著名河流是卡盖拉河北边的卡唐加河。该湖还有其他几条注入河流，但唯一的出口是维多利亚尼罗河，从北岸流出。

该湖区居民几乎全部讲班图语，是非洲人口最稠密的地区之一，沿岸方圆50英里(80公里)内居住着数百万人。靠近维多利亚湖北部湖岸有几座大城市。坎帕拉和恩德比交通便利，渔业发达。湖区西北角有塞西群岛的62个岛，其中乌凯雷韦岛最大，高出湖面650英尺(200米)，人口十分稠密。

词汇 VOCABULARY

reservoir：水库，蓄水池	papyrus：纸莎草
archipelago：群岛	swamp：沼泽
reef：暗礁	inhabit：居住、栖息
precipice：悬崖、峭壁	densely：密集地

世界上海拔最高的淡水湖与世界最高的可通行大船的淡水湖

世界上海拔最高的淡水湖措那湖，位于安多县城西南20公里处，处于念青唐古拉山和昆仑山山脉之间，属高原湖泊型自然风景区。它是世界上海拔最高的淡水湖，海拔高度4650米，面积约300平方公里，是安多县青藏铁路沿线最著名景点之一。措那湖是怒江源头湖，唐古拉山脉南部河溪均汇入措那湖流入怒江。该湖鱼类资源丰富，总量约一千万公斤左右，是重点自然资源保护区，近10年没进行捕捞。它的西岸为崖，水下有溶洞，靠岩不远有几处地热温泉使湖底局部水温常年在10度以上。

波漪涟涟的措那湖，是候鸟的栖息地。每年春季，在刚刚融化冰水的浅滩上，鱼鹰和水鸡的巢穴一坨坨点缀在岸边。远处的岛屿，候鸟在那儿栖息繁衍，天鹅、黑颈鹤、黄野鸭、班头雁……成群结队，一片喧嚣。各种鸟卵随处可见，大的约半斤重，小的如弹丸。在草原返青的季节，各种鸟卵和禽蛋均出壳成雏。这些雏鸟在措那湖继续发育成长两个月，之后和整个鸟群一起纷纷向印度洋飞去，来年早春再飞回措那湖故地。夏季的措那湖，青山绿水，鱼儿跳跃，鸥雁比翼；湖边青丘着意，湖内绿水清漪，远眺，卓革神峰隐隐作态，青山绿水遥相辉映。

措那湖相传是金刚鲁姆女神的瑶池，是当地的"神湖"。安多县牧民在藏历正月初一早早起床来接受金刚鲁姆女神的降福。神山圣湖是一个部落或地区共同崇拜的神灵的所在地，每至藏历龙年，会有成千上万的信徒前来朝拜神湖，他们成群结队的转措那湖，有的在正月初一转湖，当天返回；有的路途较远，需要几天、十几天或更长的时间。朝拜神湖是多数牧民一生的心愿，也是为了祈祷风调雨顺，牛羊兴旺。

的的喀喀湖位于秘鲁和玻利维亚两国之间的科亚奥高原上。湖长200公里，宽66公里，面积8330平方公里。湖面海拔3812米，平均水深100米，最深达304米，湖水蓄积量827立方公里。的的喀喀湖是南美洲最大的淡水湖，也是世界最高的可通行大船的大淡水湖。的的喀喀湖形成于古地质时期的第三纪，在强烈的地壳运动中，随着科迪勒拉山系隆起及巨大的构造断裂，在东科迪勒拉山脉和西科迪勒拉山脉之间，形成了一条西北—东南走向的构造盆地。的的喀喀湖就位于该构造中。经过第四纪冰川作用，湖区更加绚丽多姿。湖水源于安第斯山脉的积雪融水。有25条河流注入湖中，最大的一条是自西北注入的拉米斯河，约提供湖水补给总量的五分之二。烈日和燥风使湖水蒸发量极大，经德萨瓜德罗河排出的湖水量只相当于入湖水量的百分之五。湖内有41个岛屿，著名的有太阳岛和月亮岛。岛上有印第安人的古迹。印第安人一向把的的喀喀湖奉为"圣湖"。

08 古老而美丽的湖泊——坦噶尼喀湖

Lake Tanganyika is the second-deepest lake in the world. It lies in four countries' territories: a little in each of Burundi and Zambia, and more than 40 percent in each of Democratic Republic of Congo and Tanzania.

The main settlement on the **lakeshore** is the town of Kigoma, which is also the usual entry point to the region. Two awesome nature reserves border Lake Tanganyika: the incredibly beautiful Mahale Mountains National Park and the **chimpanzee**-famous Gombe Stream National Park.

Lake Tanganyika's crystal-clear water is contained within the hills of the Great Rift Valley. It is 675km long, an average of 50km wide, and 1,470m deep at its deepest point, holding about 18, 900km³ of **alkaline** fresh water that is claimed to be the cleanest in the world. The water on the surface averages 25ºC, the temperature of a warm day in Cape Town.

Lake Tanganyika is about three million years old and fed by at least 50 inlets and streams. Its only **outflow**, however, is the Lukuga River, which it feeds only during years of extremely high rainfall. As a body of water, it is very **isolated**: no similar **habitat**s exist in the surrounding areas.

This fact, coupled with Lake Tanganyika's age, has made it one of the most biologically rich and scientifically valuable habitats in the world. More than 500 fish species live in Lake Tanganyika. However, its great depth and lack of water turnover make its depths into "**fossil** water", which lacks oxygen. Almost all of Lake Tanganyika's fish therefore live above a depth of 600 feet.

This, at least, makes them easier for the locals to

坦噶尼喀湖是世界第二深湖。它位于四国境内：一小部分位于布隆迪和赞比亚，分别有超过40%左右在刚果民主共和国和坦桑尼亚。

人们主要在湖岸边的基戈马镇居住，这里也是进入湖区的常规入口。坦葛尼喀湖周围有两个美丽的自然保护区：美不胜收的马哈雷山国家公园和以黑猩猩闻名的冈贝国家公园。

坦葛尼喀湖清澈的湖水被包围在大裂谷的群山之中，它长675千米，平均宽50千米，最深处达1470米，储存着18900立方米的碱性淡水，号称是世界上最清澈的淡水。湖水表面的温度平均为25ºC，相当于开普敦天气晴朗时的温度。

坦葛尼喀湖约有300万年的历史了，至少有50个注水口，然而它唯一的出水口则是卢库加河，只有在降雨量丰富的时候，卢库加河才有补给水量。在这附近没有和坦葛尼喀湖类似的栖息地了。

由于这个原因，再加上坦葛尼喀湖的悠久历史，使其成为了世界上生物种类最丰富，最具有科学价值的栖息地之一。湖内生活着500多种鱼类。然而由于湖水太深，缺少进出水周转量，使其成为了"化石水"，水内缺少氧气。因此，几乎湖内的所有鱼类都居住在600英尺以上的水域。

这种情况至少为当地居民捕鱼提供了便利条件。约有一百多万人口依靠湖内的鱼类生存，晚上湖面上满是

catch and eat. About a million people depend on the lake's fish output for survival, and at night you can see the tiny lights of hundreds of small fishing vessels **bob**bing on the lake's waters.

来回晃动的小渔船，点点的灯光散落在湖面上。

背景知识 PROFILE

坦噶尼喀湖里的慈鲷

坦噶尼喀湖拥有着世界上约1／6的淡水鱼品种，其中繁衍进化最成功的鱼类要算慈鲷科了。坦噶尼喀湖中至少生活有三百种以上属慈鲷科的鱼，和150种非慈鲷科的鱼类，多数都栖息在湖底。而鱼类最多的地方则是鲁库加河流出的河口，其中坦噶尼喀沙丁鱼就至少有2到6种。而掠食性的食人鱼(和非洲维多利亚湖边的掠食性尼罗河食人鱼略有不同)就有4种，在坦噶尼喀湖中的慈鲷有98%都是湖中特有种。此外，坦噶尼喀湖中有相当多特有的无脊椎软体动物，如螃蟹、水蛭、桡足类动物（如剑水蚤）、淡水水母、淡水海绵、水蛇等等。

坦噶尼喀湖中以慈鲷最具优势，原因有几个：

1. 湖中具大量盐类物质，对盐类容忍度较高的次级淡水鱼类（如慈鲷）反而容易被保留。

2. 慈鲷鱼具有封闭式泳鳔，可以自血液中积存空气而不必到水面吸取空气，如此一来幼鱼在无水生植物遮蔽的湖中，就不必为了吸取空气而冒险游至水面，遭致掠食者的攻击。

3. 慈鲷会完善的照顾他们的后代，这是最重要的一点，多数慈鲷会保护卵，甚至以口孵方式进行，这些行为能提供完善保护及充分供应氧气，这也是他们至今仍能好好存在于此的原因。

根据对卵的照顾可以将坦湖慈鲷分两大类：基质繁殖及口孵繁殖。

基质繁殖是比口孵更原始的类型，但在演化上它们仍没有太大改变，岩石基质或贝壳是他们栖息、产卵孵化之处，代表性鱼种是N属（新锦丽鱼属）的鱼，如黄天堂鸟。

口孵慈鲷是以口当作孵卵及幼鱼场所，如此可以避开众多掠食者的觊觎而增加存活率，但他们必须具备特别的倒退技巧才行。

摄食行为也是慈鲷生存的要件，最基本的是底食性鱼，他们通常靠近底质生活、觅食或躲避敌害，慈鲷的摄食器官通常和他们的食物息息相关，在某些地区这是他们成功演化的关键，像大颚可以攫取食物，而慈鲷通常具在食道有第二副颚称为咽喉齿，是由骨板及齿组成，能进一步处理食物。

坦湖慈鲷食性也是特别值得一提，因为一般河产慈鲷大概只有无脊椎摄食者、藻食者、碎食性者而已，但在坦湖中的慈鲷却不只如此，还有更特殊的食性，如食鳞性、食海绵性、卵食性、藻类刮食性、泥食性等，这种高度分化的食性是因为他们周遭特定的生物基底及被限定在特定栖地之故，因为栖地常是限定慈鲷生存的要素，这也可以作为慈鲷饲养者的环境设定依据。

09 浩瀚大漠——撒哈拉沙漠

The Sahara Desert is located in the northern **portion** of Africa and covers over 3,500,000 square miles (9,000,000 sq. km) or **roughly** 10% of the continent. It is bounded in the east by the Red Sea and it stretches west to the Atlantic Ocean. To the north, the Sahara Desert's northern boundary is the Mediterranean Sea, while in the south it ends at the Sahel, an area where the desert landscape transforms into a semi-**arid** tropical savanna.

Around 25% of the desert is **sand dune**s, some of which reach over 500 ft (152 m) in height. There are also several mountain ranges within the Sahara and many are **volcanic**. The highest peak found in these mountains is Emi Koussi. The lowest point in the Sahara Desert is in Egypt's Qattera Depression at -436 ft (-133 m) below sea level.

Most of the water found in the Sahara today is in the form of seasonal or **intermittent** streams. The only permanent river in the desert is the Nile River that flows from Central Africa to the Mediterranean Sea. Other water in the Sahara is found in underground **aquifer**s and in areas where this water reaches the surface.

Due to the high temperatures and arid conditions

撒哈拉沙漠位于非洲北部，总面积约9000000平方公里，约占非洲大陆的10%。撒哈拉沙漠东临红海，向西延伸至大西洋，北接地中海，南达萨赫勒地区——该地区从沙漠地形变成了半干旱的大草原。

沙丘占沙漠的25%，最高的沙丘可达152m。撒哈拉内还有几条山脉，大部分是火山。其中最高峰是库西火山。最低点是埃及境内的盖塔拉洼地，为海平面以下133m。

撒哈拉的大部分水源是季节性河流或间歇性河流。唯一一条永久性河流是尼罗河。它从非洲中部发源，注入地中海。另外，撒哈拉还有一些地下溪流以及含水层和地表水。

由于撒哈拉沙漠地区气温高，这里的植被稀少，只有500种。它们大多是耐旱及高温的品种，以及那些生长在高盐度、湿润

of the Sahara Desert, the plant life in the Sahara Desert is **sparse** and includes only around 500 species. These consist mainly of drought and heat resistant varieties and those adapted to salty conditions (**halophyte**s) where there is sufficient moisture.

The harsh conditions found in the Sahara Desert have also played a role in the presence of animal life in the Sahara Desert. In the central and driest part of the desert there are around 70 different animal species, 20 of which are large mammals like the spotted hyena. Other mammals include the gerbil, sand fox and Cape hare. **Reptile**s like the sand viper and the monitor lizard are present in the Sahara as well.

It is believed that people have inhabited the Sahara Desert since 6000 BC and earlier. Since then, Egyptians, Phoenicians, Greeks and Europeans have been among the peoples in the area. Today the Sahara's population is around 4 million with the majority of the people living in Algeria, Egypt, Libya, Mauritania and Western Sahara.

Most of the people living in the Sahara today do not live in cities; instead they are nomads who move from region to region throughout the desert. Because of this, there are many different nationalities and languages in the region but Arabic is most widely spoken. For those who do live in cities or villages on fertile oases, crops and the mining of minerals like iron ore (in Algeria and Mauritania) and copper (in Mauritania) are important industries that have allowed population centers to grow.

的盐土中的植物。

撒哈拉恶劣的条件对于这里的动物亦影响很大。在最热的沙漠中部，大概有70种动物，其中20种是诸如斑点土狗的大型哺乳动物。其他的哺乳动物包括沙鼠、吕氏狐、开普兔。爬行动物有沙蝰、巨蜥。

据称，早在公元前6000年，撒哈拉沙漠已有人类居住。从此，埃及人、腓尼基人、希腊人和欧洲人也来到了这里。如今，撒哈拉沙漠的人口约400万，大部分人住在阿尔及利亚、埃及、利比亚、毛里塔尼亚和西撒哈拉。

大部分居住在撒哈拉的人口并不居住在大城市。这些游牧民族在沙漠中迁徙。因此，这些地区有很多民族和语言，不过阿拉伯语是最主要的语言。而对于那些居住在城市、绿洲中的乡村中的居民，农作物、矿产，如铁矿（在阿尔及利亚和毛里塔尼亚）和铜矿（在毛里塔尼亚）是他们最重要的工业。这些工业使得人们得以生息繁衍。

词汇 VOCABULARY

portion：比例	intermittent：断续的，间歇的
roughly：大约	aquifer：含水土层
arid：贫瘠的，干旱的	sparse：稀少的
sand dune：沙丘	halophyte：盐土植物
volcanic：火山的，爆发的	reptile：爬行动物

首次穿越撒哈拉沙漠的中国人

首次穿越撒哈拉沙漠的两个中国人经历了一场不同寻常的冒险，也是一场事关生死的博弈，他们是金飞豹和费宣。两人冒着生命的危险，用80天的时间完成了一次真爱的沟通和一种精神的传扬。他们在那片酷热的死亡之海上播下了一粒爱的种子，希望有一天，这粒种子可以成长为参天大树，通过这些爱的枝条让世界更进一步地关注非洲、关注撒哈拉。

金飞豹，云南省政协委员、民进云南省委委员、著名探险家；费宣，云南省政协委员、云南省经济管理委员会副主任、地质专家；2009年4月，金飞豹和费宣不顾非洲地区局势动荡，毅然决定启动"关注全球沙漠化，穿越非洲撒哈拉"2009中国人穿越世界第一大沙漠科学考察探险。撒哈拉沙漠是世界第一大沙漠，位于非洲北部，气候条件极其恶劣，是地球上最不适合生物生长的地方之一。80天之后，金飞豹和费宣在历经重重磨难之后终于成功完成了中国人穿越世界第一大沙漠的科考探险活动，于6月27日晚顺利返回北京。

金飞豹和费宣本次穿越撒哈拉的行程原定从非洲西部的加纳开始，穿越加纳、布基纳法索、马里、尼日尔、阿尔及利亚、利比亚、埃及7国，总行程长达7500多公里。但是让所有的人们都没有想到的是，金飞豹和费宣此行面对的最大困难不是严酷的自然环境，而是变幻莫测的非洲各国政策。当他们完成了阿尔及利亚境内的探险行程之后，却发现由于利比亚国内政策的变化，不得不被迫放弃利比亚境内的行程，改为直接进入埃及。而就在金飞豹和费宣准备从阿尔及利亚取道埃及的时候，却因为阿尔及利亚海关不承认他们的埃及落地签证而无法出境。无奈之下两人只能重新向埃及驻阿使馆申请正式的入境签证，然而就在他们在等待埃及签证的时候，两人却因为拍照事件而被阿尔及利亚警方拘留并遭到当地警方的敲诈。最后两人在中国大使馆的帮助下顺利脱困，为避免更大的麻烦，金飞豹和费宣只能在6月12日暂时返回北京，在北京重新申请埃及的入境签证。经历了一系列的波折以后，两位探险家终于拿到了埃及的签证，顺利进入撒哈拉探险活动的最后一站。

站在红海的岸边，金飞豹和费宣感慨不已，他们一路历经艰辛，感受过尼日尔河上船夫的困苦，经历过在沙漠无人区中与外界失去联系的惊恐，更险些在阿尔及利亚沦为阶下之囚。经历了风雨后的彩虹总会更加美丽，金飞豹和费宣经过了种种磨难之后得来的成功也更加珍贵，他们在沿途所到之处与当地民众友好交往，宣传环保，采集人文。传播了中华文明的传统礼仪和中国人民对非洲的友好感情，通过他们的镜头和文字也让世界进一步地了解了撒哈拉的美丽和悲哀。"关注全球沙漠化"是本次撒哈拉沙漠探险的主题，金飞豹和费宣的行程经历了热带雨林——热带草原——热带沙漠这样一个逐步演化的过程，让他们更深刻地理解了沙漠化对生态的破坏和对人民生活造成的影响。

金飞豹和费宣关注自然关注环保的活动已经不止一次了，金飞豹早在1996年就发起了清洁珠峰的环保活动。2008年，金飞豹和费宣成功完成了以"关注全球变暖对极地环境影响"为主题的徒步穿越北极格陵兰大冰盖活动，成为历史上首次完成此项探险的中国人。

从格陵兰到撒哈拉，金飞豹和费宣经历了一次冰与火的转变，但无论是在冰原还是沙漠，关注全球环球关爱自然的心愿和理念是相同的。金飞豹和费宣在探险过程中互相鼓励，互相支持，共同面对困难，发挥各自在专业领域中的优势，终于获得了最后的成功。

两位探险家在撒哈拉沙漠的穿越活动艰难而充满波折，但金飞豹和费宣知道，关注环保的道路注定不可能是舒适而安逸的，只要关注环境、关爱自然的目标还在，他们探险的脚步就永远不会停止！

10 这里生机勃勃——红海

The Red Sea is an elongated and narrow-shaped sea, which extends from north to south over a distance of approximately 2,000 km. The average width is about 280 km, with a maximum breadth of 306km in the south. The **width** of the **strait** of Bal-el-Mandeb is about 26 km and separates the Red Sea from the outer ocean via the **Gulf of Aden**. The northern tip of the Red Sea separates into two gulfs, the Gulf of Suez, which is connected to the Suez Canal and the Gulf of Aqaba. The **adjacent** land area of the Red Sea is mostly arid, having desert or semi-desert regions with no major river **inflow**. Further **inland**, the desert regions are bordered by extensive **mountain range**s.

Surface water temperature in the Red Sea varies seasonally between about 22 and 32. The surface temperature generally declines towards the Bab-al-Mandeb, due to the **influx** of cool water from the Gulf of Aden, and also gradually **decrease**s towards the northern region. The deeper waters are stable throughout the region, and below 300m the water temperature is constantly between 21 and 22.

Salinity in the Red Sea is generally high due to high **evaporation**, low precipitation and the lack of a major river inflow. Salinity is usually lower in the southern region due to the inflowing waters from the Gulf of Aden. Water **renewal** in the Red Sea is slow, and exchange with the ocean takes

红海是一片狭长的水域，南北延伸可达2000km，平均宽度为280km，最宽处位于南部，宽306km。曼德海峡通过亚丁湾将红海与外界海域分开，它的宽度大概为26km。红海北部深入两个海湾：苏伊士湾（与苏伊士运河相连）和亚喀巴湾。红海的毗邻地区大部分了无生气，不是沙漠就是半沙漠区，区域内没有主要河流。而往内陆地区，沙漠被连绵的群山所阻隔。

红海表层海水温度随季节变化，在22℃-32℃范围内。而曼德海峡的温度一般会因为来自亚丁湾冷海水的注入而有所下降，并且到北部地区温度逐渐下降。深处海水温度稳定。300m下的海水温度恒定，在21℃-22℃。

红海蒸发大，降水量小，无主要水源，所以盐度高。而南部地区因为亚丁湾水的

approximately 6 years for the 200 m above the thermocline and 200 years for the entire sea.

Sandwiched between the narrow **continental shelves** runs a deep **trench** that stretches from north to south for almost the entire sea area. The deepest region lies between 14 N and 28 N, with a maximum depth of 2,920 m. These deep areas are still geologically active and have numerous volcanic vents, emitting hot, salty and metal-rich sea water.

The two gulfs in the northern region are similar in shape but their **topography** is quite distinct. The Gulf of Suez is shallow and has a relatively flat bottom, with a depth ranging from 55m-73m. On the other hand, the Gulf of Aqaba is comprised of a deep basin and a narrow shelf. The basin is separated into two by a submarine sill, with both basins having a depth of over 1,000m.

The Red Sea is blessed with natural beauty and **astounding** biological diversity. Coral reefs, mangrove forests, seagrass beds, salt marshes and salt-pans are distributed throughout the region. These unique habitats support a diverse range of marine life, including sea turtles, dugongs, dolphins, and many endemic fish species.

注入，盐度低一些。红海的水体更新慢。与斜温层以上200m处的海水交换约需6年时间，而整个海域更新则需要200年的时间。

红海中间有一道深沟，在狭长的大陆架中夹着，它从北至南贯穿整个红海海域。最深处在北纬14°和28°之间，深度可达2920m。这些纵深区域仍然很活跃，有大量的火山口，散发着炙热、含盐且富含金属的海水。

北部的两个海湾形状大体相似，但是它们的地形迥异。苏伊士湾比较浅，海底基本平坦，最深处可达55m-73m。而亚喀巴湾是由很深的盆地和狭窄的大陆架组成。一条海底山脊将盆地一分为二。两个部分都深达1000m。

红海自然景观优美，生物物种多样。区域内遍布着珊瑚礁、红树林、海草床、盐沼以及盐田。如此独一无二的环境造就了多变的海洋物种，它包括海龟、儒艮、海豚及其他本地特有的鱼类品种。

红海旅游小贴士

如果有幸去红海旅游，请带上这些小贴士：

关于红海名字的由来

其一是红海是直接由希腊文、拉丁文、阿拉伯文翻译过来，和海的颜色没有关系，红海并不是红色的。可能的来源包括：季节性出现的红色藻类；附近的红色山脉；一个名称为红色的本地种族；指南边（对应黑海的北边）；红地的海（古埃及称沙漠为红地）等。这种解释又分为三种观点：有的说红海里有许多色泽鲜艳的贝壳，因而使水色深红；有的认为红海近岸的浅海地带有大量的珊瑚沙，使得海水变红；还有的说红海是世界上温度最高的海，适宜生物的繁衍，所以表层海水中大量繁殖着一种红色海藻，使得海水略呈红色，因而得名红海。

其二是认为红海两岸岩石的色泽是红海得名的原因。远古时代，由于交通工具和技术条件的制约，人们只能驾船在近岸航行。当时人们发现红海两岸特别是非洲沿岸，是一片绵延不断的红黄色岩壁，这些红黄色岩壁将太阳光反射到海上，使海上也红光闪烁，红海因此而得名。

其三是将红海的得名与气候联系在一起。红海海面上常有来自非洲大沙漠的风，送来一股股炎热的气流和红黄色的尘雾，使天色变暗，海面呈暗红色，所以称为红海。

其四是古代西亚的许多民族用黑色表示北方，用红色表示南方，红海就是"南方的海"。

其五，源于莉莉丝的传说，她是与亚当同时被造出的第一个女人，也是亚当的第一任妻子。原本应该是巴比伦传说中的女性，但是因为犹太教经典《塔木德》的记载而变得十分有名。莉莉丝不愿听从亚当的命令因此离开他到红海去，以每天100个的速度产下恶魔之子。主命令三个天使去找她，天使们威胁说要每天杀掉她100个小孩，莉莉丝忍受不了天使的胁迫而跳红海自杀。但由于莉莉斯是由神所创造的，并不会轻易死去，她的灵魂一直在红海沉浮，一直到天使路西法叛变上帝后，才与堕天使们一起前往了地狱。莉莉丝居住的红海意味着所有生命孕育自女性的经血，而作为从血海中诞生万物的代价，也要向血海补充鲜血（例如人祭）。

红海沿岸主要的旅游区

红海沿岸主要的旅游区有：沙姆沙伊赫、赫尔格拉、阿里什、穆罕默德角、泽哈卜、努维巴等，这些地区以闪光的沙滩、美丽的珊瑚海、丰富的海洋生物及一流的饭店等闻名于世，这里是世界上最适宜潜水的海域之一，也是水上运动者的天堂。另外，红海上的特色港口是萨法贾，拥有盐量很高的海水和黑泥沙滩，可以治疗风湿症和皮肤病，是世界上最适合疗养度假的胜地之一。

1923年，夫勒特(E. M. Forster)曾对红海海岸作过这样的描述："世界上只有这个地方才会有如此金黄色的山和五光十色的海中溶洞，这些溶洞是东方和热带地区间的纽带"。

过着退隐生活的隐者们很早就在这里建立了基督教的修道院，他们和养骆驼的贝都因部落在荒野中生活。至今东方沙漠的岩石峪和诙峪还未勘探，贝都因人在这些峪里养山羊和山鹿。红海本身有五光十色的珊瑚礁，海岸有古老的海港，水下有着各种奇异的海洋生物。

每当热风快速地向东面吹过来的时候，候鸟也迁徙到了红海海畔，这里立刻成为了鸟的天堂。今天，这个古老的海湾是世界上最好的潜水和垂钓的地方，随处能看到游人们在白沙滩上休息，沐浴着阳光，观赏着沿岸一排排葱绿的树林，潜游的游客正在水下探寻着各式各样的珊瑚礁。红海海底有着各种奇异的海洋生物：花地毯般活动着的珊瑚礁和特别诱人的鱼都正等待着你去发现它们的秘密。正如著名的潜水摄影师大卫·杜比勒（David Doubilet）所描绘的"在红海海底，每日每夜都非常热闹，珊瑚礁都在魔术般地默默地有节奏地跳着舞蹈……"

最佳旅游时间

到红海观光游览，潜水、垂钓、海上观光等亲水活动是一定要参加的。红海沿岸浪柔沙软，波澜不惊，是开展水上休闲运动的绝佳场所，赫尔格达、沙姆沙伊赫等海滨城市都有许多优良的海滨浴场和海上游乐场所。此外，红海拥有众多美丽的珊瑚、五颜六色的鱼类及各种珍奇的海洋生物，海底资源丰富，海水清澈，能见度高，是世界上最适宜开展潜水运动的场所之一。

到赫尔格达、沙姆沙伊赫等红海沿岸城市旅游的最佳时节是每年的10月~次年5月，此时是最适合到红海潜水的时节，天气凉爽，海水能见度高，水温适宜潜水，其他时间风浪较大且水较冷，潜水时需要穿更厚一些的潜水服。

购物介绍

赫尔格达是红海观光客聚集的主要区域，市中心有几条主要的购物大街，有传统市集，也有高档的精品店，喜欢购物的游客可以痛快地"挥霍"一番。一般来讲，纸莎草手工艺品、古画、珠宝、木器、咖啡壶、香料、雕刻品等，都是值得购买的纪念品。

第二章

你不可不知的非洲人文景观

科学家们早已达成共识，所有人类的祖先都来自于非洲。所以，来到非洲，一定要去看看那些非洲的古人类遗址。非洲是一个诞生诸多奇迹的地方，去胡夫金字塔走走，你会对奇迹有更好的理解。如果可能，去中非丛林里矮人村走走，你会知道，矮人们不仅仅存在于格林童话里。当然，还有很多神庙，去那里看看，可以感受历史的厚重感。

总之，非洲充满着人文的气息，本章中所列的内容只是很小的一部分。如果有幸到非洲，用自己的心去跟随非洲人文的脉动吧。

11 "世界古代七大奇迹"之一——胡夫金字塔

The Great Pyramid at **Giza**, also called Khufu's Pyramid or the Pyramid of Khufu, and Pyramid of Cheops, is the oldest and largest of the three pyramids in the Giza **Necropolis** bordering what is now Cairo, Egypt, and is the only remaining member of the Seven Wonders of the Ancient World. It is believed that the pyramid was built as a tomb for Fourth dynasty Egyptian King Khufu (Cheops in Greek) and constructed over a 20-year period concluding around 2560 BC.

The Great Pyramid was the tallest man-made structure in the world for over 3,800 years, unsurpassed until the 160 meter tall spire of Lincoln Cathedral was completed 1300 AD. Originally the Great Pyramid was covered by **casing** stones that formed a smooth outer surface, and what is seen today is the **underlying** core structure. Some of the casing stones that once covered the structure can still be seen around the base. There have been varying scientific and alternative theories regarding the Great Pyramid's construction techniques. Most accepted construction theories are based on the idea that it was built by moving huge stones from a **quarry** and dragging and lifting them into place.

Khufu's vizier, Hemon, or Hemiunu, is believed by some to be the architect of the Great Pyramid. At the time of construction, the Great Pyramid was 280 Egyptian royal cubits tall, 146.6 meters, (480.97 feet) but with erosion and the loss of its **pyramidion**, its current height is 138.8 m (455 feet). Each base side was 440 royal cubits, with each royal cubit measuring 0.524 meters.

The total mass of the pyramid is estimated at 5.9 million tonnes. The **volume**, including an internal **hillock**, is believed to be roughly 2,500,000 cubic meters.

Many of the casing stones and interior chamber blocks of the great pyramid were fit together with

吉萨金字塔亦称胡夫金字塔。在靠近埃及开罗的吉萨墓地处,一共有三座金字塔,其中吉萨金字塔最为古老、最为庞大。这座金字塔是世界上古代七大奇迹中仅存的一座。据称,吉萨金字塔建于埃及第四王朝第二位法老胡夫统治时期,被认为是胡夫为自己修建的陵墓。该金字塔耗时20年,竣工于公元前2560年。

3800年来,吉萨金字塔一直是世界上最高的人工建筑,直到1300年左右林肯尖顶大教堂完工,才取代了金字塔的位置。这座教堂高160米。最初,吉萨金字塔被石头所覆盖,有着一个光滑的外表面。我们今天看到的是外表面下的内部结构。而最初的石头表层可以在基底处看到。对于吉萨金字塔的建造技术,有各种科学理论。其中,人们较为接受的是:从采石场搬来巨石,然后托举到如今的位置。

据说,胡夫的高级官员Hemon或Hemiunu是胡夫金字塔的建筑师。完工之时,胡夫金字塔高146.6米,但因为侵蚀作用,金字塔顶失去,如今的高度降为138.8米。而每个基底为230米宽。

金字塔的总重量据估计为590万吨。如果将内部小丘算在内,体积大约为2500 000立方米。

金字塔表面的石头和内室的

extremely high **precision**. Based on measurements taken on the north eastern casing stones, the mean opening of the joints are only 1/50th of an inch wide. The accuracy of the pyramid's workmanship is such that the four sides of the base have a mean error of only 58 millimeter in length, and 1 minute in angle from a perfect square.

The Great Pyramid consists of more than 2.3 million **limestone** blocks. The Egyptians shipped the limestone blocks from quarries all along the Nile River. The stone was cut by **hammer**ing wedges into the stone. Then, the wedges were **soaked** with water. The wedges expanded, causing the rock to crack. Once they were cut, they were carried by boat either up or down the Nile River to the pyramid.

石块互相之间贴合精密。该金字塔北面表层石头的结合处平均宽度为1/50英尺。这座金字塔底座的四边长度仅均差58mm，而底座的正方形角度仅差1分。

该座金字塔由230多万石灰石建成。古埃及人从采石场沿着尼罗河用船运来石灰石，然后使用锤子将楔子凿进石头内。接着，工人们会浸泡楔子。这样，楔子会膨胀，使得石头裂开。工人们会将合乎尺寸的石材再沿着尼罗河运到金字塔处。

词汇 VOCABULARY

Giza：吉萨	volume：体积
necropolis：墓地	hillock：小丘，土墩
casing：盒，套，匣	precision：精确，精密度
underlying：潜在的，在下面的，基本的	limestone：石灰石
quarry：采石场，石矿	hammer：锤击，敲打
pyramidion：小金字塔，方尖塔的顶角锥	soaked：湿透的

背景知识 PROFILE

世界七大奇迹

古代七大奇迹

古代文明七大奇迹(The Seven Wonders of the Ancient World) 又译为"古代世界七大奇观"，指古代西方世界（尼罗河流域、两河流域、爱琴海希腊化地区）的7处壮丽的人造景观。这些建筑物和塑像，以其宏伟规模、艺术美感或独特的建造方式，代表了古代西方文明的成就，令世人惊奇不已，叹为观止。

1. 埃及吉萨金字塔
埃及开罗附近的吉萨附近；大约公元前2700年~2500年建成。
2. 奥林匹亚宙斯巨像

位于希腊雅典卫城东南面依里索斯河畔；公元前456年最后完工。

3. 阿尔忒弥斯神殿

希腊古城爱菲索斯(Ephesus)中，约在今土耳其的Izmir(Smyrna)南面50公里；约公元前550年完工。

4. 摩索拉斯基陵墓

现在的土耳其西南地区；大约公元前353年完工。

5. 亚历山大灯塔

在埃及的亚历山大港附近的法洛斯岛（island of Pharos）上；大约公元前300年完工。

6. 巴比伦空中花园

巴比伦，幼发拉底河河东，今伊拉克首都巴格达以南50里左右；大约公元前6世纪完工。

7. 罗德岛巨像

爱琴海，希腊罗德港；公元前282年完工。

新七大奇迹

在2001年，由"新七大奇迹"基金会发起新七大奇迹网上选举。由当中二百多个世界的景点中选出七十七个较优的景点，供网民投票，该活动于2007年7月8日凌晨在葡萄牙首都里斯本揭晓，中国长城、约旦佩特拉古城、巴西基督像、印加马丘遗址、奇琴伊查库库尔坎金字塔、古罗马斗兽场、泰姬陵成为世界"新七大奇迹"。

12 神秘的斯芬克斯——狮身人面像

In a **depression** to the south of Chephren's pyramid sits a creature with a human head and a lion's body. The name "sphinx" which means "**strangler**" was first given by the Greeks to a fabulous creature which had the head of a woman and the body of a lion and the wings of a bird. The sphinx appears to have started in Egypt in the form of a sun god. The Egyptian sphinx is usually a head of a king wearing his **headdress** and the body of a lion. There are, however, sphinxes with ram heads that are **associate**d with the god Amun.

The Great Sphinx is to the northeast of Chephren's Valley Temple. Where it sits was once a quarry. Chephren's workers shaped the stone into the lion and gave it their king's face over 4,500 years ago. The sphinx faces the rising sun with a temple to the front which **resemble**s the sun temples which were built later by the kings of the 5th Dynasty. The figure was buried for most of its life in the sand. King Thutmose IV (1425 - 1417 BC) placed a **stela** between the front paws of the figure. It describes when Thutmose, while still a prince, had gone hunting and fell asleep in the shade of the sphinx. During a dream, the sphinx spoke to Thutmose and told him to clear away the sand because it was **choking** the sphinx. The sphinx told him that if he did this, he would be rewarded with a kingship. Thutmose carried out this request and the sphinx held up his end of the deal.

The sphinx is built of soft **sandstone** and would have disappeared long ago had it not been buried for so long. The body is 200 feet (60m) in length and 65 feet (20m) tall. The face of the sphinx is 13 feet (4m) wide and its eyes are 6 feet (2m) high. Part of the uraeus (sacred cobra), the nose and the ritual beard are now missing. The beard from the sphinx is displayed in the British Museum. The statue is **crumbling** today because of the wind, humidity

在吉萨切夫伦金字塔南边洼地处坐落着狮身人面像。斯芬克斯的意思是"扼杀者",最初来源于希腊神话中,斯芬克斯长着女人的头、狮子的躯体,带着翅膀。而斯芬克斯最初在埃及出现是以太阳神的形象。埃及的斯芬克斯经常是长着国王的脑袋,带着国王的头饰,有着狮子的躯体。然而,也有长着羊的头,跟埃及司生命和繁殖之神亚蒙神联系起来的形象。

狮身人面像在切夫伦庙的东北方向,那里原来的位置是采石场。4500年前,切夫伦的工人们将石头塑造成狮子的样子,并且长着国王的脸庞。狮身人面像面向着升起的太阳。它的前面是一座象征着太阳庙的庙宇。这些太阳庙宇由第五代的国王修建。实际上,狮身人面像自诞生以来,很长一段时间都被沙子所覆盖。图特摩斯四世在狮身人面像的两个爪子之间放上了铭牌。据传当图特摩斯还是王子的时候,有一次去打猎,在斯芬克斯像下睡着了。他梦见斯芬克斯对他说,要将它前面的沙子清除,因为它使得斯芬克斯窒息。并且,斯芬克斯说,如果图特摩斯四世照办,它会以让他称王的方式报答。图特摩斯四世照办了,斯芬克斯也兑现了诺言。

狮身人面像是由质地柔软的砂岩建造。因为长埋于地下,而至今存留于世。狮身人面像长60m,高20m,人面宽4m,眼睛2m高。

and the smog from Cairo. Attempts to restore it have often caused more harm than good. No one can be certain who the figure is to personify. It is possible that it is Chephren. If that is so, it would then be the oldest known royal portrait in such large scale. Some say that it was built after the pyramid of Chephren was complete. It may have been set as a sort of **scarecrow** to guard his tomb. Still others say it is the face of his guardian deity, rather than Chephren himself. The image of the sphinx is a depiction of royal power. Only a pharaoh or an animal could be shown this way, with the animal representing a protective deity.

In the 1980's, a carefully planned restoration of the Sphinx was in progress. Present attempts at restoration are under the control of the Supreme Council of Antiquities' archaeologists.

眼镜蛇、鼻子以及胡须不见了。如今，斯芬克斯的胡须在英国的博物馆展出。今天，狮身人面像出现了裂痕，原因是风力侵蚀、湿度作用以及开罗的烟雾浸染。而修缮雕像的努力大多于事无补。无人能确定这个形象到底是谁。可能是切夫伦。如果是那样，那它就是现存最古老的、有如此尺寸的皇室雕像。也有一些人说，狮身人面像是在切夫伦金字塔完成之后。狮身人面像是作为一种稻草人的作用，保护切夫伦的墓地。另外一些人说，人面是切夫伦保护神的面孔，而非切夫伦本人。斯芬克斯的形象是皇室权利的一种刻画。只有法老或一种动物才可以以这种形象示人，因为动物代表着保护神。

自上个世纪80年代，狮身人面像得到了精心修复。如今此项工作由古迹最高委员会的考古学家们监管。

词汇 VOCABULARY

depression：低洼处	stela：铭牌
strangler：扼杀者，阻气门	choke：窒息
headdress：头饰	sandstone：砂岩
associate：与……相联系	crumble：（将某物）弄碎，碎成细屑
resemble：与……相似	scarecrow：稻草人

背景知识 PROFILE

斯芬克斯之谜

斯芬克斯是希腊神话中一个长着狮子躯干、女人头面的有翼怪兽。坐在忒拜城附近的悬崖上，向过路人出一个谜语："什么东西早晨用四条腿走路，中午用两条腿走路，晚上用三条腿走路？"如果路人猜不出，就被害死。俄狄浦斯猜中了谜底是"人"，斯芬克斯羞惭跳崖而死。斯芬克斯后来被比作谜一样的人和谜语。

关于这个故事，法国画家古斯塔夫·莫罗（Gustave Moreau）曾画过一幅著名的画《俄狄浦斯和斯芬克斯》。《俄狄浦斯和斯芬克斯》画的俄狄浦斯是一持杖裸体美少年，而斯芬克斯在绝美的容貌后面有一种残忍、神秘、冷僻和罪恶的力量。她那丑恶的兽身、张开的雄健的翅膀都野性勃发，越发衬托出那张少女的美丽却冷酷的脸，和成熟妇人的丰腴乳房。这是幅奇特的画，画面背景扑朔迷离的色彩似乎包含着某种暗示或隐喻。斯芬克斯紧紧缠绕着俄迪浦斯，用诱惑的胸脯抵住美男子健壮的胸膛，扬起眸子似乎在念着神秘的咒语。而俄狄浦斯带着一种戒备与男人的悲悯，以及男性对美丽异性那种无可奈何的眷恋俯视着她。这一对厮缠一处的人儿既像是一对情侣又像是两个仇敌。斯芬克斯有美丽、冷酷、淫荡的身躯，眼睛却像迷蒙的一团黑雾，在蛇形的舞姿中喷吐毒焰。

13 巨石柱下的文明——卡纳克神庙

The temple of Karnak was known as Ipet-isut (Most select of places) by the ancient Egyptians. It is a city of temples built over 2000 years and **dedicated** to the Theben **triad** of Amun, Mut and Khonsu.

This **derelict** place is still capable of overshadowing many of the wonders of the modern world and in its day must have been **awe-inspiring**.

For the largely uneducated ancient Egyptian population this could only have been the place of the gods. It is the mother of all religious buildings, the largest ever made and a place of **pilgrimage** for nearly 4,000 years, although today's pilgrims are mainly tourists. It covers about 200 acres 1.5km by 0.8km. In addition to the main sanctuary there are several smaller temples and a vast sacred lake.

Karnak is the home of the god Amun who was

对于古埃及人来说，卡纳克神庙是作为Ipet-isut（神选之地）而闻名的。这是一个庙宇的城市，建于2000多年前，是为了纪念太阳神、自然神和月亮神。

这个遭人遗弃的地方，事实上，仍然能使现代世界的很多奇迹黯然无光，让人敬畏。

对于大部分未受教育的古埃及人来说，这个地方仅仅是众神之地。它是所有宗教建筑的母建筑，是迄今为止最大的宗教建筑。近4000年以来，此地一直是朝圣之地。当然，如今的朝圣者多数是游客。卡纳克神庙占地200公顷。除了主圣堂之外，还有一些小型庙宇及一个很大的神圣之湖。

an insignificant local god until the 12th dynasty when Thebes became the capital of Egypt. He was represented in his original state as a **goose** and later as a ram, at the height of his power he was shown as a human with a head dress of feathers—all that remained of the goose.

In ancient times wars were not fought between countries but were considered as contests between gods. One deity **subduing** and replacing another, the victorious god and its people growing in strength. This is how Amon, with the help of Thutmose III and various other New Kingdom kings, rose to become the first supreme god of the known world and was **hail**ed as God of gods. His followers came from all the strata of society and he was known to some as "**Vizier**of the poor".

All Egyptian temples had a sacred lake, Karnak's is the largest. It was used during festivals when images of the gods would sail across it on golden barges. Karnak was also the home of a flock of geese dedicated to Amun.

The Eastern Gateway which once lead to a huge temple built by Akhenaten (the heretic king). In an attempt to obliterate his memory, Akenaten's enemies destroyed this shrine after his death.

12世纪底比斯成为埃及首都之前，卡纳克是当地一个小神亚蒙神的家乡。最初，亚蒙神的形象是用鹅代表的，而后是羊。而亚蒙神的鼎盛之时，人们将他刻画成人形，头戴鹅毛。

古时，国家之间无战争，反倒是诸神之战。一个神战胜另外一个，将其取而代之，胜利者和他的人民因此得势。这就是阿蒙神如何在图特摩斯三世和其他新王国国王的帮助下，成为第一个诸神之王。阿蒙神的追随者们来自社会的各个阶层，人称"贫苦人的父母官"。

所有埃及的庙宇都有一个神湖，而卡纳克湖最大。节日期间，人们会将神的形象放在金画舫内，然后在卡纳克湖内航行。此外，卡纳克湖内是一群鹅的栖息之地，旨在进献给亚蒙神。

神庙东口曾经通向一座巨大的庙宇，该庙宇是由异教徒国王Akhenaten建造的。为了抹去人们对Akhenaten的记忆，Akhenaten的敌人在其死后毁掉了这座神社。

词汇 VOCABULARY

dedicated：专注的，献身的，专用的	goose：鹅
triad：三个一组，三合会，<音>三和弦	subdue：制服
derelict：遗弃的	hail：承认……为，拥立
awe-inspiring：使人敬畏的	Vizier：（伊斯兰教国家元老，高官）维齐尔
pilgrimage：朝圣	enclosure：四周有篱笆等的场地，围场

埃及神庙简介

它属于古埃及宗教建筑，是公元前16世纪到前11世纪埃及新王国时期的主要建筑形式。多以石块砌筑，分带有柱廊的内院、大柱厅和神堂。大门前有方尖碑或法老雕像。正面墙上刻有着色浅浮雕。大柱厅内柱直径大于柱间间距，使人深感压抑，借以强化圣庙的气氛。建筑实例有古埃及卢克索的阿蒙神庙。具体如下：

阿布辛贝尔大神庙

公元前第13世纪著名的法老拉美西斯二世以他自己与阿蒙·拉，普塔和拉·哈勒刻特三位一体神的荣耀开始采岩，伴着一座献给拉美西斯二世之妻与女神哈托尔的略小一筹的神庙，坐落于尼罗河畔，俯瞰伸向南方的平原，成为埃及力量的象征、令人敬畏的纪念碑。它很可能以此来威吓南方的人们，以镇住任何一个想入侵埃及之地的人。神庙战略性的方位正对尼罗河畔，这却为它带来不幸，在二十世纪六十年代时尼罗河上一个新的水坝建筑使得水位上升，随时会淹没这座伟大的遗址，1963年到1967年间由联合国教育科学文化组织领头做了国际性援救，将神庙搬到更高更为安全的地方。

大法老自己的四座巨像俯瞰于神庙前，巨像戴着独特的头巾，冠以上下埃及的王冠，每座20米高，然而从正面看要宽于35米，高于30米。随伴着国王的是他的众多妻子、儿女，他们在他腿边，要比他小得多。在入口正顶的一座小壁龛供奉着拉·哈勒刻特神。正面顶部冠以一排狒狒。

中心入口通入一个大廊柱大厅，大厅的前面是奥西里斯国王模样的塑像。神庙的方位布置精妙，每年的2月22日与10月22日最早的太阳光线会照在最内室的后墙上，使得坐在那儿的四神像明亮发光。

拉美西斯二世庙

拉美西斯二世在塞提一世的废庙边建了令人惊叹的墓葬庙。据说这座大神庙可堪比阿布辛贝尔庙的神奇。不过拉美西斯建的这座神庙离尼罗河太近，洪水成了它们的丧钟，仅幸存了第一庭院的柱廊，废墟前是拉美西斯高17米巨像的基座，雕像可能重于1000吨，雕像倒向第二庭院，头与躯干落在那里，其他部分已成碎片分散于全世界的博物馆。

拉美西斯三世庙

拉美西斯三世整个神庙，宫殿环于一座高墙内。入口经过围墙，很像一座亚洲的堡垒。就在围墙内，向南是阿蒙尼狄斯一世、舍彭维佩特二世与尼托刻特的教堂，她们都有阿蒙的圣阿多特里斯头衔。第一塔门通向一座开阔的庭院，排以拉美西斯三世的雕像，一边是奥西里斯，另一边是未切的圆柱，第二塔门通向列柱厅，也是拉美西斯型的特色圆柱，这连着斜坡通向第三塔门，接着到了一个多柱大厅。浮雕与外国俘虏的人头也放在神庙里，这可能是国王掌控叙利亚与努比亚的象征。

14 新的城市——迦太基古城

With its **enviable** location on an **arrowhead**-shaped peninsula centrally located between east and west, the city of Carthage (from the Phoenician Qart-Hadasht "New City"), was an important city in Roman times that became a major center of early Christianity. Ruins of the once-great city can be seen not far from Tunis, in modern-day Tunisia.

Not a sacred site in itself (and with few **surviving** temples), ancient Carthage is of religious interest as a great **pagan** city, an early center of Christianity, and the home of Tertullian and St. Cyprian.

History

Originally a Phoenician trading town, Carthage was captured and destroyed by the Romans in 146 BC following the Punic Wars. A century later, in 44 BC, Julius Caesar established a Roman city there, which rose to prominence as one of the three great ports of the Roman Mediterranean. With a population of about 300,000 in the early 3rd century, Roman Carthage was second only to Rome in the western empire.

A **magnet** for trade, overseas visitors, and refugees in late antiquity, Carthage was known for its deep attachment to Roman culture and civic life.

By 200 AD, a **flourishing** Christian community was established in Carthage. Writing to a pagan audience from Carthage in 197 AD, Tertullian proclaimed that the Christians "have filled every place among you". A council of 70 bishops was held at Carthage sometime between 198 and 222. At the Council at Carthage in 397, the Biblical **canon** for the western Church was confirmed.

The Donatist **schism**, a major rift in North African Christianity, was born in Carthage in 312

"迦太基"源于腓尼基语,意为"新的城市"。迦太基城位于箭头形半岛的顶端,正好是东西方的中间。它是罗马时期一座重要的城市,而后成为早期基督教的主要中心。如今,人们能够在突尼斯不远处看到迦太基城遗址。

迦太基本身并不是圣城,而是作为一处异教城市,是早期基督教中心,是古代基督教神学家、伦理学家德尔图良和早期基督教神学家和神父圣西普里安的故乡。

历史

最初,迦太基是腓尼基的一个贸易小镇。公元前146年,罗马人占领并破坏迦太基城,而后该城市又经历布匿战争。一个世纪后的公元前44年,裘里斯·凯撒在此建立罗马城市,这个罗马城而后一跃成为地中海沿岸三个港口之一。3世纪,迦太基城人口约30万,罗马的迦太基城在西方帝国中仅次于罗马。

200年,一个蓬勃的基督教团体在迦太基城建立起来。德尔图良在197年从迦太基给一群异教徒观众的信中写到,基督徒"已经渗透到了你们所在的各个地方"。198年至222年间,一个70主教组成的委员会偶尔会在迦太基召开会议。397年,基督教义

AD. It ended officially in the Baths of Gargilius in the summer of 411, after drawing the intense attention of St. Augustine of Hippo and other theologians and authorities. The city was taken by the Vandals in the 5th century, but much of the city continued to flourish under barbarian rule. Although some public buildings fell into neglect, many church buildings, private houses, and some baths were rebuilt and decorated with mosaics and sculpture.

Carthage's economy collapsed around 650 when its harbors went out of use, and the city was captured by the Arabs in 698 AD. Today, Carthage is nothing but an area of ruins and foundations alongside the Mediterranean, not far from Tunis.

What to See

Today, it is mainly Roman sites (theatres, temples, villas and baths), which can be seen in Carthage. Among the highlights are the ruins of the Roman **amphitheatre** and the thermal Antonine Baths, which were once the largest baths built by the Romans.

You can get a great view of Carthage by climbing the nearby Byrsa Hill, on which you'll also find the Carthage Museum. The museum displays **mosaic**s, sculptures and artifacts from the period before Carthage was destroyed by Rome in 146 BC.

Also on Byrsa Hill is St. Louis Cathedral, built by the French in 1890 and dedicated to the 13th century saint-king who died on the shores of Carthage in 1270. It is now deconsecrated and used for concerts.

已在迦太基确定下来。

312年，多纳徒派从北非基督教中分裂出来，在迦太基诞生。411年夏多纳徒派正式消失。5世纪，汪达尔人占领了迦太基城。而城市的大部分仍在野蛮人的统治下蓬勃发展。尽管一些公共建筑无人管理，但是很多教堂、私人宅邸以及一些浴室却得到了重修，并且用镶嵌画和雕塑装饰一新。

大约650年，迦太基的经济开始凋敝，此时它的港口已失去用途。698年，阿拉伯人占领该城市。今天，迦太基只落得地中海沿岸一片残骸和地基，距离突尼斯不远。

景观

如今，人们能够在迦太基看到的主要是罗马的景点（剧场、庙宇、住宅以及浴室）。而最令人注目的则是罗马圆形剧场以及安东尼浴室（该浴室曾是罗马人建造的最大的浴室）。

人们还可以登上附近的比尔斯山，俯瞰迦太基城，而且还会看见迦太基博物馆。馆内展出着公元前146年迦太基城被罗马人破坏之前的镶嵌画、雕塑以及手工艺品。

另外，在山顶上还能看到圣路易斯教堂。该教堂由法国人在1890年建造，目的是纪念1270年死于迦太基海岸的13世纪圣人君主。如今，教堂已改为音乐厅使用。

词汇 VOCABULARY

enviable：让人羡慕的	flourishing：繁荣的，盛行的
arrowhead：箭头	canon：教规，标准，准则，真经
surviving：继续存在的，未死的，依然健在的	schism：分歧，分离

pagan：异教徒	amphitheatre：圆形剧场，竞技场
magnet：磁铁，有吸引力的人（物）	mosaic：镶嵌画，镶嵌图案

背景知识 **P**ROFILE

迦太基战争

迦太基战争又叫"布匿"战争，是公元前264年～公元前146年古罗马与迦太基争夺地中海西部统治权的战争。因罗马人称迦太基人为"布匿"，故名。公元前275年罗马征服整个意大利半岛后，成为奴隶制强国，开始向海外扩张，与早已称霸地中海西部的迦太基发生冲突。双方间的战争主要有三次。

15 石头城——津巴布韦遗址

The monument of Great Zimbabwe is the most famous stone building in southern Africa. Located over 150 miles from Harare, it stands 1,100 km above sea level on the Harare **Plateau**. It is thought to have been built over a long period, beginning in 1200 and ending in 1450.

The Great Zimbabwe monument is built out of **granite** which is the parent rock of the region—i.e. it predominates locally. The building method used was dry-stone walling, demanding a high level of **masonry** expertise. Some of the site is built round natural rock formations. The actual structure comprises a huge enclosing wall some 20 metres high.

Inside there are **concentric passageway**s, along with a number of enclosures. One of these is thought to be a royal enclosure. Large quantities of gold and **ceremonial** battle axes, along with other objects have been found there. There is also what is thought to be a gold workshop,

津巴布韦遗址是非洲南部最有名的石头建筑。该遗址距首都哈拉雷150英里，坐落在海拔1100km的哈拉雷高原上。据猜测，津巴布韦遗址始建于1200年，竣工于1450年。

遗址的建材为当地的母质岩——花岗岩。建筑时不用灰泥而只用石块筑墙，这就要求很高的建造石屋的技巧。遗址中的一些是建造在天然石堆的附属物。实际的构造包括地上的高达20m的墙体。

遗址内部，有中心的过道分布，并有很多圈地。其中一块儿据说是皇家用地。在此，人们发现了大量的黄金、仪式用的战斧以及其他物品。还有一座据说是黄金工作

and a shrine which is still regarded as sacred today.

The wealth of Great Zimbabwe lay in cattle production and gold. There are a number of mines to the west of Great Zimbabwe, about 40 kilometres away. One theory is that the rulers of Great Zimbabwe did not have direct control over the gold mines, but rather managed the trade in it, buying up huge quantities in **exchange** for cattle. The evidence suggests that Great Zimbabwe was at the centre of an international commercial system, which on the continent of Africa. But this trade network also extended to towns in the Gulf, in western parts of India, and even went as far as China.

There are several theories about the decline of Great Zimbabwe. One is environmental: that a combination of **overgrazing** and drought caused the soil on the Zimbabwe Plateau to become exhausted. It is estimated that between 5,000 to 30,000 people lived on and around the site. A decline in land productivity would easily have led to **famine**.

The other explanation is that the people of Great Zimbabwe had to move in order to **maximise** their exploitation of the gold trade network. By 1500 the site of Great Zimbabwe was abandoned. Its people had moved in two directions: North to establish the Mutapa state and South to establish the Torwa state.

坊的地方，以及一座神社。该神社至今仍被人们认为是神圣之地。

津巴布韦遗址的财富在于牲畜产量及黄金产量。在该遗址的西部40km处，有很多矿。一种猜测是说，津巴布韦的统治者并没有对金矿的直接控制权限，但能够管理在津巴布韦进行的贸易，他们用牲畜大量买进。另有证据显示，津巴布韦位于非洲大陆的一处国际商业系统的中心。不过，这个贸易网络遗址延伸至阿拉伯海湾，至印度的西部地区，甚至远到中国。

对于津巴布韦的衰落，有很多种猜测。一种是环境原因：因为过渡放牧以及干旱导致津巴布韦高原的土壤变得贫瘠。据估计，曾有5000~30000人居住在津巴布韦遗址所在地及其附近地区。土地生产力低下很快导致饥荒产生。

其他的解释是说，津巴布韦的人们为了最大限度地发展金矿贸易网络，不得不迁徙。到1500年，津巴布韦遗址所在地遭遗弃。人们移居到了两个方向：向北建立Mutapa state，向南建立Torwa state。

词汇 VOCABULARY

plateau：高原	ceremonial：礼仪的，仪式的
granite：花岗岩	exchange：交换顾
masonry：工技术，石屋	encompass：囊括
concentric：同中心的，同轴的	overgrazing：过度放牧
passageway：走廊，过道	famine：饥荒
maximise：使……最大化	

津巴布韦的风俗、礼节及禁忌

津法律允许"一夫多妻"制。津农村地区是以血缘关系为基础组成的农村村社的传统社会，酋长和头人是农村村落的领导人。绍纳族的酋长和头人按兄终弟继，然后再长房长子的继承顺序。恩德贝莱族社会的酋长和头人按父死子继的顺序。酋长和头人管辖其领地和人民，拥有一定的神权和世俗权力，在农村地区影响较大。

随着津与外界交往日多，城镇中的津巴布韦人开始崇尚"新风尚"，一夫一妻的家庭越来越多，农村传统风俗习惯也在逐渐改变。但在农村地区，婚姻关系和财产继承仍带有较明显的原始社会的遗风。

由于津农业传统影响深厚，津人民非常看重牛、羊等家畜在其生活的作用，把它们视为婚丧、生日和馈赠外宾的至高礼物。例如，1996年，穆加贝总统举行婚礼，穆家乡人民以牛羊作为穆的结婚贺礼。

津巴布韦人喜好文化、艺术、歌舞等，津石雕更是闻名于世。凡遇到喜庆节日，妇女均会穿上民族盛装，载歌载舞，气氛非常活跃。

津巴布韦人受教育程度在非洲国家中较高，比较注重礼节，待人彬彬有礼，热情友好，对老人、妇女尊重谦让。在任何场合，津巴布韦人都注意语言美，即便见到不认识的人也会主动问候。在社交场合，津巴布韦人多采用握手的方式问候致意；见到非常熟悉的朋友，也会热情拥抱，相互左右各亲吻一下对方的面颊，但这仅是礼节性的。妇女见到长者或尊贵客人时一般下蹲请安。

津巴布韦人有见面送礼的习惯，礼物种类繁多，有当地土特产、牛、羊以及津石雕、铜版画等。客人在接到礼物后，应表示感谢，然后交换礼物。切忌拒绝对方的礼物，因为津巴布韦人认为，拒绝礼物是对对方极大的不尊重。

津巴布韦人的主食称作"萨杂"，即用白玉米面熬成的糙粥，加以牛肉、鸡肉、猪肉和蔬菜。过去，黄玉米仅被用作饲料，现在食用的人逐渐增多。部族或个人禁食其崇拜的图腾类食物。

津巴布韦人自尊心很强，对于歧视黑人、不尊重其文化的人，会当即予以羞辱，不留情面。

16 见证南非人民的奋斗史——先民博物馆

The majestic Voortrekker Monument is located on a **hilltop** in Pretoria, and built to **honor** the Voortrekkers who left the Cape Colony between 1835 and 1854.

Designed by Gerard Moerdijk, the Voortrekker Monument was built with the idea of creating a monument that would "stand a thousand years to describe the history and meaning of the Great Trek (Groot Trek) to its **descendant**s".

History of the Voortrekker Monument

When President Paul Kruger attended the Day of the Covenant celebrations at Blood River in Natal on 16 December 1888, the idea to build a monument in honor of the Voortrekkers was first discussed. The "Sentrale Volksmonumentekomitee" [Central People's Monuments Committee] (SVK) was formed in 1931 to bring this idea to **fruition**.

Construction on the Voortrekker Monument started on 13 July 1937, with the **cornerstone** being laid on 16 December 1938 by three descendants of some of the Voortrekker leaders. The then-prime minister DF Malan **inaugurate**d the Voortrekker Monument on 16 December 1949.

Main Features of the Voortrekker Monument

The Voortrekker Monument measures 40 meters high, with a base of 40 meters by 40 meters. Several theories exist as to the **symbolism** of the monument.

Around the outside of the Voortrekker Monument, each of the four corners contains a statue: Piet Retief, Andries Pretorius, Hendrik Potgieter, and an "unknown" leader, representing all of the other Voortrekker leaders. Each statues weighs approximately 6 tones. At the eastern corner of the Voortrekker Monument, on the same level as its entrance, is the **foundation stone**.

雄伟的先民博物馆坐落于比勒陀利亚一个山顶上，旨在纪念在1835年至1854年期间离开开普敦殖民地的移民先驱们。

该博物馆由建筑师杰勒德设计，建造的灵感来源于建一座"可以巍然屹立1000年，通过它，后辈们可以记住移民先驱们的足迹"的博物馆。

历史

1888年12月16日，南非总统保罗·克鲁格出席在娜塔耳血河举行的协议纪念活动，人们首次讨论建立博物馆，纪念移民先驱。1931年，中央人民博物馆委员会成立，使得这个想法成形。

先民博物馆始建于1937年7月13日，1938年12月16日奠基石落下。1949年举行落成仪式。

主要特征

先民博物馆40米高，底座40*40m。对于博物馆的象征意义，有一种猜测。

先民博物馆外面，每一角都有一个雕像：彼得·雷蒂夫、比勒陀利乌斯、波特希特以及一位不知姓名的领导人，他们是移民先驱们的代表。每座雕塑重约6吨。在博物馆的东边角落，与入口处平行，是一块基石。

博物馆的主入口处通向英雄厅。此地有四块巨大的拱形比利时玻璃窗。英雄厅包括大理石的历

The main entrance of the Voortrekker Monument leads into the domed Hall of Heroes. The area is **flank**ed by four huge arched Belgian glass windows. The Hall of Heroes contains the marbled Historical **Frieze**, which forms an important part of the monument. Consisting of 27 **bas-relief panel**s depicting the history of the Great Trek, it is the biggest marble frieze in the world.

The set of panels describes historical scenes starting from the first Voortrekkers (1835) up to the signing of the Sand River Convention (1852). The **Cenotaph** can be viewed in the middle of the floor of the Hall of Heroes. The central focus of the Voortrekker Monument is the Cenotaph, which is located in the center of the Cenotaph Hall. The Cenotaph can also be viewed from the dome at the top of the Voortrekker Monument. Through an opening in the dome, a ray of sunshine shines directly on the Cenotaph, striking the words "Ons vir jou Suid Afrika" at exactly 12:00 on 16 December annually. The ray of light is said to symbolize God's blessing on the lives of the Voortrekkers. A **multitude** of visitors visit the Voortrekker Monument annually on this day to experience this.

The Cenotaph Hall is **decorate**d with the flags of the different Voortrekker Republics, as well as display cases containing artifacts from the Great Trek. The northern wall contains a lantern with a flame that has been kept burning since 1938.

史檐壁，这形成了博物馆重要的部分。这块檐壁由27块浮雕板组成，描述了大迁徙的历史。这是世界上最大的大理石檐壁。

一系列的浮雕板描述了从首次移民到《沙河协定》的签订。从英雄厅的地板中央能够看到纪念碑。先民博物馆中心的关注点就是纪念碑。它位于纪念碑厅的中心。从博物馆的穹顶上能看到纪念碑。通过穹顶的缝隙，每年的12月16日正午12点一缕阳光照耀在纪念碑上的字上："一切为了你——南非"。光代表了上帝对于先民们生命的祝福。每年的这一天，大量的游客来先民博物馆来体验这一刻。

纪念碑厅里，飘扬着各种先民共和国的旗帜，也展示着大迁徙时期的手工艺术品。北墙上有盏灯，自1938年以来，这盏灯一直都亮着。

南非简史

最早的土著居民是桑人、科伊人及后来南迁的班图人。1652年荷兰人开始入侵，对当地黑人发动多次殖民战争。19世纪初英国开始入侵，1806年夺占"开普殖民地"，荷裔布尔人被迫向内地迁徙，并于1852年和1854年先后建立了"奥兰治自由邦"和"德兰士瓦共和国"。1867年和1886年南非发现钻石和黄金后，大批欧洲移民蜂拥而至。英国人通过"英布战争"（1899~1902），吞并了奥兰治自由邦和德兰士瓦共和国。1910年5月英国将开普省、德兰士瓦省、纳塔尔省和奥兰治自由邦合并成南非联邦，成为英国的自治领地。1961年5月31日，南非退出英联邦，成立了南非共和国。南非白人当局长期在国内以立法和行政手段推行种族歧视和种族隔离政策，先后颁布了几百种种族主义法律和法令。1948年国民党执政后，全面推行种族隔离制度，镇压南非人民的反抗斗争，遭到国际社会的谴责和制裁。1989年，德克勒克出任国民党领袖和总统后，推行政治改革，取消对黑人解放组织的禁令并释放曼德拉等人。1991年，非国大、南非政府、国民党等19方就政治解决南非问题举行多党谈判，并于1993年就政治过渡安排达成协议。1994年4月~5月，南非举行了首次由各种族参加的大选，南非举行首次不分种族大选，非国大与南非共产党、南非工会大会组成三方联盟并以62.65%的多数获胜，曼德拉出任南非首任黑人总统，非国大、国民党、因卡塔自由党组成民族团结政府。这标志着种族隔离制度的结束和民主、平等新南非的诞生。1994年6月23日，联合国大会通过决议恢复南非在联大的席位。1996年12月，南非总统曼德拉签署新宪法，为今后建立种族平等的新型国家体制奠定了法律基础。

17 功过任评说——阿斯旺大坝

Aswan Dam (Aswan High Dam) is located in the north of the **border** between Egypt and Sudan. It is a huge rock fill dam which **confine**s the longest river of the world, Nile River, in the world's third largest **reservoirs**, Lake Nasser. It was finished in 1970 and the ten years went in to the making of the dam.

Since ancient times, Egypt has always depended

阿斯旺大坝位于埃及和苏丹的边境上。它位于世界第三大湖——纳塞尔湖上，控制着世界上最长的河——尼罗河的水量。阿斯旺大坝于1970年竣工，历时十年。

自从古时开始，埃及就因为不同的原因需要依赖尼罗河。尼罗河的两

on the water of the Nile River for various reasons. The two major **tributaries** of the Nile River are the White Nile and the Blue Nile. The source of White Nile is the Sobat River Bahr al-Jabal and that of the Blue Nile is in Ethiopian Highlands. The two tributaries **converge** in Khartoum, where they **merge** to form the Nile River. The Nile River has a total length of 4,160 miles (6,695 kilometers) from source to sea.

The Aswan Dam which is located in Aswan, Egypt, tames the Nile River and uses the power of the river for a variety of social and economic causes. There are in fact two dams at Aswan and not just one; even though when most people talk of the Aswan High Dam they refer to the Aswan Dam. Collectively, these two dams run the flow of the Nile River through Egypt, and are also used to produce **hydroelectric** power for the Egyptians. The Aswan Dam has generated a lot of debate since it was built. A group of people fear that the dam can cause major environmental damage, and so they would not support the dam construction and want it removed, although doing so would have **harsh** consequence for Egypt.

The first dam at Aswan, the Aswan Low Dam, was built in the late 1800s by British government, and later was redone a couple of times. This dam was originally designed to manage the annual flooding of the Nile, which was important event in Egypt. Since ancient times the Egyptians have lived and **cultivate** near the Nile, with the help of the annual flooding to **irrigate** and **fertilize** their fields. With the increase in population the unpredictable floods became a problem. It caused loss of life and property, and the British reacted by damming the river.

The first Aswan Dam was not a great success as it was not adequate for the task, and thus in the 1950s several countries like the United States decided to help build a dam which was further upstream. However, later on these countries did not **abide** to the deal, there by forcing

条主要支流是白尼罗河和青尼罗河。白尼罗河的源头是杰贝勒河与索巴特河，青尼罗河的源头是埃塞俄比亚高地。在喀什穆境内，两条支流汇合，汇入尼罗河。尼罗河全长6695km。

阿斯旺大坝位于埃及阿斯旺，它驯服了尼罗河，并将水利用于社会及经济等方面。实际上，阿斯旺有两座大坝——尽管当人们说起阿斯旺大坝时，多指第一座大坝。这两座大坝都截断流经埃及的尼罗河，都用于为埃及人进行水力发电。自从修建以来，阿斯旺大坝饱受争议。一些人担心大坝会引起严重的环境破坏。他们不主张大坝建设，希望大坝拆除。可这样做，对埃及可谓是后患无穷。

阿斯旺一期工程由英国政府修建，修建时间是19世纪末期，而后重修几次。大坝建造的最初目的是为了控制尼罗河每年的泛滥。自古时开始，埃及人就在尼罗河流域生息、繁衍。每年的河水泛滥能起到灌溉作用。随着人口的增长，难以预测的河水成了问题。它夺走了生命、财产。因此，英国政府决定建大坝。

因为资源不足，最初的大坝并未成功。20世纪50年代，美国等国家决定帮助建另外一座大坝。然而，这些国家变卦，迫使埃及在20世纪60年代从苏联那里获得援助。自此，阿斯旺大坝二期工程开始。

因为阿斯旺大坝的修建，尼罗河上游洪水频发，导致很多人流离失所，而对于历史遗迹来说

Egypt to take help from the Soviet Union and thus in the 1960s, construction of the Aswan High Dam started.

As a result of the construction of the Aswan High Dam, mass flooding took place upstream on the Nile, damaged people from their homes and causing huge loss to some invaluable archaeological sites. The lake which was created behind the dam is called as Lake Nasser named after the late Egyptian President Nasser. Egyptians were of opinion that the upstream flooding was a logical way to convenient seasonal flood waters and a steady source of hydroelectric power.

In the long run, quite a few problems have come up in Egypt because of the Aswan Dam. The capacity of Lake Nasser is shrinking as a result of depositions of silt behind the dam, and because of the silt there is water shortage in rest of Egypt.

也是损失惨重。因大坝而成的湖叫做纳塞尔湖。名称来自于已故总统纳赛尔。埃及人认为上游河水泛滥，相比于风调雨顺以及水利发电是值得的。

长远来看，因为阿斯旺大坝，埃及产生了一些问题。纳赛尔湖已因泥沙淤积蓄水量变小，而且由于泥沙淤积，埃及的部分地区出现了缺水现象。

词汇 VOCABULARY

border：边境	hydroelectric：水力发电的
confine：限制	harsh：严峻的
reservoirs：水库	cultivate：耕作，种植庄稼
tributary：支流	irrigate：灌溉
converge：汇集	fertilize：使肥沃，使多产
merge：合并	abide：遵守

背景知识 PROFILE

世界上著名的水利工程

世界上最大的水电站——伊泰普水电站

伊泰普大坝建在流经巴西和巴拉圭两国之间的巴拉那河上。由两国联合所建，从20世纪70年代中期开始，直到1982年才竣工，其耗资200亿美元。大坝有60层楼高，坝后的水库沿河延伸达161千米。

自1990年改进以后，伊泰普大坝成为当时世界上最大的水电站，18台水轮机组发电量达1.26万兆瓦。它的发电量比仅次于它的对手——委内瑞拉的古里大坝，要高出20%

以上。

伊泰普水电站生产的电能由巴西与巴拉圭两国分享。但是，巴拉圭只使用了发电量中极小的一部分。所以，巴拉圭将其份额中的大部分卖给了巴西。

世界高重力坝之一——胡佛大坝

工程建于1931年4月，1936年3月竣工。水库名米德湖，总库容352亿立米。水电装机1134.5万KW，两个泄洪隧洞引水明渠长约198米，泄量为11340立米/秒。4个进水塔每个底部直径25米，最大坝高222.5米。该坝于1955年被评为美国现代土木工程七大奇迹之一。该工程建成后，在防洪、灌溉、城市及工业供水、水力发电等方面发挥了巨大的作用，为开发和建设美国西部各州做出了贡献。

世界最高坝——罗贡坝

世界最高的土石坝，也是世界最高坝。工程于1975年开工，1989年完工。位于塔吉克斯坦阿姆河支流瓦赫什河上。工程主要任务是灌溉与发电。最大坝高335米，坝顶长660米，坝顶宽20米，底宽1500米。坝体体积7550万立米。水库库容133亿立米。水电装机360万KW。

18 军事要塞——耶稣堡

The **Portuguese** built Fort Jesus in 1593. The site chosen was a coral ridge at the entrance to the harbor. The Fort was designed by an Italian Architect and Engineer, Joao Batista Cairato. The earliest known plan of the Fort is in a **manuscript** Atlas by Manuel Godinho de Heredia—dated 1610 which shows the original **layout** of the buildings inside the Fort.

Fort Jesus was built to secure the safety of Portuguese living on the East Coast of Africa. It has had a long history of hostilities of the interested parties that used to live in Mombasa. Perhaps no Fort in Africa has experienced such **turbulence** as Fort Jesus. Omani Arabs attacked the Fort from 1696 to 1698.

Between 1837 and 1895, the Fort was used as **barrack**s for the soldiers. When the British **protectorate** was proclaimed on the 1st of July 1895,

葡萄牙人建造的耶稣堡始建于1953年，此堡的目的在于控制港口。耶稣堡由意大利建筑师及工程师乔安·巴蒂斯塔·凯尔拉杜设计。最早的耶稣堡设计图纸来自于Manuel Godinho de Heredia的手稿，时间是1610年，它显示了堡内建筑的原始格局。

耶稣堡是葡萄牙为了保证自己在非洲东海岸的安全而建立的。它曾引发住在蒙巴萨的有关人士之间长久以来的嫌隙。也许在非洲没有哪座古堡像耶稣堡一样经历过如此的动荡。阿曼的阿拉伯人曾经在1696-1698年间，袭击古堡。

1837年-1895年间，古堡作为了士兵的营房。而1895年7月1日，当蒙

the Fort was converted into a prison. The huts were removed and cells were built. On the 24th October 1958, Fort Jesus was declared a National Park in the **custody** of the Trustees of the Kenya National Parks. Excavation was carried out and the Fort became a Museum in 1962. The Fort is now an important historical landmark in the East African region.

The Fort Jesus museum was built with a grant from the Gulbenkian Foundation. The exhibits consist of finds from archaeological **excavation**s at Fort Jesus, Gede, Manda, Ungwana and other sites. Other objects on display were donated by individuals notably Mrs. J.C. White, Mr. C.E. Whitton and Mrs. W.S. Marchant.

巴萨成为英国的保护地区之后，该古堡便成了监狱。房间被一间间监狱所取代。1958年10月24日，肯尼亚国家公园托管会宣布耶稣堡是一所国家公园。然后1962年，古堡又成了博物馆。如今，耶稣堡是东非地区非常重要的一座历史坐标。

耶稣堡博物馆是在获古尔本基安基金会资金投入的情况下建造。展品包括在耶稣堡、盖德、曼塔等景点处发现的出土文物。另外，还有个人捐赠的物品。

词汇 VOCABULARY

Portuguese：葡萄牙人	barrack：营房
manuscript：手稿	protectorate：受保护国
layout：布局，安排	custody：监管，监护
turbulence：动荡	excavation：出土文物

背景知识 PROFILE

世界上著名的三座古堡

瑞士的西庸城堡（Chillon）

西庸城堡是为了控制军事意义重大的南北通道和湖水、山之间的小道而建立的军事要塞。从12世纪成了Savoy王族的所有，13世纪~14世纪成了王族的夏宫，作为军事要塞和司法机关。这个时期也是西庸城堡的黄金期。从1536年到1798年成了伯恩人统治的Vaud洲的所有。就是他们在城堡留下自己最美丽的装饰。随着1798年Vaud洲的独立，西庸城堡也成了他们的所有。19世纪浪漫主义时代西庸城堡因为在Jean-Jacques Rousseau，Victor Hugo，Alexandre Dumas，Byron等著名作家的故事中登场而广为人知，其中《西庸城堡的罪人》（The Prisoner of Chillon）是闻名世界的名著。

西庸城堡的内部古朴的房间里面展示着当时使用过的物品。各种器皿和银剑，头盔和刀等，可以回味当时贵族的生活。虽然笨拙，但非常协调的木床和充满美丽的墙壁，显出城堡浪漫的生活。城中的礼拜堂里面通过幻灯，重现过去的壁画，用手挡住光线，就能看见模糊的实际的壁画。走上迷宫般的台阶，就能到屋顶。

在屋顶俯视莱茵湖的绝境，还有眺望法国国境是西庸城堡的另一个魅力所在。西庸城堡将继续保持现今古朴的样子，向游客展示建筑物的历史。城堡周围的莱茵湖也值得一游。

芬兰的图尔库城堡（Turku Castle）

图尔库城堡位于奥拉河的入海口旁。这座军事防御的城堡始建于1280年，旧城堡部分用了280年时间。文艺复兴式的新堡部分则是在1574年~1588年间建的，包括国王和王后大厅。当时的图尔库还属于瑞典的领地。瑞典国王来芬兰都住在这里，有14位瑞典国王以此为行宫。二战中城堡遭破坏，战后经修复，新堡部分被改成图尔库文化历史博物馆。城堡还有18到20世纪的古钱币和徽章展览。

法国的朗热堡（Langeais）

以前，人们要想在卢瓦尔河的朗热河段上架一座桥简直就是痴人说梦。这里的河道很宽，河水湍急，冬天还要发数次洪水。直到1951年，这里才有了现在使用的这座吊桥，而在桥的对面，就矗立着朗热城堡。

朗热城堡位于法国南部历史悠久的都兰地区。卢瓦尔河在朗热地区河面开阔，成为了朗热地区的天堑，选择在这里建造一座城堡，自然会成为那些妄图夺取都兰地区的敌人不可逾越的军事工事。公元4世纪，圣马丁在此建立了一座修道院，到了9世纪朗热地区第一次建造了一座石制堡垒，这就是日后朗热城堡中的主堡，它同时也是当时卢瓦尔河流域最早建造的石制城堡。现在的朗热城堡就是在这座城堡的基础上扩建而成的。在12世纪时，英格兰国王狮心王查理占领了都兰地区，朗热城堡也自然被他占有。由于城堡最初是防御之用，所以它与后来卢瓦尔河流域的大多数被贵族用于享乐的城堡不同，不具备秀丽的外表、华丽的内室，而是依靠坚固的城墙、敦实的防御塔楼构成滴水不漏的严密防御体系。城堡底部的城墙非常厚，至少有4米，而且底部没有门，门开在离地很高的地方，而且尽可能的小，如果要进门，就要借助梯子。

19 探访人类足迹——人类摇篮遗址

The **Cradle** of Humankind Site comprises a **strip** of a dozen **dolomitic** limestone caves containing the **fossillise**d remains of ancient forms of animals, plants and most importantly, **hominid**s. The **dolomite** in which the caves formed, started out as **coral reef**s growing in a warm shallow sea about 2.3 billion years ago.

The Cradle of Humankind site lies mainly in the Gauteng province with a small extension into the neighboring North West Province, and covers 47000 hectares of land mostly privately owned.

As the reefs died off they were transformed into limestone which some time later was converted into dolomite. Millions of years later after the sea had **recede**d, slightly acidic **groundwater** began to **dissolve** out **calcium carbonate** from the dolomite to form underground **cavern**s. Over time the **water table** dropped and the underground caverns were exposed to the air. The **percolation** of acidic water through the dolomite also dissolved calcium carbonates out of the rock into the caverns, which formed **stalactite**s, **stalagmite**s and other crystalline structures. Continued erosion on the earth's surface and dissolution of the dolomite eventually resulted in shafts or avens forming between the surface of the earth and the caverns below. Bones, stones and plants washed down these shafts into the caves; and animals and hominids fell into the caves, became trapped and died. The bone and plant remains became fossilized and along with various stones and pebbles became cemented in a hard mixture called **breccia**.

At least seven of the twelve sites have yielded hominid remains. In fact, together these cave sites have produced over 850 hominid fossil remains, so that to date

人类摇篮遗址包含十多个白云石灰岩的山洞，这些山洞内有远古形态的动植物以及原始人类的遗址。这些组成山洞的白云石最初是温暖浅水海域的珊瑚礁，时间是23亿年以前。

人类摇篮遗址主要坐落在豪登省，并且稍稍延伸至西北省，占地4.7万公顷，大多数为私人占地。

珊瑚死后，便转变成了石灰岩，再然后就变成了白云石。数百万年后，海水退却，微酸的地下水开始溶解出碳酸钙，由此形成了洞穴。随着时间的推移，地下水位下降，地下的山洞便裸露出来。酸性水经过白云石的渗透作用也会溶解碳酸钙，释放到山洞中，这样就成了钟乳石、石笋以及其他水晶制结构。地球表面不断被侵蚀，白云石不断被溶解，最终在地球表面和山洞的中间导致了凹陷或落水洞的形成。而那些误落入山洞的动物或原始人类会困在此处，最终丧命。动物的骨头和植物开始石化，并且和不同的石头和卵石板结成角砾岩。

至少7/12的遗址存在原始人类遗迹。实际上，这些洞穴能够产生850处原始人类遗迹。所以，这些遗址代表了世界上最为丰富的原始人类化石的景点之一。这片区域的科学价值在于，它为我们回顾

they represent one of the world's richest concentrations of fossil hominid bearing sites. The scientific value of this area lies in the fact that these sites provide us with a window into the past, to a time when our earliest ancestors were evolving and changing. Scientists have long accepted that all humans had their origins in Africa.

Through the use of biochemical evidence they have argued that the split of the human **lineage** (Hominidae) from that of the African **ape**s took place around 5-6 million years ago. The study of hominid fossils from sites in Africa thus enables scientists to understand how these hominids have changed and **diversified** since then.

过去提供了一扇窗，透过这扇窗，我们可以看到我们最早的祖先是如何进化以及改变的。科学家们早已达成共识，所有人类的起源都在非洲。

通过生物化学的方法，科学家们认为人类从非洲猿中分离出来是发生在五、六百万年前。而非洲发现的原始人类遗址可以让科学家们更好地理解原始人类是如何改变和多元化的。

词汇 VOCABULARY

cradle：摇篮	calcium carbonate：碳酸钙	breccia：角砾岩
strip：狭长的一条	cavern：山洞	lineage：家系，直系，血统
dolomitic：有白云石的	water table：地下水位	ape：猿
fossillise：使……石化	percolation：渗透	diversify：使多样化，使变化，使不同
hominid：原始人类	stalactite：石钟乳	groundwater：地下水
dolomite：白云石	stalagmite：石笋	dissolve：溶解
coral reef：珊瑚礁	recede：后退，减弱	

背景知识 PROFILE

世界上八大古人类遗址

尼安德特人

1848年，在欧洲西南角的直布罗陀发现了一些古人类化石，这些化石所代表的古人类就是最先被发现的、后来被称做尼安德特人（简称尼人）的早期智人，但当时却没有引起人们的注意。尼安德特人的名称来自德国杜塞尔多夫市附近的尼安德特河谷，1856年8月，在这里的一个山洞里发现了一个成年男性的颅顶骨和一些四肢骨骼的化石，被命名为尼安德特人。在这以后，尼人的化石开始在西起西班牙和法国、东到伊朗北部和乌兹别克斯坦、南到巴勒斯坦、北到北纬53度线的广大地区被大量地发现。尼人的生存时代为距今20万年至3万7千年之间。

克罗马农人

1868年，E·拉台和H·克累斯提在法国多尔多涅区埃济附近趁修路之便，在克罗马农岩窟中发现古代埋葬的人类骸骨化石，并有殓衣的痕迹，至少在五具骸骨之侧，还发现石器，表示给死者未去灵界之前所需要用之工具，还有灰烬坑及驯鹿等动物骨骼。

从这些遗骸可以看出：克罗马农人的体格颇为雄伟，平均身高可达1.82米，脑容量1590毫升-1715毫升，颜面甚广，下颌发达，与现代西欧、中欧的人种几无区别。从其文化遗物判断，时代为旧石器时代晚期，同位素年龄测定，距今35000年-10000万年前。

爪哇猿人

爪哇猿人，由荷兰人类学家Eugene Dubois（1858-1940）于1891年在印度尼西亚中部州（Medium）特里尼尔（Trinil）地方发现，是世界上最早发现的猿人化石。地质年代属更新世中期。所发现的化石有头盖骨一具、臼齿二枚、左侧股骨一根。形态特征是：颅骨低平，最宽处接近颅底；额骨倾斜，眉脊呈屋檐状；脑容量约900毫升；臼齿粗大；股骨长45厘米，骨干甚直，适于直立行走。1936-1941年荷兰古生物学家Gustav Heinlich Ralph von Koenigswald在印度尼西亚三吉岭（Sangiran）一带，又发现爪哇直立猿人头骨和下颌骨多具。

能人

能人(Homo habilis)，发现于非州的东部和南部，可能有几种，其中不少特征颇与南方古猿相似。生活在距今300万年-150万年前，他的脑量明显比南方古猿大，并能制造石器。一般认为他是南方古猿向直立人进化的中间环节。他的身高约为109厘米-152厘米。大多数能人化石出现在190万年-160万年前，从生物学角度看，他更像南方古猿。与"东非人"（即南方古猿鲍氏种）同在一层位内，也就是奥杜韦河谷剖面的第一层。综合若干能人化石的特点，大致可作以下描述：头骨扁平，平均脑量大于南方古猿而小于直立人，脑的结构更接近于人，至少存在讲话能力的神经系统，但有专家认为，30万年-40万年前的人才具有语言能力。头骨顶部的中矢嵴或不明显，上下颌都小于南方古猿。门齿特大，枕骨结节比南方古猿或直立人都弱。手骨比现代人粗壮，足骨与现代人颇为相似。古人类学家认为，目前能人是人类最早的祖先，他已能制造石器了。

汤恩小孩

1924年，南非的汤恩石灰岩采石场的工人在爆破时炸出了一个小孩的不完整的头骨化石，保存有部分颅骨、面骨、下颌骨和完整的脑模（脑壳里的填充物依照脑壳内部的骨骼结构形成的与原来的脑子外形一致的化石），颌骨上保存了全部乳齿和正在萌出的第一恒臼齿。现在所有南非的南方古猿化石都被归为一个属两个种，即南方古猿非洲种（又称纤细型南方古猿）和南方古猿粗壮种（又称粗壮型南方古猿）。纤细型的年代大约在距今350万年至150万年之间，一般来说比粗壮型的时代要早。

Toumai

一个由法国和乍得科学家组成的40人考察组7月10日宣布，他们发现了距今600万年-700万年的古人类头盖骨。据报道，这是迄今为止发现的最古老的古人类化石。Toumai

在分类学上的正式名称为 Sahelanthropus tchadensis，似乎可以译为"萨赫勒人乍得种"（萨赫勒是撒哈拉沙漠以南的一个地区，近几十年来荒漠化得厉害）。昵称 Toumai 来自当地土语，意思是"在干旱季节快要开始的危险时期出生的小孩"。如果它不在人类进化树的起点位置，也应该相当接近。

露西

1974年11月，美国自然历史博物馆的科学家多纳尔德·约翰森等研究人员，来到号称"非洲屋脊"的埃塞俄比亚。他们在那里的哈达地区，发掘到一具不太完整的古人类化石。根据骨骼的形态分析，化石的主人是一个年仅20岁的女性。约翰森给她起了个名字——"露西"，并详细分析了她的身体结构特点。约翰森认为，"露西"生活在距今300万年以前，她已经能够独立行走。

365万年前的人类足迹

这是迄今为止，发现的最为古老的人科动物足迹化石，距今已有365万年。由著名的古人类学家，旧石器考古学家玛丽·利基（Mary Leakey）于1975年在坦桑尼亚的雷托立（Laetoli, Tanzania）地区发现。这个伟大的发现，用最直接的证据表明，我们的祖先，在至少365万年前，已能直立行走了。

20 童话外的矮人们——中非矮人村

Over 150,000 unreached Pygmies live in the tropical rain forests of Central Africa. They inhabit the region that stretches from Cameroon, across the Congo, into Zaire. At least one of the groups, the Akebou, also occupies parts of Togo, West Africa.

Pygmies are best known for their small size. Adults usually grow to be only three or four feet tall. In fact, their name, "Pygmy", is **derive**d from the Greek word, pyme, which means "a cubit in height".

Pygmies are the earliest known **inhabitant**s of the Congo Basin, which is located in Zaire. It is also reported that the Ituri Forest has been occupied by Pygmies for over four thousand years. The Pygmies who live there today call themselves Mbuti.

15万多矮人在中非热带雨林离群索居着。他们的居住区域从喀麦隆起，经过刚果，进入扎伊尔。而其中至少一个团体——Akebou也占据着西非多哥的一些地方。

矮人以其矮小身材而闻名。成年人也只有3、4英尺高。实际上，"矮人"这个词汇来源于希腊单词pyme，意思是"18-22英寸高"（1英尺=12英寸）。

矮人是刚果盆地最早的已知居民，他们居住在扎伊尔。据报道，矮人曾经在4000多年前住在伊图里雨林中。如今，住在此地的矮人自称为Mbuti。

Pygmies are lighter skinned than their **Negroid** neighbors. They are a gentle, peaceful people who have the ability to be **camouflage**d so well in the forest that they can be passed without ever being noticed.

Pygmies are forest **dweller**s, with most of them relying on hunting and gathering for survival. Some of them may also farm or plant fields in the middle of the forest. However, they will **abandon** them while the crops are growing to hunt and gather, since that is what they know best.

Today, Pygmies no longer inhabit the forest areas alone. Many groups of Negroid farmers have **infiltrate**d the region and built villages there. The two peoples have developed an economic, **mutual** dependence, and live together peacefully. Because of this, the Pygmies usually speak a **dialect** of the Negroid tribe.

Pygmy men hunt deer, pigs, hippos, and elephants. Some Pygmy groups use nets to hunt, while others use spears or bows and arrows. Usually, the only domestic animals that are kept are hunting dogs. Forest resources, such as meat and honey, are traded to farmers for corn, salt, clothes, and iron tools. While the men are hunting, the women are busy collecting wild fruits, roots, insects, lizards, and shellfish. They also do most of the fishing.

Pygmies live in nomadic bands that range in size from 20 to no more than 100 people. These bands wander across the hunting territories that are collectively owned by the whole group.

A Pygmy generally has only one wife, but **polygamy** does exist, especially among the Baka. A Pygmy man obtains a wife by giving a gift, or "bride price", to the girl's family. The Mbuti, as well as other Pygmy groups, also practice "sister exchanging" as a means of obtaining wives.

Pygmies typically dress in simple loincloths that are made from the beaten bark of trees. In some tribes, the back strip on the loincloth extends nearly to the ground, giving a "tail-like" appearance. They like these long strips because they look good while they are dancing.

矮人比其临近居民黑人皮肤颜色要淡一些。他们祥和宁静，爱好和平。他们有能力在森林里伪装，不被发现。

矮人是丛林里的居住者。很多的矮人靠打猎和采集生存。也有一些靠农业和养殖生存。然而，如果到了打猎和采集的时间，他们会脱离农业和养殖。

如今，很多群体的黑人也进入矮人居住的这片领域，并在那里建造房屋。黑人和矮人们逐渐形成了经济上的相互依赖，他们在一起相安无事。因此，矮人们也会说一些黑人们的方言。

矮人的男人们会猎取鹿、猪、河马以及大象。一些矮人群体用网打猎，一些用长矛、弓箭打猎。一般来说，他们只养猎狗以便打猎之用。他们会用肉、蜂蜜等森林资源换取农民的玉米、盐、衣服以及铁制工具。女人们会采集野果、根、昆虫、蜥蜴以及贝类。另外，她们还会打渔。

矮人是以游牧族群生活的，族群的数量是20人~100人。这些族群散落在猎物区域周围。

矮人们通常是一夫一妻制。但一夫多妻也存在，尤其是在Baka。男人们赢取女人的方式是送礼物给女方家庭。而在Mbuti或其他矮人族群中，男人们通过将家里妹妹作为礼物送出去，来获得妻子。

矮人的传统服饰是腰布，制衣材料是树皮。一些部落中，后背腰布的长度会及地，有点儿尾巴的感觉。他们很喜欢这些长条，因为跳起舞来，别有韵味。

derive：起源，衍生	abandon：抛弃，放弃
inhabitant：居民	infiltrate：渗透，悄悄进入
Negroid：黑人	mutual：相互的
camouflage：伪装	dialect：方言
dweller：住在某处的人或动物	polygamy：一夫多妻，一妻多夫，多配偶制

中国的矮人村

在四川省资中县的一个偏僻小山村里，有一种罕见的怪现象，就是这个村的村民长到五六岁时，健康的身体就停止了生长、发育。令人不可思议的是他们并非患侏儒症，且与之仅隔一山的邻村，却无一矮人，个中原因，无人知晓。正因如此，这小小的村子便声名远播，被人称为"矮人村"。

由于这些矮人大都出生于上个世纪三四十年代，至今岁数多半在六七十岁，只因身材矮小，家境贫穷而无法成家立业，生儿育女。因此"男的单身、女的孤寡"极为普遍。而稍微上了年纪，没有后代的矮人只得由当地政府照顾，住进村敬老院。

老人们回想起60多年前的夏天，似乎是在一夜之间一种突如其来的怪病袭击了这个原本平和安宁的村庄，猝不及防并且似乎没有停止迹象的莫名的全身关节疼痛开始在村庄里无情地蔓延着。从50多岁的老人到几岁的孩子，连续几年里恐慌的村民们接二连三地被这种可怕的怪病袭击着。

从此"矮人辈出"的阳鸣寺村有了一个新的名字——矮人村。这个方圆数十里的村庄里，身高仅1米左右的矮人随处可见，他们当中最矮的只有73厘米，更让人疑惑不解的是不仅此病怪，患病的区域也怪，在资中县方圆几百公里唯独阳鸣寺村出现了这种罕见怪病。

紧邻阳鸣寺村的村里乡里却无一人患此类病，更没有出现过一例儿童般身高的矮人。同一方水土同一片天地，这恐怖的怪病却为何仅在阳鸣寺村肆虐呢？而村中也不是所有的人个子都矮，也有的人是能健康成长的。因此这个现象的成因让人困惑不已。更让人疑惑的是患病的矮人们的父母身高都正常，以前几代人也找不出一个矮子。

资中县志里有这样一段记录：1951年阳鸣寺村发现一种奇怪病症，患者肢体短，身材矮，当地人称"矮子病"，到1985年普查时，已有119例。短短数年阳鸣寺村出现了上百个身高终身停留在童年时期的矮人，为此许多家庭陷入无尽的苦恼之中。

恐怖的气氛长久地笼罩着这个曾经宁静的小山村，一些人选择了背井离乡，举家搬迁，以期远离这片深陷恐慌的土地。恐惧使得外界对矮人村望而却步，恐惧也使得关于怪病的各种传闻弥漫乡间。有的人说是因为这个地方风水不好；有的说是因为得病的人家祖坟没有埋好；有的人说是因为修建公路铁路挖断了龙神；还有的说是因为祠堂被烧毁了……

有一种说法让很多村民信以为真：很早以前，一位姓王的村民在修房时发现了一只深埋在岩石下的大乌龟，这只乌龟的四肢看起来非常怪异，一些村民建议把乌龟弄出岩石放生，但是遭到大多数人的反对，他们建议将乌龟弄出来炖着吃，滋补身体，当天这只硕大的乌龟就被村民们烫死后炖着吃了。

怪病发生之后有人说如果当时把乌龟放生了，矮人村便不会遭此厄运了。还有人推测是因为日本兵侵占到这里施放了某种毒气造成的，但是这种推测又很快被村民们否定了，因为日本人没有来过阳鸣寺村。

虽然矮人村的怪病让许多人望而生畏，但是国家各相关机构的研究人员，仍然被"矮人之谜"深深吸引，他们排除种种恐惧和顾虑走进了这片深藏在丘陵山峦之间的矮人村。他们提取了矮人村村民的日常饮用水以及土壤等带回去研究。为彻底挖出真凶，他们还对村民的血液、毛发等进行了取样化验，最终的检验结果，让"追凶之路"看见了曙光。

研究人员发现，从矮人村几口上个世纪20年代至今的古井里提取的井水样本中，钙、磷等微量元素奇缺，而人体生长发育的必须物质含量更是几乎为零。专家们认为阳鸣寺村的水源存在着问题。

在调查中专家了解到，上个世纪20年代中期，在如今阳鸣乡7大队一带不少村民不时地感觉到大地在晃动，有人猜测是地震。这场令人心悸的震动断断续续持续了一个多月，此后几年间村民便莫名地患上了怪病。

地质专家通过实地考察并查阅了历史资料深入分析后发现，因为阳鸣寺村方圆数公里全是高山、岩石，整个村子处于山谷中部，而地震引发的地壳运动极有可能让地下深处一些有害矿物质渗透地面，污染了当地的水源和土壤。

谜底被一点点地揭开，地壳运动引发了水源问题的结论基本得到了相关专家的一致认定。而曾经弥漫在村庄里的怪病迷雾也渐渐云开雾散。到上个世纪80年代，当地政府开始着手改善水源。

1988年，当地政府专门修建了一个引水工程，1991年正式投入了使用，此后就解决了整个阳鸣寺村村民的生产、生活用水。但是渗透到土壤和水里的有害物质究竟是什么，相关专家正在进行进一步研究，希望查明矮人村灾祸的真正元凶。

　　非洲复杂的历史条件使得非洲诞生了很多争取和平、自由与解放的英雄，本章将为您简要介绍苏丹民族英雄马赫迪、联合国前任秘书长安南以及"南非国父"曼德拉。

　　一般来讲，我们中国的教育偏于向学生介绍英美国家的文学，而实际上非洲的文学界亦卓尔不群。本章的重点是向读者朋友介绍两位诺贝尔文学奖获得者戈迪默和索因卡。另外，非洲也有像雪莱、济慈、拜伦那样激情澎湃的诗人——沙比，这也是一个早逝但值得永远铭记的灵魂。

　　另外，世界体坛上又有很多非洲的体育名将叱咤风云。如莫桑比克奥运首金获得者穆托拉以及来自"非洲雄狮"喀麦隆队的姆博马。

　　此外，非洲还是一个心随乐动的乐土，所以，本章的最后将向各位讲述两位音乐人的故事。

21 苏丹民族英雄——马赫迪（1844~1885）

Mohammed Ahmed was a Sudanese religious and political leader. The son of a **shipbuilder** in Nubia, he was brought up near Khartoum. After orthodox religious study, he turned to a mystical interpretation of Islam in the **Sufi** tradition, joined a religious brotherhood, and in 1870 moved to a **hermitage** with his disciples. In 1881 he proclaimed a divine mission to purify Islam and the governments that **defile**d it, targeting the Turkish ruler of Egypt and its dependency. In 1885, after he defeated Charles George Gordon to capture Khartoum, he established a theocratic state, but he died the same year, probably of **typhus**.

His religious experiences and **contemplation**s on Aba Island caused Mohammed Ahmed to feel that Allah had selected him as the true Mahdi, the right-guided one or the **messianic** leader called to battle against **immorality** and **corruption** and for the **rejuvenation** and purification of Islam.

Mohammed Ahmed found ideal conditions in the central and northern Sudan for a mass emotional movement, not only in the religious devotion of the Moslem population of the area but especially in the **resentment** of the inhabitants toward the corruption and oppression of the Turkish and Egyptian rulers Mohammed Ahmed thus found support from the Sudanese for a variety of reasons and motives—from pious and religious believers who accepted his puritan and reformist views, from nomadic groups who opposed all governmental restrictions, and from others who profited from the slave trade and rejected efforts of the Egyptian khedive Ismail and Gen. Gordon to eliminate it.

马赫迪是苏丹的宗教和政治领袖，原名穆罕默德·艾哈迈德·伊本·阿卜杜拉。马赫迪是努比亚一名造船工人的儿子，在喀什穆附近长大。学习东正教之后，他开始转向苏非派传统中阐释伊斯兰教，而后加入一个宗教团体的兄弟会。1870年，他与门徒过起隐居的生活。1881年，他开始投入到一项神圣的使命当中，以净化伊斯兰教以及亵渎伊斯兰教的政府，目标是对付埃及的土耳其领袖以及摆脱对他的依赖。1885年，在打败查理·乔治·戈登占领喀什穆之后，他建立了一个神权政府。同年，马赫迪病死，死因可能是斑疹伤寒。

马赫迪在太平岛的宗教经历以及思考使得他认为，真主阿拉选定他作为蒙受引导者去对抗邪恶、腐败，以及复兴和净化伊斯兰教。

马赫迪发现，在苏丹中部及北部进行群众情感煽动活动有着得天独厚的条件。这不仅仅在穆斯林中进行，而且还可以利用当地人民对于土耳其以及埃及领导者的腐败和压迫所持有的憎恨态度，在当地人民中进行。因此，马赫迪由于各种不同的原因及动机得到了苏丹人民的支持。这些人包括：那些接受他的清教徒式及改革主义观点的虔诚的宗教信徒们，那些反对所有政府约束的游牧民族们，以及那些从奴隶贸易中狩利（而埃及总督及英国司令戈登要废除奴隶贸易）的人们。

Mohammed Ahmed's movement for reform and reorganization spread rapidly following his public appearance as the Mahdi in June 1881 because of its wide appeal. But the weakness and indecision of Egyptian authorities because of economic and political problems within Egypt played a key role in the success of the Mahdi's campaign.

The **victorious** followers of the Mahdi occupied most of the Sudan; Lord Cromer, the British consul general in Cairo, sent the famous Gen. Gordon to carry out and accelerate the Egyptian evacuation. Khartoum, the capital and center of the country, fell to the Mahdi in January 1885 following Gen. Gordon's legendary and **foolhardy** defense.

The Mahdi had successfully expelled foreign influences and had united most of the Sudan area in a unique religiopolitical movement. According to Mahdist theology and **theocracy**, the Mahdi held his superior power directly from Allah and then delegated power directly to others as he chose. The Mahdi died in 1885, probably of typhus, but his theocratic state continued for another 13 years under his follower and friend the caliph Abdullahi. The British general Kitchener reoccupied the Sudan primarily with Egyptian troops in 1898, not only because of any threat the Mahdist movement itself posed to the British position in Egypt but because of British imperial needs in the partition of Africa among the great powers of Europe.

马赫迪的改革和改组运动很快传播开来。1881年6月，应广大人民要求，穆罕默德·艾哈迈德以马赫迪的身份公开出现。不过，马赫迪的成功还归因于埃及政府因为经济及政治问题所表现的软弱以及缺乏决断性。

马赫迪的信徒们占领了苏丹的大部分地区。英国驻埃及的行政官员克罗默伯爵派有名的戈登司令去加快占领埃及的步伐。1885年，马赫迪占领了喀什穆——苏丹的首都及中心，打败了戈登有勇无谋的防御。

马赫迪成功地驱逐了外国势力，并通过一次独一无二的宗教政治活动统一了苏丹大部分区域。根据马赫迪派的神学及神权国家的理论，马赫迪直接从阿拉那里获得权力，然后他会将权力下发给那些他选定的人。马赫迪死于1885年，但他的神权国家继续存活了13年。1898年，英国司令基奇纳在埃及军队的帮助下重新占领了苏丹。一方面是因为马赫迪运动与埃及境内的英国政府施加了威胁，另一方面是因为英国皇室想要实现在非洲的划区而治。

词汇 **V**OCABULARY

shipbuilder：造船工人	immorality：不道德
Sufi：苏非派（伊斯兰教的神秘主义派别）	corruption：腐败
hermitage：隐居之处，隐士生活，修道院	rejuvenation：复原，再生，更新，嫩化，恢复
defile：亵渎	resentment：怨恨，愤恨

typhus：斑疹伤寒	victorious：得胜的，胜利的
contemplation：思考	foolhardy：鲁莽的，有勇无谋的
messianic：弥赛亚的，救世主的	theocracy：神权的国家

马赫迪宫

坐落在苏丹名城恩图曼的东南角，尼罗河西岸，是一座富有阿拉伯民族风格的雄伟建筑。这是苏丹人民为纪念民族英雄马赫迪而修建的纪念馆。马赫迪原名穆罕默德·艾哈迈德，他以伊斯兰教为号召，提出"建立人人平等的制度"等口号，动员苏丹人民奋起反抗英国的统治。1881 年 8 月，他在南科尔多凡地区发动武装起义，并宣布自己为马赫迪，"马赫迪"是"救世主"的意思。

宫内，有书写着"先知的哈里发穆罕默德·马赫迪"的殷红色的起义军战旗；还有马赫迪的不少书信和文告，其中包括马赫迪早在 1880 年所写的信件。在博物馆的"击毙戈登专室"里，展示了戈登的头像，他用过的铁皮箱和部分衣物、文件及书信等。其中有一杆亮铮铮的长矛，就是当年刺死戈登的锐利武器。现在，马赫迪宫被苏丹穆斯林及马赫迪子孙后代视为圣地，经常有人瞻仰膜拜。

22 诺贝尔和平奖获得者——科菲·安南（1938~）

The former US ambassador to the United Nations, Richard Holbrooke, once described Kofi Annan as "the best secretary general in the history of the UN".

Kofi Atta Annan was the seventh Secretary General of the United Nations. In 2001, he was awarded the Nobel Peace Prize jointly with the United Nations for their work for a better organized and more peaceful world.

Mr Annan's major project at the UN was reform. In a speech in September 2003 he said that the UN was at a "fork in the road". He pressed for a new philosophy—that of **intervention**. The UN must place itself above the rights of **sovereign** states when necessary to protect

美国驻联合国前任大使，理查德·霍尔布鲁克，曾评价安南为"联合国历史上最好的联合国秘书长"。

科菲·阿塔·安南先生是联合国的第七任秘书长，他曾于2001年与联合国一起荣获诺贝尔和平奖，以表扬他们为世界和平及秩序所做出的贡献。

安南在联合国任职期间的最大贡献就是改革。他在2003年9月的一次讲话中指出，联合国现正走

civilians from war and mass slaughter, he declared. He **appoint**ed a **panel** of "wise men" who drew up a report agreeing that the UN should assume a role when a state had failed in its "responsibility to protect" its citizens. In September 2005, a UN declaration stated that "every sovereign government has a 'responsibility to protect' its citizens and those within its **jurisdiction** from **genocide**, mass killing, and massive and **sustained** human rights violations". The **application** of this principle remains to be worked out in practice but the principle itself might be Kofi Annan's most important **legacy** at the UN.

Kofi Atta Annan and his twin sister were born on the 8th of April in 1938 in Kumasi, Ghana. Kumasi is known as "The Garden City" due to the wide variety of plant life in the area. Kofi Atta Annan is fluent in 5 languages including English, French and three African languages.

He made history by being the first black African to serve as Secretary General of the United Nations. He viewed the HIV/AIDS **pandemic** as one of his personal priorities, calling on a Global AIDS and Health Fund to increase support to developing countries that are trying to overcome the disease. Mr. Annan supported sending a United Nations peacekeeping mission to Darfur, Sudan and actively supported women's rights in Arab and Muslim countries. Most recently, once again making a call for peace to protect civilians, Mr. Annan demanded that the use of munitions not be used in populated areas.

Kofi Atta Annan supported the call to action for all nations to respond to global warming issues. He encouraged the positive momentum in Nepal and supported a peaceful resolution there to end 10 years of civil war. Mr. Annan also strongly urged human rights progress in Myanmar (Burma) along with democratic reform and national reconciliation.

In serving others, Kofi Atta Annan dedicated himself

在一个岔路口。他提出了一个新的理念——干涉。他强调，在涉及到保护世界公民免受战争及大屠杀威胁时，如有必要，联合国的权利将会高于主权国家的权利。他选择了一群明智的人组成了一个座谈小组，该小组一致认为，当一个主权国家没有完成对公民的职责时，联合国应充当起保护该国公民的角色。在2005年9月，联合国发表声明，任何政府都有责任保护其管辖范围内的所有公民免受种族屠杀，大屠杀或人权受损。这项声明直到现在都一直被实践着，这个声明应算是安南为联合国留下的最宝贵的遗产了。

安南和他的双胞胎姊姊于1938年4月8日出生于迦纳的库马西。安南先生精通五种语言，包括英语、法语以及三种非洲语言。

安南先生是第一位在联合国担任秘书长的非洲黑人，他将防治艾滋病视为自己的首要任务之一，并呼吁成立全球艾滋病与健康基金，以增加对发展中国家的支持，协助他们对抗艾滋病。安南先生支持派遣联合国维和部队到苏丹的达尔富尔执行任务，同时积极支持阿拉伯与回教国家的妇女权益。最近，他再次提出和平的呼吁，以保护平民百姓，并要求不要在人口密集的地区开火。

安南先生对于各国都应立即采取行动以解决全球暖化问题的这项呼吁，也相当支持。他鼓励尼泊尔采取正面积极的行动，以和平方式终止长达十年的内战。安南先生亦强烈呼吁缅甸政府当局改善人权，进行民主改革及国家和解。

在服务他人方面，安南先生全力

as Secretary General for the United Nations to support a vision that embraced security, development and human rights for all. Mr. Annan completed his second term in December, 2006; we would like to convey our best wishes to a distinguished gentleman of peace.

做好联合国秘书长的职务，以促成全人类都能享有安全、发展与人权的愿景。安南先生于2006年12月结束他的第二个任期，我们向这位杰出的和平之士致上诚挚的祝福。

词汇 VOCABULARY

ambassador：大使，使节	jurisdiction：司法权，审判权，管辖权
intervention：介入，调停，干涉	genocide：种族灭绝，灭绝整个种族的大屠杀
sovereign：至高无上的；有主权的；拥有最高统治权的	sustained：持续的，持久的，持久不变的
appoint：任命，指定，约定	legacy：遗赠，遗产
panel：座谈小组，全体陪审员	pandemic：全国流行的，普遍的
application：应用（程序），申请权	

背景知识 PROFILE

安南诺贝尔和平奖获奖演讲

国王和王后陛下，各位殿下，各位阁下：

今天，一个女孩将诞生在阿富汗。女孩的母亲将与世界上任何地方的母亲一样，搂抱她、喂她、疼爱她、照顾她。这都是人性最基本的行为，人人如此，没有分别。但在今天的阿富汗出生的女孩，她将开始过的生活，与人类的一少部分已实现的富足生活相比，相距几个世纪。她的生活条件，以我们这个大厅中许多人看来，是不人道的。我谈到阿富汗的一个女孩，其实我也可以提到塞拉利昂的一个男婴，又或一个女婴。

今天，没有人不知道世界上贫富之间的这一鸿沟，没有人能说一点也不知道这道鸿沟使一穷二白的人付出的代价多大。他们与我们一样，应当享有人的尊严、基本自由、安全、食物和教育。但代价不只是由他们承担的。最终，我们所有人都要承担，无论北方南方、富的穷的、男的女的、所有种族、所有宗教，都要付出代价。

今天真正的边界不在国与国之间，而在于强者与弱者、自由者与受压制者、特权者与困窘者之间。今天，没有一堵墙能把世界上一个地区的人道主义或人权危机与另一地区的国家安全危机隔开。科学家告诉我们，自然世界非常小，而且高度相互依存。在亚马孙雨林的一只蝴蝶扇动翅膀就能够在地球另一边造成强烈风暴。这就是人称"蝴蝶效应"的原则。

今天，我们认识到，或许比以往任何时候都认识到，人类活动世界也有自己的"蝴蝶效应"，是好是歹，都要面对。我们通过一道火焰门进入了第三个千年。如果在9.11恐怖事件之后的今天，我们看得更清楚、更远，我们就会认识到人类是不可分的。新的威胁不会把种族、国家或地区分开对待。每个人，无论贫富或社会地位如何，都从内心产生了新的不安全感。年纪轻的、年纪大的，都对痛苦时和富足时维系我们大家的凝聚力有了更深刻的认识。人们曾以为全球和平与繁荣必然逐步实现。但21世纪一开始就通过暴力去除了这种幻想。这是新的现实，再也不能视而不见，必须勇敢面对。

20世纪可能是人类历史死难最多的世纪，这个世纪被无法数得清的冲突、不能言状的痛苦和难以想象的罪行所折磨。一个集团或国家，往往出于无理性的仇恨和猜疑，或出于极度傲慢及对权力和资源的渴求，一再对另一集团或国家采取极端的暴力行动。为了应付这些灾难，世界领导人在20世纪中叶走到一起，共同努力，促使各国空前团结起来。联合国这个论坛从而产生。各国可以在这一论坛共同申明每个人的尊严与价值，为所有人民争取和平与发展。

在这个论坛，各国还可以团结一致，加强法治，确认并设法满足穷人的需要，抑制人的残忍与贪婪，保护自然资源和美丽的大自然，支持男女权利平等，同时照顾子孙后代的安全。我们从20世纪继承了一些政治手段和科技工具。只要我们有此意愿，善加利用，就有可能消除贫穷、无知和疾病。

23 南非国父——纳尔逊·曼德拉（1918~2013）

Mandela's words, "The **struggle** is my life," are not to be taken lightly.

Nelson Mandela personifies struggle. He is still leading the fight against apartheid with extraordinary **vigour** and **resilience** after spending nearly three decades of his life **behind bars**. He has sacrificed his private life and his youth for his people, and remains South Africa's best known and loved hero.

Mandela has held numerous positions in the ANC: ANCYL secretary (1948); ANCYL president (1950); ANC Transvaal president (1952); **deputy** national president

曼德拉曾说："奋斗就是我的人生。"对此，我们应给予重视。

曼德拉就象征着奋斗。即便入狱近三十载后，他仍然充满热情地领导着反对种族隔离的斗争。他已将自己的个人生活、他的青春献给了他的人民。他是南非人家喻户晓、备受爱戴的英雄。

一生中，曼德拉在非洲国民大会（ANC）任职无数：非洲国民大会青年团（ANCYL）秘书

(1952) and ANC president (1991).

Mandela **matriculate**d at Healdtown Methodist **Boarding School** and then started a BA degree at Fort Hare. Mandela was elected national volunteer-in-chief of the 1952 Defiance Campaign. He travelled the country organizing resistance to **discriminatory legislation**.

He was given a **suspended sentence** for his part in the campaign. Shortly afterwards a banning order **confine**d him to Johannesburg for six months. During this period he formulated the "M Plan", in terms of which ANC branches were broken down into underground cells.

In the fifties, after being forced through constant bannings to resign officially from the ANC, Mandela analysed the Bantustan policy as a political swindle. He predicted mass removals, political persecutions and police terror.

For the second half of the fifties, he was one of the accused in the **Treason** Trial. With Duma Nokwe, he conducted the defense.

In 1962 Mandela left the country for military training in Algeria and to arrange training for other MK members.

On his return he was arrested for leaving the country illegally and for incitement to strike. He conducted his own defense. He was convicted and jailed for five years in November 1962. While serving his sentence, he was charged, in the Rivonia trial, with sabotage and sentenced to life imprisonment.

A decade before being imprisoned, Mandela had spoken out against the introduction of Bantu Education, recommending that community activists "make every home, every shack or rickety structure a centre of learning".

Robben Island, where he was **imprison**ed, became a centre for learning, and Mandela was a central figure in the organized political education

（1948）；ANCYL主席（1950）；ANC德兰士瓦省主席（1952）；国家副主席（1952）；ANC主席（1991）。

曼德拉被寄宿学校录取，然后开始在福特哈尔大学攻读学士学位。1952年的抗法运动，曼德拉被选为全国义工总领袖。他到处游历，组织人民抵抗歧视法。

曼德拉因为参与此次运动，被判缓刑。很快，曼德拉被遣送到约翰内斯堡的监狱，在此关押6个月。这期间，曼德拉想出了"M计划"，主要是将ANC的机构分割成小的地下组织。

20世纪50年代，重重压力之下，曼德拉辞去ANC公职。曼德拉分析出班图斯坦政策就是一个政治骗局。他预言了政治迫害、警察暴乱等事件。

50年代下半年，他被告有叛国罪。在Duma Nokwe的帮助下，他实行辩护。

1962年，曼德拉离开祖国，前往阿尔及利亚参加军事训练，并为其他成员组织培训。

回来之后，他因非法出国以及发动罢工被逮捕。他进行了自我辩护。1962年，他被判有罪，锒铛入狱5年。在服刑期间，曼德拉在利沃尼亚（Rivonia）审判上被控告肆意破坏罪，被判终身监禁。

监禁10年以后，曼德拉公开发言，反对班图教育，主张社团激进分子"把每个家庭、每个棚屋或危房变成学习中心"。

曼德拉被监禁的罗本岛成为了学习中心，曼德拉成了教育课上的中心人物。

在狱中，曼德拉从未妥协，他常

classes.

In prison Mandela never compromised his political principles and was always a source of strength for the other prisoners.

During the seventies he refused the offer of a remission of sentence if he recognized Transkei and settled there.

In the eighties he again rejected PW Botha's offer of freedom if he renounced violence.

It is significant that shortly after his release on Sunday 11 February 1990, Mandela and his delegation agreed to the suspension of armed struggle.

Mandela has honorary degrees from more than 50 international universities and is chancellor of the University of the North.

He was inaugurated as the first democratically elected State President of South Africa on 10 May 1994 - June 1999.

Nelson Mandela retired from Public life in June 1999. He **reside**s in his birth place - Qunu, Transkei.

On 5th Dec, 2013, Mandela died at Johannesburg.

常是其他狱友的力量源泉。

70年代，如果曼德拉承认特兰斯凯并居住在那儿，他可以得到释放。曼德拉拒绝了。

80年代，P.W. 博塔提出，如果曼德拉放弃暴力，曼德拉可以重获自由。曼德拉再次拒绝。

1990年2月11日，南非当局在国内外舆论压力下，被迫宣布无条件释放曼德拉。曼德拉和其代表团同意暂缓军事武装斗争。

曼德拉在50多所国际大学拥有荣誉学位，是北方大学的荣誉校长。

1994年5月10日，曼德拉成为南非第一任民主选举的总统，任期5年。

1999年6月，曼德拉从公共事业上退休。他居住在其出生地——特兰斯凯的库奴。

2013年12月5日，曼德拉逝世于约翰内斯堡。

词汇 VOCABULARY

struggle: 奋斗，斗争	discriminatory: 歧视的
vigour: 活力，精力	legislation: 法律，法规
resilience: 弹性	suspended sentence: 缓刑
behind bars: 坐牢	confine: 限制，监禁
deputy: 副的	treason: 叛国罪
matriculate: 准许入学，录取	imprison: 监禁
Boarding School: 寄宿学校	reside: 居住，定居

《光辉岁月》

南非黑人领袖曼德拉从1963年起，在开普敦的罗本岛的维克托-韦斯特监狱被关押了长达27年之久，经过艰苦的斗争，终于在1990年2月11日下午4时出狱。出狱后，曼德拉继续领导南非的反种族歧视运动，终于在1994年5月9日当选为南非历史上第一任黑人总统。这也标志着这场种族歧视的斗争取得了最后的胜利。

BEYOND是一支富有博大胸怀、富有同情心、关注社会的摇滚乐队。黄家驹在1990年8月3日到6日从巴布亚新几内亚之行回来后，创作了一首《光辉岁月》，黄家驹以这首歌向黑人领袖曼德拉致敬，歌颂了曼德拉伟大而辉煌的一生，充分地表达了自己对种族歧视的厌恶与憎恨！

曼德拉在听到这首歌曲之后，立即找人来翻译了歌词内容，当他听完歌词中的含义之后，不禁潸然泪下，可能歌词里面的一字一句，都深深地冲击了这位伟人心底最柔软的地方。现在，让我们来重温一下《光辉岁月》吧。

钟声响起归家的讯号
在他生命里
彷佛带点唏嘘
黑色肌肤给他的意义
是一生奉献肤色斗争中
年月把拥有变作失去
疲倦的双眼带着期望
今天只有残留的躯壳
迎接光辉岁月
风雨中抱紧自由
一生经过彷徨的挣扎
自信可改变未来
问谁又能做到
可否不分肤色的界限
愿这土地里
不分你我高低
缤纷色彩闪出的美丽
是因它没有分开每种色彩
年月把拥有变作失去
疲倦的双眼带着期望
今天只有残留的躯壳
迎接光辉岁月
风雨中抱紧自由

一生经过彷徨的挣扎
自信可改变未来
问谁又能做到
今天只有残留的躯壳
迎接光辉岁月
风雨中抱紧自由
一生经过彷徨的挣扎
自信可改变未来
问谁又能做到
Oh…… Ha……
今天只有残留的躯壳
迎接光辉岁月
风雨中抱紧自由
一生经过彷徨的挣扎
自信可改变未来
问谁又能做到
Oh…… Ha……
今天只有残留的躯壳
迎接光辉岁月
风雨中抱紧自由
一生经过彷徨的挣扎

24 非洲文学诺贝尔奖第一人——沃雷·索因卡（1934~）

Wole Soyinka is a Nigerian-born playwright, novelist, political activist and **Nobel laureate**.

Born Akinwande Oluwole Babatunde Soyinka in 1934, he grew up in Abeokuta, Western Nigeria, which was still part of a **sprawling** British empire. The Soyinkas are members of the Yoruba tribe, a people steeped in a rich, complex culture of dance, art and drama.

Before entering college, Mr. Soyinka worked as a clerk while he wrote plays and short stories that were broadcast on Nigerian radio. In 1952 at the University College in Ibadan, he began his studies of English literature, Western history and Greek. Two years later, he moved to England to study English literature at the University of Leeds.

In the late 1950s, Mr. Soyinka completed his first two important plays, "The Swamp Dwellers" and "The Lion and the Jewel", both **tackling** the uneasy relationship between progress and tradition in Africa.

His creativity has been **prodigious**, encompassing a sequence of remarkable plays, two novels, poetry, polemical writings, critical essays, a classic **memoir** of his early life ("Aké", 1982) and a memoir devoted to his father. In 1986, he became the first African to receive the Nobel Prize for Literature. Mr. Soyinka's plays and poems depicted what the Swedish Academy called "the drama of existence".

On the occasion of Mr. Soyinka's 70th birthday, his friend, the scholar Henry Louis Gates Jr. praised him in a 2004 essay in The New York Times, saying he had "earned a reputation as the **conscience** of Nigeria, and in a nation where the **average life span** is 52, turning 70 is **achievement** enough. In his case,

沃雷·索因卡是尼日利亚剧作家、诗人、小说家、评论家，是诺贝奖获得者。

1934年，索因卡出生于尼日利亚西部约鲁巴族聚居的一个小城，在尼日利亚西部的阿贝奥库塔长大。当时，阿贝奥库塔是大英帝国的殖民地。索因卡一家是约鲁巴人，一个富有复杂的舞蹈、艺术以及戏剧文化的民族。

进大学以前，索因卡已经一边工作一边写剧本和短篇。他的作品曾经在尼日利亚的广播上播出。1952年，索因卡在伊巴丹的大学学院主修英国文学、西方历史以及希腊文化。两年后，他前往英国，开始在利兹大学学习英国文学。

20世纪50年代后期，索因卡完成了他最初的两部剧本：《沼泽地的居民》和《雄狮与宝石》。两部作品的主题关注的都是非洲的文明进程和传统之间的尴尬关系。

他的创作量非常巨大，包括一系列出色的剧本，两部小说，诗歌，议论文，评论文，对早期生活的回忆录以及献给父亲的回忆录。1986年，他荣获诺贝尔奖，成为了非洲诺贝尔奖第一人。瑞典学院称，索因卡的剧本和诗歌描述了"存在的戏剧"。

索因卡七十岁生日时，他的朋友小亨利·路易斯·盖茨学者在2004年发表于《纽约时报》的一篇文章中赞到："他已经赢得了尼日利亚良心的

though, it's nothing short of a miracle".

Mr. Soyinka has been in exile three times and remains a constant critical voice of Nigeria's government. He has also spoken out about the country's increasingly divided ethnic and religious groups. He has written that religion is the problem of the 21st century, in the same way that W.E.B. Du Bois predicted that the problem of the 21st century would be race.

He has not moderated his demands for full democracy in Nigeria. He is engaged in the movement for a new constitutional convention.

名声。在一个平均寿命只有52岁的国度里，活到70已是一种壮举。不过，对于他来说，这并不是一个奇迹"。

索因卡曾经三次遭到放逐，但对政府仍持有批判的声音。他还就国家不断分离的种族及宗教族群分裂问题发表公开言论。他曾写道，宗教是21世纪的主要问题。同样，杜波依斯预言，21世纪的主要问题是种族。

他要求在尼日利亚实现完全民主，对此，他从未妥协。目前，他参与到了一项新宪法管理的运动当中。

词汇 VOCABULARY

Nobel laureate：诺贝尔奖获得者	conscience：良心
sprawling：规模庞大的	average life span：平均寿命
tackle：处理，对待	achievement：成就，成绩，完成
prodigious：巨大的	
memoir：回忆录	

背景知识 PROFILE

索因卡主要作品介绍

《沼泽地居民》（1958）

该剧描写的是生活在沼泽地上的一个小村庄里的一家农民。马古里夫妇安贫乐道，信奉蛇神，即使自然灾害重重，也静守在沼泽地，并对城市资本主义文明嗤之以鼻。妻子认为离家10年之久的长子一定在去往城市的途中淹死了，丈夫把城市视作毁灭青年一代并使人忘却根之所系的陷阱。但是由于西方文明的冲击，城市的自由空气、颇具魔力的金钱市场对年轻一代产生了极大的诱惑，他们盼望逃离封闭自守、令人绝望的故土。长子阿乌契克逃离故乡，在城市赢得了财富，获得了成功。在他身上，体现着年轻一代黑人的叛逆性与创造性。但是，因实利思想的侵蚀，阿乌契克不顾血亲关系，把弟弟伊格韦祖当成事业上的普通对手击败，又夺去了他的妻子。伊格韦祖家破人亡，不得不重返沼泽地，因为在他心目中，"我有我的家，尽管它坐落在泥塘中央，我要回去。"但城市文明已使他开了眼界，他无法容忍沼泽地闭关自守的环境，对蛇神发出悲愤的控诉，再次离乡背井，投身于金钱统治一切、骨肉互相残杀的罪恶世界。

本剧在索因卡早期创作中风格独特，是一部充满抒情色调的诗体悲剧。

《森林舞蹈》（1960）

剧情发生在一个庞大的森林里：人类在即将举行民族大聚会之际，决定让伟大的祖先前来参加，让他们作为"民族杰出的象征"，作为"历史纽带来联系这欢乐的时节"。不料，森林之王的宠臣阿洛尼派去一对不安的男女幽灵。他们生活在16世纪的马塔·卡里布王朝：那里，国王暴躁好战，王后惯于卖弄风情，大臣们刚愎自用，致使军队首领（男幽灵前身）因拒绝参加非正义的战争被卖为奴，与怀孕的妻子含冤而死。数百年后，他们作为客人来到人间，见到4个前世是马培·卡里布王朝的王后及宫廷大臣的人，竟被驱逐，但森林之王把他们全部请来参加舞会。

本剧作于1960年尼日利亚独立之后，"民族大聚会"象征着尼日利亚独立大会。它回溯16世纪的生活，目的让人们正视不光彩的过去，重建现在。但现实是不幸历史的延续，男女幽灵仍未改变厄运，女幽灵历经300年妊娠苦痛生下的"半孩"一直大叫"我生下来就会死的"。从某种意义上讲，"半孩"象征着刚刚独立的非洲国家，意味着非洲各国虽形式上独立，实则是个早产儿，尚未具备生存的条件，前景并不乐观。该剧将欧洲现代戏剧艺术同非洲民间仪式中的舞蹈、笑剧、唱诗、音乐等奇妙地结合在一起，使用了大量的约鲁巴民间谚语，神灵们也被赋上宗教传说中人物的光晕，瑞典学院称其是"一种赋有精灵、鬼怪之神的非洲仲夏夜之梦"。

《解释者》（1965）

归国留学生塞孔尼、本德尔、科拉、艾格博、萨戈经常聚在一起，对尼日利亚现状各抒己见，争论不已。他们胸怀大志，但却怀才不遇，这是由于现实社会有着种种弊端。优秀的工程师塞孔尼不愿在办公室的杂物中湮没才华。董事长为了整他，派他到条件艰苦的边远地区修建水电站，后又收买专家指控新电站不符合要求，工程被注销，塞孔尼被冠以"疯子工程师"的绰号。因积郁在胸，塞孔尼真的发了疯，在一个漆黑的雨夜，惨死在车轮之下。当教师的本德尔从塞孔尼的死中获得重要启示，最后成为宗教与道德意识的化身。画家科拉为纪念塞孔尼，花费整整15个月的时间绘出"众神像"，希望把古老的神话同现实结合起来。就职于外交部的艾格博始终在传统与现代之间徘徊不定。他既想回到外祖父的部落中去，继承酋长之位，以获得权力、财富及无数个妻子，保留残存的高贵风

度，又想摆脱部族的束缚及复古的梦想，重新生活。最活跃的社会批判者、记者萨戈逢人便讲"粪便哲学"与"厕所理论"。在他眼中，报馆、拉格斯城乃至整个尼日利亚就建在垃圾堆中。

这是一部西非现代主义英语小说的先驱之作。它打破了线型的小说叙述形式，运用意识流、蒙太奇等手法把零散的片断联成错落有致的整体。作品中的"解释者"，即前文所述的几个人物具有象征意义，反映出某种宗教与道德思想。

《阿凯——童年纪事》（1982）

这部自传以隽永传神、幽默睿智的语言叙述了索因卡的童年时代，生动地展现了一个充满好奇、幻想、憧憬与神秘的孩提世界，淋漓尽致地勾勒出20世纪三四十年代尼日利亚西部小城的生活风貌。小索因卡生于一个知识分子家庭。父亲是当地教会学校的校长，笃信基督教，母亲是虔诚的"基督迷"，整个家庭弥漫着浓郁的宗教气息。他所受的教育和生活习惯相当西化，但外部环境仍旧保持着约鲁巴的传统遗风与信仰，它无时不在影响着索因卡。约鲁巴族祖祖辈辈敬畏的精灵鬼怪的形象亦深深投入他幼小的心灵。特别是约鲁巴的主神奥贡，成为他心目中恐怖的象征与超自然力量的化身。年幼的索因卡勇敢，执拗，自信，好争辩，聪慧过人，天生一副反抗的脾性。他伤感、孤独，喜欢到森林及其他僻静的场所，或与自然亲密地交谈，或独自沉思冥想。

这部自传曾被《纽约时报书评副刊》评为"1982年英语文学最佳作品之一"。英国报刊称它对英语文学做出了重要贡献，"必将成为童年故事中的不朽杰作"。

25 对待种族隔离，她说不——纳丁·戈迪默（1923~）

For almost 50 years an **ardent** opponent of apartheid, Nadine Gordimer was born in a small town in the Traansvaal, South Africa. The daughter of Jewish immigrants, she had a middle-class **upbringing** and education, attending private schools and the University of Witwatersrand. Her first story was **publish**ed when she was 15, but she did not attract much attention until her first novel, The Lying Days in 1953.

Gordimer writes in a controlled, **unsentimental** style that **contrast**s with her subject matter: the effect of **apartheid** on the lives of South Africans and the

纳丁·戈迪默近50年来一直是一位种族隔离的强烈反对者。她出生于南非一个叫斯普林斯的矿业小城中。作为犹太族移民的后裔，戈迪默是在中产阶级的环境中长大，接受的是中产阶级的教育，进的是私立学校，曾就读于威特沃特斯兰大学。她15岁时，她的第一个故事已经发表。而直到她的第一部小说《说谎的日子》问世，她才引起人们的关注。

戈迪默的写作风格自制、客观。这与她的主题形成鲜明对比：种族隔

frustrations of life in a racially-divided country. With a skilful use of small details, she describes the daily lives of South Africans, black, white and coloured, as they go about their affairs in a **flawed** and **artificial** society. Feelings of exile and **alienation** pervade her novels and short-story collections, such as "The Soft Voice of the Serpent" (1956) and "Not for Publication" (1960).

With The Conservationist (1974), which describes a white man's **exploitation** of his black employees, Gordimer shared the 1974 Booker Prize. In Burger's Daughter (1979), a white woman tries to come to terms with her feelings when her Communist father is imprisoned for opposing the system. Other **notable** works include July's People (1981), A Sport of Nature (1987) and My Son's Story (1990). Her most recent novel, The House Gun (1998) is set in contemporary, post-apartheid South Africa, and describes the emotional confusion of a couple whose son is accused of murder.

In 1991, Gordimer was awarded the Nobel Prize for Literature. She has always tried to preserve her privacy, but international fame and her role as a lifelong defender of free speech in a police state have forced her into the public arena.

Key works include:

The Lying Days (1953)

A Guest of Honour (1970)

The Conservationist (1974)

Burger's Daughter (1979)

July's People (1981)

My Son's Story (1990)

The House Gun (1998)

离对南非人民的影响以及种族隔离下生活的窘境。她笔触细腻、富于技巧，她描述了在存在缺陷以及虚伪的社会里，南非人民——白人、黑人以及有色人种——的生活常态。在她的小说以及短篇作品——如《蛇温柔的声音》、《不是为了出版》——中，充斥着驱逐感以及疏离感。

1974年，戈迪默因《自然资源保护论》获1974年英国布克奖。该书主要描写了白人对黑人雇员的剥削。在《伯格的女儿》中，戈迪默描写了这样一个故事：当父亲因为反对体制被监禁，一个白人女人如何平复自己的心情。另外，《七月的人们》（1981），《大自然的运动》，《我儿子的故事》也是很有名的作品。她最近的作品《屋里的枪》以当代社会，即后种族隔离的南非为背景，描写了一对夫妇的困惑，其子被控杀人。

1991年，戈迪默获诺贝尔文学奖。她总是在尽力保护自己的隐私，但是享誉世界的名声以及她自由言论捍卫者的角色不断将她推向公众视线。

主要作品一览表：

《撒谎的日子》（1953）

《尊贵的客人》（1970）

《自然资源保护论》（1974）

《伯格的女儿》（1979）

《七月的人们》（1981）

《我儿子的故事》（1990）

《屋子里的枪》（1998）

ardent：热情的	frustration：绝望，挫折
upbringing：教，抚养，培养	flawed：有缺陷的
publish：出版	artificial：虚假的，做作的
unsentimental：不感情用事的，不易动感情的	alienation：疏离
contrast：形成对比	exploitation：剥削
apartheid：种族隔离	notable：有名的

背景知识 **P**ROFILE

纳丁·戈迪默接受中国记者采访（2006年）

《环球时报》记者：作为一名读者，我阅读过您的《不是为了出版》、《屋子里的枪》和您的一些短篇小说，如果向中国读者介绍您的作品，您最希望介绍哪些？

戈迪默：你刚才提到的《不是为了出版》已经是一本旧书了，1965年出版的。《跳跃及其他短篇小说》和《士兵的拥抱》是两本比较新的短篇小说集。《屋子里的枪》是1998年出版的，这部长篇已签署了中文翻译合同。我想，像《屋子里的枪》这样的小说也许能够翻译好。这部小说是关于暴力的，我觉得这个世界上有太多的暴力。

记者：我们知道您很早就是诺贝尔文学奖的候选人，但直到1991年南非的民主曙光初现之时，您才获奖。您觉得这和南非的政治形势有什么关联吗？

戈迪默：没有任何关系。你不可能仅凭哪一本书就能获奖，而要看你主要的创作成就，这就是为什么诺贝尔文学奖的得主都是些上岁数的人，我获奖时快68岁了。

记者：能谈谈当时的情况和感受吗？

戈迪默：一位作家在真正获得诺贝尔奖前的至少五六年甚至七八年里，都会被一直排在候选人之列。每年揭晓之前，总有记者打电话给我："你已经排上名了，将获得诺贝尔奖，你有什么感想？"我总是告诉他们："如果我得了奖，我会告诉你的，再见！"然后就挂断电话。这种情况持续了一年又一年，我知道迟早有一天会获奖。在我获奖的前一年，也就是1990年，墨西哥诗人帕斯荣获诺贝尔文学奖，他是我的朋友，我为他感到高兴，因为他比我的年龄要大得多。当时的情况很显然，诺贝尔奖的得主不是他就是我。但我替他高兴完了也就再没去想什么，那几年我已经习惯了当诺贝尔文学奖候选人。第二年文学奖揭晓时，我正在纽约联系出版新书，住在儿子的公寓楼里。那天我起得很早，想打个电话又害怕吵醒家人，便悄悄去厨房。我正走进厨房要拿起电话时，电话铃响了，是瑞典的一位记者通知我，说我刚刚获得当年的诺贝尔文学奖，因为我了解这位记者，知道他不是在开玩笑。

记者：您阅读过中国的文学作品吗？

戈迪默：没有。文学的翻译沟通是我经常关注的问题之一。我们现在都在讲全球化，事实上在经济、金融、贸易等领域，也的确发生了许多变化，全球化趋势迅猛，差距正在缩小。但如果看看文化方面，则这种全球化现在的代表可以说是美国文化中最低档次的那一部分。不管你到任何地方，打开电视，到处都是美国那种粗俗浅薄的闹剧，这种闹剧居然还被翻译成各种语言，差不多充斥了整个世界，从匈牙利、赞比亚到日本，到处都一样。另一方面，谈到书籍和文学作品的交流时，翻译工作实在是做得太差太少，尤其是对非西方文化的介绍和翻译更是如此，对中国文学作品的翻译和介绍就更是少得可怜。

26 早逝的灵魂——艾卜勒·卡西木·沙比（1909~1934）

In Arab literature, especially in the Age of **Ignorance**, poets were held in high esteem due to the belief held by most Arab communities that these masters of **verse** were also blessed with the gift of **clairvoyance**.

There were a group of poets, who would write **ode**s on how the political and social situation of their **locale** would change. This **bestow**ed an **aura** of social importance on the poet.

Aboul-Qacem Echebbi (Abu al-Qasim al-Shabi) was born on February 24, 1909 in Tunisia at a time when the North African country was struggling with numerous trials as a French **colony**.

In his youth, he **channel**ed his hatred of the inhuman treatment of Arabs in North African countries like Tunisia, Algeria and Morocco and began writing odes **condemn**ing social injustice.

The poet's regretful early death denied the young genius his chance to play a **prominent** role as seer, and predict his country's political and social developments. Nevertheless, one of Echebbi's visions, **outline**d in an ode penned some 85 years ago, has come to pass.

Echebbi passed away from a wasting heart disease at the age of 25 in 1934, but his poem has survived in the hearts of generations of Arab

阿拉伯文化中，尤其是在无知的年代，诗人深受社会敬仰，原因在于很多阿拉伯群体认为这些掌握着诗行的大师们具有上帝赐予的洞察力。

有这样一群诗人，针对其所生活的地方政治及社会局势是如何改变的，他们会写颂诗。这就使得诗人格外重要。

沙比于1909年出生在突尼斯。此时，这个北非的国家正苦苦挣扎在法国殖民下。

年轻时，沙比将自己对阿拉伯人在北非的非人道做法的愤懑表现在颂诗当中，以此来谴责社会不公平。

遗憾的是，诗人英年早逝。这使得他那满腹的才华没能为他祖国的政治及社会发展出一份力。然而沙比在大约85年前的一首诗中幻想的，如今已成为现实。

1934年，沙比死于心脏衰竭，年仅25岁。但是他的诗永远活跃在阿拉伯革命者心中。对于他们来讲，他的诗是最典型的史诗。

如果人们想要生

revolutionaries as a quintessential epic ode.

When the people wants to live,

destiny must surely respond

Darkness will disappear,

chains will certainly break!

The two verses, which are part of the Tunisian **national anthem**, are followed by a warning in the original ode, entitled the "Will to Live".

And does who do not embrace the zest for life

Evaporate in the atmosphere and cease to be.

In his lengthy ode, Echebbi foreshadowed that his country would **discard** its **shackle**s and end the French colonial rule, but his short life did not permit him a glance of the dawn of independence.

One of the odes' wonders is that the young Tunisian poet somehow managed to clearly predict the current developments in the country and his poem **herald**s a time when his nation would no longer be a slave to dictators.

Today, the Mediterranean littoral state has finally managed to forsake one dictatorship which ruled a police state that would not tolerate freedom.

命运必须回应

黑暗终将结束

枷锁必将消失！

这两段诗出现在突尼斯的国歌当中，原诗名为《生命的意愿》，后面还有两行：

不珍爱生命的人

必将在大气中蒸发不见。

在沙比传奇的颂诗中，他预言了他的国家会结束法国殖民的桎梏，但他短暂的一生并不允许他一瞥自由的黎明。

这些颂诗的神奇之处在于，这位年轻的突尼斯诗人以某种方式预言了国家如今的发展，他的诗向人们预演了一个他的人民摆脱奴隶命运的时代。

如今，这个地中海沿岸的国家已经成功地摆脱了殖民统治，过上了自由的生活。

词汇 Ⅴ OCABULARY

ignorance：无知，蒙昧	channel：引导，形成河道，集中（精力）
verse：诗行，诗节	condemn：谴责
clairvoyance：洞察力	prominent：突出的，杰出的，突起的
ode：颂诗	outline：概述，画出轮廓
locale：地方	national anthem：国歌
bestow：赋予	discard：丢弃，抛弃
aura：氛围	shackle：手铐，脚镣，镣铐
colony：殖民地	herald：预报，标志

《牧歌》

（作者：沙比 译者：郭黎）

清晨来临，向酣睡的生命歌唱；
山岭在轻轻摇曳的枝条下沉入梦乡。
和风舞弄着憔悴干枯的花瓣；
暗淡的峡谷里，徐徐飘动着霞光。
清晨美妙地来临，地平线一片辉煌；
花儿、鸟儿和水波伸伸懒腰。
活生生的世界醒来，为生命而欢唱；
醒醒吧，我的羊，过来吧，我的羊！
跟我走吧，我的羊，在鸟群间穿行；
让峡谷充满咩咩叫声，还有活泼和欢欣；
听小溪的细语，闻鲜花的清香。
看那峡谷，正笼罩着光闪熠熠的雾云；
来吧，采撷大地和新牧场上的青草；
听啊，我的短笛正吹送甜蜜的乐曲；
旋律从我心间涌出，恰如玫瑰的呼吸；
然后飞上天空，像一只幸福歌唱的夜莺。
如果我们来到森林，万木把我们荫蔽；
尽情地摘吧：青草、鲜花和果实。
是太阳用光明给它们哺乳，是月亮把它们抚育；
它们在破晓时分，吮吸朝露滴滴。
在山谷，在坡上，尽情欢乐吧；
如果疲倦了，就在繁茂的绿阴下小休。
在阴影的沉默里，咀嚼青草，咀嚼思绪；
听风儿歌唱，在山间的葡萄枝头。
林中有鲜花和甜嫩的绿草；
蜜蜂在它们四周，哼着欢歌。
纯洁的香气不曾遭到豺狼呼吸的玷污；
不，狐狸不曾结伴在它们上面踩过！
清新的馨香，神奇，安宁；
微风步态娉婷，娇声娇气。
青枝翠叶，光和美在其间起舞；
常青的绿色，黑夜无法将它拭去。
我的羊呀，别在蓊郁的森林久留；
森林时代是孩童，淘气、甜蜜、美丽。

人的时代是老汉，愁眉苦脸，迟钝沉闷；

心灰意懒，在这片平原上缓行。

在林中有你的草场，你美好的天地；

歌声，琴韵都向黄昏时光而去。

柔嫩，细弱的小草的阴影已拖长；

快，快回到那安谧平和的地域。

27 莫桑比克奥运首金获得者——玛丽亚·穆托拉（1972~）

The world's fastest woman over 800 metres is Maria Mutola - and she has overcome remarkable **odds** to reach the top.

She was born in Chamanculo, a poor **shanty town** in the suburbs of the Mozambican capital, Maputo, on 27 October 1972.

She said, "It doesn't matter where you come from. If you come from a rich or poor area or family, you can always achieve your goals at school or in sports—if you focus enough and dedicate yourself."

Until the beginning of her teens, Mutola played football with men in the Chamanculo neighbourhood until Mozambican writer, Jose Craveirinha, noticed a possible **athletics** talent when she was 14.

After four months of serious training, she **excel**led and won her first international race. At 15 she was **competing** in the Olympics.

But her crowning achievement to date is without doubt the gold medal she won in the Olympic Games held in the Australian city of Sydney – Mozambique's first ever Olympic gold.

"To be the first Mozambican to be able to grab gold, I was very happy and **emotional**," Mutola said.

Her victory put Mozambique on the world map and was received back home with joy and **jubilation**.

世界上800米赛跑跑得最快的女性是玛丽亚·穆托拉。她克服重重困难才取得了如此骄人的成绩。

1972年10月27日，穆托拉出生在莫桑比克首都马普托城郊的一个贫民窟里。

她曾说："你来自哪儿没有关系。无论你的家庭是富有还是贫穷，你都可以在学习或运动上取得好成绩——如果你用尽努力，拼命争取。"

在十几岁之前，穆托拉一直在Chamanculo社区和男孩们一起踢足球。穆托拉14岁时，莫桑比克作家克拉韦里尼亚发现了她的田径天赋。

经过四个月的艰苦训练，穆托拉脱颖而出，并赢得了人生中第一场国际比赛。15岁，她参加了奥运会。

她的首金是在澳大利亚悉尼举办的奥运会上获得的——这也是莫桑比克的首枚金牌。

穆托拉说，"能成为为国摘得首金的人，我很高兴和激动。"

When she returned home from Sydney, Mutola was given a **red carpet** reception right from the packed airport.

She could hardly hide her tears as she walked past the traditional dance groups that tirelessly shouted her name and gave her messages of praise and **encouragement**.

In response Mutola said: "I dedicate this gold medal to all Mozambicans, because it's the first Olympic gold medal for our country."

During her return home, Mutola had a tight schedule, visiting central and northern Mozambican provinces. She also met the prime minister and president.

"This was my first visit to the provinces and I enjoyed seeing the smiling faces of people who came to see me to say well-done Maria, good job Maria", she explained.

After the Sydney victory, the Mozambican Government decided to, among other things, name one of the avenues of the capital after her.

The school where she did her primary education now also bears her name.

Mutola would love to **inspire** fellow Mozambicans, particularly youngsters, to take part in sports and said she hoped her victory in Sydney would help people forget about the evil things that have ravaged Mozambique, including poverty, the war, the floods and other natural disasters.

She says that like many other women and men, she dreams of having her own family, but is in no hurry.

"I'm still young and have a lot to do... I just wanna run a few more years, maybe one more Olympic games. Then, I can actually quit."

She doesn't want to think that with this year's Olympic victory she has accomplished everything, "because if I think that way, I'll start losing races."

And she says she now has set her sights on breaking the world record in the 800 metres and 1500 metres.

她的成功使得莫桑比克进入了世界版图。奥运凯旋后，她也收获了喜悦和欢呼。一下飞机，她就受到了红地毯式的欢迎。

当她走过鼓励、表扬她的传统舞蹈队时，她禁不住潸然泪下。

穆托拉说，"我把这块金牌献给所有莫桑比克的人民，因为这是我们国家第一块金牌。"

回家以后，穆托拉行程很紧。她去了莫桑比克中北部各个省份，还受到了总理和总统的接见。

穆托拉说，"这是我第一次去这些省份。看到那么多笑盈盈的人们说着'做得好，玛丽亚'，我很高兴"。

悉尼取胜之后，莫桑比克政府决定将首都一座场馆的名字命名为穆托拉。

穆托拉喜欢激励自己的国人，尤其是年轻一代，去参与体育活动。她希望她在悉尼的胜利能够使人们忘却那些万恶的事情：贫穷、战争、洪水以及其他自然灾害使得莫桑比克一片破败。

她说，她像很多人一样，渴望拥有自己的家庭，但这事儿得从长计议。

"我还年轻，我还有很多事要做……我还想再跑几年，如果可能，再参加一次奥运会。然后，我才会甘心退出。"

她不愿将此次奥运会的胜利看成是人生的巅峰，"因为那样，我会失掉其他比赛。"

她说，她的目标是要打破800米、1500米竞赛的世界记录。

odds：机率，差别，投注赔率，让步，优势	emotional：动感情的
shanty town：贫民窟	jubilation：喜悦，欢呼
athletics：体育运动，田径	red carpet：红地毯的，隆重的
excel：超越	encouragement：鼓励
compete：竞争	inspire：激励，激发

背景知识 **P**ROFILE

世界腰果之乡——莫桑比克

有"世界腰果之乡"的美誉

莫桑比克是最大的腰果生产国之一，享有"世界腰果之乡"的美誉。和大多数非洲国家的炎热不同，莫桑比克气候较温和，境内既无大涝，也无大旱，最适合腰果树的生长。全国共种有腰果树约3000万棵，再加上野生的话，数量就更多。算下来，平均每个国民就拥有6棵，"腰果之乡"的确名不虚传。

非洲植物资源丰富，大多数国家的林木都是土生土长，但莫桑比克的腰果林却是例外。16世纪，几个葡萄牙人从巴西带来几颗腰果种子，试种在莫桑比克沿海，结果大获成功。人们纷纷引种，当地数量众多的猴子也在迁移中将种子到处传播，加上这种树不娇贵，无需照管就能顺利成长，在不长的时间里便覆盖了莫桑比克全国。美洲大陆曾从非洲引进了许多热带经济作物，腰果树在莫桑比克的"无心插柳"，可以看作是南美对非洲的"回报"了。

有关腰果的歌曲脍炙人口

对中国人来说，腰果是种好吃的零食，但对于莫桑比克人来说却大不一样。腰果仁可以吃，也可以榨汁、酿酒；腰果木可以做成坚固的家具；腰果汁能做防腐涂料；腰果树皮、树根还可以当药材。难怪在莫桑比克，腰果的图案随处可见，有关腰果的歌曲、诗歌和小说更是脍炙人口呢。

腰果给莫桑比克人带来了可观的财富。据说，每吨腰果仁能卖5000多美元，腰果油因为防腐功能卓越更是价值连城，连美国航天飞机上都涂了它的提炼物。甚至有人认为国徽里不应该只有甘蔗和玉米两种作物，还应加上腰果，因为后者同样是重要的农作物。

"吃猫鼠"的老家

看过动画片《黑猫警长》的人，恐怕都记着里面曾介绍过一种能吃猫的老鼠，事实上，这种"吃猫鼠"的老家就在莫桑比克。去过当地的游客曾编顺口溜说，那里的"蜂窝像磨盘，耗子比猫大"。的确，莫桑比克的老鼠有的重达3到4公斤，堪称老鼠界的大块头，而猫却大多体形瘦小，让它们担负捕捉如此硕鼠的重任，的确有点"强猫所难"。

东南非洲有色金属矿藏丰富，地质结构复杂，长期生活在地下的老鼠摄入的微量元素远比别处的动物多，其中一些莫桑比克老鼠便逐渐长成奇特的品种，吃猫鼠就是一例。这种老鼠天生一张大嘴，猫碰上它立即变得体若筛糠、浑身酥软。此时吃猫鼠便扑上去咬住猫的喉管，先吸食其血，再拖回洞穴慢慢"享用"。据说，这种老鼠嘴里可以喷射出麻醉唾液，猫一旦沾上便会昏倒，自然任其宰割了。

有趣的是，人们对老鼠不但不讨厌，还很感激。原来当地曾因内战遗留下大量地雷。人工探雷不仅效率低，还很危险。后来比利时专家训练了一群老鼠担任工兵，这些老鼠嗅觉灵敏，能在土中任意打洞，找地雷是小菜一碟，更妙的是它们的身体比人和狗都轻得多，即使踩上地雷也不会引爆。不过承担这项探雷工作的并不是吃猫鼠，而是当地引进的另一种冈比亚老鼠。这种老鼠约有2斤重，比吃猫鼠灵活多了。

28 非洲足球先生——帕特里克·姆博马（1970~ ）

Born in Cameroon, Patrick Mboma moved with his family to France when he was two years old. He had already played professionally in France, Japan and Italy, when he hit his **peak** in 2000. Early in the year, he led the "**Indomitable** Lions" of **Cameroon** to **victory** in the **African Nations' Cup**. Considered **outsider**s at the Sydney Olympics, the Cameroon team attracted little attention during pool play, beating Kuwait 3-2 and tying both the United States and the Czech Republic 1-1. But in their quarterfinal match-up against Brazil, they began a **thrilling** and unexpected run. Mboma scored in the 17th minute to give his team a 1-0 halftime lead. They held onto their advantage deep into the second half, but then two Cameroonian players received red cards, leaving the team two men short. With seconds remaining in regulation, Ronaldinho scored on a free kick to send the game into overtime. Despite playing with only nine men, Cameroon survived the overtime and then won the penalty shootout. In the semifinals,

帕特里克·姆博马出生于喀麦隆，两岁时跟随父母移居法国。他曾效力于法国、日本、意大利，2000年达到事业顶峰。2006年初，他带领喀麦隆"非洲雄狮"队取得了非洲国家杯的冠军。悉尼奥运会时，人们并不看好喀麦隆队，在小组赛时并未引起太多关注。小组赛的成绩是：对阵科威特3:2，与美国及捷克共和国打成平局。但是在四分之一决赛对阵巴西时，喀麦隆队表现令人振奋。姆博马在17分钟时踢进一球，使得队伍在前半场以1:0的比分取得优势地位。下半场，他们守住优势，但随后，两名喀麦隆球员被红牌罚下。在比赛将要结束时，罗纳尔·迪尼奥发任意球得分，使得双方进入加时赛。在缺少两名球员的情况下，喀麦隆队挺过加时赛，并到了点球决胜的阶段。在半决赛时，当比赛还剩6分钟时，喀麦隆队负智利

Cameroon **trail**ed Chile 1-0 with six minutes to play when Mboma scored to tie the game. With only one minute left in regulation, Mboma drew a foul in the penalty box. Lauren Etame-Mayer converted the penalty and the Cameroonians moved on to the final, which they played against Spain before a crowd of 98,212. Cameroon fell behind 0-2 after the first half, but eight minutes into the second half, Mboma fired a cross that **deflect**ed off the face of a Spanish **defender** and into the goal. Five minutes later, Samuel Eto'o tapped in another cross from Mboma to tie the game. There was no more scoring in regulation or in overtime, but Cameroon won the penalty shootout 5-3 to earn the Olympic championship. Chosen African Footballer of the Year in 2000, Mboma went on to lead Cameroon to victory again in the 2002 African Nations' Cup.

1分。姆博马的一记进球，使得比赛成为平局。比赛仅剩一分钟时，姆博马犯规，进入受罚席。劳雷亚诺·比桑·埃塔姆-马耶尔又进一球，使得喀麦隆队打进决赛。决赛中，喀麦隆队在全场98212名观众面前与西班牙争夺奥运比赛分量最重的一枚金牌。在上半场，喀麦隆队以0-2落后，下半场开始五分钟后，姆博马为喀麦隆队扳回一分。五分钟后，埃托奥的进球将比分扳成2-2。随后，双方再无建树，进入加时赛，在加时赛中，喀麦隆队以5-3击败西班牙获得奥运会男子足球冠军。同年，姆博马当选为非洲足球先生。2002年，姆博马再次带领喀麦隆队获得非洲国家杯。2005年5月16日，效力于日本神户胜利船队的喀麦隆著名球星姆博马因为伤病困扰，宣布正式退役。

词汇 VOCABULARY

peak：顶峰	outsider：外行，旁观者，局外人
indomitable：不可屈服的，不可战胜的	thrilling：激动人心的
Cameroon：喀麦隆	trail：（在比赛、竞赛等中）输，失败
victory：胜利	deflect：使偏斜，使转向
African Nations' Cup：非洲国家杯	defender：卫冕者，防守队员

背景知识 PROFILE

足球术语一览表

场地名称篇：

field / pitch 足球场	midfield 中场
backfield 后场	kickoff circle / center circle 中圈
halfway line 中线	touchline / sideline 边线
goal line 球门线	end line 底线

penalty mark （点球）罚球点   penalty area 禁区（罚球区）

penalty box 受罚区   goal area 小禁区（球门区）

球队成员称谓篇：

coach 教练   head coach 主教练

football player 足球运动员   referee 裁判

lineman 巡边员   captain / leader 队长

forward / striker 前锋   midfielder 前卫

left midfielder 左前卫   right midfielder 右前卫

attacking midfielder 攻击型前卫（前腰） defending midfielder 防守型前卫（后腰）

center forward 中锋   full back 后卫

center back 中后卫   left back 左后卫

right back 右后卫   sweeper 清道夫，拖后中卫

goalkeeper / goalie 守门员

足球技术篇：

kick-off 开球   bicycle kick / overhead kick 倒钩球

chest-high ball 半高球   corner ball / corner 角球

goal kick 球门球   handball 手球

header 头球   penalty kick / shootout 点球

place kick 定位球   own goal 乌龙球

hat-trick 帽子戏法   free kick 任意球

direct free kick 直接任意球   indirect free kick 间接任意球

stopping 停球   chesting 胸部停球

pass 传球   short pass 短传

long pass 长传   cross pass 横传

spot pass 球传到位   consecutive passes 连续传球

take a pass 接球   triangular pass 三角传球

flank pass 边线传球   lobbing pass 高吊传球

volley pass 凌空传球   slide tackle 铲球

rolling pass / ground pass 地滚球   flying header 跳起顶球

clearance kick 解围   shoot 射门

close-range shot 近射   long shot 远射

offside 越位   throw-in 掷界外球

block tackle 正面抢截   body check 阻挡

fair charge 合理冲撞   diving header 鱼跃顶球

dribbling 盘球，带球   clean catching （守门员）接高球

finger-tip save （守门员）托救球   offside 越位

deceptive movement 假动作   break through 突破

kick-out 踢出界

足球战术篇：

set the pace 掌握进攻节奏   ward off an assault 击退一次攻势

break up an attack 破坏一次攻势   disorganize the defence 搅乱防守

total football 全攻全守足球战术   open football 拉开的足球战术

off-side trap 越位战术   wing play 边锋战术

time wasting tactics 拖延战术   4-3-3 formation 433阵型

4-4-2 formation 442阵型   beat the offside trap 反越位成功

foul 犯规   technical foul 技术犯规

break loose 摆脱   control the midfield 控制中场

set a wall 筑人墙   close-marking defence 盯人防守

比赛方式篇：

half-time interval 中场休息   round robin 循环赛

group round robin 小组循环赛   extra time / overtime 加时赛

elimination match 淘汰赛   injury time 伤停补时

golden goal / sudden death 金球制，突然死亡法   eighth-final 八分之一决赛

quarterfinal 四分之一决赛   semi-final 半决赛

final match 决赛   preliminary match 预赛

one-sided game 一边倒的比赛   competition regulations 比赛条例

disqualification 取消比赛资格   match ban 禁赛命令

doping test 药检   draw / sortition 抽签

send a player off 判罚出场   red card 红牌

yellow card 黄牌   goal 球门，进球数

draw 平局   goal drought 进球荒

ranking 排名（名次）

29 传统与现代的化身——帕帕·文巴（1954~）

One of the most **beloved** singers in Congo music, Papa Wemba was born Shungu Jules Wembadio in Kasai, in the lower part of Congo's massive and remote interior. A **self-proclaimed** singer from birth and an **avid** participant in that region's traditional life, Wemba inherited his father's role as "chief of customs". But city life **beckon**ed, and he headed north to Kinshasa, where in 1969 he helped to found Zaiko Langa Langa, Zaire's most popular youth band Congo music had ever seen.

For their **irreverence**, and the **sensation** they caused, Zaiko have been compared to the Rolling Stones, whom they admired. But members split off to form their own bands that **spawn**ed yet other bands: Langa Langa Stars, Grand Zaiko Wa Wa, Chock (as in shock) Stars, and, among many others, Papa Wemba's Viva La Musica.

Wemba was one of the first to split off, and he did so in a way that ensured him a special place in the **rabble** of Zaire's competing stars. In the era of President Mobutu's "authenticity" **edict**, which demanded affirmation of African heritage, Wemba worked the traditional log drum or lokole into his music, and appeared on stage in raffia skirt and cowrie shell hat, things urbanites had once dismissed as shameful **trapping**s of the bush. But after relocating in Paris, Wemba returned with a new look, which he called "Ungaru". Raffia gave way to Gianfranco Ferre, Pierre Cardin, and a host of trendy European designs.

Wemba gets credit for launching the Zaiko clan's trademark use of high fashion as a form of social **rebellion**. Wemba's **dashing** self-styled look—a 1930s throwback featuring baggy, pleated trousers hemmed above shiny brogues and hair clipped close at the sides—soon earned him the title Pope of the Sapeurs: Society of

帕帕·文巴是刚果音乐史上倍受喜爱的歌手之一，他出生于刚果开赛河边。文巴自称是天生的歌手，他积极参与当地的传统活动，继承了父亲"民俗长"的角色。但是文巴更喜欢城市生活，他开始北上到金沙萨。1969年，他在金沙萨组建了Zaiko Langa Langa乐队，这是扎伊尔最有名的青年乐队。在刚果音乐史上可谓是史无前例。

因为他们所引起的轰动，人们将该乐队与滚石乐队相提并论。而滚石也是这个乐队崇拜的对象。但后来乐队解散，他们分别成立了自己的乐队。（文巴的乐队名称为Viva La Musica。）

文巴是一个从乐队分裂出来的成员，这种做法使得他在扎伊尔复杂的明星圈内处于一个尴尬的位置。蒙博托总统的时代，非洲传统得到复兴。文巴将木鼓等传统乐器融入到音乐中。演出时，他穿着酒椰叶衬衫，头戴宝贝贝壳帽。这些东西受到了都市人的鄙夷。但迁居巴黎之后，文巴以崭新的面貌归来。他把这种新面貌叫"Ungaru"。他开始穿奇安弗兰科·费雷等欧洲时尚名牌。

文巴将时尚元素加入Zaiko中，体现了对社会的反叛，并因此获得了好评。文巴造型时尚，他身着三十年代的复古宽松、起褶的

Ambianceurs and Persons of Elegance. The wildness of soukous and the excesses of the Sapeurs can be seen as channeled expressions of free spirits in an environment of political oppression and **relentless** conformity.

In 1987, he created a band in Paris, using European and African musicians, and set about playing music that did not adhere to the core principles of Congo pop. Wemba's Afropop did not go down well with the home crowd, but it did open doors for him in Europe and America, especially when he and his new group performed in the 1988 traveling spectacle of African traditional performance arts, Africa Oyé.

Since then, Wemba has led parallel lives, performing and recording both with Viva La Musica and with his crossover group. The Viva la Musica releases have been some of the best straight Congo music releases of the late 1990s. Meanwhile, Wemba's work with his own group earned him a place in the 1998 touring festival Africa fête. In any context, Wemba preserves a shy, roguish demeanor behind his Parisian polish.

裤子，配上半统工作靴，头发别在两边。他将穿衣时尚已经演绎到了一种让人顶礼膜拜的地步。他这种风格可以被理解成在政治压迫和要求服从的环境中一种自由意志的表达。

1987年，文巴在巴黎组建了一个乐队，成员是来自欧洲和非洲的音乐家。他们的音乐不符合刚果流行音乐的核心价值观念。文巴的非洲流行乐在家乡并没有受到追捧，反倒为他在欧美的市场打开了大门。尤其是1988那场以非洲表演艺术为特征的表演，更让欧美人赞不绝口。

自那以后，文巴过着双重的生活，既有之前传统非洲风的Viva La Musica，也有跨界的融合演出。20世纪90年代末期，Viva la Musica曾发行了一些刚果音乐史上非常棒的专辑。无论是哪种语境下，在文巴巴黎式的精致中，都保有一种腼腆、无赖的举止态度。

词汇 VOCABULARY

beloved：被人爱着的	rabble：乌合之众，暴民，下等人
self-proclaimed：自称的	edict：法令，命令
avid：贪婪的，渴望的	trappings：装扮
beckon：招手	rebellion：反叛
irreverence：不敬的行为	dashing：时髦的
spawn：产卵，种菌丝于，产生，造成	relentless：无情的

背景知识 PROFILE

滚石乐队简介

滚石乐队(The Rolling Stones)的名字取自于前辈艺人Muddy Waters的一首歌曲

《Rollingstones Blues》。它是当今乐坛最伟大的乐队，音乐史上最杰出的乐队之一，流行乐史上最重要的乐队之一，摇滚史上最有影响的乐队之一，现场演出表现最棒的乐队之一。

乐队从1962年年底开始在伦敦的Marquee Club表演，自此他们开始了不凡的音乐生涯。早期的The Rolling Stones的作品走的是民谣和节奏&布鲁斯路线。1965年，"滚石"发表的第一首上榜歌曲"满足"(Satisfaction)奠定了乐队的基本音乐风格。不仅如此，这首名作在当时的西方社会取得了很大的反响，它引导了摇滚乐的创作演变为具有社会意义的一种文化表现形式。

60年代末，The Rolling Stones发行的几张出色专辑《乞丐的宴会》(Begger's Banquet)、《魔鬼陛下们的要求》(Their Satanic Majesties Request)以及后来的《任血流淌》(Let It Bleed)等都取得了很大的成功，并成为了摇滚史上的经典杰作。"滚石"乐队本身也建立了自己富有个性与时代感召力的形象。鼎盛时期的"滚石"乐队能精确、生动地演绎布鲁斯音乐，另外他们表现的成熟，丰富的硬摇滚(Hard Rock)曲风能使人激动不已。The Rolling Stones形成的夸张、豪放的音乐表现特征也使他们成为经典摇滚(Classic Rock)的奠基者之一。The Rolling Stones与The Beatles(甲壳虫)、The Kinks(奇想)还有The Who(谁人)等乐队一起开创了60年代英国新摇滚文化的新纪元。

进入70年代以后，"滚石"推出了像《Sticky Fingers》(小偷小摸)和《Exile On Main Street》(街头流亡者)这样优秀的唱片。The Rolling Stones在各地的演唱会使无数歌迷领略到了摇滚乐无穷的魅力与巨大快乐，"滚石"确实影响了后来许多出色乐队的创作和成长。

80、90年代，"滚石"依然活跃于音乐舞台，他们1988年发行的专辑《钢轮》(Steel Wheel)引起了很大的轰动。94年的专辑《Vooddo Lounge》与1997年专辑《Bridge To Babylon》(巴比伦之桥)均取得了乐评界的好评并在销量上也取得了不俗的成绩。

"滚石"乐队于1963年在英国成立，乐队成员5人：歌手米克·贾格尔（Mick Jagger）、吉他手兼歌手基斯·理查德（Keith Richards）、吉他手兼歌手布莱恩·琼斯（Brian Jones）、贝司手比尔·怀曼（Bill Wyman）、钢琴手伊恩·斯图尔(Ian Stewart)和鼓手查利·活茨。

与同时代的另一支伟大乐队"甲壳虫"相比，"滚石"具有更强的攻击性和叛逆色彩——他们是天生的坏小子，狂放不羁，处处透着锐利狡黠的气息，是后期"嬉皮"运动中绝对的"自我中心主义"的代表。从某种意义上讲，"滚石"的确具有魔鬼的一面，否则他们制作的经典作品《魔鬼陛下们的要求》也不会显得如此名副其实。邪迷黑暗的《魔鬼陛下们的要求》是一张好作品，但当真论起乐队的巅峰之作，还当首推1968的《乞丐的宴会》（Bagger's Banquet）和1969年的《任血流淌》（Let It Bleed）。经过60年代的鼎盛时期，进入70年代后，"滚石"的叛逆形象有所降低，虽有佳作问世，但已无法再现当年的盛事。

30 马里布鲁斯音乐之父——阿里·杜尔（1939~2006）

One of Africa's best known **musician**s, Ali Farka Toure, has died after a long illness in his home country of Mali, the culture ministry has announced.

He was one of the **pioneer**s of "Mali Blues" and his 1994 Talking Timbuktu **album** produced with US blues guitarist Ry Cooder was widely **acclaim**ed.

Toure, who was in his late 60s, won two Grammy awards for his work.

In 2004, he was elected **mayor** of his home town of Niafunke on the shores of the River Niger in northern Mali.

Mali's prime minister, culture minister and many of Mali's top artists have been gathering at his home to pay their respects ahead of his **funeral**.

Radio stations in the capital, Bamako, have interrupted their normal **coverage** to play his music.

He died in Bamako but is to be buried in Niafunke, 850km north of the capital on Wednesday, the authorities have announced.

Toure won Grammys for Talking Timbuktu and again in 2006, for his album in **collaboration** with another famous Malian musician, Toumani Diabate, In the Heart of the Moon.

His record label, World Circuit, said he had just finished work on a new solo album.

Although he has worked with several US blues guitarists, the "Bluesman of Africa" always insisted that the music had its roots in the traditional sounds of northern Mali, rather than the southern United States.

Malian journalist Sadio Kante says Toure was

阿里•法尔卡•杜尔是非洲最有名的音乐家之一。马里文化部长已宣布，杜尔长久病痛之后，在他的祖国马里去世。

杜尔是"马里布鲁斯"的创始人之一。1994年，他和美国布鲁斯吉他手莱•库德共同制作的专辑《话说廷巴克图》大受好评。

杜尔近70岁时，获得了两项格莱美奖。

2004年，他被家乡Niafunke镇评为市长。Niafunke镇位于马里北部尼日尔河岸边。

杜尔葬礼前，马里首相、文化部长以及马里很多顶尖艺术家都聚集到了杜尔的家乡，来悼念这位音乐家。

马里首都巴马科的广播电台都停止他们的日常节目，开始播放他的音乐。

他在巴马科去世，却葬在了离巴马科850km远的Niafunke镇。

杜尔的专辑《话说廷巴克图》获得了两项格莱美奖。2006年，他又与马里音乐家图曼尼•迪亚巴发行了又一张专辑《漫步月心》。

他的唱片公司World Circuit说，他刚刚完成了一张个人专辑的录制。

尽管他曾和一些美国布鲁斯吉他手合作，但这位"非洲布鲁斯音乐人"常常强调他的音乐是植根于马里北部的传统声音中，而不是美国南部。

马里记者Sadio Kante说，杜尔的国际声誉比在国内更大。

他出生于1939年的廷巴克图，确切生辰不详。

better known abroad than in his home country.

He was born in Timbuktu in 1939 but the exact date of his birth is not known.

"For some people, Timbuktu is a place at the end of nowhere," he was once quoted as saying.

"But that's not true, I'm from Timbuktu, and I can tell you that it's right in the centre of the world."

During the 1990s rebellion by the Tuareg people of northern Mali, Toure was seen as something of a **peacemaker** by singing in all of the region's languages—Songhai, Fulani and the Tuareg's Tamashek.

Many Bamako residents saw him as a northerner, rather than a national figure, says Sadio Kante.

But those in Mali's entertainment business are in **mourning**. "A monument has fallen. With the death of Ali Farka Toure, Mali is losing one of its greatest ambassadors," television producer Mbaye Boubacar Diarra told the AP news agency.

He leaves a widow and 11 children.

"对于一些人来说，廷巴克图是一个名不见经传的地方，但是那并不对。我来自廷巴克图，我会告诉你，它就在世界的中心"。

20世纪90年代的那场由马里北部图阿雷格人发动的叛乱中，杜尔化身成了一个和平使者，他用这个地区所有的语言——桑海语、富拉尼语以及图阿雷格的塔玛舍克语唱着歌曲。

Sadio Kante说，很多巴马科的居民将他视为一个北方人，而非一个民族领袖。

但是，马里的娱乐界却在为他的逝世而哀悼。电视制作人Mbaye Boubacar Diarra 告诉美联社新闻，"一座丰碑倒了。杜尔的死使得马里少了一位伟大的大使。"

他死后，留下妻子一人带着11个孩子。

词汇 VOCABULARY

musician: 音乐家	funeral: 葬礼
pioneer: 先驱	coverage: 报道
album: 相册，专辑，唱片	collaboration: 合作
acclaim: 欢呼，喝采，称赞	peacemaker: 调解者，和事佬
mayor: 市长	mourning: 悲伤，治丧，戴孝

背景知识 PROFILE

格莱美奖简介

格莱美音乐大奖（GRAMMY AWARDS）是美国国家录音与科学学会（The National Academy of Recording Arts & Science）举行的一个年度大型音乐评奖活动。格莱美奖被誉为"音乐界奥斯卡"。

"格莱美"（GRAMMY）是英文Gramophone（留声机）的变异谐音。以它命名的音乐奖迄今已有50年历史，其奖杯形状如一架老式的留声机。

1957年，美国洛杉矶一批音乐人和唱片公司管理人员倡议成立一个代表音乐制品艺术和科学的机构，并通过这个机构鼓励有才华的音乐家、歌手及幕后音乐制作人员。首届格莱美音乐奖于1958年颁发，以后录音学会每年举行一次颁奖仪式，奖项也由最初时的26项增加到28大类共101项。

美国当地时间2011年4月6日，美国录音艺术科学院宣布，2012年起将把格莱美音乐奖（Grammy Awards）奖项从原本的109个减为78个。

虽然格莱美奖力求公正客观，但凡走过必留下痕迹，四十年来仍留下获奖趋势可供预测。

主题健康："年度唱片"跟"年度歌曲"主题最好跟"爱"与"信（绝对不能是"性"）"有关，如"I Will Always Love You"；要对人生充满希望，如"Evergreen"、"We Are the World"；可以怀念所爱的人，如"Tears in Heaven"、"Unforgetable"；鼓励人们追求幸福，如"Somewhere Out There"；或是扭转劣势的勇气，如"Change the World"等正面意义，以上的主题比较可能得到肯定，这也是为何早期的Rolling Stones与Madonna会被拒之门外的原因。

市场肯定：以2004年为例，五张"年度唱片"都是Billboard排行榜前二十名的作品，五首"年度歌曲"都是点播大热门，近十年来的"年度唱片"得主就包括四首排行榜冠军与四首排行榜亚军，一首前五名之作。毕竟评审也是消费听众的一份子，基于相辅相成的作用，得到格莱美入围或优胜的作品，一经媒体渲染，往往会立即反映在暴增的唱片销量上。

搭配电影：这种因搭配电影曝光而广受格莱美认同的例子实在是太多了，近十年来就有八首"年度歌曲"同时也是电影主题曲或插曲的实证。

印象分数：这有两种情况，一是曾得过格莱美的老将，二是上一届才抱奖而归的新秀，只要新作成绩不是太差，（何况被格莱美肯定过的新人，来年通常都有傲人的商业表现），格莱美都会尽量给他们保留一个好位子。

有详细规则的游戏才能玩得久，美国表演艺术界的四大奖（音乐：格莱美、电影：奥斯卡、舞台：东尼奖、电视：艾米奖）全都符合这项要求。

受气候、文化等因素的影响，非洲形成了独具特色的饮食习惯。非洲食物向来就以调味艺术而闻名，将各种各样的香料及调味料，如肉桂、辣椒、豆蔻、丁香等，运用到淋漓尽致。从北非到南非，由于种族和宗教文化等方面的影响，其饮食的主要风格在于以烤煮烩炖等方式下的各种食物的"杂烩"。非洲大地原产的香料、蔬菜、水果品种繁多，所以非洲人自古以来就形成了将多种食品混在一起烹饪的习惯，对肉食大多采用烤制后再用上咖喱、番茄汁、奶昔等淋拌的制作方法，面食则多采用与水果相拌过油微炸的烹饪方法。

总之，非洲的美食是一种包容的哲学。如果有幸去非洲，请怀着一颗包容的心去品尝，给你的味觉一次享受盛宴的机会。

第四章

你不可不知的非洲美食

31 素食主义者之选——库沙里

Kushari, often **transliterate**d as koshary, kosheri or koshari, is a popular traditional Egyptian national dish. It consists of a base of rice, brown **lentils**, **chickpeas**, **macaroni**, and a **topping** of Egyptian **garlic** and **vinegar** and spicy tomato sauce (salsa). Fried onion is commonly added as a **garnish**. Koshary is normally a vegetarian and usually a vegan dish, possibly reflecting the meatless diet of Coptic Christians during Lent and other **fast**s and/or the high cost of meat for the lower classes. It is becoming common to add fried liver or shawarma meat as an additional topping.

Koshary is one of the most popular, inexpensive, and common dishes in Egypt, and many restaurants **specialize** in this one dish.

The following is a traveler who comments on Kushari.

A better description for the food is "Egyptian Chilli", the aforementioned ingredients are layered together upon a wide bowl, to be mixed together by the diner, together generous pourings of chilli and garlic sauces. The result, actually, is a lot like chilli - yet a lot easier to digest.

The dish is served in specialized eateries which serve nothing else. As I walked into this one, in downtow Cairo, the owner, from behind a table where he was counting receipts asked "Do you understand our menu?" I said I didn't, even though I knew it wouldn't be hard for him to explain.

"We only have Kushari, nothing else. It is 'Egyptian Chilli'. When the waiter comes, just tell him 'small, medium, or large.' He will understand." I nodded and passed upstairs to the dining room, where I found

库沙里又叫koshary，kosheri或koshari，是一道受人欢迎的埃及传统美食。它是用米饭、黑扁豆、鹰嘴豆及通心粉，再在上面淋上蒜蓉、醋及番茄酱做成，材料要先分开烹调。通常，油炸洋葱会作为配菜加入其中。库沙里是素食主义者的选择，是哥普特基督教徒在大斋期或其他禁食期食素的菜肴，也是贫苦人民因无钱买昂贵的肉类时的食物选择。现在，人们会放油炸肝或沙瓦玛烤肉卷在库沙里表面。

库沙里物美价廉，广受欢迎，在埃及随处可见。很多餐馆只卖这一种菜肴。

以下是一个游客在埃及吃库沙里的经历以及他对库沙里的评价。

这种食物被描述成"埃及辣椒"最合适不过了。之前说到的那些原来会被分层放在一个大碗里，要吃时再混合在一起，同时混合辣椒或蒜蓉汁。如此这般之后，味道很像辣椒，但比辣椒要容易消化得多。

这种菜在专门的小餐馆里可以吃到。当我走进开罗市中心一家餐馆时，老板问我是否懂他们的菜单。我说，我不懂。尽管我知道他解释起来也不容易。

"我们只有库沙里。它是'埃及辣椒'。一会儿服务生过来，你只要跟他说'小份儿，中份儿，大份儿就可以了'"。我点头，然后上楼落座。后来我发现周围坐着衣着简朴的

myself among a plain-looking set of Egyptians, taking a respite from whatever shopping or errands had brought them downtown on a weekend Friday.

My order was taken as promised, and the result was predictably excellent.

Here is the **recipe** for Kushari offered by Marie Henein, a vegan from Coptic Orthodox.

2 cups uncooked brown or white rice

1 pound lentils

2 Tablespoons vegetable oil, divided

1 Tablespoon crushed garlic

Two 16-ounce cans of tomato sauce

1/2 cup water

1/4 cup vinegar

1 medium onion

Cook rice according to directions. Rinse lentils and put them in a pot, covering them with water, and bring to a boil. Then simmer on low heat until almost all water is absorbed and lentils are well cooked. Add extra water if longer time is needed. To make the sauce, first saute the garlic in 1 Tablespoon oil until golden. Add both cans of tomato sauce and simmer 10-15 minutes. Add water and vinegar and bring to a boil. Remove from heat immediately and add salt to taste. Finally, slice onion in thin, small pieces and saute in remaining 1 Tablespoon oil until brown and crispy.

This dish should be arranged as a layer of lentils (on the bottom), followed by a layer of rice, then another layer of lentils and another layer of rice. Sprinkle the onions and the sauce on top before serving.

Total Calories Per Serving: 563

Fat: 7 grams

埃及人。他们可能是刚买完东西或因为某些事儿来市中心来这儿休息一会儿。

一会儿我的菜上来，结果是好吃得出乎意料。

以下是库沙里的烹饪方法，提供者名叫玛丽·赫内因，她是一个来自哥普特基督教的素食主义者。

两杯黄色或白色的生米

一磅小扁豆

两大汤匙植物油，分开放

一大汤匙蒜末

两罐16盎司番茄酱

1/2杯水

1/4杯醋

一个一般大小的洋葱

根据指示先煮饭。将小扁豆洗净放入锅内，然后加水，没过表面，开火煮沸。此时小火慢炖至小扁豆几乎将所有水分吸收，已经熟好。如果需要更多时间，需加水。做酱汁时需要在1大汤匙油内炒蒜，直至颜色变黄。然后加入两罐番茄酱，小火慢炖10分钟~15分钟。接着加入水、醋，煮沸。此时，将锅从火上马上移开，加盐品尝味道。最后，将洋葱切成小薄片，再把它放入一大汤匙油中炒成酥黄状。

食用时，将扁豆层至于碗的底部，然后盖一层米饭，接着一层扁豆，再一层米饭。上桌前加洋葱和酱。

该道菜整体热量：563卡路里

含脂肪量：7克。

transliterate：将词或字母用另一字母体系中的字母写出	fast：禁食，斋戒
lentil：小扁豆	ingredient：食材
chickpea：鹰嘴豆	digest：消化
macaroni：通心粉	downtown：市中心
topping：糕点上的装饰配料，构成顶部的东西	receipt：收据
garlic：蒜	plain-looking：相貌平平的
vinegar：醋	respite：休息
garnish：装饰，配菜	recipe：食谱，烹饪方法
specialize：专注于……；以……闻名	

背景知识 **P**ROFILE

埃及著名的美食

富尔 (Fuul) 及塔米亚 (Ta'amiyya) 可以说是非正式的埃及国菜。富尔是用蚕豆制成的，用油、柠檬、盐、肉、蛋以及洋葱加以调味；塔米亚则是将磨碎的鸡豆，和香料炸成的小丸子。把富尔和塔米亚加上一点番茄，用披塔 (Pita) 面包夹成三明治就是一道美味的小吃了。

埃及的三明治通常是用一小片肉、乳酪或熏肉卷成的，加一点芥茉酱就更美味了。沙威马在埃及也很有名，在埃及各地都可以看到卖羊肉沙威码的小贩，吃时加上腌黄瓜或腌萝卜。

除了三明治，埃及还有许多简便而价廉的小吃，菲提尔 (Fiteer)是一种类似披萨的食物，有甜咸两种口味，甜的菲提尔上放了葡萄干、核果以及砂糖，咸的非迪尔则加了起司、橄榄、碎肉或蛋。

柯夫塔 (Kofta) 和烤肉串 (Kebab) 是埃及最著名的两道菜。柯夫塔是把绞肉以香料调味后，用棍子串着烤，通常这两种东西都会和煮熟的番茄和洋葱一起吃。

莫沙卡 (Musaga) 是很可口的一道菜，它是用茄子、番茄、大蒜及香料烤成。莫洛奇亚 (Molokhiyya) 是一道绿色的浓汤，是用绿色蔬菜、米饭及大蒜炖成的 (埃及人和中国北方人一样，喜欢用大蒜调味)。夏休卡 (Shakshooka) 是一种烤的绞肉和番茄酱，再加一个蛋，也有素食夏休卡。

烤鸽子也是有名的菜，先塞麦子在鸽体内，再以炭火烧烤。另一种作法是把鸽肉和洋葱、番茄以及米或麦，放在陶罐里做成炖菜。还有一道叫做库夏里 (Kushari) 的菜，是用米、面、洋葱、黑扁豆及番茄酱做成，材料要先分开烹调，要吃时再和一起。

　　埃及最常见的面包是披塔面包及法国面包，最常见的起司有两种，一种是吉那贝达 (Gibna Beyda)，另一种是黄白色的硬起司，叫作吉那茹米(Gibna Rumi)。

32 一饭，一世界——西非炒饭

Jollof rice probably **originate**d from rice dishes eaten by the **Wolof** people of Senegal and Gambia, but its popularity has spread to most of West Africa, especially Nigeria and Ghana. Based on rice, tomatoes and usually meat or fish, it is believed by some to be the origin of Cajun jambalaya. The Gambian version is called benachin. Also spelled jolof or djolof rice.

Ingredients (4-6 servings):

Ingredients

Oil -- 1/4 cup

Chicken, cut into pieces -- 1.5 pounds

Water or **stock** -- 5 cups

Onions, **chop**ped -- 2 cups

Red or green **bell pepper**, chopped -- 1 piece

Garlic, **mince**d -- 3-4 **clove**s

Long-grain rice -- 3 cups

Tomato paste -- 1/4 cups

Tomatoes, chopped -- 2 cups

Carrots, peeled and chopped -- 2 cups

Green beans -- 1 cup

Cabbage, chopped -- 1 cup

Salt and pepper to taste

Methods

Heat the oil over medium-high flame in a large pot. Working in batches, add the chicken and **brown** on all sides. Remove the chicken to another large pot and add the water or stock. Bring to a boil, reduce heat to low and **simmer** for 20 minutes.

西非炒饭很可能是源于塞内加尔和冈比亚的沃洛夫人吃的一种米饭类食物。而如今，这种食物在西非大受欢迎，尤其在尼日利亚和加纳。主要原料有大米、西红柿、牲畜肉或鱼肉。不过，也有人认为这种饭来源于阿卡迪亚人的什锦饭。冈比亚人们称它为benachin。该单词还可以拼写成jolof或djolof米饭。

原料（4人~6人份）：

油——1/4杯

鸡肉，切碎——1.5磅

水或高汤——5杯

洋葱，剁碎——2杯

红或青椒，剁碎——1个

蒜，绞碎——3-4瓣

长颗粒米——3杯

番茄酱——1/4杯

西红柿，切碎——2杯

胡萝卜，削皮，切碎——2杯

青豆——1杯

洋白菜，切碎——1杯

盐或胡椒（根据口味）

制作方法：

在一个大锅中，加油，以中高火加热。加入鸡肉，炒至棕黄色。将炒好的鸡肉放入另一个大锅中，加水或高汤。煮沸，然后小火慢炖20分钟。

While the chicken simmers, pour all but 2-3 tablespoons of oil out of the first pot. Heat the oil over medium flame, add the onions and peppers and sauté until the onions are wilted and translucent, 4-5 minutes. Add the garlic and sauté for another 1-2 minutes.

Stir the rice into the onions and peppers and heat through for another 1-2 minutes. Stir in the tomato paste to coat the rice and give it a reddish hue. Add the chopped tomatoes and let them cook down for 2-3 minutes.

Pour in the chicken and its simmering liquid into the rice pot and add the carrots, green beans and cabbage. Season well with salt and pepper. Bring to a boil, reduce heat to low, cover tightly and simmer for 20 minutes.

Remove from heat, let rest another 10 minutes. Remove to a serving platter and serve with **slice**d hard-boiled eggs and a side salad.

Variations

There are many variations of jollof rice. Feel free to improvise using what you meats and vegetables you have on hand. Try beef, ham, shrimp, fish, goat or pork. For vegetables, add peas, potatoes, eggplant or mushrooms.

Beef Jollof Rice: substitute cubed stewing beef for the chicken. After browning the beef, simmer in liquid for 45 minutes before adding to the **sauté**ed rice mixture.

Vegetarian Jollof Rice: simply eliminate the meat and stir hot water or vegetable stock into the sautéed rice mixture.

Optional spices that can be used to flavor the dish are cinnamon, curry powder or cayenne. Some minced chile peppers can be sautéed with the onions to add extra bite.

在鸡肉慢炖的同时，将第一口锅清空，加入2-3大汤匙油，中火加热，然后加入洋葱、胡椒，4-5分钟炒至洋葱变软，色泽透明。加入蒜，再炒1-2分钟。

将米饭和洋葱、胡椒混合，加热1-2分钟。加入番茄酱，使得米饭呈红色。加入切碎的西红柿，整体再煮2-3分钟。

将鸡肉以及鸡汁倒入米饭锅内，加胡萝卜、青豆及洋白菜。加盐和胡椒调好味。煮沸，然后盖上锅盖小火炖20分钟。

然后熄火，焖10分钟。然后放到上桌的盘子内。同时，可以用煮透的鸡蛋片和配菜沙拉佐餐。

其他的变化形式

西非炒饭有很多变种。可以根据你手头的肉类和蔬菜临场发挥。可以试试牛肉、火腿肉、虾肉、鱼肉、羊肉或猪肉。而蔬菜可以试试豌豆、土豆、茄子或蘑菇。

牛肉西非炒饭：将鸡肉丁替换成牛肉丁。牛肉丁炒至橙色以后，在加入炒好的米饭混合物之前，将牛肉在汤汁中炖45分钟。

素食主义者版的西非炒饭：去掉肉类。将热水或蔬菜高汤倒入米饭混合物中搅拌。

另外，还可以加入肉桂、咖喱粉或辣椒粉调味。在炒洋葱时也可以加入切碎的辣椒，如此将别有一番风味。

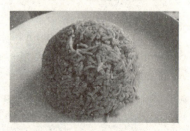

originate：起源于，发端于	clove：（复合鳞茎的）瓣
Wolof：沃洛夫人（塞内加尔和冈比亚人）	cabbage：洋白菜，卷心菜，包心菜
stock：汤汁，高汤	brown：将……变成橙色
chop：切碎，劈开，剁碎	simmer：煨，炖
bell pepper：青椒，灯笼椒，柿子辣	slice：片
mince：切碎	sauté：煎，炒（食物）

背景知识 **P**ROFILE

烹饪术语之一

烹饪中的一些烹调方法

蒸：Steam	加芥末、咖喱等烧烤：Devil
熏：Smoke	涮：Instantly Boil
腌：Salt	烙：Sear
煮：Boil	烫：Scald
炖：Double Boil	烤：Toast
炖;焖;扒：Braise	焙;烤;炙：Broil
焖;煨：Stew	熬浓：Inspissate
炙;灼：Broil; Fry	腊制：Cure
炸;油煎：Fire	扒：Fry & Simmer
炸：Deeply Fry	爆：Quickly Fry
煎：Pan-Fry	干炸：Drily Fry
油泡;炒：Stir; Fry	铁板：Sizzle
嫩煎;炒：Saute	串烧：Skewer
火焰烧：Flambe	烘;烤：Bake
烧：Burn	烩：Assort
(用叉)烧烤：Barbecue	腌制：Pickle
烧烤：Roast	油焖：Fricassee
炙烤：Grill	水煮：Poach
(用平锅)烧：Pan-Roast	抄;煮成半熟：Parboil
(用平锅)煎烧：Pan-Broil	卤水;腌泡;汁泡：Marinate
熬：Decoct	酿;填馅：Stuff
煎熬：Render	砂锅：Casserole
加辣味烧烤：Simmer	去骨：Bone

33 有趣的玉米饭团——乌伽黎

Known as ugali in Kenya and Tanzania, this **starchy**, **polenta**-like **side dish** goes by different names in sub-Saharan Africa. In Malawi and Zambia it is called nsima or nshima. The South African name for it is pap or mealie pap. Zimbabweans call it sadza.

Ingredients (4 to 6 servings):

Water -- 4 cups

Salt -- 2 **teaspoon**s

White cornmeal, finely **ground**-- 2 cups

Method

Bring the water and salt to a boil in a heavy-bottomed **saucepan**. Stir in the cornmeal slowly, letting it fall though the fingers of your hand.

Reduce heat to medium-low and continue stirring regularly, smashing any lumps with a spoon, until the **mush** pulls away from the sides of the pot and becomes very thick, about 10 minutes. Remove from heat and allow to cool somewhat.

Place the ugali into a large serving bowl. Wet your hands with water, form into a ball and serve.

Variations

White cornmeal is the most commonly used grain for ugali. But you can **substitutesorghum**, **millet** or coarse **cassava** flour or even **hominy grit**s.

More or less water can be added to achieve the **consistency** you prefer.

Stir in a little butter if you like for a richer flavor.

Notes

Ugali is usually served as an accompaniment to meat or vegetable stews, greens or soured milk. To eat ugali, pull off a small ball of mush with your fingers. Form an indentation with your thumb, and use it to scoop up accompanying stews and other dishes.

肯尼亚和坦桑尼亚将这种食物叫乌伽黎，这种含淀粉的玉米糊状的配菜在撒哈拉以南的非洲有各种各样的叫法。马拉维和赞比亚叫它nsima或nshima。南非人叫它粥或煮米粥。津巴布韦人称它为sadza。

原料（**4-6**人份）：

水——4杯；盐——2 小勺；白玉米，碾碎——2杯

制作步骤

将盐放入水中，在深底平锅中煮沸。将白玉米缓缓加入锅中，并搅拌。

将火降至中低档，继续有规律搅拌，用勺子弄碎聚在一起的疙瘩，直到玉米糊糊非常粘稠，这个过程大概需要10分钟。将锅移开，放凉。

盛入盘中，弄湿双手，将乌伽黎攥成球，上桌。

其他的变化形式：

乌伽黎中最常用的是白玉米。不过，也可以用高粱、小米、木薯粉甚至是玉米渣。

至于水，你可以根据你对粘食的喜好加相应量的水。

如果你喜欢还可以加一点黄油。

注意：

乌伽黎通常是和炖肉或炖菜、绿色蔬菜或酸奶一起端上餐桌的。吃乌伽黎的时候用手指弄成小球食用。用大拇指按压出凹陷型，然后在此处加其他炖菜。或者也可以用手弄成更大

Or you can form larger balls with your hands or an icecream scoop, place them in individual serving bowls and spoon stew around them.

Cornmeal mush is also found in Caribbean creole cuisine and was certainly brought there by imported slaves. On the islands of Curaçao and Aruba it is known as funchi, funjie in the Virgin Islands. In Antigua and Dominica it is called fungi. Haitians make mayi moulin.

的球或用冰淇淋勺子挖，将这些饭团放到每个人的碗中，然后给每个人舀炖菜。

在加勒比海地区的克里奥尔人也食用这种玉米糊，很可能是非洲的奴隶带到这里的。在Curaçao and Aruba 岛屿地区叫funchi，在维尔京群岛上叫funjie。在安提瓜岛和多米尼加叫fungi。而海地人则叫mayi moulin。

词汇 VOCABULARY

starchy：含淀粉的	mush：糊状物
polenta：玉米糊，大麦粥，栗粉粥	sorghum：高粱
side dish：配菜	millet：小米
teapoon：茶匙，小汤匙	cassava：木薯
grind：碾碎	hominy grit：玉米渣
saucepan：长柄平底锅	consistency：一致性，浓稠度
substitute：替换	

34 小面团，大智慧——坦桑尼亚炸角

Tanzania Mandazi is great when eaten for breakfast, accompanied by a nice cuppa tea!

Mandazi can best be described as an East African version of the **donut**. They are deep-fried and slightly sweet and are traditionally served in East Africa for breakfast.

Mandazi are also quite a popular "**street food**" meaning that you can easily buy them along the roadside in the larger cities and even in

早餐吃坦桑尼亚炸角配一杯茶再美妙不过了。

炸角可以被称为东非版本的炸面圈。炸角需要炸得很脆，微甜，是东非人早餐的传统食物。

无论是在大城市的街边还是在小城镇的地头，都能随处可见炸角。在当地人早餐的菜单上，炸角也是榜上有名。炸角便宜，馅儿大——对于一个囊中羞涩的背包

the smaller towns. You will find them on the menu of most local guest houses for breakfast, and they are also cheap to buy and very filling—so are ideal for the traveller on a budget!

What makes them different from the traditional donut is that they usually don't have a hole in the middle, and they are cut into a **diamond** shape instead of a traditional round donut shape. The addition of spices like **cardamom** to the dough also makes them different. Some Mandazi (typically made in the coastal areas) also have **coconut** milk added to the dough.

Ingredients:

2 cups Flour

5 tsps Sugar

1 tsp Cardamom powder

1 sachet of **Yeast**

1 cup **lukewarm** Milk

Oil for frying

Manufaltering Processes:

Sift the flour, sugar & cardamom powder into a bowl. **Sprinkle** the yeast over these ingredients and then add the lukewarm milk. Stir to **blend** and **knead** into a soft and **pliable** dough. Leave covered in a warm place until doubled in size. Punch down and roll out flat. Cut into diamond shapes & leave these covered in a warm place until doubled in size again. Deep fry in very hot oil until golden brown on both sides. Remove, drain and serve immediately.

客来说再合适不过了。

炸角和传统炸面圈的不同之处在于炸角的中间没有洞；而就形状来说，传统的面圈儿是圆形的，而炸角是菱形的。另外，还可以在面团中加入豆蔻。而沿海的一些地区还会在面团中加入椰汁。

原料：

2杯面粉

5大汤匙糖

1小汤匙豆蔻粉

1小袋酵母

1杯温热的牛奶

油炸用油

制作步骤：

将面粉、糖和豆蔻粉放到碗中。撒上酵母，然后加牛奶。搅拌，揉成柔软的面团。在一个温暖的环境中，盖上盖子，发酵，直到面团两倍大。将面团弄平。切成菱形，继续发酵到两倍大。然后大火炸透，两面色泽都呈橙黄色。关火，沥油。马上食用。

再叙坦桑尼亚美食

坦桑尼亚各部族之间的饮食习惯也有所不同，以畜牧业为主的部族就以牛、羊为主食；以渔业为主的部族就以鱼虾为主食；以种植香蕉为主的部族则以香蕉为主食。居住在北部维多利亚湖西面的哈亚族就是以种植香蕉著称，他们习惯在香蕉林中修建住宅。哈亚族还有一条戒律，即忌吃飞禽，也不吃鸡和鸡蛋。此外哈亚族也禁食昆虫，但不包括蚱蜢和白蚁。

三色鸵鸟蛋饼：

坦桑尼亚人爱吃鸵鸟肉，三色鸵鸟蛋饼在制作时分别在菠菜碎、土豆碎和金枪鱼中加入鸵鸟蛋液和适量盐调成汁，然后将三种蛋汁分别淋入锅中摊成蛋饼，并将三张蛋饼摞在一起，吃时切成三角状即可。

35 七种蔬菜相伴的摩洛哥国菜——考斯考斯

The Moroccan national dish is couscous with seven vegetables. Couscous is a small grain sized "**pasta**" made from wheat **semolina** flour. Every vegetable adds an important dimension to this famous dish. Lamb or mutton is most commonly used in this dish, but chicken can also be used.

Preparing this dish consists of two separate parts: preparing the couscous grains and preparing the vegetables with meat stock. The couscous should be prepared while the stock is cooking.

☆Steaming the Couscous

Couscous is steamed semolina grains. Its preparation involves alternating **steam**ing and mixing the semolina with salt, oil, water and butter.

Ingredients

500g. of couscous (wheat semolina grains)

100g.of butter

1/4 cup of olive (preferably) or vegetable oil

A **pinch** of salt

摩洛哥的国菜就是七种蔬菜相伴的考斯考斯。考斯考斯是一种小型谷物类面食，是由粗粒小麦粉制成。七种蔬菜分散在考斯考斯的各个方向。这道菜中通常用羔羊肉或羊肉。不过，也可以用鸡肉。

制作这道菜需要两道分开的工序：准备考斯考斯谷物和准备加肉汤的蔬菜。在做考斯考斯的同时，需要同时做高汤。

☆蒸考斯考斯

考斯考斯是蒸粗粒小麦谷物。做它需要一边蒸一边将粗粒小麦谷物和盐、油、水及黄油混合。

原料：

500g考斯考斯（粗粒小麦谷物）

100g黄油

1/4杯橄榄油或植物油

1撮盐

4 cups of water (not including the water used for steaming)

Methods

Sprinkle one teaspoon of salt and two tablespoons of oil on the couscous and spread it around by hand in a shallow pan.

Using two cups of water, soak the couscous and stir it by hand (important, to give air), making sure to break up any clumps that may have formed. Let it sit for ten minutes to **absorb** all the water.

Work the couscous by hand, lifting the grains, rubbing them gently and letting them fall back into the pan. Once the couscous has absorbed all the water and has a **flaky texture** (no lumps), slowly put the couscous; a light layer at first, then after five minutes add the remaining couscous in successive layers in the **steamer**. Let it steam for twenty minutes.

Once the steam has risen through the couscous, pour it back onto the pan. Use a wooden spoon to separate the grains and cool it down. Sprinkle the couscous progressively with a cup of cold water while stirring it by hand (be sure to give the couscous plenty of air), and break up any clumps that may have formed. Stir until the grains have absorbed all the water. Allow it to cool and dry for ten minutes.

Repeat steps three and four one more time.

Let it sit while the stock finishes cooking.

☆**Cooking the stock with Vegetables and Meat Ingredients**

1/2 kg of shoulder of mutton or chicken

1/2 cup chickpeas soaked in water over night (or canned; but please note that canned chickpeas should only be added to the stew 30 minutes before the end since they are already cooked)

500g onions

150g. **turnip**s

150g. carrots

2 zucchinis

4杯水（不包括蒸考斯考斯需要的水）

步骤：

将一小汤匙盐和一大汤匙油洒在浅锅里的考斯考斯上。

在考斯考斯内加入两杯水，没过表面，然后用手搅拌（这步很重要，因为可以使得考斯考斯内部有空气），确保没有疙瘩。将混合好的考斯考斯放置10分钟以便充分吸水。

揉搓考斯考斯。一旦考斯考斯吸收了全部的水，就会变成层状质地。然后将考斯考斯一层层放入蒸笼中，蒸20分钟。

如果蒸汽升起来，就将考斯考斯放回到锅内。用木勺将谷物分开，然后放凉。加一杯凉水到考斯考斯中，一边加水，一边搅拌（以便空气充足）。一直搅拌到考斯考斯吸收了全部的水。然后将它风干10分钟。

再次重复3、4两步。

一直等到高汤那边已经煮好。

☆用蔬菜、肉烧高汤

500g羊排或鸡排

1/2杯鹰嘴豆，用水浸泡整夜（也可以是罐装的；但注意灌装鹰嘴豆须在炖菜结束前30分钟放入，因为它本身已经是熟的）

500g洋葱

150g芜菁

150g胡萝卜

2个西葫芦

2个辣椒

1捆香菜

1/4杯高汤用橄榄油或植物油

1大汤匙黄油

2 hot peppers (chillies)

1 bouquet **coriander**

1/4 cup olive oil or vegetable oil for stock

1 tsp butter

1/4 medium sized Savoy cabbage

10 **cherry tomato**es

300 g. red pumpkins

1/4 tsp of saffron (preferably crushed saffron flowers)

1 tablespoon of black pepper powder

1/2 tsp ground **turmeric** (for color)

3 litres of water

Salt (to adjust)

Directions

Cut the lamb (or chicken) and chop the cabbage into quarters. Slice two onions **lengthwise**. Put into the pot.

Add in oil, saffron, turmeric, black pepper powder, bouquet coriander, and salt.

Stir over medium heat to sauté the vegetables and seal the meat.

Add the chickpeas and pour over water until the ingredients are submerged. Boil for fifteen minutes.

Add 2 more sliced onions, peeled and sliced lengthwise carrots, zucchini (medium size cubes), and turnips (peeled and quartered). Simmer for another fifteen minutes.

Add the pumpkin (medium size cubes), the cherry tomatoes, and hot peppers at the end. Simmer for ten minutes.

Check the seasoning of the stock. Boil any excess water in the stew, but make sure there is sufficient broth to use as a sauce. Verify that the vegetables are cooked.

☆Setting the dish for serving

Half an hour before serving, steam the couscous for ten minutes. Put the couscous back in the shallow pan, stir the couscous and mix in the butter (cut in small cubes). Sprinkle with two ladle scoops of stock progressively as you stir the couscous. Make sure the couscous is flaky, separated and moist.

1/4一般大小的皱叶甘蓝

10个小番茄

300g红色南瓜

1/4大汤匙番红花（最好是揉碎的花朵）

1大汤匙黑胡椒粉

1/2大汤匙碾碎的姜黄（为了调颜色）

3升水

盐（根据口味）

步骤：

将羊肉或鸡肉、卷心菜切块。将洋葱纵向切成片。然后将这些放入锅内。

加油、番红花、姜黄、黑胡椒粉、香菜和盐。

中火翻炒，炒蔬菜，然后将肉盖住。

加入鹰嘴豆，并加水，直到没过所有原来的表面。煮沸15分钟。

加入2片洋葱，削皮纵向切的胡萝卜片，西葫芦（中等块），芜菁（削皮、分瓣儿）。继续慢炖15分钟。

最后加入南瓜（中等块）、小西红柿，辣椒。继续炖10分钟。

尝下高汤的味道。将锅内的水煮没，但要确保有足够的汁做酱汁。确保蔬菜已经煮熟。

准备上菜

在上菜前的半小时，将考斯考斯蒸10分钟。将考斯考斯放回浅锅内，搅拌考斯考斯，并混入黄油（将黄油切成小块儿）。一边搅拌考斯考斯，一边慢慢洒两勺高汤。确保考斯考斯有层次感，不黏在一起，且很湿润。

尝考斯考斯的味道，看是否

Taste the couscous to check the salt.

Put the couscous, in a large round dish, piled into a cone.

Dig a hollow into the middle of the couscous cone.

Put the meat and vegetables on top.

Serve at once with extra stock served separately for those who prefer it moister.

还要加盐。

将考斯考斯放入大的圆盘中，堆成沙丘形状。

将考斯考斯的中间挖一个空；

将肉和菜放在顶端。

上菜；另外，可以多备一些高汤，以便喜欢多汤的人们可以随时添加。

pasta：面食	steamer：蒸笼
semolina：粗粒小麦粉	turnip：芜菁
steam：蒸	zucchini：西葫芦
pinch：少量，一撮	coriander：香菜
absorb：吸收	cherry tomato：小西红柿
flaky：薄片的，成层的	turmeric：姜黄
texture：纹理，质地	lengthwise：纵向地

背景知识 PROFILE

摩洛哥美食之一

摩洛哥菜最大的特色和最主要的贡献是能够很有技巧地将相对立的味道和不同的食材混合起来，从而制造一种丰富且印象深刻的烹饪经历。摩洛哥菜味道丰富，甜美，咸味浓，让人有兴致。菜的味道使得人们能够感受到菜谱、制作步骤的复杂。摩洛哥菜在世界上因种类繁多、历史悠久而享有盛誉。再来看一道摩洛哥汤品。配上考斯考斯，味道可谓是妙不可言哪！

摩洛哥哈里拉汤（Harira）

简介：是以西红柿为汤底，加入鹰嘴豆，牛肉或羊肉，洋葱，小面条和一些香料一起炖煮而成。将面条切成方便面渣大小的形状，混合在汤里当料；喝起来除去了浓郁的咸味。这道汤对摩洛哥人来说相当的重要，因为每当他们进行一段时间的斋戒后，开始进食的第一道食物就是它，顺便搭配着枣子、温牛奶、果汁、面包和摩洛哥煎饼一同食用。

原料：

主料：（6人~8人份）

羊肉丁　　　　　　　200克

羊骨头	1000克
鹰嘴豆（鸡心豆）	100克
棕色蓝提豆	100克
意大利细面条	80克
羊肉汤（或鸡汤）	1200毫升

配料：

洋葱碎	20克
蒜茸	20克
香菜末	15克
欧芹（法香）末	15克

调味料：

橄榄油	30毫升
番茄膏	1汤匙
藏红花	0.05克
特制香料	1茶匙
食盐	1汤匙

做法：

1. 将鹰嘴豆和蓝提豆分别浸泡过夜，漂洗干净控干。
2. 锅内烧热橄榄油，爆香洋葱碎、蒜茸和欧芹末。
3. 加入羊肉丁煸炒至变色，再加番茄膏继续煸炒。
4. 加入羊骨头、香料、藏红花和羊肉汤。
5. 烧开后加入鹰嘴豆、蓝提豆和掰碎的意大利细面条，慢火煮约十五分钟。
6. 待面条和豆子完全煮熟后，加入食盐调味。
7. 出锅撒上香菜末即可。

注意：

橄榄油可用普通植物油取代；羊肉汤也可以由鸡汤取代，当然味道就不如羊肉汤那样浓。

36 漂亮的外表，精彩的内在——帕斯蒂娅馅饼

Pastilla, which may be **alternately** called Bastilla, Bstilla, or Bsteeya, is an interesting North African dish, particularly favored in Moroccan **cuisine**, that combines the flavors and textures of savory meat, **crunchy** pastry and sweet spices. Though the traditional dish in Morocco or other parts of Northern Africa may be made with **squab** or pigeon meat, in the US, you're likely to see chicken substituted instead. The chicken is cooked and **shred**ded and may be combined with toasted and ground **almond**s.

The thing that makes pastilla unusual, is that the meat and other ingredients are then formed into a pastry made with **filo** dough. In Moroccan restaurants, pastilla is typically one of the offerings, and when the restaurants serve in the traditional manner, where hands instead of silverware are used, a large pastilla is served to the guests, who then break off pieces with their hands. Pastilla is usually topped with **cinnamon** and powdered sugar, creating an unusual but delicious taste, and making it quite different from European meat pies and pasties.

A word to the wise if you do happen to be dining in a traditional Moroccan or North African restaurant: Be careful when grabbing bits of pastilla after it is first served. The interior can be extremely hot. It's quite easy to burn the tongue or the fingers if you take too big a portion at first. Also use only the right hand for tearing off pieces of this dish or for any other food served. The left hand is used for toilet purposes in Morocco, and it is considered highly rude to use your left hand to grab food. These traditions are relaxed outside of the Arabic world, but should be closely attended to if you happen to be in Morocco.

帕斯蒂娅馅饼也可以被称为 Bastilla，Bstilla或Bsteeya。它是一道非常有趣的北非菜，是摩洛哥很有特色的美食。帕斯蒂娅馅饼将各种不同风味，各种美味的肉类，酥脆的馅饼皮及甜味的香料混合起来。尽管摩洛哥或北非其他部分的传统菜中，肉类一般使用鸽子肉，而在美国，人们会用鸡肉取而代之。将鸡肉煮熟后，会将其撕成条，也可能将烧烤好的碾碎的杏仁与之混合。

帕斯蒂娅馅饼之所以与众不同，原因在于馅饼里的肉和其他食材都会揉进薄层的生面制成的油酥面团里。在摩洛哥餐馆里，帕斯蒂娅馅饼是一道典型的菜。如果餐馆里以传统方式上这道菜，人们通常用手而不用银器吃这顿饭。人们吃的时候，会一角一角地吃。人们会在帕斯蒂娅馅饼上洒肉桂和糖粒。如此，帕斯蒂娅馅饼便与欧洲肉饼和薄脆饼不同。

如果你真有机会在摩洛哥传统餐馆或北非餐馆里吃饭，当吃一角帕斯蒂娅馅饼时，要小心。因为馅饼里面很热。心急吃不了热豆腐。要用右手吃饭，因为在摩洛哥，人们用左手上厕所；因此，当地人认为左手抓食物是粗鲁的。在阿拉伯世界之外，人们不在乎这些传统，但在当地，还是要谨慎的遵循。

帕斯蒂娅馅饼有很多种变种。你会发现很多菜利用这种做法做甜点。带有梨和蜂蜜的果馅饼可以叫帕斯蒂

There are a number of **variant**s to pastilla. You'll find many different national cuisines have adopted its use for sweet desserts. Tarts with pears and honey in filo dough may be called pastillas, though they tend toward the sweet only and not the savory. Such pastillas are found often in French cooking, and of course, French cooking not only **influence**d Moroccan cuisine but has also been influence by it.

You'll also find numerous online recipes if you wish to try to make one of these pastries. With easy to purchase filo dough on hand, it's actually not difficult to create one. The main difficulty for some is that many recipes call for the chicken and spices to be cooked the day prior, and then **chill**ed overnight. Some recipes also recommend beating eggs into the chicken prior to enveloping the chilled meat in pastry dough. This creates a more **custard**-like interior, but some recipes find this step unnecessary. You will have a drier pastilla if you omit the eggs.

娅馅饼,尽管人们偏向于甜的而非香味浓郁的。在法国菜中,也有帕斯蒂娅馅饼。当然,法国菜既影响了摩洛哥菜也受到了其影响。

鉴于薄层的生面很好买,亲手做帕斯蒂娅馅饼并不难。可能对于一些人来说,最主要的困难在于很多食谱都需要将鸡肉和香料提前一天弄好,然后夜间冷藏。一些菜谱也推荐在面团将肉包裹起来之前,打鸡蛋到鸡肉里。这就成了一种蛋奶沙司式的内在,但有些食谱认为这步并不重要。如果你不放鸡蛋,帕斯蒂娅馅饼会相对干一点儿。

alternately:交替地,轮流地,间隔地	filo:(制酥点用的)擀成极薄层的生面
cuisine:烹饪,佳肴	cinnamon:肉桂
crunchy:易碎的	variant:变体,变种,变型
squab:乳鸽	influence:影响
shred:撕成碎片	chill:使……冷却
almond:杏仁	custard:蛋奶沙司

37 地道的开普敦菜——咖喱肉沫

Bobotie is a South African dish which comes in many different variations and therefore there can be a huge difference in its **flavors**. You can get this traditional dish with fish, beef, **venison** or **ostrich**. One thing all these variations have in common: a spicy fruity taste with only a **hint** of curry.

Served with yellow rice and some green veggies, like **broccoli** or beans it is just perfect for a typical South African dinner. Enjoy with a medium sweet wine.

Ingredients for a typical South African bobotie (4 persons):

500g lean beef **mince**

2 medium onions, finely chopped

1 tsps vegetable oil for frying

1 tsps mild curry powder

1/2 tsp cardamom, chilli and coriander seeds mixed

1 tsp turmeric powder

1 tsp salt, milled black pepper

☆ **Methods**

Fry the onions in oil. Add curry powder, turmeric and spice mix, salt and pepper and fry another minute. Add in the mince and fry until browned but not dry.

Then add into the mince-mix:

2 slices of white bread, some milk to soften bread, then **mash**ed

1 tsp tomato sauce/**puree**

1 apple peeled, cored and **grate**d

2 tsps raisins

2 tsps smooth apricot jam

Juice and **zest** of one unwaxed lemon

咖喱肉沫是一道非洲南部经典菜，有很多种变种，因此，在味道上也有很大的不同。做这道传统菜，可以用鱼肉、牛肉、鹿肉或鸵鸟肉来做。不过，无论有多少种形式的咖喱肉沫，它们都有一个共同特点：一种辣辣的水果味夹杂着一丝咖喱味。

通常，咖喱肉沫和一些如花椰菜或豌豆等绿色蔬菜一起食用。这可是一道南非晚宴上非常传统的菜系。如果能配上中度的甜葡萄酒就无敌了。

南非传统菜咖喱肉沫原料（**4人份**）：

500g瘦肉沫

2个中等洋葱，切好

1大汤匙油炸用蔬菜油

1大汤匙轻度咖喱粉

1/2大汤匙香料，含肉桂、辣椒及香菜籽

1大汤匙姜黄粉

1大汤匙盐、研磨好的黑胡椒

☆ **制作方法**

将洋葱用油炒。加咖喱粉、姜黄及香料混合粉，以及盐、胡椒，继续炸1分钟。然后加入到牛肉沫中。将拌好的牛肉沫放入锅中炒成黄色，但不炒干。

然后在牛肉沫中加入：

2片面包，一些牛奶，使用牛奶将面包软化，捣烂；

1大汤匙番茄酱/泥；

1个苹果，去皮，去核，磨碎；

2大汤匙葡萄干；

2大汤匙顺滑杏子酱；

果汁及柠檬皮；

1 garlic clove, peeled and crushed

Add all the ingredients into the mince and mix. Pour into an oven-proof baking dish and if you like it sweet, add the banana slices on top.

Then make a custard mix of and pour on top of the mince mixture.

200ml milk

2 large eggs

Lay some flaked almonds or coconut flakes on top of the custard and some crushed lemon leaves or like in the traditional dish, bay leaves.

2 tsps flaked almonds

Crushed lemon leaves or bay leaves

Coconut flakes

Bake in the oven for 30 minutes at 200ºC.

Serve with yellow rice:

Boil 250g white rice with half a tsp of turmeric, 6 cloves, 1tsp salt and 50g raisins in 650ml water.

1瓣蒜，去皮，碾碎

加入这些以后，把肉沫混合物放到耐热盘中。如果你喜欢甜味的，可以在上面加香蕉片。

然后制作一个蛋奶沙司，将其倒入肉沫混合物里。

200毫升牛奶

2个大鸡蛋

然后在蛋奶沙司上放片状杏仁或椰仁碎屑，以及捣碎的柠檬叶或月桂树叶。

2大汤匙片状杏仁

捣碎的柠檬叶或月桂树叶

椰仁碎屑

烤箱温度设成200 ℃，加热30分钟。

请佐之以黄米饭：

煮饭，米和水的比例为：白米250g，650毫升水（水中含1大汤匙姜黄，6朵丁香，1大汤匙盐和50g葡萄干）。

词汇 VOCABULARY

flavor：滋味，味道	mince：切碎物，粉碎，肉馅
venison：鹿肉	mash：把……捣成糊状
ostrich：鸵鸟	puree：菜泥，果泥，浓汤
hint：暗示，细微的迹象，少许，微量	grate：磨擦，磨碎，（使）烦恼
broccoli：花椰菜	zest：（烹饪时调味用的）橙子、柠檬等的外皮

背景知识 PROFILE

开普敦美食

被誉为"海上客栈"的国际都市开普敦，各种美食应有尽有，除了西洋饮食外，还有中国、日本、印度、泰国等各国餐馆。开普敦是这个国家花销最大的地方，如果喜欢大众化的餐饮，可选择在火车站的二楼或小吃街就餐，有物美价廉的汉堡，香肠，咖哩饭等。此外，Adderley街、乔治的一些咖啡店。还有博物馆、伴侣公园（Company Garden）内的餐厅也很好。但这些餐厅都在傍晚关门。但是你可以自炊或买些东西回去，因为海角区周边还有很多关门很晚的饭店和便利店。

38 毛里求斯美食——豆儿普里

"Nou ale manze ene ti dholl puri," (let's go and eat some "dholl puri,") whose mouth does not water at this **invitation**? Who has ever had the courage to say, "No" to it? Anyone whose answer is "no" cannot be Mauritian.

"Dholl puri" has been part of Mauritian culture since time **immemorial**. The story goes that "dholl puri" came to be in an attempt on the part of our Indian ancestors to prepare Indian "parathas" (stuffed Indian flat bread). Due to a lack of ingredients, **substitute**s had to be used and the "parathas" eventually gave way to a **hybridize**d counterpart—what we today know as " dholl Puri". "Dholl Puri" is basically Indian style bread stuffed with yellow split peas—"dal gram". It can be eaten on its own or accompanied by a selection of foods, the most popular ones being "rougaille" (a tomato based sauce), **kidney bean**s and **chutney**s among others.

Buying and eating "dholl puris" at a "dholl puri" stall is one of the trademark practices of Mauritians.

Ingredients (8 servings):

500g Dholl

1/2 tsp tumeric powder

1kg white flour

salt to taste

1 tsp ground roasted cumin

2 tbs oil

Mixture of **ghee** and oil for the dholl pouri

Manufacturing processes

Boil the dholl in about 2 cups of water with some salt and tumeric.

Drain the cooked dholl and grind the grains in a foodmill (**blender**).

"Nou ale manze ene ti dholl puri。" （走，我们去吃点豆儿普里），如果你拒绝，也就说明你可算不上是正宗的岛民。

自远古以来，"豆儿普里"就已经是毛里求斯文化的一部分。关于豆儿普里的产生，有着这样一个故事。印度祖先们想要做印度的parathas（印度的填陷饼）。但因为缺少食材，人们不得不找替代的食材，这样就产生了parathas的变种——也就是我们今天所说的豆儿普里。豆儿普里做出是印度风格的黄豆饼。一餐饭中，人们可以只吃它，也可以佐之以其他事物，其中最有名的是rougaille（由番茄做成的一道地中海风味菜肴），四季豆和酸辣酱。

在一个豆儿普里的店吃上一顿豆儿普里是毛里求斯人的典型形象。

原料（**8人份**）：

500g黄豌豆

1kg白面粉

2小汤匙粉状茴香豆

1/2大汤匙姜黄粉

盐（根据口味）

2大汤匙油

制作步骤：

将黄豌豆在2杯水中煮沸，并加入姜黄粉，盐。

将黄豌豆过滤，将沸水留着，以备做馅饼皮的时候使用；将豌豆用搅拌器磨碎；

在碎豌豆中加入茴香；

Add some cumin to the grinded dholl.

Sift the flour and add in some salt.

Create a soft dough by mixing 2 tbs of oil and some water to the **sift** flour.

Leave mixture to rest for about 30mins.

Divide the dough into small balls.

Flatten the small balls and add in about 1 tbs of ground dholl in the centre.

Enclose the dough.

Roll each stuffed ball carefully with a rolling pin to a circle about 15cm in **diameter**.

Paste a little oil/ghee mixture on a hot **griddle** and allow the circles to cook on one side (about 1min).

Paste some very little oil/ghee mixture on the pouri and turn over.

Serve the hot dholl puri with a wonderful rougailles or a nice meat curry.

和面，面内加盐、2大汤匙油；面要软；

将面团放置30分钟；

然后将面团切成多个面球；

将面球擀开，中间放1大汤匙碎豌豆；

把含有碎豌豆的面皮捏好；

将每一个豆包小心擀开，大概直径15cm（以上步骤可参考家里做馅饼的流程）；

在烤饼用的烤盘中刷上油或酥油，然后将之前的豆包饼放入锅内，一面加热1分钟左右；

然后在未加热的那面放上油，翻过来继续预热；

配上rougaille或美味的咖喱肉就可以吃咯！

词汇 VOCABULARY

invitation：邀请，诱惑	ghee：印度酥油
immemorial：（因年代久远而）无法追忆的，古老的，远古的	blender：搅拌机
substitute：替代品	enclose：包，裹
hybridize：混合生成	roll：用……轧平（某物），将（某物）碾平
kidney bean：豌豆	diameter：直径
chutney：酸辣酱	griddle：烤盘
sift：筛	

背景知识 PROFILE

毛里求斯美食

　　毛里求斯烹饪风格受到了不同文化、不同烹饪传统的影响。毛里求斯人很愿意尝试各种风味的美食，最常见的是克里奥尔、中国、欧洲以及印度菜肴。来毛里求斯最不可错过的一道传统美食就是克里奥尔咖喱，这道辛辣的菜肴是由鱼肉、牛肉或者鸡肉做成，通常和米饭一起食用。其他传统的毛里求斯菜肴包括rougaille（由番茄做成的一道地中海风味菜肴）、Sounouk（咸干鱼）、Octopus stew（炖章鱼）以及Daube de poisson（炖肉）。Biryani是一道穆斯林菜肴，味道非常地辛辣刺激。您在这里还可以吃到中国食物，如炒大米、豉椒炒牛肉等，既美味又便宜。最受欢迎的毛里求斯饮料有Alooda（用琼脂、牛奶和香料，如香草或者杏仁酿造而成）。

游客们还可以尝尝毛里求斯传统的小吃，像Gateaux piment（辣糕饼）、Samoussa（咖喱角）以及Baja都是最受欢迎的街边小吃。毛里求斯大部分食物都是辛辣的，而且毛里求斯人就喜欢吃红辣椒。

毛里求斯四面环海，海鲜也就成为了餐桌上的必备美食。小米虾、鱼、牡蛎、蟹再加上红色的酱料"sauce rouge"，光看着颜色就让人垂涎欲滴，品之更是沁人心脾。

您在毛里求斯任何地方都可以找到当地的传统食物，如街头、商业区、集市以及海滩边等地方。比如在海滩，您就会看到有人提着袋子在出售菠萝。

从便宜的街头小吃到昂贵的饭店大餐，您可以按照自己的需求选择不同的就餐地点。不过只要能吃到美味的当地菜肴，您应该不会在意吃饭的场所了吧。您只需要花0.25欧元就可以买到一个烤肉（Roti），而在旅游区的饭店中您又可以吃到豪华的海鲜大餐。

和世界上其他地方一样，在过去的20年中，有许多著名的国际快餐连锁店在此开业，您可以买到汉堡包、披萨饼等。

如果您外出就餐，应该注意一下几个问题：

1. 在大部分酒店和高级饭店，付给10%的小费是很寻常的，但不是强迫的。

2. 毛里求斯会收取一定的增值税。通常饭店收取的是菜单上价格15%的增值税，但是您应该注意查看菜单价格是否已经包含了增值税。

3. 毛里求斯允许饮酒的法定年龄是18岁。

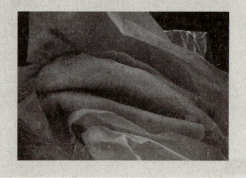

39 美味的埃塞俄比亚菜——鸡肉煲

One of the best-known of all African recipes, Doro Wat (Doro Watt, Doro Wot, Doro Wet, Doro We't, Dorowat) is a spicy **Ethiopian** chicken dish made with Berberé (a spice mixture or spice paste) and Niter Kibbeh (or nit'ir qibe, a spicy clarified butter). Berberé and niter kibbeh, basic ingredients in many Ethiopian recipes, are usually made in large quantities and kept on hand for some time. No doubt using berberé and niter kibbeh gives a special quality to Doro Wat. But a very good result can be **obtain**ed by adding the same spices directly to the Doro Wat, instead of indirectly in the berberé spice mix and niter kibbeh.

What You Need

Juice of one lemon

Two teaspoons salt

One chicken (about 3 pounds), cleaned and cut into serving-size pieces

Two (or more) onions, finely chopped

Four tablespoons niter kebbeh (or butter)

Four cloves garlic, finely chopped or minced

One piece fresh **ginger** root—cleaned, **scraped**, and chopped

1/2 teaspoon ground **fenugreek**

1/2 teaspoon ground cardamom

1/2 teaspoon ground nutmeg

1/2 teaspoon berberé—or—1~2 tablespoons of a combination of cayenne pepper and **paprika** (if berberé and niter kebbeh are not used)

1 small tomato, chopped or a few tablespoons tomato paste or tomato sauce (optional)

1 cup chicken stock, water, or **dry red wine**

Hard-boiled eggs (1 per person), pierced with a **toothpick** or the **tine** of a long fork.

在所有非洲美食中，鸡肉煲是其中一道。它是一道融合Berberé（混合香料或香料糊）和Niter Kibbeh（辣味黄油）的埃塞俄比亚辣味鸡肉菜。Berberé和Niter kibbeh是埃塞俄比亚食谱里的基本食材，人们往往会一次做很多，以备不时之需。毫无疑问，使用Berberé和Niter kibbeh使得鸡肉煲别具风味。当然，也可以把制作Berberé和Niter kibbeh的香料直接加到鸡肉煲里。

原料：

1个柠檬汁

2小汤匙盐

1只鸡（3磅重），洗净、切好

2个（或多个）洋葱，切好

4大汤匙niter kebbeh（或黄油）

4瓣蒜，捣碎

1片新鲜姜片——洗净，去皮，切好

1/2小汤匙碾好的葫芦巴

1/2小汤匙碾好的肉桂

1/2小汤匙碾好的肉豆蔻

1/2小汤匙berberé或者如果没有berberé 和 Niter kebbeh，可以用1~2大汤匙辣椒粉和甜辣椒粉的混合

1个小西红柿，切好；或者几小汤匙番茄酱（可选）

1杯鸡汤，水，干红

煮熟的鸡蛋（每人一个），插牙签或者用叉

步骤：

在一个玻璃碗中，将柠檬汁（一

What You Do

In a glass bowl, combine the lemon juice (some cooks use **lime juice**), half the salt, and chicken pieces. Let chicken marinate for 30 minutes to an hour.

Cook the onions over medium heat for a few minutes in a dry (no oil) pot or dutch oven large enough to eventually hold all of the ingredients. Stir constantly to prevent them from browning or burning; reduce heat or remove the pot from the heat if necessary.

Add the niter kebbeh or butter to the onions, along with the garlic, ginger, fenugreek, cardamom, nutmeg, remaining salt, berberé (or cayenne pepper and paprika), and tomato. Stir and simmer for a few minutes. The onions should be soft, tender, and translucent, but not browned.

Add the chicken stock, water, or dry red wine. Bring the mixture to a low boil while stirring gently. Cook for a few minutes, then reduce heat.

Add the chicken pieces, making sure to cover them with the sauce. Cover and simmer for 30 to 40 minutes while turning the chicken a few times.

After the chicken has been cooking for 20 minutes, gently add the hard-boiled eggs and ladle sauce over them.

Serve hot. The only traditional way to serve doro wat is with a spongy flat bread called injera, which can only be properly made with difficult-to-obtain teff flour. While it's not the way Ethiopians would serve it, doro wat is very good with Couscous, Rice, or Middle-Eastern or Indian style flat bread.

The wine and tomato seem to be recent non-Ethiopian influences, but they are so widely used that they need to be reported here, even if their use is not traditional.

些人会用酸橙汁），一半（1汤匙）盐和鸡块混合。放置30-60分钟。

中火煸炒洋葱几分钟。不放油。采用能承载下所有原料的荷兰炖锅。不断翻炒，以防炒糊。

将niter kebbeh或黄油加入洋葱中，并同时加入蒜、姜、葫芦巴、肉桂、肉豆蔻、盐、berberé及西红柿。翻炒，焖炖几分钟。洋葱应该柔软、娇嫩、透明，但没变黄。

加入鸡汁、水或干红。将这些在小火下煮沸，并翻炒。煮几分钟之后，关小火。

加入鸡块儿，汁要将鸡块儿覆盖。盖上锅内，焖炖30-40分钟，中途翻炒几次。

在焖炖20分钟时，缓缓加入煮熟的鸡蛋，并把鸡蛋用汁覆盖住。

趁热吃。传统和鸡肉煲一起吃的是一种柔软的面包片，叫injera，这种面包片需要一种很难获得的埃塞俄比亚画眉草才能做成。既然这样，我们用考斯考斯，米饭或中东及印度风味的面包一起食用，味道也很不错。

最后说一句，加入红酒和西红柿并不是埃塞俄比亚的传统做法，但现实生活中，人们经常使用，所以尽管不传统，还是值得一试。

Ethiopian：埃塞俄比亚的	paprika：甜辣椒
obtain：获得，得到	dry red wine：干红
ginger：姜	toothpick：牙签
scape：刮掉，擦掉	tine：尖
fenugreek：葫芦巴	lime-juice：酸橙汁

背景知识 **P**ROFILE

埃塞俄比亚美食——英吉拉

英吉拉（Injera）是埃塞俄比亚人世代流传的主食，在埃塞人的食物中占有"统治"地位。埃塞人偶尔也吃面包和米饭，但量较少。总的来说，英吉拉在这儿比馒头在中国北方的地位还要高。

英吉拉所需主料苔麸（TEFF）有一个非常好听的中文译名叫"埃塞俄比亚画眉草"。埃塞是唯一食用苔麸的国家，在世界其他地方苔麸只是一种普通的草，这一点从它的中文名字上也可以得到印证。苔麸产量非常低，其亩产只有小麦的15%，每150颗苔麸的重量才相当于一颗小麦粒。但其营养价值非常高，富含氨基酸、蛋白质、各种微量元素、植物纤维等。它的钙含量比牛奶还高，铁含量是小麦的两倍。

英吉拉是发酵食品，其制作过程一般需要2—3天。大致做法为：将苔麸粉加水、发酵粉、少量面粉混合后置于室温下两天使其充分发酵；然后像摊煎饼那样将发酵后的面糊在平底锅上摊成圆饼；将圆饼卷起，切成约10公分的小段，就是成品的英吉拉了。因为经过发酵，英吉拉靠近平底锅的一面为平的，另一面则多孔状。

吃英吉拉有专用的酱汁，通常是用各种肉类（小块或肉末）、蔬菜等加上辣椒粉、盐等调味品慢火煨制而成，当然也有当地人非常喜欢的土制奶酪和生牛肉等。吃英吉拉的时候有一定讲究，首先撕下一小块英吉拉，用手拿住，多孔的一面朝下，包住部分酱汁或肉，然后整个送到自己的嘴里。不过要注意，整个过程只能用一只手。对待尊贵的客人，热情的埃塞人经常会亲自将包好的英吉拉送到客人嘴里。

英吉拉本身微酸、柔软、易于消化，其酱汁美味可口，软嫩细滑，因此英吉拉受到不少外国人的喜欢。

40 清香宜人，有益健康——洛依柏丝茶

Not only tasty, this **herbal** tea is good for your health too.

Technically, Rooibos is not a true tea. It comes from the plant Aspalathus linearis, rather than the Camellia plants that produce traditional teas. The name Rooibos comes from the **Afrikaans** word for "red bush".

The Rooibos plant is a small **shrubby bush** that only grows in South Africa. The bush grows anywhere from 1/2 to 1 metre in height, with very thin, needle-like leaves. The leaves are green, but turn the characteristic red after **fermentation**.

The Rooibos seeds are precious, because the plants produce few of them. The seeds also pop out of the fruits as soon as they are ripe, making harvest difficult. Many farmers still **raid anthill**s looking for Rooibos seeds.

It is a rather delicate plant, and the **cultivation** has not changed much over the years. The plants **thrive** best when left along in their natural soil. The farming of Rooibos has always been very close to nature and remains so today.

The locals have known that Rooibos can be used to make a delicious **beverage** for a very long time, but it was only "discovered" in 1904 by a Russian **immigrant** named Benjamin Ginsberg. He was a settler in the area and thought that the tea was so enjoyable that it should be available to people everywhere. He was the first to market Rooibos tea.

Rooibos tea is a distinctive red color and its taste is also unique with a very sweet and slightly nutty flavor. Its delicious taste and numerous healthful qualities have helped Rooibos become a popular tea

这道清凉茶不仅清香宜人，而且有益身体健康。

严格说来，洛依柏丝并不是一道真正的茶。它产自植物Aspalathus linearis，而非传统产茶植物山茶属植物。洛依柏丝来源于南非荷兰语"红色灌木"。

洛依柏丝茶树是一种矮小灌木丛，只在南非遍地生长。植株高度在0.5~1米之间，树叶呈针形。叶子绿色，在经过发酵之后变为红色。

洛依柏丝的种子非常珍贵，因为洛依柏丝植株产量小。而且种子一成熟就会掉出来，所以收种子很难。很多茶农会"洗劫"蚂蚁窝，因为那里有蚂蚁搬到窝里的洛依柏丝种子。

这种植物较娇弱，其培植方法多年来变化不大。这种植物在它们最适应的土壤中长势良好。洛依柏丝的培植亲近自然，今天亦是如此。

当地人很早就知道洛依柏丝可以用来做好喝的饮料。而最早发现这种茶的外国人是俄罗斯移民本杰明•金斯伯，时间是1904年。他在当地定居，然后发现这种茶味道好极了，认为世界各地的人都应该喝到，是他第一个将洛依柏丝茶推向市场。

洛依柏丝茶呈鲜明的红色，味道独特，很甜微含坚果香气。不仅如此，它还有益身体健康。其美妙的味道和功效使得洛依柏丝茶风靡全世界。不过，整体来说，洛依柏丝茶是相对比较新的品种，越来越多的人开

all over the world. It is still fairly "new" but more and more people are coming to love this unique red tea.

Rooibos has increased in popularity not only because of its wonderful colour and taste, but because of all the great things it can do for your health.

Rooibos has no caffeine and is low in tannin, so it can be enjoyed all day long without any unpleasant **side effect**s. This also makes it a great tea for pregnant women and nursing mothers.

Various studies have shown the many health problems that can be helped by drinking Rooibos tea:

Eases **irritability**, headaches, nervous tension and insomnia.

Acts as an anti-spasmodic agent, to relieve stomach cramps and colic in infants.

Can be used to treat hay fever, **asthma** and **eczema**.

Placed directly on the skin, it can slow the aging process.

Boosts the immune system.

Rooibos tea contains no oxalic acid, so it can safely be consumed by people who are prone to kidney stones.

There are so many minerals in the tea, that it can almost be considered a nutritional supplement:

Copper, Iron, Potassium, Calcium, Fluoride, Zinc, Manganese, Alpha-hydroxy (great for the skin), Magnesium.

It's always such a pleasure to discover a delicious new beverage, especially one that is so good for you!

始喜欢这道特殊的红茶。

洛依柏丝茶不含咖啡因，丹宁酸含量低，因此，可全天饮用，而无副作用。这也使得它成为了孕妇及哺乳期的妈妈的宠爱之物。

多项调查研究表明，很多健康问题可以通过饮用洛依柏丝茶得到缓解：

缓解愤怒、头疼、紧张及失眠；

可以对付间歇性痉挛，缓解胃阵痛以及婴儿的绞痛；

可用于对付花粉热、哮喘和湿疹；

直接涂于皮肤表面，可以抑制衰老；

强化免疫系统；

洛依柏丝茶不含草酸，所以肾结石患者也可以安全饮用。

该茶含多种矿物质：所以是一种营养增补剂。

铜、铁、钾、铝、氟化物、锌、锰、护肤物质。

发现一款味道好的饮料是一件幸事，况且它还对你的健康大有裨益。

词汇 VOCABULARY

herbal：草本的	thrive：茁壮成长，蓬勃发展，繁荣
Afrikaans：荷兰南非语	beverage：饮料
shrubby bush：灌木丛	immigrant：移民
fermentation：发酵	side effect：副作用
raid：袭击	irritability：易怒
anthill：蚁穴	asthma：哮喘
cultivation：培植	eczema：湿疹

世界各地茶文化

茶是世界三大饮料之一，世界上许多饮茶国家都与茶文化有着千丝万缕的联系。全球性的文化交流，使茶文化传播世界，同各国人民的生活方式、风土人情，以至宗教意识相融合，呈现出五彩缤纷的世界各民族饮茶习俗。

（一）中国茶文化

中华茶文化源远流长，博大精深。唐代茶圣陆羽的茶经在历史上吹响了中华茶文化的号角。从此茶的精神渗透了宫廷和社会，深入中国的诗词、绘画、书法、宗教、医学。几千年来中国不但积累了大量关于茶叶种植、生产的物质文化，更积累了丰富的有关茶的精神文化，这就是中国特有的茶文化，属于文化学范畴。

中国人饮茶，注重一个"品"字。"品茶"不但是鉴别茶的优劣，也带有神思遐想和领略饮茶情趣之意。在百忙之中泡上一壶浓茶，择雅静之处，自斟自饮，可以消除疲劳、涤烦益思、振奋精神，也可以细啜慢饮，达到美的享受，使精神世界升华到高尚的艺术境界。品茶的环境一般由建筑物、园林、摆设、茶具等因素组成。饮茶要求安静、清新、舒适、干净。中国园林世界闻名，山水风景更是不可胜数。利用园林或自然山水间，搭设茶室，让人们小憩，意趣盎然。

中国是文明古国，礼仪之邦，很重礼节。凡来了客人，沏茶、敬茶的礼仪是必不可少的。当有客来访，可征求意见，选用最合来客口味的茶和最佳茶具待客。以茶敬客时，对茶叶适当拼配也是必要的。主人在陪伴客人饮茶时，要注意客人杯、壶中的茶水残留量，一般用茶杯泡茶，如已喝去一半，就要添加开水，随喝随添，使茶水浓度基本保持前后一致，水温适宜。在饮茶时也可适当佐以茶食、糖果、菜肴等，达到调节口味和点心之功效。

中国茶文化的内容主要是茶在中国精神文化中的体现，这比"茶风俗"、"茶道"的范畴深广的多，也是中国茶文化之所以与欧美或日本的茶文化分别的很大的原因。

（二）日本茶道

中日两国一衣带水，隋唐以前，两国已有文化交往。随着中国佛教文化的传播，茶文化也同时传到了日本。饮茶很快成了日本的风尚。日本茶道即是通过饮茶的方式，对人们进行一种礼法教育和道德修养的一种仪式。日本茶道20多个流派，沿袭至今。

现代日本茶道一般在面积不大、清雅别致的茶室里进行。室内有珍贵古玩、名家书画。茶室中放着供烧水的陶炭（风）炉、茶锅（釜）。炉前排列着专供茶道用的各种沏茶、品茶用具。日本茶道的规矩比较讲究，友人到达时，主人在门口恭候。待宾客坐定，先奉上点心，供客人品尝。然后在炭炉上烧水，将茶放入青瓷碗中。水沸后，由主持人按规程沏水泡茶，依次递给宾客品饮。品茶时要吸气，并发出吱吱声音，表示对主人茶品的赞赏。当喝尽茶汤后，可用大拇指和洁净的纸擦干茶碗，仔细欣赏茶具，且边看边赞"好茶！"以表敬意。仪式结束，客人鞠躬告辞，主人跪坐门侧相送。整个过程，都洋溢着

"敬、和、清、寂"的精神。

（三）亚洲其他国家的茶文化

东南亚如马来西亚、新加坡等国家受汉文化影响较深，习惯冲泡清饮乌龙、普洱、花茶。南朝鲜因受中国和日本双重文化影响，兴起"茶礼"习俗。港澳地区则沿袭闽粤饮茶习俗，以饮普洱、水仙、花茶为主。泰国、缅甸和云南地区相似，习惯吃"腌茶"，将生茶腌制成酸味制品，吃时拌入食盐、生姜、花生之类，干嚼佐餐。南亚的印度、巴基斯坦、孟加拉、斯里兰卡等国家饮甜味红茶，或甜味红奶茶。印度饮茶总量为世界第一位，喜欢浓味的加糖红茶。巴基斯坦一般以茶、奶、糖按1：4：3的比例冲泡调饮，喜味浓的红茶。西亚地区的土耳其人，不论大人小孩都喜欢红茶，城乡茶馆普遍，出门饮茶也方便。伊朗和伊拉克人更是餐餐不离浓味红茶，用沸水冲泡，再在茶汤中添加糖、奶或柠檬共饮。

（四）欧洲各国的饮茶文化

英国饮茶之风始于17世纪中期，先由皇室倡导，后普及到城乡，成为英国的社交风俗。英国人喜欢饮滋味浓郁的红茶，并在茶中添加牛奶和糖。上流社会设置家庭茶室，收集陈设名贵茶具，讲求传统身分和闲情逸致的饮茶风度，以显示英国绅士的气派。爱尔兰人饮茶之风更甚，为欧洲首位，喜欢味浓的红碎茶。荷兰是西欧最早饮茶的国家。茶中放糖，多喜泡红茶和香味茶。西欧的其他国家也都习饮高档红茶和甜式调味红茶，青年人则多喜欢香味茶。

（五）美州国家的茶文化

美国的饮茶习俗与众不同，主要以红茶泡用或用速溶茶冲泡，放入冰箱冷却后，饮时杯中加入冰块、方糖、柠檬，或蜂蜜、甜果酒调饮，甜而酸香，开胃爽口。加拿大人多为英式热饮高档红茶，也有冰茶。

（六）非洲国家的茶文化

非洲的多数国家气候干燥、炎热，居民多信奉伊斯兰教，不饮酒而饮茶，饮茶已成为日常生活的主要内容。无论是亲朋相聚，还是婚丧嫁娶，乃至宗教活动，均以茶待客。这些国家多爱饮绿茶，并习惯在茶里放上新鲜的薄荷叶和白糖，蒸煮后饮用。当今世界各国、各民族的饮茶风俗，都因本民族的传统、地域民情和生活方式的不同而各有所异，然而"客来敬茶"却是古今中外的共同礼俗。

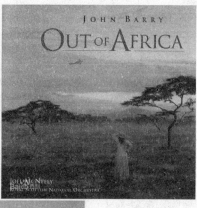

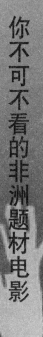

第五章

你不可不看的非洲题材电影

　　非洲是片充满矛盾的土地，既有贫困与战争交织，又有淳朴人民的安静祥和；既有狮子等各种热带动物的激情共舞，又有沙漠与绿洲造就的一片静美；既有"尼罗河畔妖妇"——埃及艳后的美貌，又有"埃及王子"摩西的传奇……总之，非洲是片神奇的土地。这片广袤的土地孕育着这些不同的文化，它们或发人深省，或美轮美奂。在这一章，我们将通过介绍关于非洲题材的十部经典影片，来共享一场关于非洲自然与文化的视觉盛宴。

41 人道主义赞歌——《卢旺达饭店》

Hotel Rwanda is not about hotel management, but about heroism and survival. Rusesabagina rises to the challenge in the film. The film works not because the screen is filled with meaningless special effects, formless action and vast digital armies, but because Cheadle, Nolte and the filmmakers are interested in how two men choose to function in an impossible situation. Because we sympathize with these men, we are moved by the film.

—Roger Ebert

Hotel Rwanda is a 2004 American **drama film** directed by Terry George. It was adapted from a **screenplay** written by both George and Keir Pearson. Based on real life events in 1994 Rwanda, the film stars Don Cheadle as hotelier Paul Rusesabagina, who attempts to save his fellow citizens from the ravages of the Rwandan Genocide by **grant**ing them shelter in the **besieged** Hôtel des Mille Collines. The film, which has been called an African Schindle's List, explores **genocide**, political corruption, and the **repercussions** of violence.

Plot

Tensions between the Hutu and Tutsi peoples lead to a war in Rwanda, where **corruption**s and **bribe**s between politicians are routine. Paul Rusesabagina (Don Cheadle), the manager of the Sabena Hôtel des Mille Collines is Hutu, but his wife Tatiana (Sophie Okonedo), is Tutsi. His marriage is a source of friction with Hutu **extremist**s.

As the political situation in the country worsens, Paul and his family observe neighbors being killed in ethnic violence. Paul **curries favor with** people of influence, bribing them with money and alcohol,

《卢旺达饭店》无关酒店管理，而是关乎英雄主义和生存的主题。在影片中卢斯赛伯吉纳勇敢应对挑战。此电影大受欢迎，与屏幕中充斥着的无意义的特效、无形的行为、大量的数字军人不相关联，而是与钱德尔、诺尔特以及电影制作人对于在绝境下两个男人如何做出抉择的关注密切相关。因为我们同情这些男人，感动于这部电影。

——罗杰•埃伯

《卢旺达饭店》（Hotel Rwanda）是一部由特里•乔治执导的美国剧情片（drama film），发行于2004年，改编自乔治和凯尔•皮尔森的电影剧本。该片取材于1994年发生在卢旺达的大屠杀，主演唐•钱德尔扮演了饭店经理保罗•卢斯赛伯吉纳（Paul Rusesabagina）。该片讲述了保罗•卢斯赛伯吉纳在卢旺达种族仇杀中，通过允许难民住在其被围困的米勒•科林斯饭店的方式，设法挽救了1268位图西族难民生命的故事。该片被誉为非洲的《辛德勒的名单》，探讨了大屠杀、政治腐败及暴力后果的问题。

故事简介

胡图族与图西族两部族之间矛盾重重，这导致了卢旺达境内的战争。从此，卢旺达境内腐败、贿赂肆意横行。主人公保罗•卢斯赛伯吉纳（唐•钱德尔饰）是米勒•科林斯饭店的经理，是胡图族人。其妻塔莎娜（苏菲•奥康尼多饰）却是图西族的。对于胡

seeking to maintain sufficient influence to keep his family safe. When civil war erupts and a Rwandan Army officer threatens Paul and his neighbors, Paul barely negotiates their safety, and brings everyone to the hotel. More refugees come to the hotel from the overburdened United Nations camp, the Red Cross, and orphanages. Paul must divert the Hutu soldiers, care for the refugees, be a source of strength to his family, and maintain the appearance of a functioning high-class hotel, as the situation becomes more violent.

The UN Peacekeeping forces, led by Canadian Colonel Oliver (Nick Nolte), are unable to take assertive action against the Interahamwe since they are forbidden to intervene in the genocide. The foreign nationals are evacuated, but the Rwandans are left behind. When the UN forces attempt to evacuate a group of refugees, including Paul's family, they are ambushed and must turn back. In a last-ditch effort to save the refugees, Paul pleads with the Rwandan Army General, Augustin Bizimungu (Fana Mokoena) for assistance. However, when Paul's bribes no longer work, he blackmails the General with threats of being tried as a war criminal. Soon after, the family and the hotel refugees are finally able to leave the besieged hotel in a UN convoy. They travel through retreating masses of refugees and militia to reach safety behind Tutsi rebel lines.

The film's **epilogue** displays a series of graphics stating that Rusesabagina saved 1,268 Rwandan refugees at the Hôtel des Mille Collines, and now lives in Belgium with his family. It also notes that General Bizimungu was tried and convicted by the UN for war crimes in 2002, as almost a million people died by the time the genocide ended in July 1994.

As an independent film, it had an initial

图族极端分子来说，保罗的婚姻是摩擦冲突中的一个引子。

随着卢旺达国家政治形势的恶化，保罗和家人们目睹了邻居们在种族暴力中遇害的惨况。为了保证自家安全，保罗采取了向政要送钱、酒行贿的方式。内战爆发时，一名卢旺达军官威胁保罗及其邻居。保罗未与之就所有人的安全进行协商，而是允许所有人都住进了他的饭店。接着，更多的难民从超负荷的联合国营地、红十字会及孤儿院中逃出，而涌入保罗的饭店。随着局势的恶化，保罗必须引开胡图战士，关爱难民，成为家庭力量的源泉，维持一座高级饭店表面上的日常运营。

而由加拿大奥利佛上校带领的联合国维和部队，却因无权干涉大屠杀而未采取任何反对行动。在卢境内的外国人已经撤离，但卢旺达人民却被抛在水深火热之中。当联合国军队尝试要撤离包括保罗一家在内的一批难民时，却遭埋伏而不得不撤退。在救难民的最后努力中，保罗向卢旺达军队司令奥古斯丁·比兹蒙谷（范纳·莫库纳饰）发出请求，寻求帮助。然而，保罗的贿赂也于事无补，于是他威胁该司令说，如果他拒绝施救，将面临一名战争犯的审判。很快，保罗的家庭和饭店其他难民能够在联合国军队势力的护送下离开被围困的饭店。他们在大量撤退的难民和民兵流中穿过，跨过图西族反叛者的防线，而得以安全到达（目的地）。

在电影后记中出现了一系列文字，其中叙说了卢斯赛伯吉纳一共挽救了住在米勒·科林斯饭店内的1268名难民，他与他的家人现居住于比利时。另外，后记中还提到，比兹蒙谷司令于2002年受到了联合国的审判，并因战争犯罪而获刑。此外，在1994年7月的大屠杀中有近一百万人罹难。

作为一部独立制作的片子，此片在影

limited release in theaters, but was nominated for multiple awards, including Academy Award nominations for Best Actor, Best Supporting Actress, and Best Original Screenplay. The film also won a number of awards including those from the Berlin and Toronto International Film Festivals.

院上映之初，票房有限。然而，此片却获众多奖项，包括奥斯卡最佳男演员提名、最佳女配角提名、最佳原创剧本提名。另外，在柏林及多伦多国际电影节中，这部电影也获得了众多奖项。

词汇 VOCABULARY

drama film：剧情片	genocide,：种族灭绝，大屠杀
besieged：受困的	corruption：腐败
repercussion：影响、后果	curry favor with sb.：拍某人马屁
screenplay：电影剧本	epilogue：结尾, 收场白
grant：同意给予或允许（所求）	extremist：极端分子
bribe：贿赂	

背景知识 PROFILE

卢旺达大屠杀

卢旺达种族大屠杀（Rwandan Genocide）又称卢旺达内战，是发生于1994年4月6日至1994年6月中旬在卢旺达的胡图族对图西族及胡图族温和派有组织的种族灭绝大屠杀。大屠杀共造成80万至100万人死亡。

大屠杀背景

卢旺达地处非洲中部，有"千丘之国"之称，是一个落后的农业国家，1992年被联合国列为世界47个最不发达国家之一。胡图族和图西族两个民族占到了全国总人口的99%，其中胡图族人口占85%，图西族人口占14%。

16世纪，图西族人在卢旺达建立了封建王国。自19世纪中叶起，英国、德国、比利时等西方殖民势力相继入侵。1890年，卢旺达沦为"德属东非"保护地。1916年，比利时获得卢旺达的委任统治权。第二次世界大战结束以后，卢旺达成为联合国托管地，但仍由比利时统治。20世纪60年代以前，仅占人口10%—15%的图西族在卢旺达占据统治地位，88%的政府官员都是图西族人，并拥有绝大部分可耕地。1959年，卢旺达南部的胡图族农民开始反抗图西族贵族的统治并掌握政权，把土地重新分配给无地的人，许多图西族贵族逃到了邻近国家。1962年，卢旺达宣布独立后，图西族和胡图族多次发生冲突，战事持续不断。

大屠杀过程

1990年，侨居在乌干达的图西族难民组织卢旺达爱国阵线
（RPF）与胡图族政府军爆发内战。在周边国家的调停和压力下，
1993年8月，卢旺达政府和爱国阵线在坦桑尼亚北部城市阿鲁沙签
署旨在结束内战的和平协定。即将到来的和平令卢旺达政府高层
中的极端势力感到恐惧，他们逐渐对朱韦纳尔·哈比亚利马纳总统
感到不满，认为他在与爱国阵线的谈判中让步太多。

1994年4月6日，载着卢旺达总统朱韦纳尔·哈比亚利马纳和布
隆迪总统西普里安·恩塔里亚米拉的飞机在卢旺达首都基加利附近
被击落，两位总统同时罹难。该事件立即在卢旺达全国范围内引
发了胡图族人针对图西族人的血腥报复。7日，由胡图族士兵组成
的总统卫队杀害了卢旺达女总理、图西族人乌维林吉伊姆扎纳和3名部长。在当地媒体和
电台的煽动下，此后3个月里，先后约有80万至100万人惨死在胡图族士兵、民兵、平民的
枪支、弯刀和削尖的木棒之下，绝大部分受害者是图西族人，也包括一些同情图西族的胡
图族人，卢旺达全国1/8的人口消失，另外还有25万至50万卢旺达妇女和女孩遭到强奸。

同年7月，卢旺达爱国阵线与邻国乌干达的军队反攻进入卢旺达首都基加利，击败了
胡图族政府。200万胡图族人，其中一些屠杀参与者，由于害怕遭到图西族报复，逃到邻
国布隆迪、坦桑尼亚、乌干达和扎伊尔（现在的刚果民主共和国）。数千人由于霍乱和痢
疾死于难民营。

国际的反应

由于美国在索马里进行的"黑鹰坠落"行动的失败，因此美国并不想介入卢旺达内
战。对此美国总统克林顿于1998年3月访问卢旺达时，在基加利机场对大屠杀幸存者发表
讲话时婉转地表达了歉意。

比利时政府以10名比利时维和军人遭到杀害为由，撤出了全部在卢旺达的部队，并带
走了所有的武器。

联合国在卢旺达种族大屠杀事件中表现消极。大屠杀发生的第四天，联合国安理会通
过投票，决定象征性地在卢旺达保留260名维和人员，职责仅仅是调停停火和提供人道主
义援助。在卢旺达种族大屠杀持续了近一个半月后，联合国才决定将联合国驻卢旺达援助
团人数增加到5500人，扩大其行动授权，并说服其他国家参与救援。

法国在基伏湖附近建立了野战医院，尝试收容难民。加拿大、以色列、荷兰和爱尔兰
也提供了一些援助。红十字会、无国界医生等国际救援组织无惧炮火，到达当地，拯救平
民百姓。

大屠杀影响

1994年的卢旺达内战和种族大屠杀给卢旺达带来了巨大灾难，使这个原本贫困的国家
雪上加霜，大批劳动力丧失，国家经济处于崩溃边缘。大屠杀还使这个国家的人口结构产

生了很大的变化，全国14岁以下的儿童约占总人口的40%，许多妇女成为寡妇，大量逃亡邻国的胡图族极端主义分子渗入邻近国家，给这些国家的安定带来负面影响。

成立纪念日

1994年联合国在坦桑尼亚的阿鲁沙成立卢旺达问题国际刑事法庭，审判高级政府官员或军人。卢旺达政府则负责审判较低层级的领导人或平民。

联合国大会于2003年12月23日宣布将每年的4月7日定为"反思卢旺达大屠杀国际日"。

2004年3月26日，联合国秘书长科菲·安南在纽约联合国总部举行的"卢旺达大屠杀10周年纪念会"上发表讲话，呼吁国际社会采取行动，防止卢旺达大屠杀事件重演。同年4月7日，卢旺达举行卢旺达大屠杀10周年的全国性纪念活动，以哀悼大屠杀遇难者。

42 关于占有与失去——《走出非洲》

From 1913 to 1931 Karen Blixen (penname: Isak Dinesen) (1885-1962), the Danish writer lived in British East Africa, now Kenya, where she ran a large coffee **plantation**. She had originally come out to Africa to marry the Swedish-born **Baron** Bror Blixen, who was her cousin as well as the twin brother of Hans Blixen, the man she really loved but who had **jilt**ed her.

As man and wife, Bror and Karen were friends and occasional lovers, but Bror was an **ebullient**, unashamed **philanderer**, something that Karen seems to have accepted with **equanimity** until she contracted **syphilis** from him. They separated—Karen remaining on the farm while Bror went off to pursue his living as a great white hunter.

After Bror's departure, Karen developed what seems to have been the most profound emotional attachment of her life with Denys Finch Hatton, an English Earl's younger son, a charming aristocrat who had enough money to live pretty much as he pleased.

1913-1931年期间，丹麦作家卡伦·布里克森（笔名伊萨克·迪内森）住在英属东非今肯尼亚地区。在那里，她拥有着一座大型咖啡农场。卡伦最初走进非洲是为了嫁给生于丹麦的男爵布罗·布里克森。布罗是卡伦的堂兄，是卡伦的旧爱汉斯·布里克森的胞弟。

婚后，布罗和卡伦过着朋友兼恋人般的生活。然而，布罗为人热情奔放，善于戏弄女人。对此，卡伦似乎心如静水，默然不语。可最后，布罗竟将梅毒传染给卡伦，这导致了二人分离。卡伦继续留在农场上，布罗外出开始寻求一个伟大猎人的生活。

自此，卡伦开始了和丹尼斯·芬奇·哈顿的爱情。丹尼斯（罗伯特·雷德福饰）是一位英国伯爵的年轻子嗣，他英俊潇洒，生活富有。在回英国的

Between trips back to England, Denys led wealthy tourists on safaris, hunted on his own, **dabble**d in various business deals and, from time to time, visited Karen on her farm, usually arriving unannounced and staying only as long as it suited him.

They shared a love of books and music. She fed him well and he took her up in his plane to show her the face of Africa from the air.

It's this affair of Karen Blixen that provides the elusive heart of Sydney Pollack's "Out of Africa," a big, physically elaborate but wispy movie. Miss Streep's Karen, accompanied by family china, crystal and silverware, sweeps grandly into Africa as if entering a world created for her own intellectual stimulation. She's nothing if not possessive. She speaks of native servants as "my Kikuyus." The plantation is "my farm." The continent is "'my Africa". She eventually comes to understand, as Denys Finch Hatton (Robert Redford) tells her, that "we're not owners here, Karen. We're just passing through."

The film's Karen Blixen is part Scarlett O'Hara fighting to save Tara, part insensitive tourist marveling at the quaint customs of the local folk. There is far greater emotional **rapport** between Karen and Bror Blixen, beautifully played by Klaus Maria Brandauer ("Mephisto," "Colonel Redl"), than there is between Karen and Denys. The film's most moving moments are those that recall what life was like back in the good old days on the plantation.

With the exception of Miss Streep's performance, the pleasures of "Out of Africa" are all peripheral - David Watkin's photography, the landscapes, the shots of animal life —all of which would fit neatly into a **National Geographic layout**.

"Out of Africa," which has been rated PG ("Parental Guidance Suggested"), contains several explicit, animal-eat-animal shots and some mildly vulgar language.

旅途中，因各种商务，丹尼斯过起了在非洲狩猎的生活。他开始时不时拜访卡伦，又常常不告而别，来去只听内心声音。

卡伦和丹尼斯都热爱读书，爱听音乐。她供给他膳食，他驾飞机带她冲上云霄，领略非洲的美。

正是卡伦的这个故事深深打动了西德尼·波拉克，使他创作了这部宏大的、精致的却略带朦胧的电影《走出非洲》。梅丽尔·斯特里普版的卡伦，伴着居家的瓷器、水晶、银器，带着一种奢华进入了非洲，一个好似为了她的能力而设计的世界。如果一无所有，她身无长物。她称当地的仆人为"我的基库尤人"，庄园为"我的农场"，大陆为"我的非洲"。最后，就像丹尼斯告诉她的那样，她终于明白，"我们不是这儿的主人，我们只是过客。"

电影里的卡伦，有点儿像斯嘉丽·奥哈拉，也有点儿像惊叹于当地人民风俗习惯的游客。卡伦和布罗之间的情感交流要远胜于卡伦和丹尼斯。克劳斯·马里亚·勃莱德尔的精彩演绎使得那些旧日的庄园生活成了影片中最动人的情节。

除了斯特里普的精彩表现以外，大卫·沃特金镜头下的非洲美景，非洲动物的生活图景成了该影片中动人的背景陪衬。

《走出非洲》电影分级属于PG，即需家长陪同观看的电影，包括一些清晰地动物之间相互厮杀的场面以及某些较粗俗的语言。

plantation：种植园	equanimity：心情平静
baron：男爵	syphilis：梅毒（一种性传播疾病）
jilt：抛弃	dabble：涉足、涉猎
ebullient：精力充沛的，热情洋溢的	rapport：融洽和谐的关系
philanderer：玩弄女性的男人	layout：布局，安排，设计

背景知识 **P**ROFILE

丹麦及英国贵族爵位分级

丹麦贵族爵位分为公爵（Hertug）、侯爵（Marki）、伯爵（Greve）、子爵（Vicegreve）和男爵（Baron）五个等级。

这里，我们重点介绍下英国贵族爵位的分级。英国贵族爵位（peerage）分为公爵（Duke）、侯爵（Marquis或Marquess）、伯爵（Earl）、子爵（Viscount）和男爵（Baron）五个等级。原来贵族爵位都是世袭的，而且只能有一个继承人。长子是法定继承人，只有在贵族没有儿子的情况下，其爵位才能由首先到达继承年龄的直系后代来继承。自1958年以后，才允许将非继承性的"终身贵族爵位"（Life peerages）授予某一个人。

对公爵、公爵夫人（Duchess）尊称为"Grace"。直接称呼时用"Your Grace"（大人，夫人），间接提及时用"His (her) Grace"，用在信封或信的开头可尊称为"His Grace the Duke of …"或"Her Grace the Duchess of …"。

侯爵、伯爵、子爵和男爵都可以称为"Lord"（勋爵），直接称呼时，都可称"Your Lordship"，间接提及时可用"Lord + 姓"或"Lord + 地名"。信封上或信的开头分别称"My Lord Marquis"或"My Lord"（主要用于伯、子、男爵）。

侯爵夫人（Marchiness）、伯爵夫人（Countess）、子爵夫人（Viscountess）、男爵夫人（Baroness）均可称为："Lady"（夫人），即用"Lady + 丈夫的姓或丈夫勋称中的地名"。

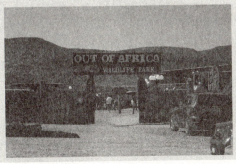

43 美艳与智慧的结合体——《埃及艳后》

It is virtually impossible to separate Cleopatra the movie from Cleopatra the spectacle—and that's because they are truly and rarely **intertwine**d.

A legend of Hollywood, the 1963 production of Cleopatra has so much curiosity surrounding it. It was budgeted at $2 million and eventually cost (up to) $44 million to produce—close to $300 million in today's dollars. The production was forced to move from Rome to London and back to Rome again. Two of its stars fell in love (Taylor and Burton) on the set, ruining both of their marriages. 20th Century Fox essentially went bankrupt, leading to the ousting of its chief. The first director was fired after burning $7 million with nothing to show for it. The second director (Mankiewicz) was fired during editing, only to be rehired when no one else could finish the picture. Taylor threw up the first time she saw the finished product. Producer Walter Wanger never worked in Hollywood again. And the original six-hour epic was cut to a little over three.

The first American cut—a bit over four hours—is finally released on DVD, an exhaustive three-disc set that provides as much information about the movie.

But enough of the gossip—the movie itself is hardly the best film ever made. Its first half, tracing Cleopatra's dealings with Julius Caesar (Rex Harrison), dealings which ultimately lead to his downfall, is a great bit of cinema. It's a tight 1:50 and tells a powerful tale of greed for power and duplicity in politics. On the famed **Ides of March**, Caesar gets his **comeuppance**, and Mark Antony (Richard Burton) becomes the focus of the film. His love affair with Cleo is a sick **monstrosity**, an inexplicable mess of

实际上，很难把《埃及艳后》这部电影跟历史上埃及艳后克利奥帕特拉本人的传奇分离开来——这是因为二者是确确实实相互交织着。

1963年好莱坞大片《埃及艳后》曾传奇一时，关于影片本身让人好奇点众多。该片预计200万美元，而实际上耗资4400万，大约相当于现在的3亿美元。该片拍摄地点从罗马转移到伦敦，而后又折回罗马。泰勒（饰演埃及艳后）和伯顿（饰演安东尼）因为本片而坠入爱河，纷纷离婚，组建家庭。二十世纪福克斯电影制片公司（20th Century Fox）因为此片几近破产，这也导致了公司领导人的更换。第一任导演被炒，因为在烧了700万之后，一无所成。第二任导演在电影的编辑期被炒，而后却因为无人能完成此片，得到继续聘用。当泰勒第一次看成片时，大为不满。本来六个小时的史诗巨制被删减成三个小时稍多一点。

而在美国上映的影片大概四个小时，最终以DVD的形式出版发行，三张碟片的形式提供了丰富的信息。

电影本身并不算最好。第一部分（电影的前1小时50分钟）是关于埃及艳后和凯撒（雷克斯·哈里森）之间的纠葛，而其中的交易导致了凯撒的身败名裂。这部分的主题是对权力的贪欲和政界里的欺骗。最终，在著名的3月15日凯撒受到了应有的惩罚，退出权力舞台，马克·安东尼（理查德·伯

gluttony and **gaudiness**. Part II of Cleopatra is the return of Cleopatra to Rome in a monumental procession is one of the centerpieces of grandiose filmmaking. Perhaps it had something to do with the fact that most of the movie was shot without a real script by a director receiving daily injections just to keep on working... Better yet to skip over all this nonsense and head straight to Octavian's rule.

Cleopatra ruined so many careers it's amazing that it's still remembered mostly fondly by Hollywood insiders and movie fans.

顿）成为了电影的中心。安东尼和埃及艳后的风流韵事丑陋无比，充满怪诞。他们的生活骄奢淫逸，傲慢无礼。《埃及艳后》的第二部分讲述了克利奥帕特拉回归罗马的故事，这一段展示了里程碑式的游行队伍，是电影制作中的精彩片段之一。不过评论家们因为此段并没有实际内容，建议人们直接过渡到电影的第三部分——屋大维的统治。

坦率的说，《埃及艳后》毁了很多人的职业生涯，但很奇怪的是，好莱坞业内人士和电影爱好者们依然记得这部影片。

词汇 VOCABULARY

intertwine：交织	comeuppance：报应，罪有应得
tracheotomy：气管切开术	monstrosity：畸形
unearth：挖掘	gluttony：暴饮暴食
Ides of March：三月十五日	gaudiness：华而不实

背景知识 PROFILE

历史人物及电影公司简介

埃及艳后：即克利奥帕特拉七世（又译克利欧佩特拉七世；约前70年12月或前69年1月—约前30年8月12日）是古埃及托勒密王朝的最后一任法老。文艺或电影上，她被认为是为保持国家免受罗马帝国吞并，曾色诱凯撒大帝及他的手下马克·安东尼。

恺撒大帝：罗马共和国末期杰出的军事统帅、政治家。他公元前60年与庞培、克拉苏秘密结成前三巨头同盟，随后出任高卢总督，花了八年时间征服了高卢全境（大约是现在的法国），还袭击了日耳曼和不列颠。前49年，他率军占领罗马，打败庞培，集大权于一身，实行独裁统治并制定了《儒略历》。公元前44年，恺撒遭以布鲁图所领导的元老院成员暗杀身亡。恺撒死后，其甥孙及养子屋大维击败安东尼开创罗马帝国并成为第一位帝国皇帝。

马克·安东尼：凯撒的心腹。在凯撒遇刺后，在凯撒墓前发表著名演说，使得叛乱者失去人心。

盖乌斯·屋大维(Gaius Julius Caesar Octavianus)：罗马帝国的开国君主，元首政制的创始人，统治罗马长达43年，是世界历史上最为重要的人物之一。他是凯撒的甥孙，公元前44年被凯撒收为养子并指定为继承人。凯撒被刺后登上政治舞台。公元前1世纪，他平息了企图分裂罗马共和国的内战，被元老院赐封为"奥古斯都"，并改组罗马政府，给罗马世界带来了两个世纪的和平与繁荣。

二十世纪福克斯电影制片公司（20th Century Fox）：香港称为二十世纪霍氏公司，是美国的电影公司，成立于1935年5月。在好莱坞的八家大公司中，二十世纪福克斯是创立最晚的，而且经受的波折也最多，几次经历险些破产的厄运。创始人之一的威廉·福克斯虽然能够把姓氏写在公司名里，但实际上，在1935这家公司正式挂牌时，威廉·福克斯已经是局外人。

44 苦难、隐忍和自由——《埃及王子》

For many centuries, those producing mass entertainment have recognized the inherent drama and majesty in the story of the Hebrew exodus from Egypt. The tale has inspired countless plays, a renowned **oratorio** (Handel's "Israel in Egypt"), and one of the most beloved epic motion pictures of all time (Cecil B. De Mille's The Ten Commandments). Now, the Exodus has been used as a basis for The Prince of Egypt, which marks Dreamworks SKG's entrance into the field of glossy, big budget animation. Like Fox (with Anastasia) and Warner Brothers (with the disappointing The Quest for Camelot), Dreamworks intends to challenge Disney's reign as the King of Animation. The Prince of Egypt is a worthy starting point. It ranks alongside the Magic Kingdom's Mulan at the top of the year's traditional-style animated pile.

Of course, telling a Biblical story has forced Dreamworks to do a great deal of creative **tap-dancing** to avoid offending potential viewers. The last thing the studio wanted was an organized protest outside theaters on opening day. Muslim, Christian,

多年来，很多娱乐制作团队意识到《圣经：出埃及记》中的戏剧性。出埃及的故事启发了多部剧作、一部著名的清唱剧（亨德尔的《以色列人在埃及》）、一部深受众人喜欢的史诗性动作片（塞西尔·B·戴米尔的《十诫》）。如今，《出埃及记》已成了《埃及王子》的原型，这部片子也是梦工厂进入巨资制作动画片世界的敲门砖。就像福克斯电影公司（Fox）（《真假公主》）和华纳兄弟（Warner Brothers）（《魔剑奇兵》）一样，梦工厂想要挑战迪士尼"动画片之王"的美誉。而《埃及王子》正是这样一个良好的开端。在一年的传统动画片集中，《埃及王子》和神奇王国（Magic Kingdom）的《木兰》问鼎排行榜。

当然，讲述一个圣经故事"逼迫"着梦工厂做了大量的创造性的规避工作，以避免冒犯潜在的观众。梦

and Jewish religious leaders were consulted about the script. Every effort was made to follow the source material faithfully, although a disclaimer appears before the opening sequence reminding viewers that, while the movie uses "artistic and historical license," every effort was made to remain "true to the essence" of the tale as related in the first 14 chapters of the Book of Exodus (Moses' birth, exile, then return to lead his people out of Egypt).

As in Mulan, the subject matter is fairly sophisticated for animated **fare** (witness the PG rating). In keeping with Exodus, the **mistreatment** of the Hebrew slaves is depicted (albeit not graphically), as the mass slaughter of Egyptian firstborns that leads to the Pharaoh's freeing of the slaves. And, as if the story wasn't grim enough to begin with, the screenwriters invented a friendship between Ramses and Moses to elevate certain aspects of The Prince of Egypt to the level of a **Shakepearean tragedy**. At times, Moses is depicted as a **brood**ing, Hamlet-like hero. Like Antz (another Dreamworks production), The Prince of Egypt seems aimed at an older crowd, although the core audience of children will still find plenty to enjoy.

The Prince of Egypt neither skims over nor **dwells upon** the least happy elements of the story. Overall, it's a story of triumph and adventure—of oppression ended and freedom begun. The comedy elements that have become an integral part of animated features are **downplay**ed. The **Pharaoh**'s two chief priests are **sly** and **fatuous**, and some of their **antics** are amusing, but they offer little more than occasional, momentary comic relief. For the most part, The Prince of Egypt plays it straight. As for the other "necessary" aspect of the successful animated feature—the musical numbers—The Prince of Egypt features about a half-dozen (from Hans Zimmer and Stephen Schwartz, who wrote the lyrics for Pocahontas and

工厂可不想看到在电影公映的当天剧院外挤满了抗议示威的人。因此，梦工厂向穆斯林教、基督教、犹太教的领导人们就圣经进行咨询。梦工厂力求忠实地反应《圣经：出埃及记》中前十四章的内容（摩西的诞生，放逐，然后重返埃及领导他的人民出埃及）。

就像《木兰》，主题对于动画片的票价来说，是十分复杂的（孩子需要在家长的陪同下观影）。在与《出埃及记》一致的基础上，对希伯来奴隶的粗暴对待被刻画成了埃及出生的人的大屠杀，这也导致了法老对于奴隶给予自由的特赦。在影片中，编剧似乎觉得圣经原著的开端不够严肃，而创造了在拉美西斯和莫斯之间的一段友谊，从而将《埃及王子》的某些方面上升到了莎士比亚悲剧的层面。摩西有时被刻画成疑虑重重，哈姆雷特式的英雄。如梦工厂的另一部作品《蚁哥正传》一样，《埃及王子》的观影年龄似乎也更大一些，不过大多数孩子还是非常喜欢这部影片。

《埃及王子》既没有掠过故事本身的快乐元素，也没有对这些快乐元素进行长久思考。总体上来说，这是一个关于胜利和历险的故事——始于压迫，结束于自由。在该影片中，传统动画影片必不可少的戏剧元素并未得到过多彰显。法老的两个重要牧师既狡黠又愚昧，虽然他们的一些夸张表演惹人发笑，但他们所提供给关注的只是偶尔的欢笑。《埃及王子》的大部分是准确、无渲染的。动画片的另一重要元素是音乐——该影片中歌曲高达六首左右。尽管这些音乐并无达到早期迪斯尼那些让人无法忘却的

The Hunchback of Notre Dame). And, while none are as memorable as those from the early entries into Disney's recent wave, they fold nicely into the story.

The animation in The Prince of Egypt is truly **top-notch**, and is easily a match for anything Disney has turned out in the last decade. The artists effectively mix hand-drawn and computer-generated images to good effect, the colors are rich and vibrant, and the characters' lip movements are in synch with the soundtrack. The final product is polished, with a number of standout sequences (the chariot race, the plagues, and the parting of the Red Sea). While last year's Anastasia managed to come close to Disney's visual elegance, The Prince of Egypt matches it. This impressive achievement uncovers yet another chink in Disney's once-impregnable animation armor.

As far as vocal talents are concerned, the film makers have gathered an impressive cast, with even the minor characters being voiced by recognizable names. The plum roles of Moses and Ramses, the leader of the captive Hebrews and the King of Egypt, belong to Val Kilmer and Ralph Fiennes, respectively. Michelle Pfeiffer supplies the voice of Moses' wife, Zipporah; Sandra Bullock is his sister, the prophetess Miriam; Jeff Goldblum is his brother, Aaron; and Danny Glover is his father-in-law, Jethro. Other voices include Patrick Stewart and Helen Mirren as Ramses' parents, and the team of Martin Short and Steve Martin as the foolish Egyptian priests.

Jeffrey Katzenberg (the former Disney honcho who is the "K" in "Dreamworks SKG") has gone out of his way to emphasize that The Prince of Egypt is not a religious movie, despite the nature of the source material. This is not intended to be a big budget Bible Story cartoon, but a rousing animated adventure. However, even without resistance from religious groups, The Prince of Egypt still faces a significant obstacle: the large number of family-oriented features

作品的高度，但它们和故事实现了巧妙的结合。

该影片中的动画效果是一流的，能与迪士尼任何一部过去十年的作品相媲美。艺术家们有效地将手绘和电脑生成的形象进行了完美结合，色彩丰富，富于动感。片中人物的唇部活动和电影原声实现同步。最终的作品精雕细琢，有很多可圈可点的场景（战车比赛，瘟疫，红海之别）。《真假公主》成功地与迪士尼的仿真效果相靠近，而《埃及王子》亦不逊色。这一巨大成功向迪士尼曾经不可战胜的动画传奇形象发出挑战。

而在电影的声音方面，电影制作人集结了一个非常强大的团队。即使片中的小角色也是由那些大人物来操刀。摩西和拉美西斯、被俘的希伯来人首领和埃及国王分别由方·基默、拉尔夫·范恩斯来配音。而米歇尔·法伊弗则为摩西妻子西坡拉赋予生命；桑德拉·布洛克为摩西的妹妹，女先知米里亚姆，杰夫·高布伦为摩西的弟弟艾伦，丹尼·格洛弗为其岳父杰思罗。而其他配音演员包括帕特里克·斯图尔特和海伦·米伦，他们分别扮演拉美西斯的父母，而马丁·肖特和史蒂夫·马丁则替那两个愚蠢的埃及牧师说了话。

杰弗瑞·卡森伯格曾强调《埃及王子》非宗教电影，尽管有着宗教题材。这不是一部大制作的圣经故事动画片，而是一场让人激动的动画冒险。然而，尽管宗教团体并未抗议，《埃及王子》仍然面临着一个很大的窘境：在假期档的影院里充斥着大量的家庭亲子题材的影片。然而，即使在《虫虫危机》、《小猪进城》、

clogging the theaters this holiday season. Nevertheless, even in a field that includes A Bug's Life, Babe: Pig in the City, The Rugrats Movie, and Mighty Joe Young, this movie is worth a trip to the local multiplex by viewers of all ages, races, and religious persuasions.

《淘气小兵兵》以及《巨猩乔扬》这样一个高质量影片云集的世界里，《埃及王子》仍值得所有年龄、种族以及宗教信仰的人们进入电影，一探究竟。

背景知识 PROFILE

圣经故事及电影公司

《出埃及记》：《出埃及记》是摩西五经的第二卷，卷名源于旧约希腊文七十士译本，与19章1节的描述契合。《出埃及记》犹若一道桥梁，把《创世纪》和另外三卷记载以色列人旷野四十年生活的历史书连贯起来。它同时也是一本重要的典籍，解释了为什么约瑟时代集体下埃及、备受欢迎的以色列民族，后来竟沦为奴隶，替法老用泥和草造砖建城；又介绍了他们怎样出埃及，并在去往迦南地之前，建立律法、宗教体制和详细的道德规范。

摩西：纪元前十三世纪的犹太人先知，旧约圣经前五本书的执笔者。带领在埃及过着奴隶生活的以色列人。到达神所预备的流着奶和蜜之地——迦南（巴勒斯坦的古地名，在今天约旦河与死海的西岸一带），神借着摩西写下《十诫》给他的子民遵守，并建造会幕，教导他的子民敬拜他。历史上没有谁能够像摩西那样，拥有如此众多的崇拜者。

摩西十诫：根据《圣经》记载，是上帝耶和华借由以色列的先知和首领摩西向以色列民族颁布的律法中的首要的十条规定，这大概是公元前1500年的事情。以十诫为代表的摩西律法是犹太人的生活和信仰的准则，也是最初的法律条文。在基督教中也有很重要的地位。

梦工厂（Dreamworks SKG）：始建于1994年10月，三位创始人分别是史蒂文·斯皮尔伯格（代表DreamWorks SKG中的"S"），杰弗瑞·卡森伯格（代表DreamWorks SKG中的"K"）和大卫·格芬（代表DreamWorks SKG中的"G"）。梦工厂的产品包括电影、动画片、电视节目、家庭视频娱乐、唱片、书籍、玩具和消费产品。

45 宗教与爱的包容——《拉姑莱特的夏天》

To the old-timers, the beach city of La Goulette, **Tunisia**, is **paradise**, but three teenage friends view it as a world away from their desires.

Set in 1967, A Summer in La Goulette is a 1996 comedy/drama about pretty 17-year-olds who ache to depart from their religious and cultural traditions, and long for freedom from their parents' dated ideals of **courtship**. Thus, the trio — Meriem (Sonia Mankaï), a **Muslim**; Gigi (Sarah Pariente), a **Catholic**; and Tina (Ava Cohen-Jonathan), a **Jew**—decide to take control of their **destinies** and "become women." The best friends make a pact to lose their virginities by Aug. 15, which happens to be the day of the Madonna (Virgin Mary).

However, the girls' first attempt is **foil**ed and, worst of all, the fathers catch their little angels in a darkened room with three neighborhood boys of the wrong (different) religions. Trust is broken, fingers are pointed, viewpoints are challenged and long-standing friendships between the girls' dads are ruined, creating **strife** in the apartment complex where the families live.

Simultaneously, the film takes place as "great

对于怀旧的人们来说，突尼斯拉姑莱特美丽的海滩可谓是天堂。然而，对于《拉姑莱特》影片中的三个少女来说，此地却是一个欲望无处实现的地方。

该片时间定格于1967年，拍摄于1996年。这部喜剧/戏剧讲述了三个急于摆脱自己的宗教和文化传统的女孩，渴望拥有异于父母期望的恋爱方式。因此，三人——穆斯林教徒梅里姆（索尼娅·曼卡饰）、天主教徒吉吉（萨拉·帕连特饰）和犹太教徒蒂娜（阿娃·科昂·若纳唐饰）——决定掌控自己的人生，成为一个"女人"。三个好朋友约定在8月15日（圣母玛利亚日）失去自己的童贞。

但是，女孩的第一次尝试却失败了。最糟糕的是，三位老爸在一间黑屋子里，当场发现他们的天使正和邻家不同信仰的男孩厮混在一起。瞬间，信任不复存在了，她们变成了千夫所指的坏女孩，因为她们，长久以来的观点受到了挑战，而这一系列的时间使得女孩们父亲之间的友谊也破裂开来。最后，三个女孩的居住地冲突应声而起。

tension" mounts in the Middle East, just before the second Arab-Israeli War. The national conflict appears to be a veiled metaphor for the **rift** among the fathers.

Further complicating matters, the **lecherous** landlord, Hadj Beji (Gamil Ratib), has eyes for Meriem, who is decades his junior, and offers her father a calculated **proposal** to make the ingénue his wife.

A Summer in La Goulette presents an interesting **dilemma** that seems somewhat foreign during a time when, in American society, sexuality is loosely regarded. Nonetheless, writer-director Férid Boughedir does an excellent job of portraying the struggles between elders and youths, and strikes a **balance** between seriousness and humor.

同时，电影发生在中东"极度紧张"的山区，时间刚好是在第二次阿以冲突之前。因此，民族冲突可看成是三位父亲之间的情感裂痕的隐喻。

更为复杂的是，好色的房东对梅里姆的觊觎。他要长于梅里姆几十岁，处心积虑的他竟然向梅里姆的爸爸提出，要娶梅里姆为妻。

《拉姑莱特的夏天》向观众展示了一种有趣的两难境地，这在当时性放纵的美国社会看来，是那么的格格不入。然而，编剧兼导演费力德•布格蒂尔在刻画老人和年轻人两代人冲突方面表现极为出色，而且在严肃和幽默之间维持了很好的平衡。

此片是2010年突尼斯电影展的上映作品之一。

词汇 VOCABULARY

Tunisia：突尼斯（是非洲最大的磷酸盐和天然气储藏地之一，石油藏量丰富。服务业、农业、轻工业，以及生产和出口石油和磷酸盐是经济的重要项目。以突尼西亚海岸风光和罗马遗址为主的旅游业也很重要。）	
paradise：天堂	foil：挫败
courtship：恋爱期	strife：冲突、争斗、争吵
Muslim：伊斯兰教信徒	rift：不和，裂痕
Catholic：天主教信徒	lecherous：好色的
destiny：命运	proposal：求婚
Jew：基督教信徒	dilemma：(进退两难的)窘境，困境

世界三大主要宗教

伊斯兰教　世界主要宗教之一，公元7世纪初由穆罕默德在阿拉伯半岛创立。"伊斯兰"一词意为"顺从"——特别是顺从唯一真主安拉的意志。伊斯兰教是严格遵守一神论的宗教，其信徒称作穆斯林，认为先知穆罕默德是真主的使者中最后一位并且是最完美的一位，其他使者包括亚当和夏娃、亚伯拉罕、摩西、耶稣等人。伊斯兰教的圣典是《古兰经》，载有真主对穆罕默德的启示。

基督教　基督宗教是一个一神论的宗教，指所有相信主耶稣基督为救主的教会。虽然耶稣基督所建立的是一个合一的基督教会，但基督教在历史进程中却分化为许多派别，2013年全世界范围当中有超过一万个基督教派，主流的派别主要有天主教、东正教、新教三大传统教派，以及一些在信仰人数上虽不如传统教派多，但也有了相当的规模的非传统教派，如：摩门教、耶和华见证人等。其他的则大多为信徒人数较少的边缘教派。值得注意的是在中文称呼上，由于基督教新教往往简称为基督教，于是容易造成误解，所以中文学术界通常将天主教、东正教和新教统称为基督宗教，用基督教称呼新教；神学界又称新教为更正教会；民间又称之为耶稣教。基督教是世界上信仰人口最多的宗教，有20亿以上的人信仰基督教。

佛教　佛教的内容概括来讲，可分为佛、法、僧三个基本层次：

1."佛"是梵语"佛陀"的音译简称。原意指的是"觉者"、"觉悟者"，泛指彻悟人生真谛、掌握最高真理、证得佛教修行的最高境界者。具体则是指释迦牟尼佛，即佛教的教主。

2."法"是梵文"达摩"的音译。"法"有两层含义：一是指事物的规范或规则，人们可以籍由这些规范或规则，对事物进行考察和识别；二指的是事物的自性或本质。从某种层面上说，"法"表示宇宙人生的一切万事万物，具体则是指记录佛的言教、阐发佛教教义的宗教典籍。

3."僧"是梵文"僧伽"的音译，含义是"和合众"、"法众"。僧，就是众多的出家人和合相处在一起。所以佛教的僧实际上是一种集体称呼，一名出家人不能称为僧，由四个以上信奉佛法、遵守佛教戒律的人所组成的组织才能称为"僧"。

"佛教"是佛陀对九法界众生至善圆满的教育。时间上，讲过去、现在、未来；空间上，讲眼前的生活、浩瀚无边的宇宙。所以佛教是教育，是智慧、觉悟、宇宙人生真相的教育。

46 小人物的自由和梦想——《黑房子》

While Moroccan films are traditionally **relegated** to arthouse cinemas, Casanegra is **hip**, stylish and **engaging** enough to break out further—if it weren't for its two-hour running time. Lakhmari takes too long to set up the main premise, and then too long to see it through.

The film begins with the protagonists running from the police, then flashes back to explain how they got there. Adil (Omar Lotfi) lives with mother and violent **stepfather** and dreams of moving to **Sweden**. Karim (Anas Elbaz) is secretly in love with an older, upper-class French woman and his family struggles with the burden of his sick father.

The two make petty money through petty crimes, some for local heavy Zrirek (a deliciously over-the-top Mohamed Benbrahim), whose **sadism** is equaled only by his neurotic love for his little dog.

The more **street-smart** Karim is **leery** of getting further involved with Zrirek, but Adil needs to score big to buy fake documents for Sweden, and hopes to take his **buddy** with him. You know things will go downhill when Adil talks his friend into accepting just one big job that will solve all their troubles.

The film caused a scandal at home, presumably for offering a different view of the infamous city. Like Lakhmari's **anti-hero**es, no one in the developing or developed world wants to work **menial** jobs anymore, and class divisions widen especially in poorer countries. Even Karim, the brains of the duo, would rather continue selling contraband cigarettes than gut fish for his

传统的摩洛哥电影一般只能在艺术电影院放映，而《黑房子》却入流时尚、魅力非凡，使得该片能够有所突破，实际上，两个小时的放映时间已属非比寻常。而导演诺尔·艾丁·拉克马里花了很长时间想这个故事，很长时间润色这个故事。

影片开始，镜头定格在逃避警察追捕的两位主演身上，然后采用倒叙的手法解释出现如此一幕的原因。该影片主演之一是阿迪尔（奥马尔·卢特菲饰），他和母亲及暴力的继父生活在一起，梦想着有朝一日移居瑞典。第二位主流是卡里姆（阿纳斯·埃尔巴兹饰），他和法国一个年老的贵族女人产生了隐秘的恋情，他的家庭因为卡里姆生病的父亲而陷入困境。

这两个年轻小伙子通过小偷小摸挣得一些小钱，而其中一些会给地头蛇兹里海克，这是一个有着施虐狂的人，对他的小狗有着精神病般的热爱。

熟悉都市人生活方式及世态的卡里姆对于进一步和兹里海克纠缠警惕心很强，而阿迪尔却要继续犯罪以便花钱买到瑞典的假文件，他希望好朋友卡里姆能和他一起。当阿迪尔让卡里姆接受一份足以解决他们所有问题的工作时，麻烦来了。

这部电影在摩洛哥被视为耻辱，它提供了一种不同的方式看待臭名昭著的城市。就像诺尔·艾丁·拉克马里的平凡主角一样，无论是在发达国家还是发展中国家，人们都不愿意做仆人的工作，而在赤贫的国家，阶级分化尤其严重。甚至是卡里姆都宁愿继续贩卖违禁的香烟，而不愿为父亲曾经那为富不仁的雇主工作。

father's exploitative former employer.

The acting from **newcomer**s Lotfi and Elbaz is first-rate. Their chemistry is good and they easily walk that fine line of making audiences care about two characters with relatively flexible morals. Shot mostly at night, the film's color palette is predominantly seedy yellows and washed-out blues.

电影新人卢特菲和埃尔巴兹的演技一流。他们之间的化学反应非常奇妙，使得观众在观影过程中能够带着比较灵活的道德感来真正关心两位人物。因为电影主要拍摄时间是晚上，所以电影的主要色调是黄色和水洗蓝。

背景知识 PROFILE

摩洛哥电影节

提起摩洛哥电影大多数人可能都不太熟悉。但作为阿拉伯、非洲、欧洲三种文明交汇之地，它与众不同的文化底蕴和气质吸引了众多欧美电影人来此拍摄。为促进中摩电影文化交流，由中国国家广电总局电影局、摩洛哥国家电影中心及摩洛哥王国驻华大使馆主办，北京新影联院线、北京百老汇电影中心承办的"摩洛哥电影周"展映活动于2011年7月5日在北京百老汇电影中心拉开帷幕。

这次"摩洛哥电影周"带来4部不同类型的电影作品。从开幕影片《纳吉布的烦恼》到《罗拉的心愿》再从《黑房子》到《飞马》（《飞马》则讲述了一个发生在精神病院里的故事，着重探讨人物的内心）每部影片都会给观众带来独特的观影感受。作为摩洛哥近年来最受欢迎的喜剧片之一《纳吉布的烦恼》，它不仅讲述了一出通俗易懂的家庭闹剧，还在嬉笑之余让观众明白生活的哲理。

摩洛哥电影代表团在开幕式上介绍，由著名法国摩洛哥籍导演Nabil Ayouch执导的《罗拉的心愿》讲述了由女主角罗拉远赴埃及习舞的过程，不仅呈现了东西文

明的差异与交融，更勾勒出一幅寻求爱情与梦想的美好蓝图。而诺尔·艾丁·拉克马里执导的，获得2008年迪拜国际电影节最佳摄影奖的《黑房子》则用轻松俏皮的风格讲述了两位失业的摩洛哥青年的遭遇。

47 女性的声音——《沙漠之花》

Desert Flower, a well-made film that **depict**s the remarkable life of the model Waris Dirie, manages to be both a classic feel-good story and about as far from a feel-good story as you can get.

Ms. Dirie escaped an **impoverished** childhood in Somalia and, largely through **serendipity**, became a **sought-after** model. Eventually, in a magazine interview, she told of being forced to undergo ritual **female circumcision** as a young girl, a brutal process also known, more accurately, as female genital **mutilation**. She became a United Nations **spokeswoman** against the practice.

Liya Kebede, herself a model, gives a **credible** performance as Ms. Dirie, who fled her family at 13 to avoid a forced marriage and ended up in London. Sally Hawkins is a treat as the **salesclerk** who reluctantly befriends her there, and Timothy Spall provides his usual quirkiness as the **photographer** who discovers her scrubbing floors in a humble restaurant.

The film, based on Ms. Dirie's **memoir** of the same title, is heartening both for Ms. Dirie's **rise-and-overcome** tale and for the reminder that a helping hand from a stranger can still occasionally be found in this unkind world. But, of course, it's also disheartening because of what was done to Ms. Dirie, a moment revisited in a hard-to-watch flashback. The film makes bluntly clear that this is a trauma that lasts a lifetime.

Desert Flower is rated R (Under 17 requires

《沙漠之花》是一部制作精良的电影，讲述了名模华莉丝·迪里的传奇一生。本片既会让观众感觉到经典的魅力，又会感受到超乎经典的意义。

迪里女士通过机遇奇缘的运气逃离了家乡索马里的贫苦的童年，而后成为了一名倍受欢迎的模特。最后，在一次杂志采访中，她讲述了少年时被迫接受的妇女割礼。后来，她成了联合国反对女性割礼的代言人。

模特出身的莉亚·科贝德出演迪里女士。她演绎了迪里13岁为逃婚而出逃到伦敦。莎莉·霍金斯所饰演的售货员在伦敦较为不情愿地照顾了迪里，而蒂莫西·斯波则演绎了一个个性颇为怪异的摄影师，他在一个破餐馆里发现了擦洗地板的迪里。

本片基于迪里女士同名回忆录，影片的动人之处在于迪里女士的坎坷成名之路以及它提醒世人在这样缺少善良的世界上依然有雪中送炭存在。但是，也因为迪里所受的割礼而让人愤慨。该影片刻画了这一童年遭遇成了迪里一生的创伤。

《沙漠之花》因为其中的性爱

accompanying parent or adult guardian) for sexual situations and the scenes related to genital mutilation.

场面和女性割礼而被定为限制级，17岁以下的观众需要家长或成年人陪同。

背景知识 PROFILE

电影分级

电影分级制度的出现主要是为了青少年发展教育，以便区分其等级和适宜度。起到指导看片的作用。本次知识拓展让我们来看一下常规的电影分级：

G，代表general audience 无年龄限制；

PG，代表parental guidance suggested 家长指导级；

PG-13，代表parents strongly cautioned 特别辅导级，强烈建议家长监督，此级别可能不适合13岁以下未成年人观看；

R，代表restricted，限制级，包含成人内容，家长在带孩子看电影前一定要先查清楚这部电影讲什么；

NC-17，代表no one 17 and under admitted，17岁以下禁止观看。

48 生活的强者与伟大母爱——《永不遗忘的美丽/昨天》

Set against the **backdrop** of some beautiful but **isolated** South African Zululand, Yesterday is the story of a woman called Yesterday (Leleti Khumalo), so named by her father as he said that yesterday was always better than today. Yesterday lives a simple existence with her seven-year-old daughter Beauty (Lihle Mvelase) and her errant husband working underground in mines in **Johannesburg**. Yesterday rarely sees her husband and so she is basically left to **fend for herself** and Beauty in a village where there is no electricity, water is obtained after walking to the local well each day and where westernised medical aid is **unobtainable**.

Yesterday becomes ill and seeks help at a neighbouring village, walking with Beauty for over two hours to get there, but being too late is sent away to return the following week. This happens again until eventually Yesterday is seen by the doctor who in due course diagnoses HIV and urges Yesterday to find her husband as it is likely that he too has the virus. Yesterday is determined to stay alive until Beauty's first day of school the following year and then nurses her husband through his illness after he **reluctantly** returns home.

Yesterday is a moving and emotional journey as Yesterday deals with her **diagnosis**, her daughter's future and her husband's illness. After her diagnosis is revealed, Yesterday receives little support from the **tight-knit** village where she lives, once she was part of the community but now she is **ostracise**d, her only friend being a teacher she befriended on the road to the neighbouring village.

Never sinking into sentimentality or becoming a tool to preach regarding HIV issues, Yesterday is

《永不遗忘的美丽》发生在南非祖鲁兰一个遥远的村庄。影片讲述的是一个叫"昨天"（雷丽迪·辜马洛饰）的女人的故事。她之所以叫昨天是因为父亲认为昨天总比今天好。昨天与七岁的女儿美丽、行为不端的丈夫过着简单的生活。她丈夫在约翰内斯堡的矿井里做煤矿工人。昨天很少看见丈夫，独立与生活奋战。她和女儿住在一个没有电的村庄里，而生活用水要每天走路去当地的井内自取。西方的医疗服务是到不了那个村庄的。

后来，昨天生病了，她领着美丽步行两小时去附近的村庄寻求帮助，结果还是因为迟到了，而被迫回家只能下周再来。而后，昨天被一个诊断HIV的医生发现患有艾滋病，医生催促昨天去找丈夫，因为丈夫体内可能也有病毒。昨天下定决心一定要活到明年女儿美丽上学的那天。虽自己身患疾病，昨天仍然悉心照顾患病回家的丈夫。

影片之所以感人至深是因为这是一场昨天与病魔作斗争，为女儿的将来谋划，为丈夫的疾病操心劳苦的情感历程。当乡亲们得知她患艾滋病后，昨天并没有从他们那里得到支持，尽管她曾是这个社区的一员。可现在，她却受到了排斥，她唯一的朋友是邻村的一名教师。

《昨天》并未陷入多愁善感的老路或是成为关注艾滋问题的传道工具，它很简单，但非常真实。昨天对

simplistic but also brutally honest. Yesterday's love and devotion for her child is **paramount** as is her loyalty to her husband and it is these virtues that are central to the movie, combined with the visually dramatic and often harsh landscape. It is hard not to feel touched by Yesterday's story as she strives to deal with her life and it is a reality check that human emotions know no boundaries.

孩子的爱和奉献以及她对丈夫的忠诚是第一位的。正是艾滋病病毒是这部电影的中心，且融合了虚拟的艺术表现书法和艰苦的现实环境。当昨天和她的生活相抗争，她的故事就深深地感动了我们。其实，人类情感是无界的。

词汇 VOCABULARY

backdrop：背景	reluctantly：极不情愿地
isolated：偏僻的，少有人烟的	diagnosis：诊断
Johannesburg：约翰内斯堡	tight-knit：紧密相连的
fend for oneself：照顾自己，自谋生计	ostracize/se：（对人的）排除，排斥，不理睬
unobtainable：无法获得的	paramount：首要的，第一位的

背景知识 PROFILE

关于艾滋病

联合国艾滋病规划署（UNAIDS）

联合国艾滋病规划署（UNAIDS）于 1996 年初在华设立办事处，其主要职责是协调和提供支持，积极开展倡导和资源动员工作，以便资助并支持中国的艾滋病防治工作。

联合国艾滋病规划署的十个共同发起机构（联合国难民事务高级专员署、联合国儿童基金会、世界粮食计划署、联合国开发计划署、联合国人口基金、联合国毒品和犯罪问题办事处、国际劳工组织、联合国教科文组织、世界卫生组织和世界银行）都以各自的方式全面参与在华的有关艾滋病的活动。特别是世界卫生组织，联合国开发计划署和联合国儿童基金会已经与中国合作了许多项目，如监测、倡导和培训等。

在联合国驻华协调员的支持下，正式成立了联合国艾滋病中国专题组，专题组在华工作顺利。专题组不只局限于联合国在华机构，它鼓励政府、双边援助机构和非政府组织参与专题组的活动。专题组每两个月召开一次会议。

专题组的工作职责与联合国艾滋病规划署关注的重点是一样的，即加强国家应对艾滋病的能力，确保长期持续地采取行动应对艾滋病的流行。为实现这些目标，专题组的主要活动包括加强十个共同发起机构间的合作，采取一致行动，一起开展监测和评估；向国内有关机构提供技术支持，广泛宣传国际上的先进经验；促进中国领导对艾滋病工作的协调和监测；倡导政府进一步做出承诺，动员多部门参与，以及共同合作动员更多的资源投入。

专题组的工作具体由联合国艾滋病规划署驻华办事处国家协调员、办事处的官员及工作人员负责。联合国艾滋病规划署驻华办事处积极参与扩展艾滋病工作的伙伴网络，因为防治艾滋病需要各部门的参与，以及跨部门合作往往会遇到困难。联合国艾滋病规划署驻华办事处向在华开展艾滋病防治工作的伙伴提供技术、政策及管理方面的建议，主要是推广全世界上以往和现行的应对艾滋病流行的先进经验。

尽管联合国艾滋病规划署驻华办事处向中国的艾滋病防治工作提供支持，促进协调，但并不是替代中国政府的工作。相反，是中国政府负责艾滋病工作的全面协调工作，包括各级有关工作的协调，以及来自联合国及联合国艾滋病规划署等外界援助。

卫生部是指定的多部门协调单位，也是联合国艾滋病规划署驻华办事处的政府归口协调单位。国家成立了由各部门高层领导组成的多部门参与的国务院艾滋病防治工作委员会，委员会在国务院的领导下定期召开会议。委员会成员有卫生部、外交部、商务部、铁道部、公安部、国家教委、全国妇联等。委员会是联合国艾滋病中国专题组的国家对口单位。

世界艾滋病日

为提高人们对艾滋病的认识，世界卫生组织于1988年1月将每年的12月1日定为世界艾滋病日，号召世界各国和国际组织在这一天举办相关活动，宣传和普及预防艾滋病的知识，2009年世界艾滋病日的主题为："普遍可及和人权"。

2010年12月1日是第23个"世界艾滋病日"。主题为："正视艾滋，重视权益，点亮反歧视之光"。

49 女性的声音——《遮蔽的天空》

The Sheltering Sky is the kind of "art" film that **discriminating** audiences either embrace or find incredibly boring and pretentious. And, in the end, that seems to pretty much sum up most of Bernardo Bertolucci's movies.

Take them or leave them, The Conformist, Last Tango in Paris, 1900, Tragedy of a Ridiculous Man and even Bertolucci's most **accessible** picture, the Oscar-winning The Last Emperor, are not easy films. They

《遮蔽的天空》是那种有鉴赏力的观众爱不释手或觉得极无聊做作的电影；而这差不多概括了贝纳尔多·贝托鲁奇大多数影片的特点。

无论是哪种观众，对于贝托鲁奇的电影，如《同流者》、《巴黎最后的探戈》、《1900》、《荒谬人的悲剧》或是奥斯卡获奖作品《末代皇帝》都不会觉得它们简单无内容。这

are daring, risky ventures all, and the Italian writer-director seems to love rolling the dice.

Likewise, The Sheltering Sky is a **demanding** film. Based on Paul Bowles' 1949 novel, the film focuses on Kit Moresby (played by Debra Winger) and, to a lesser extent, her husband, Port (John Malkovich), who are remnants of the postwar idle rich. They consider themselves intellectuals, noting that they are "travelers", not "tourists". They are also rather **arrogant** in their romantic notions about North Africa and seem to be in the dry-rot final stages of a disintegrating marriage.

As the film opens, they **embark** on a voyage of self-discovery in Tangiers, in the company of their friend, George (Campbell Scott), who is not so secretly in love with Kit. As their trip becomes more of a trial, however, George abandons them.

Kit and Port explore North Africa in an attempt to understand the **exotic** and the forbidden, while becoming more **self-indulgent** along the way. Initially there seems to be a desire to save their marriage, but it becomes gradually less important the farther they get from the "civilized" world.

Eventually, a tragedy occurs — or is it? — plunging Kit into something akin to a state of shock as she links up with a wandering **tribe** and becomes a sex-slave of sorts.

Over the course of the film's nearly 2 1/2 hours, Bertolucci seems more interested in painting pretty pictures than telling a story, and there are long stretches when even the most patient **moviegoer**s will wonder if it's worth all the **vapid** dialogue spouted by vapid characters. True, the pictures are very pretty, and there are some intriguing ideas set up periodically.

It is no doubt quite difficult to portray self-indulgence without the work itself taking on an air of arrogance; and certainly The Sheltering Sky fails on that level, despite the impressive location

些影片充满了果敢、危险的冒险。这个意大利剧作家兼导演似乎喜欢玩转电影，呈现不同的侧面。

同样，《遮蔽的天空》是一部让人觉得吃力的电影。该影片根据保罗·鲍尔斯1949年的小说改编而成。影片女主角为姬特（德博拉·温格饰），其次是她的丈夫波特（约翰·马尔科维奇饰）。这对夫妇是战后无所事事的富人。他们视自己为知识分子，认为他们是"旅行者"，而非"游客"。他们对北非怀有浪漫的想法，他们的婚姻似乎处于崩溃的边缘。

电影一开场，二人在朋友乔治的陪伴下在丹吉尔开始了自我发现之旅。而乔治与姬特的恋情是一种公开的秘密。随着他们的旅行变成三人的旅行，然而，乔治却离开了他们。

一方面，姬特和波特在北非不断探索那些异域风情，那些被禁之事，而另一方面，二人愈加地自我放纵。旅程的开端好像有一种要挽救婚姻的以为，但随着他们越来越远离"文明的"世界，这种目的逐渐削弱。

最终，悲剧发生了——其实，这是否是出悲剧值得商榷——这使得姬特和一个流浪的部落相互纠缠，她甚至成了一种性的奴隶。

在全片两个半小时的时间里，贝托鲁奇似乎更喜欢描绘美丽的风景，而非讲述故事。即使是电影爱好者也会怀疑那些无聊的演员说的那些无聊的对白是否有价值。诚然，画面很美，有一些内在的有趣想法不时出现。

如果想要刻画自我放纵，毫无疑问，表现自负是必要条件。当然，《遮蔽的天空》在这点上可以说是

photography, a fine score by Ryuichi Sakamoto and an excellent lead performance by Debra Winger.

Some moviegoers will also no doubt be offended by the film's graphic sex scenes. The Sheltering Sky is rated R for quite a bit of sex and nudity, with some profanity and violence.

失败的，尽管地点的拍摄让人印象深刻。

一些观众可能会发现电影的性爱场面无法忍受。影片因为性、赤裸及一些亵渎的言语、暴力，而被定为限制级。

背景知识 PROFILE

重量级导演——贝纳多•贝托鲁奇简介

贝纳多·贝托鲁奇于1940年3月16日出生于意大利的帕尔马。早在24岁时，他便导演了轰动一时的影片《革命前夕（Before the Revolution）》(1964)，并因之而奠定了他的事业基础。

贝托鲁奇擅于把富有家庭气息的浪漫情节和内蕴的心理批判作为表现的核心，并结合一些政治、社会内涵，形成了他独特的创作风格。1968年，由他执导的影片《同伴Partner》就颇具当时兴起的新浪潮电影的特质。此后，他在影片中开始探索那些具有心理困惑的人物身上所折射出来的深厚魅力并在《蜘蛛的计划（The Spider's Stratagem）》(1970) 一片中首获成功。

1971年，贝托鲁奇导演了影片《同流者（The Conformist）》。在该中，他表达了跳舞是一种暗喻的创作主旨。两年后，在其导演的《巴黎的最后探戈（Last Tango in PARIS）》(1973) 中他又再度表露了这种创作思想。1977年，贝托鲁奇更是以大手笔制作了颇具史诗气息的《1990》。该片讲述了两个出生背景不同的男人在世纪交替的45年间的友情与斗争，并以此折射出了广阔的社会内容和尖锐复杂的阶级斗争，获得了评论界的交口称赞。不久，贝托鲁奇又拍摄了《Luan》(1979)一片，口碑不菲。

进入80年代，贝托鲁奇更是佳作迭出。先是1981年导演了《一个荒唐男人的悲剧 Tragedy of a Ridiculous Man》。1987 年，他更是推出了力作《末代皇帝（The Last

Emperor）》。该片获得了九项国际大奖，它无疑成了贝托鲁奇导演生涯中的一座重要里程碑。

92年之后，贝托鲁奇着手执导了一个三部曲《L'-esppit Edl'exil》(1992)、《De Domeinin Ditvoor-st》(1993)和《The True Life of Antonio》(1994)，并在1994年导演了影片《Little Buddha》，都有较好反响。贝托鲁奇总是喜好把一个简单的情节与相对不令人满意的戏剧性结局相结合并以此来阐述他的创作主旨。在1996年导演的新片《偷香（Stealing Beauty）》中，他精心构建了一位19岁美国少女孤身去意大利找寻生父的故事情节。影片透过抒情表象表达了包容性较大的思想内涵，倾倒了诸多影迷。

50 原生态下的欢乐——《上帝也疯狂1》

It's no wonder The Gods Must Be Crazy was a huge **hit** upon its **release** some 20 years ago, as the film contains enough elements to please the majority of audiences. The film is **jam-packed** with moments of **physical comedy**, romance, and even abrupt violence. It's a **bizarre** mix that nevertheless manages to entertain, primarily due to writer/director Jamie Uys' obvious **enthusiasm** for his material.

There's not a single storyline at work here, though the most famous (not to mention effective) remains Xi (N!xau) and his efforts to throw a seemingly **demonic** coke bottle off the edge of the world. The said bottle has brought his tribe nothing but bad luck, so he's taken it upon himself to **extricate** the item from their lives the only way he knows how. Meanwhile, romance is in the air for a **fetching** young teacher (Sandra Prinsloo) and a bumbling scientist (Marius Weyers). The third plot strand, involving an evil revolutionary, is easily the film's weakest—but does serve to unite the other two stories in the movie's last act.

The Gods Must Be Crazy works best during

《上帝也疯狂1》自20年前上映以来，受到了极大的欢迎。这也毫无疑问，片子中那些肢体戏剧，富于想象力的故事，甚至是突然出现的暴力场景，这些所有的元素都使观众满意。虽然片子中混合各种元素，让人感觉奇怪，但还是很使人开心，原因就在于作家兼导演珍妮丝·尤易斯对于故事素材的极大热情。

本片中不仅仅是单线故事，在其中一个故事中，最有名的角色是基（历苏饰），他曾经努力将一个魔鬼式的可乐瓶子丢出他们的世界。他说，瓶子除了给部落带来厄运无他，所以他竭尽心力，将这个东西从他们的生活中剔除，因为这是他知道的唯一办法。另外，一个迷人的年轻教师（莎拉·宾斯露饰）和一个笨手笨脚的科学家（加美·尤伊斯饰）之间又有着浪漫故事的元素。第三条线涉及到一个罪恶的革命，这是本片中最弱的部分，不过该部分在电影的最后将其他

the opening sequences, in which the film apes a documentary—complete with voice over from a stuffy British narrator. It's an intriguing way to introduce the various characters, and nicely sets the absurd tone that follows. The oddly named N!xau, who was actually a bushman when he was cast, proves to be a natural actor, winning us over with his charm and memorable facial expressions (and without speaking a single word of English!)

It's not hard to understand why the film was such a worldwide sensation, as it's entirely possible to watch the movie without understanding any of the dialogue. The Gods Must Be Crazy contains enough moments of physical comedy - along the lines of The Three Stooges or Abbott and Costello—to keep the majority of audiences semi-entertained. While there is no denying that the film is overlong by at least 20 minutes, primarily because of that needlessly violent subplot dealing with the villainous **rabble rouser**, the easy-going nature of the characters makes it easy enough to overlook such flaws.

两个故事联系起来。

影片以模仿纪录片的形式开始，效果不错，画外音是一个呆板的英国叙述者的声音。这是一种引入不同角色的有趣的方式，很好地奠定了整个片子荒诞的基调。历苏这个名字很奇怪，他本人是布西曼族，后来证明了他是一个天生的演员。通过迷人的、让人难以忘怀的面部表情，他赢得了观众的喜爱（他甚至无需说一个英文单词）。

观众完全可以在不理解对话的前提下观看影片，因此，影片也自然在全世界造成了轰动。《上帝也疯狂1》包含了很多肢体的戏剧——伴随着《活宝三人组》或《两傻双人秀》惹得观众发笑不止。尽管本片可以通过删减那些毫无意义的对付煽动暴民者的暴力的方式，至少将影片删去20分钟，但剧中人们随和的性格使观众很容易忽略掉这些不足。

词汇 VOCABULARY

hit：红极一时的人物或事物；成功	enthusiasm：热情
release：发行	demonic：魔鬼般的
jam-packed：塞满的，充满的	extricate：使免除纠缠或困难
physical comedy：肢体喜剧	fetching：迷人的
bizarre：怪诞的	rabble rouser：煽动暴民者

背景知识 PROFILE

《上帝也疯狂2》

这是非常好的一部反映非洲风情的电影。全片把四个互不相干的人物故事幽默自然地融合到一起，最终以喜剧的方式结局，让观众既从中领略到非洲土著居民的智慧和友善又委婉含蓄地向世人展现了那片古老原始的大地上充盈着的一种简单而乐观的人生哲学。

故事情节：奇哥的两个孩子不小心上错车，开始了他们为期不长的奇妙旅行。一路上他们和一堆象牙作伴，摘食树上的果实；也不小心掉入水箱，见到了他们这一辈子都没有见过的水。发觉两个孩子丢失了，土著人奇哥又一次踏上了征途。他上一次的旅途，是为了丢掉给家族带来无尽麻烦的可乐瓶子，而这一次，是为了寻回亲人。

动物学家和女博士驾驶着飞机不幸误入沙漠，于是也开始了他们艰险也尴尬的冒险。来自于大城市的女博士，一旦遇到危险就形如超人捷过猴猿；临危不惧的动物学家也开始了与蜜獾和蝎子的死磕⋯⋯

同样还有永远会出现的坏人——免费带两个孩子观光旅游的偷猎者先生，带着满车的象牙，去与传说中的老大接头；此外，在片中客串的，还有两个水火不容的军人，一路上忙忙碌碌追追赶赶打打杀杀⋯⋯

后来，来自于不同地方的三类人偶然碰头，寻亲的终于一家团圆，逃难的总算性命无忧，作恶的不免作茧自缚，让我们难忘的是其中令人开怀的故事、简单的讽刺、可爱的非洲小动物，还有两个孩子重逢的拥抱⋯⋯

两部《上帝也疯狂》，都有着两条主线：一条是纯朴善良的非洲好居民奇哥及其一家老小，一条是误打误撞闯入非洲的所谓文明人，包括好人与坏人。

于是前者因为外界"文明"的到来，而感到新奇、疑惑而质朴可爱，还有点小滑稽。就像是第一部电影里，奇哥跋涉千里，就是为了丢掉带给他们家族无尽麻烦的小小可乐瓶子。后者则因为突然闯入了陌生的"自然"，而显得惊慌、尴尬，乃至手足无措。就像是第二部的动物学家，遇见那只死缠烂打英勇无畏咬定鞋子不放嘴的蜜獾⋯⋯

当前者与后者相遇，两者尴尬相视，尴尬一笑，仿佛上帝善意的一个玩笑，但反衬出的是自然的"单纯"与文明的"莽撞"。

反思之处：本片依然可见导演延续着第一部的反思：如果人类当初是从非洲走出来的，当他们重新回归非洲时，表现出更多的却是惊恐、笨拙与手足无措；在那里，所有的行程安排都得听命于上帝的规划；文明人读取电脑里的信息，土著居民阅读沙上的新闻。

在物质时代，这样的影片自然引起我们的思索。人与人，人与自然如何和谐相处。

如果上帝真的存在，不知他是否会在天堂里静静俯瞰着自己创造的众生万物？包括那些叫作"人类"的子民。不知他是否会为他们的愚蠢、自私、贪婪与无知而频频皱眉、摇头叹息，又是否会为他们的善良、真挚、悔悟与思考而连连点头、暗自发笑？

其实，文明究竟该不该发展？由不由我们控制？它将走向何方？所有这些问题都是人类自身无法也无力解答的，那就调侃着推给上帝好了，让他和我们一起疯狂吧。

非洲横穿赤道，气候多种多样。既有开普敦迷人的地中海风光，也有喀土穆炎热少雨的热带景观……

非洲地质资源丰富，既有石油丰富的罗安达，又有磷酸盐储量大的卡萨布兰卡，还有"黄金之地"约翰内斯堡……

非洲西邻大西洋，东临印度洋，丰富的海岸线使得非洲城市旅游资源引人入胜。无论是科托努美丽的水村还是开普敦独特的海洋动植物景观，对于一个爱好自然、爱好旅游的人来说，都绝对是旅游簿上的首选。

非洲历来与中国友好，在2008年北京奥运会的火炬传递中，达累斯萨拉姆成为了非洲大路上唯一一个火炬经过的城市。

总之，非洲是一个神奇、复杂而有趣的地方。本章将通过非洲各种各样的城市，力图为你呈现一个既熟悉又陌生的非洲。

第六章

你不可不到的非洲城市

51 现在与过去的完美融合——开罗

Cairo, Egypt has always been attracting travelers, dating back over 10 centuries ago to the time of the Mamluks. However, the beautiful, **hectic**, crowded, surprising, **enchanting** (and every other cool sounding adjective) city of Cairo is still in the eyes of the Egyptians the City Victorious, known officially as al-Qahirah or simply "Masr", the name for Egypt as a whole. Cairo is one of the world's largest urban areas and offers many sites to visit. It is the administrative capital of Egypt and, close by, is almost every Egypt Pyramid, such as the Great Pyramids of Giza on the very edge of the city. There are also ancient temples, tombs, gorgeous Christian churches, magnificent Muslim monuments, and of course, the Egyptian **Antiquities** Museum all either within or nearby to the city.

As long as you're willing to loosen your senses and lose yourself to this majestic city, you can discover the sweetness of Cairo; the coziness of small cafes and the pleasure of **strolling** along narrow streets. It would be impossible to accurately describe Cairo fairly; it is truly one of a kind.

Cairo is an amazing city full of life and movement, and it is that way almost 24 hours a day, with the noisy honking of horns, children playing in the streets and **merchant**s selling their wears and services.

The city provides great culture; including art galleries and music halls, such as the Cairo Opera House, Sawy Culture Wheel, Ahmed Shawky Museum as well it should, being one of the largest cities in the world. It also provides accommodations fitting every budget from the grandest in the world, such as the Four Seasons and the Cairo Marriott to budget hotels and hostels.

When you're done with the sightseeing and

埃及首都开罗自1000多年以来一直吸引着众多游客。然而，这个美丽的、繁忙的、拥挤的、惊人的、迷人的（以及其他听起来很酷的形容词）城市开罗，在埃及人眼中仍然是City Victorious，官方名称是al-Qahirah或简单为Masr，即"埃及"。开罗是世界上最大的现代城市之一，旅游景点众多。它是埃及行政首都，几乎和每一座埃及金字塔相近，如吉萨大金字塔就在该城市边缘。城内或城附近还有古庙、坟墓、华美的基督教堂、辉煌的伊斯兰教纪念碑，当然还有埃及古博物馆。

只要你愿意放松放松筋骨，想要看看这个皇家城市，你会发现开罗的甜美：在小咖啡馆里闲坐的舒适，漫步在窄小街道上的乐趣。总之，很难准确地形容开罗，因为任何描述都只是一方面。

开罗是一个让人惊奇的城市，每天充满了生命力和活力。城市里有汽车鸣笛的声音，孩子在街上玩耍的声音，小商贩叫卖各种衣服和提供各种服务的声音。

作为世界上最大的城市之一，开罗文化气息浓郁，包括：艺术画廊，音乐厅，如开罗歌剧院、Sawy Culture Wheel、Ahmed Shawky博物馆。另外，开罗还有世界上最辉煌的旅店，如四季和万豪国际酒店，以及便宜实惠的旅馆

morning exhaustion, embrace Cairo's **incredible** selection of shopping, leisure and nightlife activities. Shopping ranges from the famous Khan el-Khalili souk, (or bazaar) largely unchanged since the 14th century, to modern air-conditioned centers displaying the latest fashions. All the **bounty** of the East can be here. Particularly good buys are spices, perfumes, gold, silver, carpets, brass and copper-ware, leather work, glass, ceramics and mashrabiya. Try some of the famous street markets, like Wekalat al-Balaq; for fabrics, including Egyptian cotton, the Tentmakers Bazaar; for appliqué-work, Mohammed Ali Street; for musical instruments and, although you probably won't want to buy, the Camel Market makes a fascinating trip. This is, and has been for over a thousand years, truly a shopper's **paradis**e.

Go for shisha (water pipe) in one of the old cafes on the street, you can try cool **flavor**s like apple, coconut or even Red Bull. Get yourself a nice meal of koshari for as little as 4 pounds, and eat like a true Egyptian. Have a nice Faluka ride down the Nile, and enjoy the cool **breeze** glancing at the different Felucca decorations.

In a city as lively as Cairo, with diversity, culture and good-hearted people who are always willing to help, you'll never run out of things to do.

和招待所。

如果你已经游览了那些景观名胜，你可以尽享埃及各种购物、娱乐以及夜间活动。你可以在自14世纪起就经久不变的著名的哈利利市场购物，也可以在展示各种最新时尚的现代空调大厦里猎奇。在这里，你可以买到所有东方的物品。尤其是那些倍受人欢迎的香料、香水、黄金、银币、挂毯、铜器、皮革制品、玻璃制品或瓷器。你还可以去那些Wekalat al-Balaq等著名的街边市场逛逛，或Tentmakers集市买埃及的棉花制品，或到Mohammed Ali街购买织品，或者到骆驼市场去看看乐器，不买也不影响这引人入胜的旅行。一千年以来这里一直是购物者的天堂。

另外，你还可以去街边老咖啡馆里抽水烟筒，品尝苹果、椰子等各种美妙的口味，甚至还有红牛。你可以像埃及人一样，花4磅吃上一顿美味的杂豆饭。你还可以乘着三角帆船泛舟尼罗河上，享受微风拂面，一瞥船上各色装饰。

在开罗这样一个异彩缤纷、文化丰富、人们热情好客的城市里，你将享受不尽。

词汇 VOCABULARY

hectic：忙碌的，繁忙的	incredible：难以置信的
enchanting：迷人的	bounty：礼品
antiquity：古董	paradise：天堂
stroll：漫步	flavor：口味
merchant：商人	breeze：微风

全球十大"不夜城"

据新华社电全球哪些城市的居民喜欢过夜生活，每天熬夜到很晚才睡？伦敦、纽约还是巴黎？

英国一项调查结果出乎人们的意料。调查结果显示，埃及首都开罗才是真正的"不夜城"。

位于英国伦敦的社交网站Badoo.com分析全球180个国家和地区1.22亿人的网络聊天数据，统计各地网友最喜欢在什么时间上网聊天以及聊天时长。

统计结果显示，埃及首都开罗的网友在半夜12点45分时仍然活跃。这一时间比英国首都伦敦网友的最活跃时间晚75分钟，比美国纽约网友晚更多，差距近三个小时。

排名第二的是乌拉圭首都蒙得维的亚，第三名为黎巴嫩首都贝鲁特。"不夜城"第四位到第九位被西班牙六个城市包揽。这六个城市分别为马拉加、萨拉戈萨、马德里、巴塞罗那、巴伦西亚和塞维利亚。阿根廷首都布宜诺斯艾利斯排名第十。

路透社27日引述Badoo.com市场部负责人劳埃德·普赖斯的话分析说："（2010年南非）世界杯西班牙球队夺冠，自那时起，西班牙人开始情绪高涨。他们（国家）的经济形势也比其他国家，比如希腊，好得多。"

普赖斯说，西班牙人对时间的观念不同，这也是造成他们喜欢晚上活动的原因之一。

一些以夜生活闻名的大城市，如美国纽约、英国伦敦等都没有进入排行榜前十位。美国纽约排在32位。

"有些人说，纽约变得缺少生气和困顿，调查也证实了这种说法，"普赖斯说，"调查显示，人们晚上可能不再像以前那么消费，不再有那么多的人出门、熬夜、聚会和饮酒。"

他说，调查显示，纽约人准备上床睡觉时，开罗人正准备出门，"他们喜欢充满活力"。

十大"不夜城" 排名顺序

1. 开罗（埃及）

2. 蒙得维的亚（乌拉圭）

3. 贝鲁特（黎巴嫩）

4. 马拉加（西班牙）

5. 萨拉戈萨（西班牙）

6. 马德里（西班牙）

7. 巴塞罗那（西班牙）

8. 巴伦西亚（西班牙）

9. 塞维利亚（西班牙）

10. 布宜诺斯艾利斯（阿根廷）

52 意想不到，惊喜连连——约翰内斯堡

"Err...so, where are the guys with the guns?" may be your first thought on arriving in Johannesburg. Whilst Johannesburg has a **fearsome reputation** and people like speaking about how many times they've been killed there, in reality it's not too frightening. For most people the closest sign of the **potential** violence are the bricked up walls hiding beautiful residential houses, with electric fences and **razor wire** above them and a sign indicating "armed response".

Johannesburg represents the spirit of South Africa, and in some ways a visit to the country is not complete without an introduction to the city. It is the capital of Gauteng province and the largest city in the country; and is endearingly known to locals as Joburg, Jozi or Egoli (place of Gold). Indeed, mine dumps are never far away, rubbing shoulders with the fruits of its labour—shiny modern **skyscraper**s **intermingle**d with 19th century architecture, Indian bazaars & African muti-shops (where traditional healers **dispense** advice & traditional medicine). Johannesburg is the largest city in the world not situated on a lake, navigable river or by the coast (the only reason that it was born because of gold). It is home to Africa's tallest building, the Carlton Centre.

Top 10 things to do in Johannesburg

1	Visit "Mrs Ples" and "Little Foot" (ancestors), at the Sterkfontein Caves at the Cradle of Humanity, Maropeng. Combine this with a visit to the Origins Centre at Wits University, where you can view exhibits of Khoisan and Rock Art that gives the **background** to the origin of humans.
2	Pet the lion **cub**s at the Rhino & Lion Park and visit the Elephant **Sanctuary** near the Hartebeespoort Dam.
3	Tour of Soweto (cycle, drive or walk), including seeing the Hector Petersen memorial and museum, sampling a grilled sheep's head, locally known as a "smiley", bungee jumping from the Orlando Towers and eating at Wandie's restaurant in Dube. The Hector Pieterson museum focuses solely on the 1976 Soweto uprising, when police opened fire on school children and killed many, including the 12-year-old Hector Petersen.
4	The Apartheid Museum which you enter through either the whites or the non-whites entrance. And pop by Constitution Hill, the site of the Old Fort Prison Complex, where Mahatma Gandhi and Nelson Mandela were detained.
5	View the city from the top of the Carlton Centre or via a Helicopter trip.
6	Gold Reef City amusement park, which is built on an old gold mine, with one of the rides dropping you from the top below ground level down into the shaft.
7	Shopping or theatre. Shopping at Rosebank Rooftop Market (open Sundays). Enjoying the drama at the People's theatre
8	Play a round of golf at Houghton Golf Club or break in your hiking boots at the Suikerbosrand Nature Reserve or Watch a game of rugby at Ellis Park or watch cricket at the Wanderers Cricket Ground or watch football at Soccer City, South Africa's largest stadium.

| 9 | Walk through the Walter Sisulu National Botanical Gardens on the West Rand. |
| 10 | Hot Air Ballooning at the Hartbeespoort Dam. |

"呃……那么，那些拿枪的家伙去哪儿了？"可能是到达约翰内斯堡以后的第一印象。尽管约翰内斯堡有着让人生畏的名声，人们喜欢谈论在这里他们多次遭受袭击，但实际上，约翰内斯堡并不恐怖。对于很多人来说，暴力隐患藏在那些人们触手可及的标志物上面，如美丽的民居被高墙遮挡，墙上带着电篱笆、铁丝网以及一个"武装保全"的标识。

约翰内斯堡代表了南非的精神，在某种程度上来说，去南非而不到约翰内斯堡是不完整的旅行。它是南非的首都，也是南非最大的城市。当地人亲切地叫约翰内斯堡为Joburg、Jozi或Egoli（黄金之地）。的确，矿井随处可见，人们可以看到辛勤劳动的工人，以及这些工人们的作品——那些熠熠发光的现代摩天大楼。这些大楼和19世纪的建筑、印度式的集市、非洲的多功能商店（传统的医疗师在这儿给人建议或是卖传统药物）融合在一起。约翰内斯堡并没有位于湖上、运河上或海岸边，它是世界上这种类型的最大城市（因为这里有黄金）。此外，约翰内斯堡还是非洲最高的建筑物卡尔顿中央办公大楼的所在地。

在约翰内斯堡不可不做的十件事

一、	在人们文明的摇篮斯泰克方丹山洞看"普莱斯夫人"和"小脚丫"（南非的祖先们）。另外，去维斯大学探访发源中心，在这里你可以欣赏到科伊桑人的展品以及各种石器工艺，这些将会让人更加了解人类的起源。
二、	去犀牛&狮子公园拍拍小狮子，去哈比斯普特水库附近的大象保护区看看。
三、	体验索韦托之旅（可骑车，自驾或徒步），包括饱览赫克托尔·彼得森纪念馆及博物馆，在烤羊头上取骨做样，从奥兰多塔上体验蹦极的无限刺激，在杜布旺迪的餐馆里大吃一顿。赫克托尔·彼得森纪念馆的展品仅限于1976年索韦托的起义，当时警察对学生开火，造成很多人死亡，其中也包括一个12岁名叫赫克托尔·彼得森的人。
四、	种族隔离博物馆之行。你可以通过白人通道或非白人通道进入馆内。或是去宪法山参观，这里是古代监狱的集中地，其中玛哈特玛·甘地和纳尔逊·曼德拉都曾被关押在此。
五、	在卡尔顿中央办公大楼顶端或乘直升机俯瞰整座城市。
六、	黄金城是个用成为废墟的黄金挖掘地改建成的主题公园，人们可以来此参观游玩。在这里可以到地下深处。
七、	购物或看戏。在玫瑰岸屋顶市场等地尽享购物的乐趣，在人民剧院等地享受戏剧的瑰丽。
八、	在霍顿高尔夫俱乐部打局高尔夫球，在自然生态保留区进行远足，在埃利斯公园球观看橄榄球比赛，在Wanderers板球场看场板球比赛，或是在南非最大的体育馆——足球城里看场足球赛。
九、	可以去西兰德沃特西苏鲁国家植物园走走。
十、	在哈特比斯普特水坝享受乘热气球的快乐。

词汇 VOCABULARY

fearsome：让人生畏的	intermingle：与……混合
reputation：名声，声誉	dispense：分发
potential：隐含的	background：背景
razor wire：铁丝网	cub：幼兽
shyscraper：摩天大楼	sanctuary：保护区

背景知识 PROFILE

南非主要大学一览表

开普敦大学（University of Cape Town）

金山大学（Wits University）

斯坦陵布什大学（Stellenbosch University）

比勒陀利亚大学（维斯特大学的玛洛迪校区并入）（University of Pretoria）

纳塔尔大学（University of Natal）

约翰内斯堡大学（由原兰德阿非利加大学、金山理工学院和维斯特大学的东兰德校区合并组成，2004年底挂牌）（University of Johannesburg）

自由州大学（University of the Free State）

祖鲁兰大学（University of Zululand）

西北大学（由波彻斯卓姆大学、原西北大学和维斯特大学的塞勃肯校区合并后组成，2004年底挂牌）（University of North West）

西开普大学（University of the Western Cape）

罗德斯大学（Rhodes University）

文达大学（University of Venda）

福特哈尔大学（罗德斯大学的东伦敦校区并入）（University of Furt Hare）

林波波大学（由原南非医科大学和北方大学合并组成）（University of Limpopo）

纳尔逊·曼德拉大学（Nelson Mandela Municipal University）

南非大学（由原南非大学、南非理工学院和维斯特大学伍德克校区合并组成，2004年初完成）（University of South Africa）

茨瓦尼科技大学（由原比勒陀利亚理工学院、北豪登理工学院和西北理工学院合并组成，2004年1月挂牌）（Tshwane University）

53 美丽的高原城市——内罗毕

Nairobi, city, capital of **Kenya**, in Nairobi District, situated at an elevation of about 1660 m (about 5450 ft) in the **highlands** of the southern part of the country. Nairobi is Kenya's principal economic, administrative, and cultural center and is one of the largest and fastest growing cities in Africa. **Manufactures** include processed food, **textiles**, clothing, building materials, and communications and transportation equipment. The city also has a large tourist industry. The University of Nairobi (1956), Kenya Polytechnic (1961), and Kenya Conservatoire of Music (1944) are here. Points of Interest Nairobi National Park, a large wild life preserve on the **outskirts** of the city, is a major tourist attraction. Other points of interest include the National Museum of Kenya, known for a display on early humans in Africa; the Parliament buildings; the law courts; City Hall; McMillan Memorial Library; the busy Municipal Market and nearby bazaar; the Kenya National Theatre; and Sorsbie Art Gallery. History Located in an area once frequented by the **pastoral** Masai, Nairobi was founded in the late 1890s as a British railroad camp on the Mombasa-to-Uganda railroad. From 1899 to 1905 it served as a British provincial capital. In 1905 the city became the capital of the British East Africa Protectorate (called Kenya **Colony** from 1920 to 1963). In 1963 Nairobi became the capital of independent Kenya and **annexed** neighboring areas for future growth.

肯尼亚的首都内罗毕位于肯尼亚中南部的高原地区，海拔约1660米，是全国政治、经济和文化的中心，同时也是非洲发展得最大和最快的城市之一。制造业包括食品类、纺织类、服装类、建筑材料类、交通运输设备类等。其旅游业也非常发达。内罗毕大学（1956）、肯尼亚理工学院（1961）、肯尼亚音乐艺术学院（1944）都坐落于此。其中一个名胜是位于城市郊区的大型野生动物保护区的内罗毕国家公园，它是内罗毕的一个主要旅游景区。其他的景点还包括以展示非洲早期人类文化而闻名的肯尼亚国家博物馆；议会大厦；法庭；市政厅；迈克米兰纪念图书馆；繁忙的市政证券市场以及周边的集市；肯尼亚国家大剧院及Sorsbie艺术画廊。内罗毕在19世纪90年代后期由蒙巴萨至乌干达铁路的英国铁道营发展起来，马赛族人经常在这里放牧。1899年至1905年间，内罗毕曾被设为英国的一个行省的省会。1905年内罗毕成为了英国东非洲保护区（在1920-1963年被称为肯尼亚殖民地）的首都。1963年，内罗毕成为独立后的肯尼亚的首都并且为了未来的发展，把其邻近地区也收入囊中。20世纪90年代期间，内罗毕发生了国内动乱，其原因是越来越多的民众反对当时

During the early1990s, Nairobi suffered from civil unrest because of the growing population opposition to Kenyan President Daniel Arap Moi.

的肯尼亚总统丹尼尔•阿拉普•莫伊的领导统治。

背景知识 PROFILE

内罗毕国家公园

内罗毕国家公园在内罗毕市中心以南8公里处，A104国道西侧，有一处120平方公里的热带草原和林地，这就是非洲第一个野生动物园-内罗毕国家公园。 内罗毕公园也是世界上唯一位于国家首都真正的野生动物园。它是开放的，动物来去自由。公园占地117平方公里，东、西、北三面用电网与城市隔离，南部为开放边界，是动物随季节迁徙的通道。

内罗毕公园相对比较小（但要转遍，开车也得一天工夫），公园内地形复杂，有好几条山脉和山谷。有河流、瀑布、湖泊、沼泽，还有5个动物舐盐区。总的来说，北面有小片林地，其余以草原为主。

公园有100多种哺乳动物和400多种特有的迁徙鸟类。园中主要动物有：羚羊、斑马、猎豹、金钱豹、长颈鹿、角马、河马、犀牛、狮子、野牛、猩猩、狒狒、鸵鸟、珍珠鸡等。大象是公园唯一没有的大型动物，据说主要原因是：大象对园中树叶消耗太大，易引起动物食物危机；大象凶猛，易对周围居民造成人身威胁。经常迁徙于公园内外的动物有：角马、斑马、长颈鹿、羚羊等，它们雨季迁徙出去，旱季迁回。动物的迁徙减少了对公园资源的压力。

为保护非洲大象，肯政府严禁象牙及象牙制品的贸易。1989年，莫伊总统亲自引火，在此公园焚烧了25吨象牙及狩猎战利品。为纪念这次著名的行动，公园内圈留了象牙焚烧地，并设立了纪念碑，使这里成为公园一个别有意义的观赏点。

内罗毕公园一共有7个门，正门在公园西北角。正门旁边是肯尼亚野生动物服务总部和1964年建立的动物孤儿园。每年有20多万人参观动物孤儿园。

动物孤儿院收留、治疗被遗弃的小动物和伤病动物，直至它们具备重返大自然的生存能力。

54 意想不到的消费最高的城市——罗安达

Luanda, the capital of oil-rich **Angola**, is the most expensive city in the world for **expatriate**s to live in while London is now cheaper than Rio de Janeiro, Hong Kong and Sydney, a survey has **reveale**d.

The southern African city won the **dubious accolade** in 2011, narrowly edging out Tokyo, which was followed in third place by the Chadian capital N'Djamena, Moscow and Geneva.

The survey of the cost of living in 214 cities was **compile**d by **human resources** firm Mercer which compares the prices of 200 everyday items around the world along with the strength of local currencies against the dollar. Governments and international companies use the **ranking**s to decide how much to pay their overseas workers.

Luanda tops a list increasingly **dominate**d by developing Asian and African economies which are expensive because of the short supply of accommodation, locally-produced goods and competing services such as taxis and mobile phone providers.

The Angola city has seen an **influx** of oil workers and executives since it became sub-Saharan Africa's second biggest oil producer after Nigeria.

But it was also the victim of a 27-year civil war destroyed much of its basic infrastructure, meaning that up to 90 per cent of its food is imported, along with cars and other manufactured goods.

That means that expatriates face paying up to £12 for a fast food meal, £2.46 for a litre of milk, £7.99 for a trip to the cinema and £4.99 for 100g of spaghetti. The most basic of hotels, those living there say, can cost

一项调查显示，安格拉首都罗安达这个石油丰富的城市对外国人来说是世界上消费最高的地方，而伦敦排在了里约热内卢、香港、悉尼之后。

这个位于非洲南部的城市2011年饱受争议地位居榜首，稍高于东京，其次是乍得首都恩贾梅纳、莫斯科和日内瓦。

该项在214个城市中进行的生活消费调查由世界上分布最广的人力资源管理咨询机构美世人力资源咨询公司着手完成，该调查比较了200件日常用品的价格，最后都按该国货币水平兑换成美元。各国政府和国际公司利用此项排名来决定为他们的海外员工发多少薪水。

越来越多的亚洲、非洲发展中国家的经济榜上有名。而消费水平之所以昂贵的原因在于住房短缺，当地物资短缺，以及出租车及手机制造商之间的激烈竞争。

自从成为撒哈拉沙漠以南非洲的仅次于尼日利亚的第二大石油出产国之后，大批石油工人和经理涌入安哥拉的罗安达。

而罗安达亦是27年内战的受害者，城内基础设施大多遭到毁坏。这意味着90%的食物需要进口，而汽车和其他制造业的商品也不例外。

这意味着外国人要付12磅吃顿快餐，2.46磅买升牛奶，7.99磅去趟影院，4.99磅吃顿100g的意大利面条。

around £250 a night and a 20-minute taxi journey can come in at £30.

Conversely, the plenitude of oil means they pay just £0.37 for a litre of unleaded petrol. Meanwhile, more than 60 percent of the Angolan population lives on less than £1.25 a day.

即便最简陋的旅馆每晚也要花费250磅，而20分钟的出租车路程要花30磅。

当然，因为石油的极大丰富，人们只需要花0.37磅就可以买到一升无铅石油。另外，60%以上的安哥拉居民每天的生活费只有1.25磅。

词汇 VOCABULARY

Angola：安哥拉	compile：编纂
expatriate：移居外国者，外派雇员	human resources：人力资源
reveal：显示，表明	ranking：排名
dubious：怀疑的	dominate：主导
accolade：嘉许	influx：大量涌入
conversely：相反地	

背景知识 PROFILE

2014年度世界十大消费最高城市

1. 新加坡，新加坡
2. 巴黎，法国
3. 奥斯陆，挪威
4. 苏黎世，瑞士
5. 悉尼，澳大利亚
6. 加拉加斯，委内瑞拉
7. 日内瓦，瑞士
8. 墨尔本，澳大利亚
9. 东京，日本
10. 哥本哈根，丹麦

55 有河流也炎热——喀土穆

Khartoum is the capital and largest city of **Sudan** and of Khartoum State. It is located at the **confluence** of the **White Nile** flowing north from Lake Victoria, and the **Blue Nile** flowing west from **Ethiopia**. The main Nile continues to flow north towards Egypt and the **Mediterranean Sea**. Khartoum derives from Arabic kart m meaning "end of an elephant's **trunk**", probably referring to the narrow strip of land **extend**ing between the Blue and White Niles.

Divided by the Niles, Khartoum is a tripartite **metropolis** with an estimated **overall** population of over five million people consisting of Khartoum proper, and linked by bridges to Khartoum North (al-Khart m Bahr) and Omdurman (Umm Durm n) to the west.

Khartoum features a hot **arid** climate, with only the months of July and August seeing significant **precipitation**. Khartoum averages a little over 155 millimetres (6.1 in) of precipitation per year. Based on annual mean temperatures, Khartoum is one of the hottest major cities in the world. Temperatures may exceed 53 °C (127 °F) in mid-summer.

After the signing of the historic Comprehensive Peace Agreement between the government of Sudan and the Sudan People's Liberation Movement (SPLA), the Government of Sudan has begun a massive development project. The biggest projects taking place right now in Khartoum are the Al-Mogran Development Project, two five-star hotels, a new airport, Mac Nimir Bridge (finished in October 2007) and the Tuti Bridge that links Khartoum to Tuti Island.

Khartoum has a **thriving** economy. In recent years Khartoum has seen significant development, driven by Sudan's oil wealth. The center of the city is well-planned, with tree-lined streets.

喀土穆是苏丹的首府，喀土穆州最大的城市。它位于发源于埃塞俄比亚向西流的青尼罗河及发源于维多利亚湖向北流的白尼罗河的交汇处。尼罗河主干向北流向埃及和地中海。喀土穆原意起源于阿拉伯单词kartūm，意为"大象鼻子的末端"，这很可能是因为青、白尼罗河在喀土穆交汇向北流去，颇似大象鼻子。

因为青、白尼罗河流经喀土穆，所以喀土穆的地形分三块，它是一个大都市，人口过500万。通过众多桥梁，喀土穆和西部的北喀土穆、乌姆杜尔曼相连。

喀土穆气候炎热、干燥，只有七八月份降雨丰沛。该城市每年平均降雨155毫米。根据每年平均气温，喀土穆是世界上最热的地区之一。盛夏的温度可能超过53°C。

自苏丹政府和苏丹人民解放运动签订具有历史意义的《全面和平协议》之后，苏丹政府开始推行大规模的发展规划。目前在喀土穆内开展的是Al-Mogran发展计划，两座五星级酒店，一个新的飞机场，Mac Nimir 桥（2007年已竣工）和Tuti桥（连接喀土穆和Tuti岛）。

喀土穆经济发展迅速。近年来，喀土穆因为苏丹丰富的石油储量，发生翻天覆地的变化。市中心

The largest museum in Khartoum, and indeed all of Sudan, is the National Museum of Sudan. Founded in 1971, it contains works from different epochs of Sudanese history. Among the exhibits are two Egyptian temples of Buhen and Semna which were originally built by Queen Hatshepsut and Pharaoh Tuthmosis III respectively but relocated to Khartoum upon the flooding of Lake Nasser.

Another museum in Khartoum is the Palace Museum, located **adjacent** to the historical Presidential Palace on Blue Nile Street.

Khartoum is home to a small botanical garden, in the Mogran district of the city.

规划良好，树木林立。

喀土穆最大的博物馆是苏丹国家博物馆，这也是苏丹最大的博物馆。它成立于1971年，内藏有苏丹史上不同历史时期的作品。其中，有埃及布亨庙和塞姆纳庙，两座庙宇分别最早由哈特舍普苏特皇后和法老图特摩西斯三世建造，曾因为纳塞尔湖洪水而迁至喀土穆。

喀土穆另一座博物馆为故宫博物馆，毗邻青尼罗河街古迹总统府。

喀土穆内还有一座小的植物园，其位于该城市的Mogran区。

背景知识 PROFILE

奇特的世界旱城

"旱城"是指年降水量不足250毫米，或连续几十、上百天不下雨的干旱城区。那里，植物难以生存，生活条件严酷。然而不少世界名城却建在这种"绝地"上。

开罗——一年下雨不到10天

埃及首都开罗是阿拉伯地区的最大城市，人口1000多万，但年降水量仅26毫米，是世界最干旱的首都。它一年下雨不到10天，灰尘常年蒙罩在植物和建筑物上，城市一派土黄色，天空灰蒙蒙的，是座"蒙尘之城"。

奇怪的是，如此旱都的喝水、用水却充足。原来是尼罗河养育着这座旱城。全城建在四个河心岛和河两岸的平原上，"近水楼台先得月"，人们尽情享受着尼罗河的淡水。

伊基克——14年滴雨不下

伊基克是智利北部最大海港，年平均降水量2.1毫米，历史上曾经有14年滴雨不下的纪录。这里是茫茫大漠，热气逼人，偶尔能在海滨见到稀疏的地衣和仙人掌。这一点点降水量，只能沾湿毛巾，怎能养活9万市民？原来，没有淡水，人们就从100公里外的安第斯山脉引来雪水；没有粮食、蔬菜、水果，就从南方调来或从国外进口。

利马——不出售雨具

秘鲁首都利马，年降水量29毫米。全城人口400多万，商店几万家，天下商品无所不有，唯独不见雨伞、雨衣、雨鞋之类的雨具。市民都不知雨具是什么东西。这里的房屋无雨檐，一般街巷都不建地下水道，因为污水向地上一泼立即渗透、蒸发掉了。

利马虽旱，但气候宜人。夏季气温一般在21-27摄氏度，冬季为16-18摄氏度。号称"雨季"的6月~9月，降水以浓雾形成的露珠飘落下来，万绿挂"水晶"，煞是好看。正因为如此，这里气候不干不热，四季如春。

喀土穆——跳到河中避暑

苏丹首都喀土穆号称世界火炉，年平均气温29.2摄氏度，绝对最高温度47.8摄氏度，中午多在40摄氏度上下。若将鸡蛋埋在沙里，一小时便煮熟可吃。这里全年的降水量只有161毫米。沙漠干热尘暴刮起来时，昏天黑地，沙粒可将汽车打成"麻子"。

280万市民对付旱热自有办法。人们清晨和上午连续上班。下午放假，妇女躲在荫凉处，男人泡在尼罗河中。当不少人被炎热折磨得昏昏欲倒时，特种饮料"苏丹红"加上糖和冰块，一杯下肚，顿时精神抖擞。

56 中坦友谊地久天长——达累斯萨拉姆

The Olympic Torch is **schedule**d to relay in mid-April next year through Dar es Salaam, the only city on the African **continent**, before reaching Beijing for the 2008 **Olympic Summer Games**.

The **torch relay** schedule for Dar es Salaam was announced on Friday by the Chinese **Embassy** along with the Tanzanian Ministry for Information, Culture and Sports and the **City Council** of the Dar es Salaam.

"No one should be surprised by the choice of Dar es Salaam as the only city in Africa to host the Olympic Flame during the Torch Relay," said Chinese Ambassador Yu Qingtai at the conference to **announce** the scheduled relay to the Tanzanian city.

"The United Republic of Tanzania has a solid track record of being a country of peace, **harmony** and progress. The people of Tanzania are well known for their friendliness and **hospitality**. The country is blessed with an outstanding leadership which is widely recognized for its devotion to achieving economic and social development," added the ambassador.

Tanzanian Information, Culture and Sports Minister Muhamed Seif Khatib said at the occasion that the Tanzanian people had witnessed another good event of extended relationship and **brotherhood** expressed by the Chinese people by selecting Dar es Salaam to host the Olympic Torch.

"The arrival of the Olympic Torch in our city will foster sports development and it is a motivation to our young people to participate in sports and eventually to become Olympians," said the minister.

The city mayor of Dar es Salaam, Adam Kimbisa, added that city dwellers were greatly honored to host the Olympic Torch in Africa.

达累斯萨拉姆是到2008年北京奥运会前,非洲大陆上唯一一个圣火经过的城市。

达累斯萨拉姆的火炬传递日程由中国大使馆,坦桑尼亚信息、文化、体育部以及达累斯萨拉姆市议会共同宣布。

"在奥运火炬传递过程中,无人会对达累斯萨拉姆成为唯一一个传递圣火的非洲城市这一事实表示惊讶,"中国大使于庆泰在新闻发布会上说。

"坦桑尼亚联合共和国素来是和平、友好、进步之邦。坦桑尼亚人以友好、好客著称。长期以来,这个国家的领导力强,且因致力于经济和社会发展而得到广泛认可",大使补充说。

坦桑尼亚信息、文化、体育部部长卡提布在这一会议上说,坦桑尼亚人感受到了中国人们的友谊和兄弟情谊,因为中国选择了达累斯萨拉姆作为奥运会火炬传递城市。

"奥运火炬的到来将促进这个城市的发展,对于年轻人来说,这会激励他们积极参加体育运动,而后成为运动健将,"该部长说。

"很荣幸,达累斯萨拉姆将成为非洲唯一一个奥运会火炬传递城市,"达累斯萨拉姆市的市长说。

根据既定的奥运火炬路线,奥运火炬从南美阿根廷的布宜诺斯

"It is a great honor that Dar es Salaam will be the only African city to host the Olympic Torch," said the mayor.

According to the scheduled torch relay program announced in Beijing late on Thursday, the Olympic Torch arrive in Dar es Salaam from **Buenos Aires** of Argentina in South America and will leave the Tanzanian city for Muscat of Oman to continue its relay before ending up in Beijing on August 8, 2008.

The torch relay is scheduled to start on April 1 of 2008 and to last 130 days in all, making it the longest Olympic Torch Relay in history.

Brief Introduction to Dar es Salaam

Dar es Salaam (**Haven** of Peace in Arabic) was founded in 1862 by Sultan Seyyid Majid of Zanzibar on the site of the village of Mzizima. Mzizima's history dates back to the time when the Barawa people started to settle and cultivate the area around Mbwa Maji, Magogoni, Mjimwema, Gezaulole and Kibonde Maji Mbagara.

Present day Dar es Salaam's origins have been influenced by myriad of Sultans, the Germans and the British. The city started as a fishing village in the mid 19th century, is now Tanzania's largest city, and has become one of East Africa's most important ports and trading centers.

With its great atmosphere, mix of African, Muslim, and South Asian influences, picturesque harbour, beaches, chaotic markets, and historical buildings, it is well worth extending your stay beyond the time between flights.

Dar es Salaam is Tanzania's financial and political hub despite having lost its status as official capital to Dodoma in 1973.

艾利斯转至达累斯萨拉姆，而后到阿曼首都马斯喀特。圣火传递将一直持续到2008年8月8日。

在达累斯萨拉姆，奥运火炬从2008年4月1日起传递，总共持续130天，这是奥运史上最长的奥运火炬传递路线。

达累斯萨拉姆简介

达累斯萨拉姆（阿拉伯语"和平之地"）成立于1862年。

如今，达累斯萨拉姆的起源受到了苏丹人、德国人及英国人的影响。19世纪中叶，该城市从一个渔村发展而来，是目前坦桑尼亚最大的城市。它亦是东非最重要的港口及贸易中心之一。

达累斯萨拉姆环境宜人，受非洲、穆斯林、南亚文化的影响，还拥有风景如画港口、海滩，此外还有热闹的集市及历史建筑，所以到此一游非常值得。

尽管1973年坦桑尼亚议会决定把首都迁往内地城镇多多马，但是达累斯萨拉姆仍然是坦桑尼亚的金融和政治中心。

schedule：将某事列入进度表	announce：宣布
continent：大陆	harmony：和谐
Olympic Summer Games：夏季奥运会	hospitality：好客
torch relay：火炬传递	brotherhood：兄弟情谊
embassy：大使馆	Buenos Aires：布宜诺斯艾利斯
city council：市议会	haven：安全的地方，憩息处，避难所

57 美丽的海滩城市——开普敦

Cape Town's beautiful **coastline** extends for 307 km along the West Coast, around the Cape **Peninsula**, and beyond False **Bay** to the Kogelberg coast in the east. The combination of the warm Agulhas current that sweeps down the east coast, and the cold Benguela current that flows up the west coast, results in an incredibly rich and varied marine **flora** and **fauna**.

Its mild Mediterranean climate allows residents and visitors to enjoy the beautiful coastline all year round. While winter brings cold and wet weather, there is always a break in the rain long enough for a **brisk** walk on the beach, and surfers love the large swells generated by winter's northwesterly winds.

In spring and summer, warm and sunny weather returns, but is accompanied by the prevailing southeasterly wind—popularly known as the "Cape doctor", as it blows the city's air pollution away. The southeaster flattens the **swell**, but whips up **white horses** further out to sea, and may give beachgoers a sandblasting if they do not find a sheltered spot. Fortunately, many of the beaches along the

开普敦美丽的海岸线一直沿西海岸延伸307千米，然后绕过开普半岛，越过科斯海湾，向东一直到Kogelberg海岸。厄加勒斯暖流和本格拉寒流在此交汇，造就了开普敦地区丰富且多样的海洋动植物群。

开普敦地区是温暖的地中海气候，居民们和游客们可以终年在美丽的海岸线上休憩。虽然冬季会带来寒冷和湿润的气候，但雨水总会出现短暂的间歇，使得人们可以沙滩漫步，而冲浪爱好者则非常喜欢冬季西北风带来的波浪起伏。

在春夏，温暖和煦的天气回归开普敦，同时也伴随着强劲的东南风——当地人都将这股强风称为"开普医生"，因为这股风将清新的空气带到当地，并把空气中的污染物吹走。东南风使得近海海面平静，远海白浪滔天。此时，如果去沙滩的人们没有找到一个遮蔽的地方，将忍受风沙的侵袭。幸运的是，很多位大西洋

Atlantic Seaboard lie in the **lee** of Table Mountain, and are well-protected from the wind. Clifton, in particular, is recognised as a **fail-safe** option when the southeaster blows and discourages people from the city's other beaches.

It is also the southeaster that is responsible for the marked difference in sea temperature between False Bay and the coastal waters west of Cape Point. Indeed, the West Coast and Atlantic Seaboard are often referred to simply as "the cold side", and only the **hardy** can withstand more than a quick dip in the sea without a wetsuit.

The southeaster, which reaches galeforce at times, pushes and pulls the surface layer of seawater along with it. In False Bay, this has the effect of piling warm water up along the coast, so summer water temperatures generally stay within the 16ºC -22ºC range. West of Cape Point, the southeaster pushes surface water in a northerly direction, but it is deflected offshore due to the earth's rotation to the east. Cold water from the dark depths of the ocean rises up to replace it in a process known as upwelling, so sea temperatures typically **hover** in the 10ºC -15ºC range.

岸边的海滩在平顶山的背风处，因此很好地躲避了这股风。当东南风吹起，人们不便去开普敦其他海滩的时候，克立夫顿将会成为很好的去处。

也正是这股东南风造成了科斯海湾和开普角西岸海水之间明显的海水温度变化。实际上，西海岸和大西洋岸通常被称作"冷岸"，只有那些非常强壮且耐寒的人们才能够在不穿防寒泳衣的情况下下水一游。

这股东南风有时可达到大风的力度，它来回推动着海水表层。在科斯海湾，东南风使得表层海水温暖，夏季水温可达16ºC ~22ºC。而开普角西岸，东南风会将表面海水吹向北，可由于地球自西向东运转，东南风发生了偏向。冷海水从海洋深层来到表层，所以海水温度一般为10ºC ~15ºC。

词汇 VOCABULARY

coastline：海岸线	swell：海浪
peninsula：半岛	white horses：白浪
bay：海湾	lee：背风处
flora：植物群	fail-safe：安全的
fauna：动物群	hardy：强壮的，坚强的，能吃苦耐劳的
brisk：轻快的；兴隆的；寒冷而清新的	hover：盘旋，徘徊

热闹的开普敦

在开普敦很容易就能找到人声鼎沸的地方，因为每周都有各类文化体育活动。

在开普敦举办的两大洋马拉松节和开普敦自行车赛都吸引了成千上万的游客，而开普敦也从中获利颇丰，还拉动了当地的就业，许多商人也趁着参加活动察看了当地市场。

场馆方面，开普敦已有可容纳51 900人的纽兰兹橄榄球体育馆，1995年的橄榄球世界杯曾在这里举行。还有撒哈拉公园纽兰兹板球馆，也可容纳25 000人，那是2003年板球世界杯和刚刚过去的印度板球超级联赛的比赛场地。

大海也是开普敦的天然活动场地。比如世界第二大的冲浪比赛"非洲狂浪"就是在这里的Hout湾举行。在海湾入口处的暗礁区域有冲浪爱好者们最爱的高度足，驾驭性高的海浪。

如果巴黎伦敦时装周的东西已经看腻，开普敦时装周或许能给你不同的感觉。作为国际知名时装周之一，开普敦时装周却坚持呈现更多的本地设计师作品，服装也多由本地模特展示。开普敦人热衷社交聚会，节日是他们的生活，公共及私人派对全年无休。最著名的新年游行，起源于19世纪末，又称小丑嘉年华，是为纪念废除奴隶制。市郊各社区数十万居民化妆成小丑或怪兽在市中心游行，元月二日达到高潮。二月的J&B MET赛马节已有25年历史，同样是开普敦旅游指南推荐的盛事。慈善公益和体赛事都是城市的节日。

58 赤道附近的明珠——科托努

While the total population of **Bénin** is about 6 million peoples, well one million persons are living in Cotonou. As everywhere it pulls the people also here into the large cities, because they expect there better living conditions.

Cotonou lies on the map at 06º20.699' N, 02º16.050' E, and almost on the equator. It is narrow, restricted by a **lagoon** in the north, and the ocean in the south, and can thus only expand to the east and west. The centre is divided by the lagoon's **outlet** to the sea, and joined by two bridges: the Nouveau Pont and the Ancien Pont.

贝宁总人口600万，居然有100万居住在科托努。像世界其他的地方一样，人们来到大城市，以便更好地生活。

科托努位于北纬06º20.699'，东经02º16.050'，非常接近赤道。它是狭长状的城市，北面是泄湖，南临海洋，所以只能向东西方向延展。城市被泄湖一分为二，有两座桥相连彼此：新桥和旧桥。而正在

A third bridge is being built **parallel** to the Ancien Pont to carry motorway traffic from the east and from Nigeria directly into the city! The bridge itself was completed by the builders Diwidag in December 2003, the connecting roads are not yet completed.

A huge amount of construction work is being done in Cotonou, periodically cement cannot be found anywhere in the city. For fear of **inflation**—the last **devaluation** of 50% was on 13th Jan 1994—nobody keeps more ready money than necessary. Instead, one starts a building project, and adds another part whenever money becomes available.

The most **salient** buildings are the 2 multistoried buildings close to the "Marché Dantokpa", one belongs to a marketing lady, the other the Ecobank. Another is that of the catholic church "Notre Dame des Apôtres" close to the Ancien Pont. The church even, is by the way one of the most terrible of modern buildings in the city. Still about 80% of the buildings are one-story, therefore also the huge surface size of the city.

Similarly as in Switzerland (Zurich—Berne), Porto Novo is the capital of Bénin, while Cotonou is considered as the industrial capital. The **parliament**, most of the Ministries and all diplomatic representations reside in Cotonou.

Compared with other cities of West Africa, Cotonou is small. What makes Cotonou the secret capital of Bénin is the airport, the port and the **pulsating** life. Not to be overseen in Cotonou are the many motorbike taxis, called in the language Fon "Zemidjan" (speak Semidjan, in english "take me with you") or "Kêkênon".

A sign with the hand is sufficient and one is driven to any place. It's preferably to discuss the price in advance of driving; otherwise it can become very expensive. In the city you pay between 100 **FCFA** (short distance) up to approximately 300 FCFA, depending upon distance. Also abstruse luggage, like a goat or 12m long iron staffs (construction steel), may be taken. Everything that is possible will be transported.

建设中的第三座桥与旧桥并行，是为了承载由东而来的机动车交通以及实现从尼日利亚直接进城。桥本身已于2003年建好，但相连的公路仍在施工当中。

科托努内大量施工，水泥随处可见。处于对通货膨胀的恐惧——1994年货币贬值50%——人们不再舍得花钱。人们开始修建工程。如果当时钱不够，就先建一部分，等闲钱到位，再继续建。

城内最显著的两座建筑有多层高，距Dantokpa集市很近，其中一座的主人是一个从事营销工作的女士，另外一座是贝宁经济银行的。另外还有一座天主教堂"使徒圣母院"，离旧桥很近。其实，该座教堂是一座并不漂亮的现代建筑物。城内大多数建筑都仅有一层，因此占地面积大。

就像瑞士的首都是伯尔尼（尽管苏黎世是瑞士最大的城市），波多诺伏才是贝宁的首都，虽然科托努是重要的工业中心。议会以及大多数的部委和所有的外交机构都设在科托努。

与其他西非的城市，如拉各斯等相比，科托努很小。但它之所以是贝宁的秘密首都是因为科托努拥有机场，港口及节奏感强的生活。科托努常见的交通工具是摩托出租车。

你只需打个手势，司机就会把你拉到地方。在开车之前，你最好先讲好价钱，省得被敲竹杠。根据车程的远近，车费一般在100非洲法郎和300非洲法郎之间。乘车期间可以携带重物，如一只羊或者12米长的铁杖。所有的东西都能搭载。

Bénin：贝宁	devaluation：货币贬值
lagoon：泻湖	salient：显著的，显要的
outlet：出水口，排水口	parliament：议会
parallel：平行的	pulsating：快节奏的，极为兴奋的
inflation：通货膨胀	FCFA：非洲法郎

背景知识 PROFILE

非洲威尼斯

贝宁有30多个水上村，其中冈维埃水上村最大。该水上村坐落在科托努市北面与大西洋相连的天然泻湖诺库埃(NOKOUE)湖面上，距科托努市约25公里，其中陆路17公里(乘车约35分钟)，水路8公里(乘机动船约15分钟)，是目前非洲保存最完整的水上居民区，有"非洲威尼斯"之美称。

水上村始建于十八世纪初。当时的贝宁境内诸王并立，酋长争雄，战乱频繁。为躲避战祸，一些难民流落到诺库埃湖地区，他们用木桩在湖底打樯，在湖面上搭建草房栖身，以后逐渐形成了今日规模的水上村庄。战乱年代，冈维埃村以其优越的地理条件，成为居民们良好的避难所。"冈维埃"是当地阿贾族语，意为"得救的地方"。

水上村东西长5.5公里，南北宽4.25公里，村内有居民2.5万，房屋1.95万间。村内主要水路有两条，一为"情人街"，一为"渔夫街"，独木舟穿梭其间，或运物、或经商、或游览。湖水中，高脚茅屋、水葫芦、船和人相互交织，相映成趣。村中有商店、学校、教堂、卫生所、邮电所、集中供水点、水上市场、旅馆、文化中心和公墓等，与陆地生活几乎无异。

村民以捕鱼为生，除撒网、钓钓外，主要采用一种名为"阿卡夹"的方式捕鱼：将树桩、枝杈密集插入湖中，造成一个适于鱼群生长的小环境，鲫鱼、上尉鱼等幼鱼自然进入，八个月后便可围网捕鱼。泛舟于湖上，展现在眼前的是一幅赏心悦目的非洲风情画。

59 非洲最小的首都——班珠尔

Banjul is the capital of **Gambia**, West Africa (former name Bathurst), as well as the administrative city of the country & seat of government. The capital resort is one of the smallest cities in Africa, and is situated on an island at the mouth of the Gambia River called St. Mary's Island. The small port city has a sleepy **ambience reminiscent** of a large village. (Geographical co-ordinates 13°27'N, 16°33'W).

Places to See:

While in Banjul look out for the War Memorial & Fountain, near MacCarthy Square, erected to **commemorate** the coronation of Britain's King George VI in 1937. MacCarthy Square has a colonial atmosphere, with pleasant 19th-century architecture. There is also a children's playground with a modern play area.

Another place well worth looking at is the African Heritage Centre displaying and selling objects of art from all round the Gambia.

The **skyline** of Banjul is also graced by the twin minarets of the King Fahad **Mosque** and the State House, built by the Portuguese.

Other places worth visiting are the National Museum of the Gambia. The Museum is located around half way down Independence Drive.

Another place on Independence Drive is the July 22 Arch. Standing high at 35m it offers great views over the city and coastal areas. The Arch was built to commemorate the July 22 1994 bloodless coup when a young army officer Yahya Jammeh took control of the country ousting President Jawara.

Whenever you have had enough of the hustle and bustle local, you can get a **pirogue**s (skinny wooden boats with an outboard motor) **ferry** on the quiet

班珠尔是西非冈比亚的首都（曾用名巴瑟斯特），同时也是国家和政府的行政中心。班珠尔是非洲国家首都中最小的旅游景点。班珠尔位于圣玛丽岛（或班珠尔岛），冈比亚河在此汇入大西洋。班珠尔的地理绝对位置是北纬13°28'，西经16°36'。班珠尔与其说是首都，更像是一个大型乡村，在这里可以享受度假的悠闲。

可游览的地区：

游客们可以去看在麦卡锡广场上的战争纪念碑和喷泉，此地是为了纪念1937年英国国王乔治六世在此加冕。麦卡锡广场有着一种殖民的氛围，广场上19世纪的建筑让人赏心悦目。另外，这还有一个儿童游乐场，有着现代的游乐设施。

另外，还可以去看非洲遗址中心，这里展出冈比亚境内所有的艺术品，且供出售。

因为法赫德国王墓和议会大厦的存在，班珠尔这个城市的轮廓非常漂亮。

或者游客可以去冈比亚国家博物馆。该博物馆坐落于独立路上。或者去看独立路上的7月22日门。这个门高35米，在上面可以很好的俯瞰城市和海岸区域。门的修建是为了纪念1994年7月22日的那场不流血的政变。当时，一名年轻军官取代总统掌握了国家政权。

waterways of Oyster Creek, the main waterway separating Banjul island and the mainland. The creek is a popular destination for bird-watchers, anglers and anyone keen to just laze around on a boat. The dense **mangrove**s are particularly interesting and home to a variety of fish and other wildlife. For those wishing to cross over the estuary to Barra Point you need to get to the Banjul Ferry Terminal.

如果你看厌了城市的热闹与喧嚣，你可以乘坐独木舟泛舟于宁静的牡蛎小溪。这个小溪汇聚了很多鸟类爱好者和那些喜欢闲适的游客。茂密的红树林也非常有趣，这里是各种鱼类和其他野生生物的家园。如果有游客想要越过溪口到Barra Point，游客需要到班珠尔渡船中转站。

词汇 VOCABULARY

Gambia：冈比亚	mosque：清真寺
ambience：环境，气氛	thoroughfare：大道，大街，通衢
reminiscent：回忆的，话旧的	pirogue：独木舟
commemorate：纪念	ferry：n. 渡船；vt. 渡运
skyline：地平线，以天空为背景的轮廓	mangrove：红树属植物

背景知识 PROFILE

福布斯评出的八个会消失的城市

San Francisco(旧金山)，地震

加利福尼亚大学(University of California)的研究称在2086年之前，San Francisco 有75%的可能遭遇一场7级以上的大地震。

Detroit(底特律)，人口缩减

据报道，从1950年至今底特律的登记人口减少了约1/3，预计未来该市的人口会持续减少，直到2100年完全消失。

Ivanovo(伊凡诺沃)，人口缩减

这个前苏联的纺织中心，拥有大约44.8万的人口。自从1990年开始该地女性人口超过男性、出生率下降、死亡率增加等多种原因令其人口锐减，再加上不断有人迁移到莫斯科，导致该城市可能会从地图上消失。

Mexico City(墨西哥城)，水资源短缺、土地下沉

墨西哥城在含水土层(aquifer)之上，城中2000万居民的用水大多来自地下，长期循环可能造成塌陷。估计该城中部分地区比100年前

下降了9米。

Naples(那不勒斯)，火山爆发

Naples 港湾的Vesuvius 火山每100年就会爆发一次，当年就是它在18个小时之内摧毁了庞贝，而上一次爆发是在1944年。

Banjul(班珠尔)，水位上涨

海平面的不断上升可能导致冈比亚首都班珠尔被淹没。

Timbuktu(通布图)，沙漠化

撒哈拉沙漠南部边缘的Mali(马里)首都Timbuktu 可能会遇到严重的沙漠化，而被埋于沙中。

Venice(威尼斯)，下沉

Venice 在过去的1000年里一直在下沉，近几个世纪它的速度加快，据统计在过去的100年里Venice下沉了24厘米，政府已经开展了各种保护工程。

60 一座古老而现代的城市——卡萨布兰卡

It is the capital of Grand Casablanca region with 3.7 million **inhabitant**s (2005 estimate) and an area of 1,615 km².

Situated on the Atlantic, Casablanca has one of the largest **artificial** ports in the world. It is the major city in Morocco and the country's economic capital. Casablanca has excellent connections with the rest of Morocco, through its railways and excellent roads.

The most important part of Casablanca's economy is **phosphate** export for which Casablanca is one of the main ports as well as an administrative centre. It is also the centre of the most intensive industrial activity in the country: a **sizeable** portion of the city's products is exported. Among Casablanca's own industries are fishing, fish **canning**, **sawmilling**, furniture making, building materials, glass, textiles, electronics, leather work, beer, spirits, soft drinks, and cigarettes. Casablanca is also the center for more than

卡萨布兰卡是大卡萨布兰卡地区的首都，有370万居民（2005年的估计数字），占地面积1615平方千米。

卡萨布兰卡位于大西洋沿岸，世界上最大的人工港口之一。它是摩洛哥主要的城市之一，是该国的经济中心。卡萨布兰卡交通发达，通过铁路和公路与摩洛哥其他城市相连。

国家主要的经济来源是磷酸盐出口。因此，它也是主要的港口之一以及行政中心。卡萨布兰卡是工业高度密集区：城市大部分的工业产出都供出口。卡萨布兰卡的工业主要有：渔业、鱼罐头制造业、锯木业、家具制造业、建筑材料、玻璃、纺织、电力、皮制品、啤酒制造业、烈酒制造业、软饮料制造业及烟草业。卡萨布兰卡也是摩洛哥过半的银行交易中

half of all bank **transaction**s in Morocco.

Casablanca's **landmark** is the new **mosque** of Hassan II, the world's largest, which can be seen at great distance. Apart from this there are few landmarks in Casablanca.

In Casablanca one finds both the richest and most sophisticated groups of the Moroccan society, as well as the most desperate poverty of the country.

The modern town of Casablanca is based on the plans of the French architect, Henri Prost, who placed the center where the main market of Anfa had been. From this point all main streets **radiate** in eastern and southern directions. Additional city plans were first developed in 1946, and later in 1984.

Casablanca is the setting of the 1942 film of the same name starring Humphrey Bogart and Ingrid Bergman. The film has achieved worldwide popularity since then, having also won three Oscars and been nominated in five additional categories.

心。

卡萨布兰卡的地标是哈桑二世大清真寺，这也是世界上最大的清真寺。人们可以远观。除此以外，卡萨布兰卡地标性的建筑不多。

城中，既有富人，亦有穷人，也有成分复杂的群体。

现代城镇卡萨布兰卡是基于法国建筑师亨利·普斯特的图纸建造。他将市中心建于Anfa市场所在地。从市中心看去，所有的主路向东及向南伸展开去。城市后来在1946年和1984年得到了扩建。

卡萨布兰卡是1942年同名电影的拍摄地。电影《卡萨布兰卡》的主演是英格丽·褒曼和亨弗莱·鲍嘉。此电影在世界各地广受好评，曾获得三项奥斯卡大奖（最佳影片、最佳导演和最佳剧本）及其他五项提名。

词汇 VOCABULARY

inhabitant：居民	sawmilling：锯木业
artificial：人工的	transaction：业务，交易
phosphate：磷酸盐	landmark：界标，里程碑
sizeable：相当大的	mosque：清真寺
canning：罐头制造业	radiate：（指线路等）自中心向各方伸展

背景知识 PROFILE

同名的卡萨布兰卡

电影《卡萨布兰卡》：在纳粹的铁蹄之下，要从欧洲逃往美国，必须绕道摩洛哥北部城市卡萨布兰卡。这使得这座城市的形势异常紧张。里克夜总会的老板里克是位神秘的男子。一日，捷克反纳粹领袖维克多拉斯洛和妻子伊尔莎来到里克夜总会，希望通过里克获得通行证。里克发现伊尔莎正是自己的昔日恋人，过去的误解解开后，伊尔莎徘徊在丈夫与情人间。而仍深爱着她的里克，却决定护送伊尔莎和她的丈夫离开卡萨布兰卡。在机场，里克开枪射杀了打电话阻止飞机起飞的德军少校后，目送着心爱的女人离开。

歌曲"卡萨布兰卡"：这首歌曲的创作和演唱者是著名音乐人Bertie Higgins（贝特·希金斯），他是18世纪德国著名诗人歌德的后代，出生于美国佛罗里达州。Bertie Higgins（贝特·希金斯）说："这首歌是我为当时的女朋友、现在的妻子写的。我记得那是1982年，《北非谍影》是我们共同喜爱的电影，这部爱情片让我们如痴如醉。结合这部电影给我的感觉，我为女朋友写了《卡萨布兰卡》，她非常感动，还答应了我的求婚，成了我的妻子。" 歌曲《卡萨布兰卡》之所以受人喜爱，是因为它唱出了许多无奈离别之人的心声。它贴切地再现了影片的主题，以至于许多人都以为它是电影《卡萨布兰卡》的主题曲。歌曲充满着怀旧、追忆、思念的复杂的情绪，情感真挚，曲调优美。

花名卡萨布兰卡：卡萨布兰卡是百合中的一种。卡萨布兰卡西班牙语意为"白房子"，花语是永不磨灭的爱情。经常在百合科花朵上见到的斑点，在它的花瓣上是看不到的。所以，它纯白的花瓣总是能开得那么自傲。它是世上最美的百合花，而在希腊神话中，那是悲剧之花。传说中，遇见卡萨布兰卡的情侣无不以死亡作为这段无望恋情的终结。然而，它还有另一个鲜为人知的含义，那就是——幸福。

非洲横跨赤道，南北所跨纬度大，这造就了非洲多变且复杂的气候条件。

因此，非洲有耐旱的动植物，有喜干燥且向阳光的植物，有世界上独一无二的动植物，有塑造现代文明的植物……

总之，请跟随编者的脚步，来非洲的世界里瞧瞧那些让人肃然起敬的生命吧！

第七章

你不可不知的非洲动植物

61 神奇而美丽的鸟类——非洲火烈鸟

African Flamingos are very large with the males being up to 5 feet tall and the females about 4 feet tall. They have a unique looking head that is bent forward and a large **bill**. They also have a round body that is found on two **skinny** but very **sturdy** legs. Many people wonder why this particular flamingo is light pink instead of featuring a dark pink or red coloring.

This is due to the lower amount of **carotene** that is found in its diet. The colors will vary based on their diet and what they consume. This is why African Flamingos in different locations can have quite a variation when it comes to their overall coloring. They also have some black on the insides of the features which they show when they fly.

Many people will argue that flamingos can't fly but all of the **species** can. They **tend** to do so mainly at night but they can during the day as well. The do look kind of silly though with those long legs stretched out. They will only fly when there is **sufficient** wind to help them move without using too much energy.

They have different formations that they can follow as well. This will help to ensure they are able to use the direction of the wind to their advantage. The young African Flamingos will be ready to fly when they are about 11 weeks old. Their young bodies develop very fast and it can often be hard to tell the young from the adults when you are viewing a flock.

Don't worry about those long legs of the African Flamingo not allowing them to be able to stand up like they should. They are very strong and they keep them balanced. Sometimes you will see them standing on one leg. This is to help them with **circulation** and when they need to change their body temperature.

Even though we are **positive** that birds have been

非洲火烈鸟体型很大，雄性鸟高达5英尺，雌性高达4英尺。它们的脑袋很独特，总是弯向前方，且鸟嘴很大。身体浑圆，腿细长却强壮。很多人都很奇怪，为什么非洲火烈鸟是浅红而非深红或纯红色？

其实，原因在于它们的饮食中胡萝卜素的含量很低。而鸟的颜色会因为它们的饮食而有所变化。这就是为什么不同地区的非洲火烈鸟整个身体颜色会有差异。飞行时，它们身体内侧的一些黑色的羽毛也会显露出来。

很多人认为火烈鸟不会飞，其实不然。它们主要在夜间飞行，白天也能。它们飞行时看起来有些笨拙，因为它们的大长腿是伸展着的。它们只会在风力足够的情况下飞行，因为这样可以帮助它们节省力气。

飞行时，它们的队形时有变化。不同的队形是根据风向对它们的有利程度设计的。小火烈鸟11周大的时候就可以飞行。这些小家伙儿们长得很快。人们很难将小火烈鸟和成年火烈鸟分开。

不要担心非洲火烈鸟的大长腿，因为它们一样能够支撑它们的身体。它们的腿非常强壮，能够维持身体平衡。有时，它们还会单腿直立。这样有助于改善它们的血液循环，从而改变体温。

on the Earth for millions of years, we don't have all of the details about them and their past. Many of those today have evolved from those that roamed Earth along with the dinosaurs. Perhaps the African Flamingo is derived from one of them. One of the biggest beliefs is that their filtering feeding system and the environment they are able to live in is so different from other animals that they are definitely the result of **evolution**.

尽管火烈鸟已在地球上存活数百万年，但对于火烈鸟的过去及它们的具体情况，我们并不全都了解。很多火烈鸟是自从恐龙时代就已经存在了。而且很可能，非洲火烈鸟是恐龙的一种。其中一个可以确信的想法是它们的过滤进食系统、它们的生存环境都跟其他进化的动物存在天壤之别。

背景知识 PROFILE

关于火烈鸟

全世界共三属:大火烈鸟、小火烈鸟和阿根廷火烈鸟。

火烈鸟体型大小似鹳；嘴短而厚，上嘴中部突向下曲，下嘴较大成槽状；颈长而曲；脚极长而裸出，向前的3趾间有蹼，后趾短小不着地；翅大小适中；尾短；体羽白而带玫瑰色，飞羽黑，覆羽深红，诸色相衬，非常艳丽。

火烈鸟栖息于温热带盐湖水滨，涉行浅滩，以小虾、蛤蜊、昆虫、藻类等为食。觅食时头往下浸，嘴倒转，将食物吮入口中，把多余的水和不能吃的渣滓排出，然后徐徐吞下。性怯懦，喜群栖，常万余只结群。火烈鸟以泥筑成高墩作巢，巢基在水里，高约0.5米。孵卵时亲鸟伏在巢上，长颈后弯藏在背部羽毛中。每窝产卵1～2枚。卵壳厚，色蓝绿。孵化期约1个月。雏鸟初靠亲鸟饲育，逐渐自行生活。因羽色鲜丽，常被人饲为观赏鸟。

人们又将大火烈鸟称为红鹳、红鹤、火鹤等，雄雌相似，是一种羽色鲜艳、多姿多彩的大型涉禽，体长在130厘米～142厘米。全身的羽毛主要为朱红色，特别是翅膀基部的羽毛，光泽闪亮，远远看去，就像一团熊熊燃烧的烈火，因此得名。

它的体形长得也很奇特，身体纤细，头部很小。镰刀形的嘴细长弯曲向下，前端为黑色，中间为淡红色，基部为黄色。黄色的眼睛很小，与庞大的身躯相比，显得很不协调。细长的颈部弯曲呈"S"形，双翼展开达160厘米以上，尾羽却很短。此外，它还有一双又细又长的红腿，脚上向前的3个趾间具红色的全蹼，后趾则较小而平置。整体形态显得高雅而端庄，无论是亭亭玉立之时，还是徐徐踱步之际，总给人以文静轻盈的感觉。

它们主要栖息在盐水湖泊、沼泽及礁湖的浅水地带。通常仅有几厘米深的水中生长着丰富的各种藻类。

大火烈鸟的分布范围很广，包括亚洲、欧洲、非洲和美洲的很多地方，共分化为两个亚种。指名亚种又叫茜红鹤、加勒比火烈鸟等，分布于北美洲南部、中美洲和南美洲；另一亚种又叫玫瑰色火烈鸟，分布于欧洲南部、亚洲中部和西部，以及非洲等地。其羽色与指名亚种有很大区别，主要是淡淡的玫瑰红色，远看时为白色，只有翅膀上的覆羽为朱红色，飞羽为黑色，但在不飞行时，几乎完全被覆羽所遮盖。

非洲的纳古鲁湖被称为"大火烈鸟的天堂"。每天，湖水之上，总是浮动着一条条红色的彩练，如落英逐逝水，似朝霞映碧池，给雄险的大裂谷平添了几分优柔妩媚的韵致。织成这美丽彩练的，就是大火烈鸟。远远望去，周身红得就像一团烈火，两腿则红得就像炽燃的两根火烛。

待走近一看，一只只火烈鸟，羽衣的粉红色有深有浅，显得斑斓绚丽；双腿修长倒映水中，好像把火引烧到湖底；两翅不时轻舒慢抖，在湖面掀起道道红色的涟漪。而一旦成千上万只大火烈鸟积聚在一起，一池湖水就顿时被映照得通体红透，成为一片烈焰蒸腾的火海。纳古鲁湖的大火烈鸟群，历来被称为"世界上火光永不熄灭的一大奇观"。

火烈鸟的羽毛一拔下，羽毛就会莫名其妙的变成白色，因为羽毛离体就与体内色素分离。

62 并非来自南极洲的绅士——非洲企鹅

African penguins look much like the Humboldt penguins. African penguins have a broad **band** of black that is in the shape of an **upside-down horseshoe** on their fronts. There have black spots **scatter**ed over their chest area. They make a loud **bray**ing sound that has given them the name the "**Jackass** penguin". They stand about 27 inches (60 cm tall) and weigh from 7 to 11 lbs. (2.5kg to 4 kg).

非洲企鹅很像洪堡企鹅。非洲企鹅的黑色带很宽，从它们的身体前面看来，是倒挂的U型。另外，它们的胸前区域还有黑色斑点。它们的叫声很像驴叫，所以又有"公驴企鹅"之称。身高60cm，重2.5kg-4kg。

African penguins live and breed on the coast of South Africa and on the **off-shore** islands. During the 17th and 18th century the African penguin was killed for food and oil. More recently the collection of **guano** has destroyed nesting areas. At one time the population was estimated to be in the millions. This number has decreased to about 160,000 in 1993.

The African penguin is a protected species, but their habitats continue to be damaged by oil spills from tankers off the Southern coast of Africa. Recently a successful effort has been made to establish new breeding colonies of the African penguins in the area. There are also rescue services to aid penguins that have been harmed by the **oil slick**s.

The nests are built far apart from other nests. They can be built under bushes or on sandy beaches. Two eggs are usually laid and in years when there is plenty of food both **chick**s will survive. Incubation takes 38 to 41 days for the eggs to hatch. This task is shared equally by both parents. The chicks are kept warm and protected for about 40 days after hatching by both parents. The chicks get their adult feathers when they are 70 to 100 days old. At this time they go to sea and are on their own.

非洲企鹅居住在南非海岸及离岸岛屿上，并在此生息繁衍。17世纪~18世纪期间，人们通过杀害非洲企鹅来获取食物和油。而最近的鸟粪收集活动又破坏了企鹅的栖息地。曾经，企鹅的数量据估计有数百万。而1993年时，它们数量已降至16万。

非洲企鹅是受保护物种，可它们的居住地依然持续遭到非洲南岸石油泄漏的破坏。最近，人们在这个区域成功地新建起非洲企鹅的保护区域。另外，其他的一些使企鹅免受海面浮油的救助活动也在进行当中。

企鹅的巢穴彼此之间是分开的。它们会建在灌木丛下或沙滩上。一般，企鹅一次产两枚卵，如果食物充足，两个幼仔都能成活。孵卵期一般需要38天~41天。企鹅爸爸和妈妈会共同承担孵卵的工作。幼仔出壳以后，会在父母温暖的保护下生活40天。而当它们70天~100天大的时候，它们会长成年企鹅的毛。这时，它们会奔向大海，开始独自生活。

词汇 VOCABULARY

band：带，条纹	jackass：公驴
upside-down：颠倒的	off-shore：离岸的
horseshoe：马蹄铁	guano：鸟粪
scatter：分散	oil slick：海面浮油
bray：发出似驴叫的声音	chick：幼仔

六大类企鹅简介

王企鹅属(Aptenodytes)

有两种，帝企鹅和王企鹅，是最大型也是最漂亮的企鹅。

帝企鹅：身高一米以上，体重可超过30千克，是唯一在南极大陆沿岸一带过冬的鸟类，并在冬季繁殖，帝企鹅每次只产一枚卵，孵化时由雄企鹅将其放在两脚的蹼上并用肚皮盖住，此其间，雄企鹅停止进食，完全靠脂肪维持生命，直到幼企鹅孵出，其体重可减轻1/3。

王企鹅：体型稍小些，嘴则比较长，颜色更加鲜艳，主要分布于南大洋一带及亚南极地区，最北可到新西兰一带。

阿德利企鹅属（Pygoscelis）

有三种，巴布亚企鹅、阿德利企鹅、南极企鹅。

巴布亚企鹅（Pygoscelis Papua）：又叫金图企鹅，分布于南极半岛和南大洋中的岛屿上。

阿德利企鹅（Adelie Penguin）：数量最多的企鹅，可在南极见到大规模的群体，游荡于南极有浮冰的水域。阿德利企鹅是一夫一妻制的动物。它们在产卵之前会先筑巢，找一些小石子围成一个窝的形状，可以有效地防止卵的滚动。但在南极，由于到处是冰雪覆盖，小石子成了稀缺资源，被严格控制起来。每个阿德利企鹅所分配的小石子数量是相当有限的。如果有雄性企鹅妄图去偷窃邻居家的小石子，会被人家毫不客气地赶出家门。但这时候雌性企鹅会悄悄地跟男邻居偷情，而后，邻居就会默许雌性把自家的小石子衔几颗回去。

南极企鹅（Pygoscelis Antarctica）：又叫帽带企鹅，主要分布于南极一带，有时游荡到南极以外。

角企鹅属(Eudyptes)

企鹅中种类最多，分布最广的一属，有六种，头部有黄色羽冠，在陆地上活动比较敏捷，在新西兰的有些种群可进入森林。

黄眼企鹅属(Megadytes)

只有一种，即黄眼企鹅，分布于新西兰南岛一带。

白鳍企鹅属(Eudyptula)

有两种，是最小型的企鹅。包括小鳍脚企鹅、白翅鳍脚企鹅。

环企鹅属(Spheniscus)

环企鹅属，有四种，是分布最靠北的企鹅。包括非洲企鹅（斑嘴环企鹅、黑足企鹅或公驴企鹅，产于南非）、洪堡企鹅、麦哲伦企鹅、加岛环企鹅。

63 跑得快的大鸟——非洲鸵鸟

The African ostrich (Struthio camelus) holds three **record**s: it is the world's largest and fastest running living bird and **lay**s the largest eggs.

4,000 years ago, ostriches **roam**ed Syria. 6,000-8,000 years ago, in a **savanna**-like environment, herds of ostriches roamed what is now Sahara. More recently, the African ostrich became **extinct** in Northern Africa, Arabia, southern South Africa, surviving just in savannas south of Sahara.

In South Africa, ostriches are used for **defend**ing sheep and cattle herds. The same role is being held by the Australian ostrich, emu, in Australia. Their impressive bodies and attitude even makes thieves fear them.

This is the only bird having only two toes. The ostrich can reach a top speed of 70 km (42 mi) per hour (as much as a racehorse) and can maintain 50 km (31 mi) per hour on long distances for 15-20 minutes. In full run, the bird's steps measure 5 m (17 ft).

The bird's feet are so strong, that a kick can kill a man. People can avoid the kicks by lying down, but in this case they are not safe as the bird hits with its beak as well. The chicks reach adult speed at the age of only one month.

Most birds do not even have a **copulatory** organ, but ostriches (and related groups, like kiwi and tinamous), ducks, geese and swans do have. The presence of a copulatory organ in these birds is a sign of primitiveness.

Ostriches swallow stones (**gastrolith**s) and use them as "gastric mill". The gastroliths make about 1% of the body mass of the ostriches. An adult ostrich consumes 7 kg (16 pounds) of food daily. The ostrich

非洲鸵鸟保持着三项世界纪录：鸟类中体型世界最大，鸟类中跑得最快，产的卵最大。

4000年前，鸵鸟在叙利亚的领土内漫步。6000年-8000年前，鸵鸟群在大草原似的撒哈拉徘徊。而最近，鸵鸟在北非、阿拉伯半岛以及南非南部已经绝迹，它的存活区域仅限于撒哈拉以南的草原地区。

在南非，人们用鸵鸟保护羊群和牛群。而澳大利亚的鸵鸟、鸸鹋有同样的作用。它们那让人印象深刻的身形和态度令小偷闻风丧胆。

它是只有两个脚趾头的鸟类。鸵鸟的最大速度可达70km/小时（这已经达到了赛马的水平），能够在15分钟~20分钟内，保持50km/小时。全速赛跑时，鸵鸟的步幅可达5m。

鸵鸟的脚非常有力，它踢一脚可使人丧命。人可以卧倒来躲避鸵鸟的一踢。不过，这并不是完全安全的，鸵鸟也可能会用它的嘴啄。小鸵鸟在仅一个月大的时候都能达到成年鸵鸟的速度。

大部分鸟类没有交配器官，但鸵鸟（以及其他群体，如几维鸟等）、鸭子、鹅、天鹅是有的。这些鸟所具有的交配器官是一种原始性的体现。

鸵鸟吞咽石子（胃石），并用它们来帮助胃消化。胃石的重量约占鸵鸟整个体重的1%。一只成年鸵鸟每天需消耗7kg食物。鸵鸟是杂食动物，它们的食物包括植物类、啮齿类、蜥

is **omnivorous**, consuming from plant food to rodents, lizards, bird chicks, turtles and insects. The gut of an ostrich is 14 m (47 ft) long.

Eggs are regarded as some of the most fragile things in nature. But when African ostrich eggs were tested, they successfully handled a pressure of 120 kg! Of course, they are the largest eggs: 4.3-6.4 pounds (or 1.5-2 kg, of which 280 g are represented by the shell) and equal about 36 chicken eggs. **Crocodile**s, even if they can reach up to a ton, lay small eggs compared to their mass, about the same size of the goose egg. Bushmen use ostrich eggshells to keep fresh water.

In the wild, ostriches can live up to 30 years; when in captivity, their lifespan increases to even 70 years.

蝎、小鸟、乌龟以及昆虫。鸵鸟的肠子长14米。

一般来讲，蛋的本质是很脆弱易碎的。而非洲鸵鸟蛋能够承受120kg的重量。当然，鸵鸟蛋很大：4.3磅~6.4磅（或1.5kg~2kg，而壳的重量占280g）。鸵鸟蛋的重量相当于36只鸡蛋的重量。尽管鳄鱼的重量能够重达一吨，鳄鱼的蛋才及鹅蛋大小。布须曼人会用鸵鸟蛋壳盛干净水。

在野外，鸵鸟能活30年。而如果圈养的话，鸵鸟能活70年。

词汇 VOCABULARY

record：记录	defend：保卫，保护
lay：产卵	copulatory：交配的
roam：漫游，闲，徜徉	gastrolith：胃石
savanna：大草原	omnivorous：杂食的
extinct：灭绝的，熄灭的，消亡的	crocodile：鳄鱼

背景知识 PROFILE

鸵鸟心理与鸵鸟蛋

鸵鸟心理

鸵鸟生活在炎热的沙漠地带，那里阳光照射强烈，从地面上升的热空气，同低空的冷空气相交，由于散射而出现闪闪发光的薄雾。平时鸵鸟总是伸长脖子透过薄雾去查看，而一旦受惊或发现敌情，它就干脆将潜望镜似的脖子平贴在地面，身体蜷曲一团，以自己暗褐色的羽毛伪装成石头或灌木丛，加上薄雾的掩护，就很难被敌人发现。另外，鸵鸟将头和脖子贴近地面，还有两个作用，一是可听到远处的声音，有利于及早避开危险；二是可以放松颈部的肌肉，更好地消除疲劳。

遇到危险时，鸵鸟会把头埋入草堆里，以为自己眼睛看不见就是安全。事实上鸵鸟的两条腿很长，奔跑得很快，遇到危险的时候，其奔跑速度足以摆脱敌人的攻击，如果不是把头埋藏在草堆里坐以待毙的话，是足可以躲避猛兽攻击的。

后来，心理学家将这种消极的心态称之为"鸵鸟心态"。"鸵鸟心态"是一种逃避现实的心理，是不敢面对问题的懦弱行为。

鸵鸟蛋

鸵鸟是世上最大的禽类动物；鸵鸟蛋，则是世上最大的蛋，一粒鸵鸟蛋，可供24人享用。此外，人们在鸵鸟蛋蛋壳上通过彩绘、浮雕等手段制作成相应的艺术品，即所谓的"鸵鸟工艺蛋"，亦有很高的观赏和收藏价值。

在超市里，鸵鸟蛋重达1.5公斤，价格卖到230元一只。日前，在中国的超市中，产自市郊的鸵鸟蛋悄然上市。据了解，鸵鸟蛋口感与鸡蛋差别不大，营养成分却高出许多。每百克鸡蛋含蛋白质14.7克，鸵鸟蛋则含22.54克。

鸵鸟工艺蛋有彩绘、浮雕、镂空、景泰蓝镶雕四种绘制工艺。现有的图案以祝福、动物、山水、诗境为主。可以根据客户需要，订制各种图案和文字，如旅游景点、开业纪念、自警诗词、个人纪念等。

彩绘：鸵鸟蛋壳表面有一层透明釉质，一般颜料不易附着，所使用的颜料由高薪聘请的工艺师精心调配而成，着色效果奇佳，不但色彩鲜艳，而且时间越久越牢固，用水冲洗也不会褪色。

浮雕镂空：采用浮雕镂空工艺最能体现象牙般的质感，图案具体鲜明的层次感，自然、和谐、高雅，保存时间久远。

景泰蓝镶雕：在浮雕镂空的基础上，揉合具有500年历史的景泰蓝国技。彩色部分用各种天然彩色石粉，色彩特别纯正。此工艺品是采用鸵鸟蛋壳做载体，使用国家级的专利技术——"彩沙工艺"，纯手工精制而成，既体现了中国传统的景泰蓝样的神奇，又不失现代时尚，画面多种多样。色彩艳丽、高贵典雅、富丽堂皇、异彩纷呈，是家居装饰、收藏和馈赠亲朋好友的上佳礼品。还可按客户要求设计。

64 精力充沛的动物——非洲角马

The wildebeest is also known as the gnu, it comes under the **antelope** family as a hooved **mammal**. They have an appearance of features much like a **cros** between a cow and a horse.

The Wildebeest is native to Africa and there are 2 species: the Black Wildebeest, or white-tailed gnu and the Blue Wildebeest, or **brindled** gnu. Gnus belong to the family Bovidae, which includes antelopes, cattle, goats, and other **even**-toed horned **ungulate**s.

The main food source of wildebeests is grasses. The seasonal nature of the African grasslands forces wildebeest to migrate. They like to drink daily when water is available, but can go for a few days without water.

Its habitat consists of grassy plains and open **woodland**s in southern, central, and eastern Africa. They are especially **prolific** in the Serengeti National Park.

Wildebeest grow to 1.15–1.4 meters at the shoulder and weigh between 150–250 kilograms. Wildebeest can live more than 20 years.

The gestation period in a female is eight and a half months, producing one offspring. The calf is able to stand within minutes of the birth. In a few days it is able to keep up with the herd.

The number of wildebeest has increased steadily over recent years but human habitation leads to less grassland which threatens their long term numbers. The Wildebeests main **predator**s are lions and hyenas.

The Wildebeest Migration in Kenya and Tanzania:

The Wildebeest Migration in East Africa, also known as "The Great Migration" takes place between Tanzania's Serengeti National Park and Kenya's Masai Mara and is one of the greatest wildlife spectacles on the planet.

The precise **timing** of the annual wildebeest

角马也叫gnu（也是角马的意思），和羚羊同属一科，是有蹄类哺乳动物。它看起来像牛和马的杂交品种。

角马产自非洲，分为两类：黑角马（白尾角马）和蓝角马（斑纹角马）。角马属牛科，这一类包括羚羊、牛、山羊以及其他偶数角类的有蹄类动物。

角马的主要食物是草。非洲草原的季节性特点迫使角马大迁徙。如果水源充沛，角马喜欢每天都喝水。如果不充沛，可以在没水的情况下存活好些天。

角马居住在非洲南部、中部及东部有草的平原上或开阔的林地上。而在东非坦桑尼亚中北部的塞伦盖蒂国家公园，角马尤其多产。

角马1.15米~1.4米高，重150kg-250kg，寿命在20多年。

雌角马的妊娠期是8个半月，一胎产一仔。小角马刚出生后的几分钟之内就能够站起来。几天后，小角马就能够和大部队一起奔跑了。

近年来，角马的数量在稳定地增长。但人类的居住场所导致草地减少，这就威胁了角马的数量。角马的主要天敌是狮子和土狼。

肯尼亚和坦桑尼亚境内的角马大迁徙：

东非的角马大迁徙发生在坦桑尼亚的塞伦盖蒂国家公园及肯尼

migration depends on the rains. It is a very unpredictable and spontaneous natural event, with calving season taking place in the Serengeti between January and mid-March. The wildebeest migration starts to head towards the Western Serengeti in May or June. The best time to see the migration is generally between June and August when the wildebeest congregate and prepare to cross the famous Grumeti River.

If you are in the Masai Mara you can expect the wildebeest to make their arrival as early as July, but they generally arrive between August & September and remain in the Masai Mara between October & November. Between the end of November and January the wildebeest gradually begin their migration from the Masai Mara back towards the Serengeti.

亚的马赛马拉国家保护区,这场迁徙是地球上最为壮观的野生动物奇观。

每年角马迁徙的时间是由雨水决定的。这很难预测,是一场自然而然的事件。而产仔一般发生在1月到3月间,在塞伦盖蒂国家公园里。角马在5月或者6月前往西部的塞伦盖蒂国家公园。而参观角马的最佳时期一般在6月到8月,此时,角马聚集在一起,准备过格鲁美河。

如果你在马赛马拉国家保护区,最早7月可以看到角马到达,不过一般是在8月或9月。它们在马赛马拉国家保护区会一直待到10月或11月。而在11月末和次年1月间,角马会开始从马赛马拉国家保护区回到塞伦盖蒂国家公园。

词汇 VOCABULARY

antelope:羚羊	ungulate:有蹄类动物
mammal:哺乳类	woodland:林地
cross:杂种	prolific:多产的,多育的
brindled:有斑纹的	predator:食肉动物,掠夺者
even:偶数	timing:时间的掌握,时间的安排,时机

背景知识 PROFILE

适者生存

马拉河中有两种动物是角马们在渡河时必然要遇到的杀手:一种是世界上最大、最为凶残的尼罗鳄,一种是被称为"非洲河王"的河马。马拉河是角马们要渡过的最后一条河,渡过去,就进入了水草丰美的"伊甸园"。渡不过去,它们中的绝大部分将会因缺草缺水而死。每年的10月份和次年的3月份,马拉河都会上演一场场惊心动魄的情景:狂野、惊险和悲壮的瞬间被演绎得淋漓尽致。但是,角马依然乐此不疲,纵然在这场争斗中，更多是充当弱者的角色。

有一年10月，马拉河的河水不再湍急，甚至有的地方可以清楚地看到河底，对于人类来说，卷起裤腿就可以过河了。成千上万的角马聚集在马拉河岸边，这个地点是角马每次的必经之地。河里的尼罗鳄和河马依然在注视着角马，等待着丰盛的大餐。这时，几头年幼的角马发现在离准备过河的地点不远处河水很浅，而且尼罗鳄和河马在那里根本没有施展的空间。于是，不少年幼的角马聚集过去，准备从那里过河，躲避尼罗鳄和河马的攻击。令人吃惊的一幕发生了，几十头看上去像是头领且年老的角马过来驱赶那些年幼的角马回到原处，不允许它们从较浅处过河。角马们注视着这个举动，没有一头出来阻止。接着，角马开始在原路线过河。后果可想而知，角马死伤众多。

这一场面被《动物世界》摄制组真实地记录下来。工作人员问导游，角马明明知道马拉河里有凶恶的尼罗鳄和河马。为什么不从较浅且没有尼罗鳄和河马的地方过河，而是依然选择以前的路线呢？这不是找死吗？

导游说，是的，角马知道河浅处没有尼罗鳄和河马，从那里过河可以说是很安全的。但是角马也知道，马拉河像今年这样的情况难得一见，很多角马一辈子也遇不上。如果角马尤其是那些年幼的角马选择了从较浅处过河，并顺利到达对岸，那么次年3月，它们又要回来，再经过马拉河时，面对成群的尼罗鳄和河马，它们还敢过河吗？年幼的角马是角马种群繁衍生息的希望。它们过不了河就意味着死亡，那对整个角马种群意味着什么呢？所以，角马必须要教育年幼的角马放弃那老天疏忽的"恩赐"，以免丧失了抗争命运的本能，而是选择始终贯穿角马生命的危险——与尼罗鳄和河马的斗争。

面对鲜有的安全和屡见的危险，角马为了更好地生存和繁衍生息而选择后者，这就是角马的生存法则。这也许就是为什么角马面对凶险的生存环境能繁衍至今的原因之一吧。

65 优雅的高族群——非洲长颈鹿

Early written records described the giraffe as "**magnificent** in appearance, bizarre in form, unique in **gait**, **colossal** in height and **inoffensive** in character". Ancient cultures in Africa **revere**d the giraffe, as some modern cultures do today, and commonly depicted it in **prehistoric** rock and cave paintings. Unknown outside of Africa, this animal so excited man's **curiosity** that it was sometimes sent as a **diplomatic** gift to other countries. The animal was thought to be a cross between a camel and a leopard, it's a mistake **immortalize**d in the giraffe's scientific name of Giraffa camelopardalis.

The giraffe is the tallest living animal, uniquely adapted to reach **vegetation inaccessible** to other **herbivore**s. Giraffes have a distinctive walking gait, moving both right legs forward, then both left. At a **gallop**, however, the giraffe simultaneously swings the hind legs ahead of and outside the front legs, reaching speeds of 35 miles an hour. It has unusually elastic blood vessels with a series of valves that help offset the sudden buildup of blood (and to prevent fainting) when the head is raised, lowered or swung quickly. Giraffe "horns" are actually knobs covered with skin and hair above the eyes that protect the head from injury.

Giraffes are found in arid and dry-savanna zones south of the Sahara, wherever trees occur.

The giraffe is non-territorial and social; it lives in very loose, open herds with no specific leaders or **coordination** of herd movement. This structure reflects that a giraffe's size makes a "safety in numbers" tactic unnecessary, and that the trees they feed on tend to be spaced apart. Dominance between males is established by "necking"—swinging heads at

早期的报道称长颈鹿"外表美丽，形状奇怪，仪态独特，个头巨大，性格却温和不具攻击性"。非洲古代的文化敬畏长颈鹿，而如今的有些现代文化依旧如此。通常，长颈鹿会被描述成史前岩石和山洞中的壁画。因为只有非洲大陆有，而外界对长颈鹿知之甚少的状况引发人们对长颈鹿的好奇。甚至，有时，非洲国家会将长颈鹿作为外交礼物送给其他国家。据说，长颈鹿是骆驼和豹的杂交。实际上，这是一个来自于长颈鹿学名——camelopardalis（camel+leopard）的错误。

长颈鹿是世界上最高的动物，所以能够够到其他食草动物所不能够到的植物。长颈鹿的步态很特别，它会一起出右腿，然后一起出左腿。然而，奔跑时，长颈鹿会同时将后腿飞奔起来，位置在前腿两侧。它的速度可高达35英里/小时。长颈鹿的血管富有弹性，有很多的阀门，这就使得它能够对付抬头、低头或摇头时血液的突然增加。长颈鹿的角很小，经常被皮肤和眼睛上的毛发所覆盖，可以保护头部，使其免受损伤。

长颈鹿出没在撒哈拉以南干燥的草原地区，这里树木茂盛。

长颈鹿是非地域性的动物，群居。其群体松散，没有特定的领导，族群里也没有彼此的协调活动。这种结构证明了长颈鹿的身高使得"族群优势"不是那么必要，而它们赖以生

one another in tests of strength.

Giraffe tails are highly prized by many African cultures. The desire for good-luck bracelets, fly whisks and thread for sewing or stringing beads have led people to kill the giraffe for its tail alone. Giraffes are easily killed and poaching (now more often for their meat and hide) continues today.

Despite its long neck, the giraffe has only seven vertebrae, exactly the same number as man and most other mammals.

存的树也是分开分布的。雄性之间的优势是通过比拼脖子力气获得的。

长颈鹿的尾巴在很多文化中都含有特殊意义。人们会为了编织好运手环、蝇拂、缝补的线或穿珠子的绳，杀害长颈鹿，获取尾巴。长颈鹿很容易被杀死，现在猎杀行动仍在继续。

尽管长颈鹿脖子很长，却只有7块椎骨，这跟人和多数哺乳动物的椎骨数量是一模一样的。

词汇 VOCABULARY

magnificent：壮丽的，宏伟的	diplomatic：外交的
gait：步态，步法	immortalize：使永恒，使不灭，使不朽
colossal：巨大的	vegetation：植物
inoffensive：无害的，没恶意的，不讨厌的	inaccessible：难以到达的
revere：崇拜，敬畏	herbivore：食草动物
prehistoric：史前的	gallop：奔跑
curiosity：好奇	coordination：协调

背景知识 PROFILE

长颈鹿何时来到中国

1985年7月11日，原邮电部发行 J. 113《郑和下西洋五八零周年》纪念邮票一套4枚，最后一枚"航海史上的壮举"描绘的是郑和一行在非洲的场景，其中出现了两头长颈鹿，这是中国邮票上首次出现长颈鹿的图案。为纪念郑和下西洋600周年，国家邮政局、香港和澳门特区邮政部门联合发行了同主题纪念邮票一套3枚及小型张，各自设计了不同的图案和内容。香港、澳门特区纪念邮票的第二枚不约而同地都用长颈鹿来表明郑和船队的非洲之行。

现在世界最高的动物长颈鹿，是非洲的代表性野生动物。中国自古不出产长颈鹿，但1979年，在徐州贾旺发现的东汉画像石上绘有多只"麒麟"，其中至少三只具有非洲长颈鹿的典型特征。600年前明代的郑和远航世界，史有定论地远达非洲。之所以跑那么远，据说就是为寻找中国人心目中的吉祥神兽"麒麟"。中国古代传说中描述若有麒麟出，是国泰民安、天下太平的吉兆，可谁也没见过这种古籍中形容为鹿身、牛尾、独角神兽的模样，故一直有人怀疑它是否真的存在。明永乐十二年（公元1414年）九月二十日，郑和手下的杨敏带回榜葛剌国（今孟加拉）新国王赛弗丁进贡的一只长颈鹿，明朝举国上下为之喧腾。因为长颈鹿的形态、习性与中国古籍中描述的麒麟太过吻合，进一步了解后更发现长颈鹿的原产地在东非一带，当地的索马里语称之为"基林"（Giri），发音与麒麟非常相近，使得中国人确信长颈鹿就是麒麟。于是郑和的船队第四次下西洋前往西亚后，绕过阿拉伯半岛，首航东非，到了长颈鹿的故乡，时间是永乐十三年。同一年，郑和的船队回到了中国，一同前来的各国使者中，包括了东非的麻林国（其所在地，一说是肯尼亚的马林迪；一说是坦桑尼亚的基尔瓦·基西瓦尼）使者，他向永乐帝献上了产自本国的长颈鹿。永乐十四年（公元1416年），麻林国第二次向明朝进贡"麒麟"。马欢所撰《瀛涯胜览》一书中就此瑞兽有如下描述："麒麟，前二足高九尺余，后两足约高六尺，头抬颈长一丈六尺，首昂后低，人莫能骑。头上有两肉角，在耳边。牛尾鹿身，蹄有三跲，匾口。食粟、豆、面饼。"不难看出，所谓"麒麟"即长颈鹿也。《明史》记载，正统三年（公元1438年）榜葛剌国又进贡过一次"麒麟"。不产长颈鹿的南亚榜葛剌为何能屡屡进贡？史学研究者认为，这和当时的国际形势、海上贸易有关。在地理大发现之前，阿拉伯人控制了东西方海上贸易。他们的单桅三角帆帆船除了载运一般货物，还将阿拉伯半岛和索马里的马匹输往印度，甚至将缅甸和斯里兰卡的大象运往印度。单桅三角帆船既然能够载运马匹和大象，阿拉伯人把长颈鹿从其部分占据的东非载运到同样信奉伊斯兰教的榜葛剌当然不成问题。

近年海外有媒体称，在非洲肯尼亚发现貌似亚洲人的土著，自述系郑和船队水手后裔，透露其祖先曾送长颈鹿给中国。

66 神奇的造纸草——纸莎草

Cyperus papyrus is a **stately** aquatic member of the sedge family. The plants are easily cultivated and suitable for medium to large water features, especially in warmer climates.

The most **conspicuous** feature of the plants are the bright green, smooth, rounded **culm**s (flowering stems) which are up to 40mm thick at the base and may be up to 5m tall in ideal conditions. Each is topped by a dense **cluster** of thin, bright green, shiny stalks, which resemble a feather duster when young. The stalks **elongate** later and bend gracefully downward under their own weight so that the cluster becomes almost **spherical** in shape.

Cyperus papyrus grows in full sun, in wet **swamp**s and on **lake margin**s throughout Africa, Madagascar and the Mediterranean countries. In deeper waters it is the chief constituent of the floating, **tangled** masses of vegetation known as sudd. In southern Africa it is limited to the lower altitude, warmer parts of Namibia, Botswana, Limpopo, Mpumalanga and KwaZulu-Natal. Plants cultivated on the Highveld do seem to tolerate a few degrees of frost; the plants are more-or-less **dormant** in winter and as long as the rhizomes are protected from freezing, the old weathered culms of the previous summer's growth will be replaced by new ones in spring.

In its natural habitat Cyperus papyrus occurs in large, dense populations, often lining bodies of water such as in the Okavango Swamps of Botswana. The "feather-duster" flowering heads of papyrus make ideal nesting sites for many social species of birds. As in most sedges, **pollination** is effected by wind, not insects, and the mature fruits after release are distributed by wind and water.

The plant's use in paper-making in Ancient Egypt is mentioned. It can be said that this invention was the

纸莎草是莎草科中的一种水生植物。在中大型的水域中，纸莎草很容易成活，尤其是在温暖的环境中。

纸莎草最明显的特征就是草茎呈鲜绿色，质地平滑且呈圆形。草茎根部40mm厚。在理想的环境下，可长到5m高。纸莎草有紧密呈丛状的草冠，而每根梗是细的、鲜绿色的且很光亮，其形状很像动物掸帚。随后，梗不断长长，因为自身重量，开始往下垂，这样，这个丛状的草冠将近乎球形。

纸莎草在充足光照的环境中生长，遍布非洲大陆、马达加斯加岛及地中海国家内潮湿的沼泽及湖边。在深水域，纸莎草是大片的浮游植物——大块漂浮植物的主要组成部分。在非洲南部，纸莎草的生长区域仅限于低海拔处，如纳米比亚、博茨瓦纳、林波波河、姆蓬马朗加及夸祖鲁纳塔尔的温暖地区。而在高草原上生长的纸莎草也能忍受一定程度的冰霜。冬天，这种植物会有点冬眠的习性。只要根茎免于霜冻的侵袭，来年春天时，旧的草茎会被新的替代。

在纸莎草的自然生长环境中，它是以大量、密级的植物群出现的。"羽状冠"会成为很多鸟类的理想巢穴。像很多莎草科植物一样，纸莎草通过风力和水流传播花粉。

foundation of modern civilization. To this day expensive papers are made from papyrus using the original techniques. In southern Africa the starchy **rhizome**s and culms are eaten, raw or cooked, by humans. The culms are also used for building materials. Young **shoot**s are frequently grazed by livestock.

Ideally, the plants need a muddy or sandy substrate in water at least half a meter deep so that the tall culms will not **topple**. They need full sun but also need to be sheltered from strong winds and for best effect should be allowed to form a large colony. In winter the oldest culms dry off and can be removed with a sharp implement. New culms will be formed in spring from the growing point of the rhizome.

Propagation is by division of the rhizome in spring. **Germination** from seed is not recommended. The time period from seed to flowering is not known but it is undoubtedly several years.

No pests have been observed to attack Cyperus papyrus, with the exception of a rust fungus which appears to be specific to the family.

在古埃及，纸莎草的造纸功能是人们常提及的。可以说，这是现代文明的基础。迄今为止，造纸原料依然来源于纸莎草，且使用最初的技术。在非洲南部，富含淀粉的根茎及草茎是可以为人类食用的，可以生食或熟食。草茎也是建筑材料，而牲畜会吃那些嫩嫩的植株。

理想情况下，这些植物需要一种泥质火沙质基底，这在水中至少半米深，这样，高大的草茎才不会倒下。它们需要全日照的环境，但需要躲避强风的吹拂。冬天时，旧的草茎会变干，用利器可以割下草茎。新的草茎在春天会在根茎新的生长点上形成。

春天时，纸莎草会通过根茎的分离而繁殖。而通过种子生长、发芽并不是一个好的办法，不知道这一过程要多久，可能需要几年的时间。

人们还没有发现昆虫会食纸莎草，但纸莎草会长锈菌。

stately：庄严的，堂皇的，高贵的	tangled：纠缠的，紊乱的
conspicuous：显要的	dormant：休眠的
culm：草茎	pollination：授粉
cluster：簇	rhizome：根状茎
elongate：延长，伸长	shoot：幼芽，幼枝
spherical：球状的	topple：倒下
swamp：沼泽，湿地	propagation：繁殖
lake margin：湖边	germination：发芽，萌芽，共生，晶核化

纸莎草纸专家——哈桑·拉加卜

哈桑·拉加卜（Hassan Ragab），1911年生于埃及亚历山大一个名门望族，曾是一位电力工程师。他的一生充满传奇色彩。他参过军，积极参加了1952年7月推翻法鲁克封建王朝的革命，后被任命为国防部次长，并被授予少将军衔。他曾是一位出色的外交家，1956年至1961年先后出任驻中国、意大利和南斯拉夫大使。1968年，他潜心纸草学研究并成功研究出了失传千年的纸草造纸术，成为著名的纸草学专家。

他一生中曾与埃及共和国历史上的三位总统纳赛尔、萨达特和穆巴拉克有过亲密接触。作为军人，他曾荣获纳赛尔总统颁发给他的一级共和国勋章；作为外交家和著名实业家，萨达特总统和穆巴拉克总统曾先后为他授勋和颁奖。在以他的名字而命名的纸莎草纸博物馆里，至今还陈列着纳赛尔、萨达特和穆巴拉克三位总统为他授勋、颁奖时的珍贵照片。

但真正使埃及人民记住哈桑·拉加卜的并不是他辉煌的政治生涯和三位总统为他颁奖时的耀眼光环，而是失传千年之久的纸草造纸术在他的努力下获得再生。

据说，拉加卜当年研究纸草造纸术曾历经艰辛。首先摆在他面前的严酷现实是，造纸原料纸莎草已在埃及绝迹。没有造纸原料，造纸便无从谈起。为解决这一难题，拉加卜从苏丹进口纸莎草种子进行试种，但遭到失败。他没有气馁，又改作对进口纸莎草的根部进行试栽。经过反复试验，终于获得成功。其次，没有关于古造纸工序的任何详细资料。拉加卜知难而进，潜心研究。他查阅历史书籍，与专家们进行交流，认真学习古墓画，细心观察从法老古墓中发现的纸草文书的纹理。在发掘造纸工序的过程中，他几乎成了真正的历史学家、考古学家和画家。真是"工夫不负有心人"，在攻克了重重难关后，拉加卜终于研究出了纸莎草纸制造术，成为当之无愧的纸莎草纸的再生之父。

67 沙漠中的一片绿荫——金合欢

Umbrella Thorn Acacia is one of the most **recognizable** trees of the African savanna. It grows in sand dunes and rocky grounds of Africa's grasslands. Acacias grow in areas with annual **rainfall** as low as 4 cm. This tree can survive in 122°F temperatures during the day, and freezing temperatures at nights. The savanna that the Acacias live in is hot and dry in the **respective** summer of the Southern Hemisphere. During the winter months the savanna gets a lot of rain.

The Umbrella Thorn Acacia grows up to 20 meters high and has a spreading, flat-topped crown that gives it its name. The **bark** on the Acacia is black to gray in color and feels rough. The branches on the Acacia are **gnarl**ed. It has two types of thorns on the branches; long, straight, brownish thorns and shorter, hooked thorns that grow alongside each other. The thorns grow in pairs and disguise themselves in the clusters of flowers that grow on the Acacia. The flower clusters have up to 400 white, **puffball** flowers that grow on a twig on the Acacia. The Acacia's leaves are composed of small alternate leaflets on a central rib. The Acacia's leaves are 2.5 cm long and 1 mm wide. The seeds are 8 to 12cm long twisted pods. The Acacia's belong to the family "Mimosaceae", and until recently was known as the "Mimosa Tree".

One of the Acacia's adaptations to hot and dry conditions is a deep **taproot**, which can reach 115 ft under the ground. This adaptation helps it get the water during the dry **spell**s. A second set of roots spread out just under the ground about twice the area of the crown. The little leaves of it prevent water loss. The Acacia's umbrella-shaped tops enable the tree to capture large amounts of sunlight with the smallest possible leaves. The thorns are used to keep the savanna animals away from

在非洲草原上，金合欢是很容易辨认的树种之一。它生长在非洲草原中的沙丘以及石地中。金合欢可以长在年降水量只有4cm的地方。它可以抵抗白天122华氏度的高温，也可以忍耐夜间的零度气温。金合欢树生长在夏季炎热干旱的南半球，那里冬季月雨水充沛。

金合欢树可高达20m，树冠平，呈张开状。金合欢的树皮是黑色或灰色的，很粗糙。它的树枝是扭曲的，有两种类型的刺：长长的棕黄色直刺以及短短的弯刺。这些刺成对生长，并且躲在花丛的掩映下。金合欢一条细枝上可长多达400朵白色、羽毛状的花。而金合欢的叶子是在一条中心的叶脉上由小的叶子组成。金合欢的叶子2.5cm长，1mm宽。种子长在8cm~12cm长的豆荚内。金合欢属"含羞草科"，而且直到最近才更名为"含羞草树"。

金合欢适应的干热的环境其中一种原因便是金合欢有条很深的主根，能达地下115英尺深。它的主根可以使金合欢在干旱期从很深的地下汲水。那些副根在地下蔓延的面积是树冠的两倍。金合欢的小型叶子可以防止水分流失。金合欢伞状的树冠使得金合欢可以利用细小的叶子吸收大量的太阳光。而金合欢树上的刺可以防止草原动物吃叶子、花朵和种子。不

eating the leaves, flowers, and seedpods. The only animal that is **immune** to the thorns is the giraffe.

The Acacia provides shade for the animals of the savanna. The **trunk** of the tree makes very good **charcoal** and firewood. The flowers on the Acacia provide a good source of honey in some regions. The stem of the tree is used to treat asthma, and **diarrhea**. The bark of the Acacia is used as a disinfectant, and the pods are used to make porridge.

The Acacia is not endangered, and it is actually plentiful. There are over 700 species of the Acacia in Africa.

过，长颈鹿对这种刺是具有免疫能力的。

金合欢会为草原上的动物提供阴凉。金合欢的树干是很好的柴火。而金合欢的花在一些地区是很好的蜂蜜来源。树茎可用来对付哮喘、痢疾。金合欢的树皮可作为一种消毒剂，而豆荚可以用来做粥。

金合欢树数目众多。非洲大约有700多种金合欢树。

词汇 VOCABULARY

recognizable：可辨认的，可识别的	taproot：主根
rainfall：降水量	spell：一段时间
respective：各自的，各个的，分别的	immune：有免疫力的，不受影响的，免除的
bark：树皮	trunk：树干
gnarl：扭曲，长瘤	charcoal：树干
puffball：羽状实	diarrhea：痢疾

背景知识 PROFILE

上海世博会非洲联合馆

非洲联合馆是上海世博会最大的联合馆。展馆外立面的图案设计具有强烈的非洲元素和特征：繁茂葱郁的非洲金合欢、沙漠、非洲特有的动物和建筑物勾勒出非洲大陆自然并具有多样性的风貌，象征着古老而充满生机的非洲大陆。馆内还有一个公共展演区域，由公共舞台、真人秀台及专题展区组成。

41个国家和非洲联盟入驻非洲联合馆，这是历届世博会上数量最多的一次。非洲联合馆通过集中与分散的布局方式，为非洲各国提供了一个综合的展示平台。除了42个独立展馆外，馆内还拥有一个公共展演区域，由公共舞台、真人秀台及专题展区组成，其空间色彩、图案、功能的设计，以及互动项目和展演内容的选择，将在充分尊重非洲各参展国意愿的前提下来完成，呈现给大家的是真实的非洲风采。更为令人喜悦的是，馆内还建了个非洲集市，每个参展国拥有约68平米的售卖点，参观者可以寻获来自非洲本土的艺术品。视觉、味觉、触觉、听觉、动感在这里汇集，让参观者全方位地互动感受充满生机和活力的非洲，自始自终沉浸在浓浓的非洲氛围里。客流路线和公共区域是设计的重点，馆内设置了6个观众出入口，4个货物专属进出口，以及除出入口之外的8个紧急通道。参观的人流由集中到分散，在避免了拥挤的同时，使展区的展示效果得到保证，增大空间的有效利用率。

非洲联合馆位于世博园区的C片区，建筑面积26000多平方米。以非洲联合馆为中心的非洲展区，是组织方在选址的最初就预留的宝地。它是整个世博会园区最佳选址之一，不仅拥有濒临黄浦江的极佳景观，还和每天上演精彩创意演出和多媒体秀的后滩地区仅十步之遥，而且紧邻一个主要的浦东出入口。交通尤其便捷，周围充满看点。非洲联合馆室内净高9米，每个国家占地面积约为289平方米，总用地面积3.45万平方米，大大超过前几届世博会的非洲馆展区面积。4个外立面的面积总和达9500平米，是上海世博会11个联合馆中规模最大的一个，充分营造非洲联合馆大空间的整体氛围。

外墙图案创意根源——非洲有人类的根和源。在过去，非洲诞生了人类的早期文明。在如今，许多艺术、音乐和文化都可以在非洲找到根源，非洲为人类的发展做出了巨大贡献。外立面的图案设计富有强烈的非洲元素和特征。繁茂葱郁的非洲大树，象征非洲大陆强大坚韧的生命力。盘亘粗壮的树根深深的扎入地下，暗示非洲是人类的起源地。树根汲取营养让大树向着辽阔的天空自由生长，象征着非洲从本土文化根源摄取力量，必将造就一个充满希望和机遇的大陆！沙漠、海鸥、动物、建筑物勾勒出非洲大陆自然并具有多样性的风貌，象征着古老而又充满生机的非洲大陆。

非洲炎热干燥的空气、明亮清澈的天空、纯净浓郁的色彩、深色细腻的肌肤、热情奔放的性格、特殊节奏的音乐、载歌载舞的狂欢、狂奔迁徙的动物——这是我们印象中活泼的非洲。

层层分布的地理位置、各具领地的丰富物种、千差万别的部族文化——这是非洲国家经久的魅力所在，也是其发展的潜力。

68 生命之树——非洲猴面包树

The baobab tree of Africa is known as the upside-down tree; an ancient tree of life, the baobab tree is capable of storing water vital for the survival of local nomads.

One of Africa's ancient trees, the baobab (Adansonia digitata) is **synonymous** with the African plains; **prevalent** throughout Africa, Adansonia digitata can also be found on the island of Madagascar, where other species of the baobab tree grow. One species of the baobab tree, Adansonia gregorii, can only be found in northern Australia.

Adansonia digitata is most well known for its wide trunk, in which it can store vital life-saving water; the African baobab tree is **deciduous** and some are said to be thousands of years old. It produces large, **aromatic** flowers up to 7 inches wide; the baobab tree of Africa also produces fruit, which hangs from the branches of the tree. The fruit of the African baobab tree is particularly appealing to **baboon**s, hence its nickname monkey-bread tree.

The African baobab tree is known as the tree of life; it is capable of storing life-saving water during the drought season which is vital to local nomadic people who may not have any other means of obtaining water. Large baobab trees are said to contain more than 30,000 gallons of water; to access this water, the Kalahari bushmen use hollow pieces of grass (much like a straw) to **suck** the water out.

The African baobab tree is a vital nutrition source for many local tribes; the fruit of the baobab tree contains both **pulp** and seeds which are eaten. The pulp can also be mixed with water and made into a drink; the seeds of the baobab tree can be eaten alone or mixed with millet. The seeds can also be traded for the **extraction** of the oil or eaten in a paste; seedlings and young leaves are eaten

非洲的猴面包树是一种上下颠倒的树，一种古老的生命之树。猴面包树能够贮水，这对于当地游牧民族的生存至关重要。

猴面包树是非洲古老的树种之一，意思是平原之意。在非洲大陆，猴面包树随处可见。马达加斯加岛上也有此种树，而且该岛上还有其他猴面包树的树种。而Adansonia gregorii猴面包树只能在澳大利亚北部才能找到。

猴面包树最为有名的是它粗大的树干，在树干里能够储存生命之源——水。猴面包树每年落叶，一些猴面包树已活数千年。它的花芳香四溢，形状很大，最宽可达7英寸。猴面包树也产果子，果子长在树枝上。而狒狒尤其喜欢猴面包树上的果实。因此，便有了"猴面包树"的昵称。

非洲猴面包树素有生命之树的美誉。旱季时，猴面包树贮存的生命之水对于那些没有其他途径获得水源的游牧民族来说非常重要。大的猴面包树据说能储水3万多加仑（1加仑=4.5升）。卡拉哈里沙漠地区的布须曼人会将草叶弄成吸管的样子，从树干中吸水。

猴面包树对于很多当地的部落来说，是很重要的营养元素来源。猴面包树的果实含果肉和可吃的果籽。果肉可以和水混合，然后作为饮料；猴面包树的种子可以单

like asparagus or are used in salads.

The hollow trunk of the baobab tree (either aged naturally or through human intervention) is a place where native people have stored grain, water or livestock. The size of some baobab trees is so great that natives have used the hollow of the baobab tree trunk in which to live.

The African baobab tree has many medicinal uses; the baobab tree is high in vitamin C and calcium and therefore the leaves and fruit are eaten to protect against illness. The bark of the African baobab tree is used to treat **fever**; its medicinal use was considered to be of such value that Europeans used the bark in place of cinchona bark (from where quinine was obtained) to protect against malaria.

The inner workings of the African baobab tree provide a fiber which **indigenous** people have used to make cloth, rope, nets, musical instrument strings and waterproof hats. The bark of the baobab tree has to be removed to obtain the fiber; the baobab tree can regenerate the loss of bark if it is cut away.

独吃或者和小米混合吃。种子也可以卖，买家会利用种子榨油或混在面团中吃。而幼苗和嫩叶可以当作芦笋吃或用在沙拉中。

当地人可以利用猴面包树的空树干贮藏谷物、水或牲畜。而有些树干很大，当地人会在里面睡觉。

非洲猴面包树有很多药用。猴面包树富含维他命C和钙，因此，食用树叶和果实可以防病。树皮可以用来对付发烧。欧洲人还会利用树皮代替金鸡纳属的树皮，来对抗猩红热。

而猴面包树的内部机理给当地人做衣服、绳子、网、乐器的琴弦以及防水帽提供了纤维。为了获取纤维，人们要先刮掉树皮。猴面包树可以重新长出树皮。

词汇 Ｖ OCABULARY

synonymous：与……同义的	suck：吮吸
prevalent：普遍的	pulp：果肉
deciduous：每年落叶的	extraction：提取
aromatic：有香味的	fever：高烧
baboon：狒狒	indigenous：当地的

背景知识 Ｐ ROFILE

猴面包树名字的由来与猴面包树树林

猴面包树名字的由来

在非洲有两种说法：一种说，这是黑非洲土著人的称谓，意为"瓶状树"；另一种说法，认为这是从一个阿拉伯语词汇演变而来。那是很早以前，此种树的荚果被贩运到埃及，当地人不知为何物。但是，他们发现，荚果多籽，就以"布希波布"这个词名之，意为"多籽的水果"。"布希波布"后来演化成"包波布"。而这种树的学名则鲜为人知，直译为"指状阿当松"。米歇尔·阿当松是法国著名的植物学家。1749年，他奉派到塞内加尔工作。在逗留的四年中，他搜集到大量植物标本，尤为详尽地描述了包波布树的情状。1759年，瑞典著名植物分类学家卡尔·林奈就以阿当松的名字将这种树命名。考虑到这种树的叶子呈伸展的手指状，故又加上一个形容词，称"指状阿当松"。

因为它的果实鲜美，猴子爱吃它的果实。猴面包树学名叫波巴布树，又名猢狲木，别称猴面包树或酸瓠树，是大型落叶乔木。猴面包树树冠巨大，树杈千奇百怪，酷似树根，远看就像是摔了个"倒栽葱"。

它树干很粗，最粗的直径可达12米，要40个人手拉手才能围它一圈，但它个头又不高，只有10多米。因此，整棵树显得像一个大肚子啤酒桶。远远望去，树似乎不是长在地上，而是插在一个大肚子的花瓶里，因此又称"瓶树"。

猴面包树的树形壮观，果实巨大如足球，甘甜汁多，是猴子、猩猩、大象等动物最喜欢的美味。当它果实成熟时，猴子就成群结队而来，爬上树去摘果子吃，所以它又有"猴面包树"的称呼。

全世界唯一的猴面包树林

如果要选择马达加斯加的代表植物，相信很多人会选择猴面包树，而不是马达加斯加的国树"旅人蕉"。

猴面包树作为这个地球上古老而独特的树种之一，尽管并不是马达加斯加所独有，但全世界目前也只有马达加斯加岛还保存有成片的猴面包树林，而且全世界8种猴面包树中有7种能在马达加斯加见到。除了种类齐全之外，该岛的猴面包树还以高大粗壮、造型奇特闻名。

这里的猴面包树，树高从十几米到几十米不等，"腰围"粗大，活像硕大的啤酒桶，最粗的甚至要数十人合抱。猴面包树也是植物王国中的"老寿星"，最能活到4000岁~6000岁，有着极强的生存能力。每当旱季来临，为了减少水分的蒸发，它会迅速地落光身上的叶子。雨季来临后，便靠自身松软的木质，拼命地吸水贮存在树干内。此时，身躯已完全代替了根系的吸水作用。

据说，在热带草原旅行的人们干渴难耐时，只要找到猴面包树，就可以从树身上吸水解渴。为此，人们叫它"生命树"。猴面包树"吃饱喝足"以后，会长出了掌状复叶，开出很大的白色花。花后结出褐色椭圆形的呆实，外壳坚硬有葫芦般大小，果肉汁多味酸甜，是猴、猩猩十分喜爱的美味佳肴。

要观看猴面包树林的壮美，一定要到"猴面包树大道"。大道距离马达加斯加西部穆隆达瓦约20公里，猴面包树非常密集，而且能同时看到4种不同的种类。

一路西来，原野上、低谷中处处都可领略到它那高大耸立的英姿，执著而孤独地守望着这片原始而沉默的土地。最美的画面是，日落时分，云霞披红，大地抹彩，巨大沉重的树影投射到地面上，偶有当地的村民驾着牛车从树下经过，扬起微微土尘，又消失在了视野之外。

69 娇艳的植物——非洲白鹭花

Hyndora africana is one of the most bizarre-looking plants on the African continent and certainly not the most common of plants to be **encounter**ed in the **veld** on any casual hike.

Hydnora africana is a **parasitic** plant on species of the **genus** Euphorbia. It has such an unusual physical appearance that one would never say it is a plant. It looks astonishingly similar to **fungi** and is only distinguishable from fungi when the flower has opened.

The plant body is completely leafless, **void** of chlorophyll and is brown-grey. As it ages, the plant turns dark grey to black. A network of thick rhizophores or subterranean stems and roots **traverse** the soil around the host plant. These fleshy, angular, **warty** stems bear a series of vermiform (shaped like a worm) outgrowths commonly referred to as roots. The plant body is only visible when the developing flowers push through the ground.

The buds of these **bisexual** flowers develop underground and eventually emerge, reaching a height of about 100 to 150 mm. The flower is spherical, brown on the outside and bright salmon to orange on the inner surface, and has 3 or 4 thick, fleshy, perianth lobes, fused in the beginning but later rupturing vertically as the flower matures, at which point the bait bodies are exposed. The exposed inner surface of the perianth lobes are covered by many stout bristles. The stamens are peculiar and situated halfway down the perianth tube which is 10-20 mm wide. Flowers may not appear for a number of years until sufficient rain has fallen. The fruit is a subglobose (half-round), underground berry with a thick, leathery wall epidermis/skin. The seeds are numerous and small and **embed**ded in a gelatinous, edible fleshy pulp which is rich in starch. The fruit is delicious when baked on a fire and has a sweetish taste.

非洲白鹭花是非洲大陆上看起来非常奇特的植物之一。当然，游客也就很难通过一次随随便便的草原远足碰到这种植物了。

非洲白鹭花是一种寄生植物，属大戟属。从外形上看，很难说非洲白鹭花是一种植物。它和菌类惊人的相似。如果不开花，人们很难将菌类和非洲白鹭分开。

非洲白鹭花没有叶子，不含叶绿素，整株植物呈褐灰色。随着成长，植物会变成深灰色，然后变黑。地下，根系遍布。只有花从地下钻出来，才能看到植物。

非洲白鹭花是雌雄同体的植物，花蕾在地下形成，最终钻出地面，高度一般为100mm～150mm。花朵成球状，外面是棕色，里面是橙红色。花苞由3片~4片厚实、新鲜的花叶组成，成熟后会裂开。暴露出的表面有很多粗壮的毛毛。雄蕊很特别，位于花粉管的一半偏下，花粉管大概10mm~20mm宽。如果雨下不够的话，花朵可能很多年都不开。果实近似球形。籽多，且小，籽嵌在粘粘的、可食用的果肉里。它的果肉富含淀粉。如果放在火上烤，果实很美味，有甜甜的味道。

encounter：邂逅，偶遇	void：无效的，没有的
veld：草原	traverse：横渡，横越
parasitic：寄生的	warty：有疣的，多疣的，似疣的
genus：属	bisexual：雌雄同株的
fungi：菌类	embed：使插入，使嵌入，深留脑中

背景知识 PROFILE

世界上十大奇异植物

巨型猪笼草

本来猪笼草就是一种奇怪的食肉植物，而能够吃老鼠的猪笼草更是其中最怪异的代表。吃老鼠的猪笼草学名为"Nepenthes attenboroughii"，发现于2009年8月。它被认为是世界上最大型的食肉植物，它们的笼子甚至可以吞噬一只老鼠。科学家是在菲律宾的维多利亚山上发现这种植物的。这种植物能够通过其瓶状叶里面的酸酶将捕获的猎物消化。其瓶状叶长约30厘米，宽16厘米，是其他地区的普通猪笼草体积的两倍。

降落伞花

降落伞花学名为"Ceropegia woodii"。这种奇异植物的花朵呈现降落伞形状，内部的花瓣好像灯丝一样连接四周，花朵中心就像是一根毛茸茸的棒棒糖从内部伸出。整个花朵收拢起来就会形成一个管状物，边缘有许多细小的茸毛向外伸展。当有昆虫被花朵的气味吸引而来时，就会被管状物包裹其中，从而成为降落伞花的营养餐。不过，降落伞花从来不吃苍蝇。当苍蝇飞来时，降落伞花会将其包裹于花朵中，直到茸毛最终松开，苍蝇才得以逃脱。当苍蝇飞走时，它也带走了降落伞花的花粉。苍蝇只是它们传粉的工具而已。

蛇头菌

蛇头菌学名为"Mutinus Caninus"，可以称得上是最丑陋的菌类。蛇头菌菌柄呈圆柱形，菌盖呈鲜红色，菌盖顶端长有恶臭气味的粘稠状孢子。

跳舞草

跳舞草学名为"Desmodium Gyrans"。这种植物最奇异的特点就是叶片会随温度变化或音乐伴奏而上下舞动，因此得名"跳舞草"。当跳舞草受到阳光直射时或是处于较温暖的环境下，它们就会快速地舞动自己的叶子。当音乐响起时，跳舞草也会做出一些反应。在跳舞草每一片叶子的根部，都有一个相当于铰链装置的结构，叶子可以围绕它沿着椭圆形路径旋转。

巨花马兜铃

巨花马兜铃学名为"Aristolochia grandiflora"。这种植物的奇特之处在于它们美丽而怪异的花朵。花朵的主要部分只有一片，看起来好像是一个巨大的、带有纹理的兜状物，而不像普通的花朵那样拥有对称的花瓣。观赏者千万不要太靠近它，否则它所发出的死老鼠味道会在你们身边数小时不散。不过，巨花马兜铃虽然会发出死老鼠味道，但它们并不像巨型猪笼草那样吃老鼠，它们这种气味不过是用来吸引传粉昆虫帮助它们传粉而已。

含羞草

含羞草学名为"Mimosa pudica"。当人们用手触摸它时，甚至只是向它吹口气，它的叶子就会收缩起来，似乎受到了惊吓而做自我保护。当含羞草受到外界干扰时，它们的茎部会释放出一种化学物质。这种化学物质会迫使水份流出细胞，使得叶子看起来像是萎缩了一样。对于含羞草为什么会进化出这种特性，科学家们至今未能找到明确答案，他们认为这可能是用于威吓捕食者。

伍德苏铁

伍德苏铁学名为"Encephalartos woodii"。这是世界上最稀有的植物之一，已被列入野外灭绝物种。全球发现的唯一一株野生伍德苏铁位于南非诺耶森林边缘的一个斜坡上。目前，伍德苏铁实际上已经相当于完全灭绝，因为它是一种雌雄异株植物，而植物园中所有现存的伍德苏铁都是雄性的。科学家开始尝试将它们与最近的近亲物种进行杂交，希望能够培育出伍德苏铁的新苗，三代以后即可再现纯种伍德苏铁。

白星海芋

白星海芋学名为"Helicodiceros muscivorus"。这种植物花朵巨大，而且会释放出一种难闻的腐肉味道。这种气味可以吸引雌性大苍蝇为其传粉。当大苍蝇飞到它们身上时，它们就用自己巨大的花朵将其捕获并困于花朵之中一整夜。第二天，白星海芋才会张开花朵，将粘满花粉的大苍蝇释放。当大苍蝇飞临第二株白星海芋花朵之上时，传粉任务就完成了。

百岁兰

百岁兰学名为"Welwitschia mirabilis"，有时也叫千岁兰。百岁兰是一种非常怪异的沙漠植物，可以忍耐极为恶劣的环境。百岁兰的叶子是植物界寿命最长的叶子，而且只有一对。两片叶子从短矮而粗壮的树干上端长出，不断增宽增长，形成长带状，最长可达12英尺（约合3.7米）。百岁兰也被称为植物界的活化石，最长可以存活2000年。

囊泡貉藻

囊泡貉藻学名为"Aldrovanda Vesiculosa"，也被称为"水车植物"。它是一种水生浮游植物，与维纳斯捕蝇草是近亲。囊泡貉藻以主茎为中心向四周辐射出多条"轮辐"式的支茎，在每条支茎的顶端，都有一个与捕蝇草类似的捕虫夹结构。每个捕虫夹上都有长"触发茸毛"。当"触发茸毛"受到猎物刺激时，捕虫夹就会合拢，将猎物包夹起来。

斯诺登水兰

斯诺登水兰学名为"Snowdonia Hawkweed"。这种植物看起来并不是外观最奇怪的，也不是体型最大的，更不是气味最臭的，它的奇特之处在于它是世界上最罕见的植物。植物学家曾一度认为它于几十年前就已经灭绝。2002年，它又再次被发现于英国威尔士的一个山谷斜坡上。

70 南非的国花——帝王花

A king protea is a woody shrub that is native to South Africa. It is also the national flower of South Africa. Of all the different species of protea, the king protea has the largest flowers, measuring between 6 inches (15 cm) and 1 foot (30 cm). What appear to be flowers are actually brightly colored, **petal**-like leaves called **bract**s that contain clusters of true flowers, which are usually **dull**er in color. The bracts are usually considered the flowers on all the protea species.

Grown commercially in New Zealand, South Africa and Hawaii, the large, bright, dramatic flowers of the king protea are popular as cut flowers for use in **bridal bouquet**s and large **floral** displays. The mature plants make a spectacular addition to large gardens or as a striking landscape feature. King proteas are slow-spreading plants that can reach more than 6 feet (2 m) in height and width.

There are approximately 80 varieties or **cultivar**s of the king protea species. Because the plant has such a huge native range, it has evolved and adapted to differing environmental influences in different locations. These locally adapted cultivars have resulted in a wider variety of flowers, ranging from bright white through shades of pale pink to deep **crimson** or red.

King protea cultivars have also evolved with different disease and pest resistances, different plant and flower size and different soil and water preferences. The wide range of available cultivars can be found growing from sea level to altitudes above 4,920 feet (1,500 m) above sea level. While some king protea varieties will tolerate heavy soils, no variety will tolerate long periods of **waterlogging**, and all varieties prefer light, well-draining or sandy soils.

A useful plant for landscaping in areas with poorly conditioned soil containing few nutrients, the king protea has a large, elaborate root system that allows the plant to

帝王花是产自南非的木本灌木。帝王花也是南非的国花。在所有山龙眼属植物中，帝王花的花朵最大，大概在15cm~30cm。那些看起来是花瓣的部分其实是颜色鲜艳、成花瓣形的叶子，学名叫苞片。苞片内才是真正的花朵，花朵的颜色要暗一些。在山龙眼属植物中，苞片通常被当成花。

帝王花在新西兰、南非以及夏威夷是一种经济类植物。在新娘的花束上或大型花卉展览中会出现帝王花的身影。成熟的帝王花会为花园增添韵味。帝王花扩展很慢，高度和宽度都可达2m。

有近80种或栽培变种的帝王花。因为帝王花的生长范围比较广，所以帝王花能适应不同地区的不同环境影响。那些适应本地的品种会产生更多类型的帝王花。颜色从白色、浅粉、大红到深红。

帝王花的品种是随着不同的疾病、抗虫害、不同的植物及花朵形状以及不同的土壤和水的喜好而逐渐进化而来的。帝王花的生长范围可以低到海边，可以高到海拔1500米处。尽管一些帝王花的品种能够适应较为贫瘠的土地，但没有帝王花能够忍受长时间的浸泡。

gather resources from a wide area. King proteas will not tolerate temperatures below 59° Fahrenheit (15° Celsius). In containers, the king protea can also be grown as a house plant.

In small gardens or as a house plant, the king protea will most likely need to be vigorously **prune**d to keep it at a manageable size. King proteas can be fertilized, but this species does not tolerate phosphorous, so a low-phosphorous fertilizer must be used. Most cultivars are prone to **magnesium** deficiency, which results in poor health, reduced flower production and even death, so—especially in containers—it may be necessary to add magnesium in the form of fertilizer.

所有的帝王花都喜阳，喜欢沙质土壤。

作为一种在贫瘠土地中具有观赏价值的植物，帝王花的根系系统很发达，这使得植物能从很广大的地下吸收资源。帝王花的生长环境不能低于15℃。而且帝王花已作为室内植物。

小花园或家庭中，帝王花需要剪枝，来控制比较适合的尺寸。人们可以给帝王花施肥，但是肥料不能含磷。所以帝王花的肥料最好低磷。很多的帝王花品种容易缺镁，这会导致帝王花不够健康，花朵减小甚至是死亡。所以，盆养时，最好在帝王花的肥料中加镁。

词汇 VOCABULARY

petal：花瓣	cultivar：培植品种
bract：苞片	crimson：深红色
dull：呆滞的，迟钝的，无趣的，暗的	waterlogging：水浸泡
bridal bouquet：新娘花束	prune：修剪
floral：花朵的	magnesium：镁

背景知识 PROFILE

非洲各国的国花

刚果 Enpandrophragma sp. 香桃花心木（楝科）猴面包树

埃及 Nymphaea caerulea 睡莲（睡莲科）草棉

埃塞俄比亚 Zantedeschia aethiopica 马蹄莲（天南星科）咖啡

加蓬 Spathodea campanulata 苞萼木（紫葳科）

加纳 Phoenix dactylifera 海枣（棕榈科）可可、非洲鹅掌楸

利比亚 Punica granatum 石榴（安石榴科）

利比里亚 Piper nigrum 胡椒（胡椒科）油椰、香草果

马达加斯加 Ravenalamadagascariensis 旅人蕉（旅人蕉科）

摩洛哥 Qeurcus suber 栓皮储（壳斗科）

塞拉利昂 Elaeis guineensis 非洲油椰（棕榈科）

坦桑尼亚 Syzygium aromaticum 丁香（桃金娘科）

塞内加尔 Adansonia digyfafa 猴面包树（木棉科）

突尼斯 Acacia farnesiana 金合欢（含羞草科）油橄榄

阿尔及利亚 Iris tectorum 鸢尾（鸢尾科）澳洲夹竹桃

阿扎尼亚Brodiaea californica 卜若地（百合科）

津巴布韦 Glorilsa rothschildiana 嘉兰（百合科）

非洲是片热土，这里聚集了各种各样的顶级庆典。世界杯上，无数球迷的目光撒向了南非；狂欢节上，人们可以尽情舞蹈、尽情欢唱；芦苇舞蹈节中，少女用自己的童贞舞蹈着纯美的青春；音乐节上，音乐迷们可以放纵自己的心，逐音乐而动；民族艺术节上，鉴赏家们的寻宝活动全面开始；而在别具一格的骆驼节上，你会欣赏到"沙漠之舟"的另外一面；当然，还有男人的选美大赛，相信这一定会让游客大开眼界；最后一个美酒加美食的节日，相信它将成为您的喜爱之物。

第八章

你不可不知的非洲庆典

71 足球迷们的盛典——2010南非世界杯

The 2010 **FIFA** World Cup was the 19th FIFA World Cup, the world championship for men's national association football teams. It took place in South Africa from 11 June to 11 July 2010. The **bidding** process for hosting the tournament finals was open only to African nations; in 2004, the international football federation, FIFA, selected South Africa over Egypt and Morocco to become the first African nation to host the **final**s.

The matches were played in ten **stadium** in nine host cities around the country, with the final played at the **Soccer City** stadium in South Africa's largest city, Johannesburg. Thirty-two teams were selected for participation via a worldwide **qualification tournament** that began in August 2007.

In the final, Spain, the European champions, defeated third-time finalists the Netherlands 1–0 after **extra time**, with Andrés Iniesta's goal in the 116th minute giving Spain their first world title, the first time that a European nation has won the tournament outside its home continent. Host nation South Africa, 2006 world champions Italy and 2006 **runners-up** France were eliminated in the first round of the tournament.

Five new stadiums were built for the tournament, and five of the existing venues were upgraded. Construction costs were expected to be R8.4 billion (just over US$1 billion or €950 million).

South Africa also improved its public transport infrastructure within the host cities, including Johannesburg's Gautrain and other metro systems, and major road networks were improved. In March 2009, Danny Jordaan, the president of the 2010 World Cup organising committee, reported that all stadiums

2010年世界杯足球赛是国际足联第十九届世界杯男子足球赛，于2010年6月11日至7月11日举行。此次世界杯的举办地只允许非洲国家竞标。2004年，国际足联选择南非作为世界杯决赛举办地。这样，南非战胜埃及和摩洛哥成为第一个举办世界杯决赛的非洲国家。

球赛在南非9个城市的10个球场举行，由从2007年8月开始来自世界各地的在资格赛中胜出的32支球队参加赛事，进行64场比赛决定冠军队伍。总决赛在南非最大城市约翰内斯堡的足球城举行。

总决赛中，欧洲杯冠军西班牙队对决世界杯三次卫冕冠军荷兰队。最终，西班牙队球员安德列斯·伊涅斯塔在加时赛116分钟时，踢进一球，由此将西班牙队推向世界杯冠军的领奖台。这是第一次欧洲国家在家门口以外的大陆夺冠。主办国南非、06年世界冠军意大利和亚军法国在联赛时就出局了。

为了此次足球联赛，南非新建了5座体育馆，并将现有的5座进行了修缮。修建体育场的费用预计为84亿人民币（即10亿美元）。

另外，南非还改善了举办城市的交通基础设施状况，主要包括约翰内斯堡的铁路快运线路豪登及其他地铁系统，主要公路线路。2009年3月，南非组委会首席执行官丹尼·乔达安公布联赛所有的举办场馆需要在6个月内

for the tournament were on schedule to be completed within six months.

The country implemented special measures to ensure the safety and security of spectators **in accordance with** standard FIFA requirements, including a temporary restriction of flight operation in the airspace surrounding the stadiums.

At a ceremony to mark 100 days before the event, FIFA president Sepp Blatter praised the **readiness** of the country for the event.

竣工。

为了确保观众的安全，南非严格遵守国际足联的要求，采取了特别的措施，其中包括在比赛场馆的上空，飞机暂时性限飞。

在足球联赛开赛前100天的庆典上，足联主席赛普·布拉特高度赞扬了南非出色的准备工作。

FIFA：(International Association Football Federation) 国际足球联合会	
bidding：竞标	knockout：淘汰赛
final：决赛	extra time：加时赛
stadium：体育馆	runners-up：亚军
Soccer City：足球城	in accordance with：与……一致
qualification tournament：资格赛	readiness：准备就绪，敏捷

背景知识 PROFILE

南非世界杯九大趣闻

不愿出狱只为世界杯

英国人阿瑟·克鲁克在2010年7月5日将刑满出狱，但他却死活不愿意离开监狱，理由竟然是想要和狱友一起观看世界杯。在世界杯之前，克鲁克因为妨碍公共秩序等罪名被关进监狱，没想到进入监狱的克鲁克非常享受和一大堆狱友看球的氛围，因此他极度不愿意离开监狱。克鲁克说："我还跟狱友们打了赌，我估计，那场球（决赛）应该会在阿根廷与巴西之间进行。"正所谓，"自由诚可贵，出狱价更高，若为看球故，两者皆可抛。"

球迷赌儿子世界杯进球

英国人恩提科特在全球最著名的博彩公司——威廉希尔公司用120欧元投注，赌自己将在6月底出生的儿子能够在2034年的世界杯上为英格兰代表队取得进球。如果他的赌博能够实现，那么2034年他将会得到一笔1200万欧元的奖励。而威廉希尔公司在接受了恩提科特的投注请求后表示，他获得这笔奖金的概率为万分之一。

看球不成反遭判刑

名为马杜尔的德国球迷可能是本届世界杯最倒霉的球迷，到现场看球不成，反被法院判决三个月有期徒刑，缓期一年执行。马杜尔被判刑的原因是为了观看德国同西班牙的半决赛，他乘坐飞机赶往比赛现场，结果因为交通原因，航班无奈返回。愤怒的球迷眼看着无法观看比赛，只能将愤怒发泄到机场人员身上，马杜尔也是其中之一，因此遭受有期徒刑。

勒夫幸运羊毛衫14天未洗

自人类诞生的那一天起，迷信就无处不在，因为实在有太多科学无法解释的现象。在世界杯上，也从不缺少迷信，除了非洲球队的巫医之外，本届世界杯最离奇的迷信当然是德国主帅勒夫的蓝色羊毛衫。据勒夫本人透露，从小组赛打败加纳到半决赛被西班牙击败，他的蓝色羊毛衫就一直没有洗过，时间长达14天。遗憾地是，这件幸运羊毛衫并未让德国队晋级决赛，不过勒夫本人已经表示，这件幸运羊毛衫会进行拍卖，所得款项会用作慈善事业。

最神预言帝章鱼保罗

预测比赛是世界杯必不可少的花边话题，但大多数人预测的结果往往非常离谱，球王贝利就是此种典型。不过本届世界杯居然有一位预言帝保持了100%的正确率，那就是章鱼保罗，在预测有关德国队的比赛之时，章鱼保罗7场比赛全部命中，堪称最神奇预言帝。而章鱼保罗的高准确性也引发了鹦鹉帝，猩猩帝，海豚帝……等一系列的动物预测家。看来在预测这事上，动物要比人可靠。

神奇未来哥现身

不要迷恋哥，哥来自未来。在百度贴吧之中，来自未来的网友准确地预测了2010世界杯决赛将在荷兰和西班牙之间展开，且自称来自未来，因此被网友称之为"未来哥"。未来哥还预言了荷兰将击败西班牙捧杯成功。虽然已经被证实为炒作，但未来哥在百度贴吧的人气直逼去年最火的贾君鹏。有道是，未来哥一出，贾君鹏不再被妈妈喊回家吃饭。

大家一起来裸奔

拉美球迷奔放由来已久，但即便如此，裸奔也是不常见的。不成想，一个世界杯，本不够开放的中国球迷瞬时走在了世界潮流之前。在本届世界杯中，随着微博这一新媒体的兴起，多名球迷自爆私人照片，更多球迷实现诺言，裸奔。正是，你裸奔，我裸奔，大家一起裸奔，不裸奔，无铁杆。

看球48小时疲劳撞大树

6月16日下午，在世界杯开赛不到一周之时，37岁的金先生出名了，不过这次出名却让金先生付出了惨痛代价。为了观看世界杯和NBA总决赛，金先生连续48小时没有睡觉，在连续两大观看激烈比赛之后，金先生开车去父母家过端午节，未曾想，极度疲劳导致金先生开车时反应迟钝，撞到大树，导致左腿两处骨折，左手臂粉碎性骨折。

呜呜祖拉红遍世界

若干年后，回想起南非世界杯，球迷首先想起的或许不会是最终的冠军，而是呜呜祖啦。这个响声难听的看球辅助工具，在2010年，无论是世界杯赛场内外，着实火了一把。影响球员发挥，制造多起冷门暂且不谈，场外就有英国流行音乐巨星罗比·威廉姆斯因为呜呜祖拉和妻子分居，酒店订房送呜呜祖拉等奇闻，呜呜祖拉俨然成为南非世界杯最抢戏配角。

72 狂欢节爱好者们的盛宴——塞舌尔狂欢节

The Seychelles unique "**carnival** of carnivals," which was held in early March 2011, was the biggest event ever organized in the Creole Islands of the Seychelles, and it is today widely accepted as having been the most popular event held in these islands. Mass participation of the Seychellois population, and the involvement of the tourists who were holidaying in the Seychelles brought to life the spirit of this event organized under the theme "the **melting pot** of cultures". Since its debut, written press and TV stations from the four corners of the world have been bringing out reports of the Seychelles islands' **annual** carnival and all have been **echo**ing the one qualifying statement—"simply a success".

Last week, the respected newspaper "Le Mauritien" from the neighboring island of Mauritius brought out dedicated pages on the Seychelles Carnival with the heading "The First Carnival of the Seychelles a success" with colorful pictures of the island's unique March carnival. The pictures printed brought to life the

西印度洋上的岛国塞舌尔在2011年三月初举办了岛上最盛大的狂欢节，这被公认为是这些岛上最受欢迎的活动。大多数参加者是塞舌尔当地居民，而碰巧在这休假的世界游客们亦加入到了这个"文化大熔炉"当中，并为此次狂欢节增添了活力。自从狂欢节举办以来，世界上四面八方的各种书面报道、电视媒体开始全程报导了塞舌尔岛上的这次一年一度的狂欢节。所有媒体一致认为，塞舌尔狂欢节"非常成功"。

上周，毛里求斯媒体"Le Mauritien"为塞舌尔狂欢节设置了专栏，标题时"首届塞舌尔狂欢节举得巨大成功"，并配以狂欢节彩色照片。这些照片生动地展示了此次狂欢节参加者——美国著

diversity of participants of the "carnival of carnivals" of the Seychelles with one of Lima Calbio - the Soca Queen from Trinidad, Brazilian dancing stars, the French Float, **immaculately**-dressed Russian Sailors, an Arts School participant from the Seychelles, Indonesian dancers, Zimbabweans dancing group, and the **delegation** from the big island of Madagascar.

Twenty-one delegations from overseas **descend**ed on Seychelles for the March carnival, and they joined over sixty local groups and floats to make the first edition of the unique "carnival of carnivals" a total success. The Seychelles Tourism Board is the responsible body for the organization of the carnival, and they have said that they are over satisfied with the success of their event.

George Michel, the photo journalist from the island of Mauritius who prepared the report for the respected "Le Mauritien" newspaper explained that the official opening of the March 2011 Carnival in the Seychelles was made by the President of the Republic of Seychelles Mr. James Michel in the presence of the Mauritius Vice Prime Minister Mr. Praving Jugnauth, the Vice President of Zimbabwe Mrs. J.T.R. Mujuru, the Vice President of Zanzibar Tanzania Mr. Seif Ali Iddi, the Seychelles former President Sir James Mancham, the Seychelles Vice President Mr. Danny Faure, and the Mayor of Victoria Mrs. Antoinette Alexis, among many other dignitaries.

Alain St. Ange, the CEO of the Seychelles Tourism Board, contacted by the press about the coverage being given to the Seychelles unique carnival said that they felt humbled by the ongoing coverage being received. "We wanted to offer to the world an event where the Community of Nations could participate together. We wanted to offer an event that went beyond politics and where everyone was respected. This we have today succeeded, and we can only say that we are looking forward to an even bigger 'carnival of carnivals' from March 2-4, 2012. We say a 'carnival of carnivals' because it is the only carnival staged to bring together the best

名雷鬼音乐女歌手，特立尼达岛的Soca Queen，巴西舞蹈家，法国彩车，完美装扮的俄罗斯水手，塞舌尔当地的艺术学校学生，印度尼西亚舞者，津巴布韦舞蹈团以及马达加斯加岛代表团——所呈现出的各异的生命力。

来自世界各地的21个代表队慕三月狂欢节之名而来到塞舌尔。他们加入到当地60多个团体和彩车当中，使得独一无二的首次"狂欢节之桂冠"大获成功。塞舌尔旅游局负责组织此次狂欢节，他们说2011年的狂欢节成功程度出人意料。

毛里求斯"Le Mauritien"摄影师乔治•米歇尔说，2011年三月的官方开幕日当天，塞舌尔总统詹姆斯•米歇尔、维多利亚市市长玛丽－安托瓦妮特•亚力克西斯亲临现场，而其他国家的多位领导人亦亲自到场。

塞舌尔旅游局CEO，阿兰•圣安格在媒体连线时说，对于各国媒体对塞舌尔狂欢节的报导如此之多，他们是始料未及的。"我们曾想办一项活动，能够让国际社会参与其中，一项超越政治的活动，能够让每一个参与人员都得到尊重。而这次我们成功了。我们想说，我们期待2012年3月2日~4日，塞舌尔更大规模的狂欢节上我们再见。我们之所以叫'狂欢节桂冠'，原因在于塞舌尔狂欢节是现在仅有的将世界上最好的狂欢节、最好的狂欢群体聚在一起的活动。"

塞舌尔的旅游事业的发展任务如今落在现任总统任期之内。它能够使得总统詹姆斯•米歇尔实现

carnivals of the world and the best cultural groups of the world," Alain St.Ange said.

The portfolio for tourism in the Seychelles today falls under the Office of the President. This was to enable President James Michel of the Seychelles to bring to life his **vision** for his country's tourism industry, which he declared as the "Seychelles Brand" of tourism. Today, the island tourism industry is flourishing, investments in the Seychelles are gathering pace, and air access is peaking with increased flights to these **mid-ocean** islands.

他曾经的誓言：打造塞舌尔自己的旅游品牌。今天，岛上的旅游业蒸蒸日上，岛内的投资势头正猛，来岛的航班不断增加。

词汇 VOCABULARY

carnival：狂欢节	delegationy：代表团
melting pot：熔炉	descend：登陆
annual：一年一度的	mid-ocean：海中央
echo：重复仿效；共鸣	vision：愿景
immaculately：完美无瑕地	

背景知识 PROFILE

世界各地有名的狂欢节

巴西狂欢节

每年2月下旬，号称"地球上最大聚会"的巴西里约热内卢狂欢节就会如期拉开帷幕。狂欢节开幕前两个月，市民会选出狂欢节国王："莫莫王"。狂欢节开幕当天，里约热内卢市长会在官邸将城门金钥匙亲手交给"莫莫王"，象征一年一度的狂欢节正式开始。在长达一周的狂欢中，"莫莫王"不会坐到市长办公室发号施令，而是在沸腾的城中带领大家尽情跳舞、尽情享乐，这就算出色地完成市长的使命了。

意大利威尼斯狂欢节

意大利威尼斯狂欢节也在2月粉墨登场，它是世界上历史最悠久的狂欢节之一。威尼斯狂欢节最大的特点是它的面具，这个传统可追溯到16世纪，面具背后权贵和穷人终于融合到一起。据说在1769年，奥地利皇帝也乔装成平民前来参加威尼斯狂欢节。现在的狂欢节上，面具后的年龄差异被消除，老人极力将自己装扮得很年轻，甚至越愚蠢越好；年轻人和小人物则借助面具代表的权威，把自己扮成大人物过瘾。

西非儿童狂欢节

如果你有孩子，可以带他们到西非参加那里的儿童狂欢节。西非大部分国家认为儿童的成长需要能使他们感情奔放的环境，使他们的智慧能够得到尽情的展现。正是基于此，每年四五月，这些国家都会举行为期一个月的儿童狂欢节。节日期间，4到15岁的孩子会在村中"孩子王"的组织下举行各种庆祝活动。他们戴上自制的动物面具，表演自己编排的文体节目。家长为鼓励他们，在观看演出时会送些礼物给他们。表演结束，孩子们会聚集到"孩子王"家里，分取大人们赠送的礼物。

英国诺丁山狂欢节

诺丁山狂欢节是欧洲规模最大的街头文化艺术节，每年在英国伦敦西区诺丁山地区举行。

诺丁山区的黑人居民多半不是来自非洲，而是来自加勒比海或拉美其他地区。正是诺丁山的移民文化孕育了诺丁山狂欢节。20世纪60年代，聚居在诺丁山地区的西印度群岛移民因思乡情重而举办狂欢节，当时不过只有一小群人穿着民族服装，敲着钢鼓在街上走一圈而已。几十年后，它发展成为规模盛大的多元文化节日和伦敦最炙手可热的旅游项目之一。

在世界各地的狂欢节中，诺丁山狂欢节的规模仅次于巴西里约热内卢的狂欢节。诺丁山狂欢节一向以浓郁的加勒比海情调著称。论服装和面具，诺丁山狂欢节如同一场奇异华丽的化妆舞会；论音乐，钢鼓乐队、卡里普索歌曲、索加音乐则是诺丁山狂欢节的灵魂。钢鼓的强烈节奏足以令心跳立即合着节拍提速；卡里普索歌曲每每根据最新时政和社会热点即兴改动歌词，唯有词曲幽默讽刺的本色不变。

法国尼斯狂欢节

为了既尊重传统又跟上时代，自20世纪50年代起，每届尼斯狂欢节都确定一个尼斯狂欢节主题，马戏、小丑、美食、欢笑、疯狂、爱情、20世纪、新千年、欧洲等概念都为狂欢节提供了灵感，并为艺术家们提供了发挥想象力的舞台。狂欢节是尼斯冬季的亮点，也是城市投资的重点。花车穿插彩车一起游行、花车上美丽的姑娘不断向游人投掷鲜花是尼斯狂欢节一大特色，仅为鲜花埋单就是一笔巨大的开支。有了这一年一度的狂欢节，因海滩和阳光而夏日爆满的尼斯在旅游淡季也不乏热闹。

73 少女的节日——斯威士兰的芦苇舞蹈节

The **reed** dance is a **spectacular** annual event which has attracted thousands of tourists to the **Kingdom of Swaziland**. Performing at the reed dance ceremony are thousands of Swazi **maiden**s in their traditional attire. These Swazi girls come from all around the country and gather for the ceremony which lasts for about eight days. The Umhlanga Reed Dance takes place towards the end of the month of August, when the seasons are changing and the reed is matured and ready for harvest. This event presents the maidens with an opportunity to honor the Queen Mother. Only childless, unmarried girls can take part in this exciting event.

The dates of the Umhlanga reed dance are set according to the moon's **cycle** and are never determined on the calendar; the exact dates of the event are announced over the radio by the maidens' captain (indvuna yetintfombi), who is appointed by Royalty. She is appointed on the basis of being an expert dancer and being **knowledgeable** on royal **protocol**. She is expected to lead the girls with one of the princesses as her **counterpart** when they set off to cut the reed on the first day.

The aims of the ceremony are to:

(1) Preserve girls' **virginity**: This tradition is aimed at encouraging young Swazi women to **abstain** from sexual activities and preserve their virginity until they are matured enough to get married. (2) Provide tribute labor for the Queen mother and (3) promote a spirit of oneness and solidarity among the girls by working together.

The activities of these 8 days:

Day 1: The Swazi girls gather from their communities to Ludzidzini.

Day 2: From Ludzidzini the girls walk to Engabezweni,

芦苇舞蹈节是斯威士兰王国一年一度的盛会，每年吸引数千名游客前来。在芦苇舞蹈节上表演的是斯威士兰少女，她们会身着传统服饰。这些少女来自国家的各个地区，为了此次为期8天的盛会集合在一起。乌兰加芦苇舞蹈节一般在8月末举行。此时，季节开始变化，芦苇开始成熟，可以准备收割。此次盛会对于少女们来说，是一次向皇后致敬的好机会。只有无子嗣、未婚的少女才能参加这次令人激动的盛会。

乌兰加芦苇舞蹈节的日期是根据月亮的活动选定的，而非根据日历。确切日期是由少女们的首领来宣布的。而这位首领是由皇室指派。她需要是一位超群的舞者，且将皇室礼仪了然于心。当少女们第一天收割芦苇时，会由这位首领和一位公主共同带领。

盛会的目的是：

（1）保护少女贞洁：这个活动的目的是鼓励威斯兰少女戒除性活动保持贞洁直到她们成人结婚。

（2）像皇后致敬。（3）让少女们团结一致。

八天的活动安排如下：

第一天：少女们从各自社区聚集到Ludzidzini;

第二天：她们来到Engabezweni，受到国王的祝福。然后按照年龄分成年轻组（8岁~13岁）

another palace where the girls meet the King who blesses them for the long journey they are about to embark on. They are then separated into two groups, the older (about 14 to 22 years) and the younger (about 8 to 13 years) who then take different routes to the selected destinations for cutting the reed.

Day 3: The Swazi girls cut the reeds, and tie them in **bundle**s. There's a long-held belief that the bundle must add up not to an even number but an odd number because the even number curses the royal family.

Day 4: In the afternoon the girls set off to return to the Queen Mother's household, carrying their bundles of reeds. Again they are transported to Engabezweni by trucks where both groups meet then take their long walk to the royal kraal by night.

Day 5: This is a day of rest where the girls are free to do their own things, like going to town and mixing around. By the end of the day they must have made final preparations to their hair and dancing costumes.

Day 6: This is the day when the girls drop their reeds outside the Queen Mothers quarters. They move to the arena in a train form and dance keeping in their groups and each group singing different songs at the same time.

Day 7: This is the day of dancing. They dance all afternoon in their groups. On this day the king delivers a speech **address**ing his subjects on wide ranging issues like HIV/AIDS and so do other known personalities of the country depending on who is featured on the program.

Day 8: This day marks the end of the ceremony. The King commands that a number of cattle be slaughtered for girls. They collect their pieces of meat and can go home afterwards.

和年轻稍大组（14岁~22岁）。根据分组不同，少女们会在各自首领的带领下，选取不同路线，到达不同的芦苇收割地点；

第三天：收割芦苇，并捆好。一般芦苇捆是单数，因为双数被认为是对皇室的诅咒；

第四天：下午，女孩们携带芦苇捆，出发前往皇后的住处。两组女孩会在Engabezweni重新会合，然后连夜赶到皇室所在地；

第五天：休息日，女孩可自行安排。但在这一天结束之时，女孩们要梳好发髻，着上舞装；

第六天：女孩将芦苇放在皇后住处外。然后她们排队进入舞场，并且行且歌；

第七天：跳舞日。女孩会整个下午都在跳舞，当天，国王会就某一议题，如艾滋病等，发表讲话。如果有其他大人物在场，他们也会发表讲话。

第八天：盛会闭幕。国王命令宰杀牲畜。女孩们会带着牲畜的肉回家。

reed：芦苇	protocol：外交礼节，协议
spectacular：壮观的，精彩的	counterpart：对应物/人
Kingdom of Swaziland：斯威士兰王国	virginity：贞洁，贞操
maiden：少女	abstrain：戒除
cycle：周期	bundle：一捆
knowledgeable：有丰富知识的，博学的	address：发表讲话

背景知识 **P**ROFILE

世界各地有趣的女性节日

掌权日　每年的1月4日，是瑞士某些地区的"妇女掌权日"，在为期4天的节日中，家里大小事务全由妇女说了算，男人统统"闭幕"。

求爱日　每逢闰2月29日这天，是英国旧俗中的"妇女求爱日"。这一天，妇女可以摆脱世俗的清规戒律，大胆向意中人或未拿定主意的情人示意。

女市长节　西班牙的"女市长节"，也在2月份。当日，由女性主持市政公务，发号施令，男人如违抗，就会被公众群起攻之。

少女节　3月3日是日本的"少女节"，又称"姑娘节"，是全国性的节日。日本人认为，这时正值红桃报春，是女性美的象征，所以也叫"桃花节"。

妈妈节　4月，在尼泊尔有一个历时3天的妇女节，来自各地的妇女，披着红色"纱笼"，成群结队地涌向首都加德满都的帕苏帕蒂庙。她们在吃饱了由丈夫烹煮的美食后，便在神像前大唱赞歌。在印度，也有一个"妈妈节"。这一天，已为人母者穿上彩色缤纷的"纱笼"，带上各种首饰，显得风姿绰约。这日也是一年中她们最受尊重的一天。5月29日，是中非的"妈妈节"，母亲要带着孩子参加游行。

母亲节　5月的第二个星期日，是美国、加拿大和欧洲一些国家的母亲节，其主要内容是尊敬母亲。这一天，美国的家庭成员要按习惯佩戴石竹花，做一些使母亲高兴的事。

百女节　5月的第三个星期日，是西班牙的"百女节"，订了婚还未过门的少女们持花登高，互相祝福。

太太节　8月23日至9月15日，是德国汉堡的"太太节"。由妇女组成的演艺团体，专演一些宣传男女平等的戏，以示庆祝。8月12日，则是泰国的"母亲节"。

狂欢节　10月10日至15日，是德国莱茵地区的"妇女狂欢节"。在此期间，妇女"大自由"。男人们不得查探妇女活动的内容，违者会被抓问罪。

休息日　12月31日到第二天中午，是希腊的"主妇休息日"。这天，妇女在家里什么也不干，一切家务全由男人承担。

74 心随乐动——桑给巴尔岛Sauti za Busara音乐节

The Sauti za Busara (Sounds of Wisdom) music festival - Zanzibar features a rich **variety** of African music from the region with more than four hundred musicians participating over five days in historic Stone Town supplemented with **fringe** events around town and across the island including a festival street **parade**. Sauti za Busara is the annual music event in East Africa and widely known as "the friendliest festival on the **planet**".

The 9th edition of Sauti za Busara takes place 8 – 12 February 2012, featuring:

400 **musician**s: that's forty groups, with twenty from Tansania and twenty from other parts of Africa; urban and **rural**, **acoustic** and electric, established and **upcoming**.

Carnival Street Parade: setting alight the streets on the Opening Day, including beni **brass band**, ngoma **drummer**s, mwanandege umbrella women, stilt-walkers, capoeira dancers, **acrobat**s... and surprises.

Swahili Encounters: Four days of artistic **collaboration**s, for invited local and visiting musicians who get to reinterpret Swahili songs and present these on main stage. Seminars and Training Workshops: building skills for artists, managers, music journalists, filmmakers, sound and lighting technicians from the East Africa region.

Movers & Shakers: Daily networking forum for local and visiting arts professionals.

African Music Films: documentaries, music clips, videos and live concert footage.

Festival marketplace: local food and drinks, music, jewellery, clothing and handicrafts.

桑给巴尔岛上的Sauti za Busara（意为"智慧之声"）音乐节是一场各种类型非洲音乐的盛宴，有四百多名音乐家参与，全程5天多，举办地点是历史古城——石头城。另外还有一些街边游行等相关活动会在镇子附近或岛上其他地方举行。Sauti za Busara是东非一年一度的音乐盛典，公认为是"地球上最友好的节日"。

第九届Sauti za Busara在2012年2月8日~12日期间举行，当时有：

400名音乐家：他们来自40个组合，其中20个来自坦桑尼亚，二十个来自非洲其他地区。他们风格各异，有的是城市风，有的是乡村风，有的是原声音乐，有的是电子乐，有的是成立已久，有的是后起之秀。

狂欢节街边游行：开幕式当天，游行在街上举行，其中包括贝尼铜管乐队，恩戈麦鼓鼓手，mwanandege伞妇女，踩高跷，卡波耶拉舞，杂技……和各类惊喜。

斯瓦希里语盛典：受邀的当地艺术家们和来访的艺术家会进行四天的艺术合作，他们会重新阐释斯瓦希里语的歌曲，并在主舞台上为观众倾力奉上。研讨会和培训班培养东非地区艺术家、管理者、音乐记者、电影工作者、音响及灯光技师的技能。

具有号召力的人物：为当地及来访的艺术专家们举办每天的网络论坛。

非洲音乐电影：纪录片、音乐片段、录像及现场音乐会片段。

Busara Xtra: Around the festival, Zanzibar and Pemba are buzzing with a range of fringe events: traditional ngoma drum and dance, fashion shows, dhow races, open-mic sessions, after-parties and performances of Zanzibar's oldest taarab orchestras are all arranged by the local community.

The main aim of Sauti za Busara is to bring people together and celebrate the wealth and diversity of African music. A majority of groups participating are from the Swahili speaking region, with some visiting artists from other countries. A rich and vibrant mix of styles is showcased each year, including traditional ngoma, taarab, kidumbak, mchiriku, rumba, "muziki wa dansi", Swahili hiphop "bongo flava", r'n'b, mystic and religious music, theatre, comedy and dance.

节日集会：当地饮食、音乐、珠宝、服装和手工艺品。

其他，除了音乐盛典之外，桑给巴尔岛、奔巴岛上有很多其他活动：传统的恩戈麦鼓和舞蹈，时装秀，独桅帆船比赛，开放式麦克风会议，聚会之后的活动以及桑给巴尔岛上最古老的taarab管弦乐队的表演。

Sauti za Busara的目的在于，将人们聚到一起，来纪念非洲音乐的丰富和多样性。参加者大部分是讲斯瓦希里语的，还有其他一些国家的来访艺术家。每年，一种充满活力的风格都会在桑给巴尔岛上上演，这包括传统的恩戈麦鼓、节奏布鲁斯、宗教乐、戏剧、舞蹈等。

词汇 VOCABULARY

variety：变化，多变（性），多样（化）	acoustic：（乐器）原声的
fringe：（地方、群体或活动的）外围	upcoming：即将来临的
parade：游行，检阅	brass band：铜管乐队
planet：行星	drummer：鼓手
musician：音乐家	acrobat：杂技
rural：乡村的	collaboration：合作

背景知识 PROFILE

世界上九大有趣的音乐节

多巴哥普利茅斯爵士音乐节，多巴哥岛

上千人聚集在一个破旧的板球球场上，不是为了观看板球比赛，而是为了欣赏爵士音乐节那美妙的音律。这是加勒比海边的一个让人陶醉的夜晚，各种各样的音乐包括爵士乐，瑞歌舞，卡离骚蓝调，庞克音乐以及蓝调都可以在这里欣赏到。这个音乐节自四年前开始兴起，如今已经成为多巴哥岛最盛大的户外音乐狂欢节。这个融合各种音乐的大杂烩

吸引了西印度群岛无数的音乐狂热者，同时也有越来越多的岛外音乐粉丝参与进来。

布宜诺斯艾利斯年度探戈盛会，阿根廷

每年的2月份，持续10天的年度探戈盛会就会在布宜诺斯艾利斯市举行。对于其他国家的人们来说，探戈只是一种很性感的舞蹈。而对于阿根廷人来说，探戈是必须和音乐联系在一起的。音乐节期间，游客每天晚上都可以在各大剧院、公园甚至街角听到美妙的音乐。而一些世界级别的音乐大师们就可以顺势炫耀一下自己的作品。盛会包括了一个全市范围的音乐节和舞蹈比赛，同时也提供舞蹈课程并举办艺术展览和时装展示会。

瓦胡岛夏威夷四弦琴音乐节，美国夏威夷岛

夏威夷人称四弦琴为Ki-ho'alu，这是一个标准的地方化岛屿口音。该音乐节在上个世纪80年代早期兴起，后来分化为几个分支，分别在茂伊岛、考艾岛和夏威夷群岛的主岛瓦胡岛举办。音乐节为期一天，举办时间是每年的八月，通常是在怀基基海滩和宝石头中间的檀香山卡庇奥拉尼公园举行。

怀特岛音乐节，英国

这是英国版的伍德斯托克音乐节，曾在1968年-1970年间举办了三届，时间都在夏天。此摇滚节喧闹异常，参加人数在1970年达到顶峰，接近百万人。因为人数众多，英国议会在1970年取消了此音乐节。2002年恢复了此音乐节，喧闹程度不亚于以往的三届。近年来，来这里的头号乐队包括头酷玩、喷火战机、神童、金制绳索等。音乐节在六月举行，门票在二月份就开始出售，建议在网上订购。

菲斯世界圣乐节，摩洛哥

此节日的主题是"让我们学会和睦相处"。每年六月份，节日都会在北摩洛哥的菲斯城举办。从教皇合唱团到古典福音歌合唱团，再到南印度的卡纳提克唱腔大师以及西班牙犹太低音歌手，节日吸引了全球众多有宗教信仰的音乐大师的参与。日出前，节日在Merinides Quarry开幕，夜晚以在Batha博物馆天井内的表演闭幕。游客只需购买一张540美元的"节日&邂逅"通行证就可以欣赏到包括音乐盛会、电影、展览、晨间座谈会等各项节日。

ACL音乐节，美国德克萨斯州

ACL是美国最盛大的年度音乐盛会，于每年9月15日到17日举办。每到这时，大约有130多个乐队分别在8个舞台上蹦来跳去地展示才艺。最初节日是为乡村音乐土风舞创办的，后来融合了各种音乐。买一张850美元的VIP票，你就可以随意在公共酒吧，空调浴室和VIP树林里享受节日了，同时还可以免费品尝各种食物。节日场所从Ziler公园延续到市区中心，几乎临街的所有酒吧都提供现场音乐演奏。

塔姆沃斯乡村音乐节，澳大利亚

音乐节在每年1月份举行，历时10天。节日期间，有超过800名的艺术家登台献艺。其中较为出名的是在两百年公园内的"自由生活"音乐会和沿皮尔大街举办的有600多名街头艺人参加的集会。

萨尔茨堡音乐节，奥地利

这是世界范围内的最重大的音乐盛会之一，历时一个月的狂欢在阿尔卑斯山脚下举行。节日包括音乐会、戏剧和歌剧等项目，举办地从巴洛克式风格的教堂、宫殿和花园延伸到一个古老的谷仓和盐矿。更主要的是，举办地是莫扎特的故乡，这样就更加吸引人了。节日票从1月份开始预订。

口切拉谷地音乐节，美国加利福尼亚州

此音乐节号称全美最大的音乐节，通常在4月份举行，历时3天，举办地是土著区的帝国马球俱乐部。节日期间，酷热的天气难挡人们的激情。主要乐队包括红辣椒、北极猴和米卡。因为这里紧挨好莱坞，游客常常可以很惊喜地发现一些熟悉面孔。

75 艺术盛典——南非民族艺术节

The National Arts Festival is one of the most important events on the South African cultural **calendar**, and the biggest annual celebration of the arts on the African continent.

Starting at the end of June/beginning of July, it runs for 10 days and is held in the small **university city** of Grahamstown, which is situated in the Eastern Cape, 130km from Port Elizabeth.

The Festival **consist**s of a Main and Fringe programme both **administer**ed by the National Arts Festival Office. The Festival is **reliant** on **sponsorship** with the core sponsors being the Eastern Cape Government, Standard Bank of South Africa, National Lottery Distribution Trust Fund, National Arts Council, Transnet, Sunday Independent and MNet.

The programme **comprise**d drama, dance, physical theatre, comedy, opera, music, jazz, visual art **exhibition**s, film, student theatre, street theatre, lectures, craft fair, workshops, tours (of the city and surrounding historic places) and a children's arts festival.

民族艺术节是南非文化领域的重大活动之一，是非洲一年一度的最大的艺术盛典。

民族艺术节通常在六月末或七月初登陆，为期十天，举办地点在小的大学城格雷厄姆斯敦。该城市位于东开普省，据伊丽莎白港130米。

艺术节包括主要活动和其他活动，是由民族艺术节办公室来组织。艺术节的成功举行离不开赞助，其中，东开普敦政府，南非标旗银行，国家彩票分配信托基金，国家艺术理事会，国家运输网公司，星期日独立报及MNet是核心赞助商。

主要活动涵盖了戏剧、舞蹈、形体戏剧、喜剧、歌剧、音乐、爵士、视觉艺术展、电影、学生戏剧、街头戏剧、讲座、手工艺品展销会、艺术工厂、巡回演出（环城市和历史景点）以及儿童艺术节。

不分种族、肤色、性别及信仰，

The event has always been open to all **regardless** of race, colour, sex or creed. As no censorship or artistic **restraint** has ever been imposed on works presented in Grahamstown the Festival served as an important forum for political and protest theatre during the height of the apartheid era, and it still offers an opportunity for experimentation across the arts spectrum. Its significance as a forum for new ideas and an indicator of future **trend**s in the arts cannot be **underestimate**d.

A committee of experts in the various disciplines selects the content of the Main programme. The planning process takes into account what is available locally and from outside South Africa. Three considerations that influence decisions are the artistic merits of any **submission**, the creation of a varied and balanced programme, and the costs involved. The Committee **strive**s for excellence in all aspects of the programme, an approach that has assisted in bringing in sponsorship money for world class shows from a number of foreign governments and large multinational corporations.

The Festival has shown phenomenal growth since its inception. In 1974 there were 64 events on the Main Programme. The Fringe started in 1979 with 10 events. Now the Festival comprises of more than 350 events with over 1 200 performances.

The Transnet Village Green craft fair was introduced in 1989 with approximately 90 stalls. Now it attracts close to a 1 000 stallholders. The fair offers visitors the chance to buy a dazzling array of goods.

所有人都可以参加这个艺术节。因为艺术节没有任何审查制度，没有任何艺术限制，所以在种族隔离严重的时代，该艺术节是一个政治、抗议戏剧展出的重要论坛。如今，该艺术节仍然为所有艺术领域的人们提供了一个试验的机会。作为一个新思想萌发，新潮流产生的场所，该艺术节不容小觑。

主项目的内容由不同领域的专家委员会选定。他们的选题范围会考虑到当地资源和外部资源。另外，还有三点：提交作品的艺术特质，节目整体的丰富性和平衡性以及涉及费用。该委员会竭尽全力，力求在各个方面做到完美，这使得很多外国政府和大型跨国公司愿意出钱赞助一流的作品。

自开办以来，该艺术节的受欢迎程度不断上升。1974年，主节目环节有64项活动。1979年，开始有了10项其他活动。而如今，艺术节上已经有350多个活动，1200多场表演。

1989年，国家运输网公司绿色村庄手工艺品展销会首次亮相民族艺术节，所设站台近90个。现在，手工艺品展销会已经吸引了近1000多个展销商。通过展销会，游客们可以购买到五光十色的商品。

calendar：日历	exhibition：展览
university city：大学城	regardless：不管，不顾
consist：包括	restraint：限制
administer：管理	trend：潮流
reliant：依赖的	underestimate：过分低估
sponsorship：赞助	submission：提交（物）
comprise：包括	strive：努力，奋斗，力求

背景知识 **P**ROFILE

南非传统节日

南非节假日一方面保留宗教色彩，一方面突出纪念反种族隔离斗争的历史事件和团结融和的政治气氛。如自由日是新南非首次不分种族的大选日，为南非国庆节；青年节纪念索韦托起义；和解日教育国人吸取黑白人"血河之战"的历史教训。如公共节日适逢星期天，则星期一补假一天。

主要节日介绍：

人权日（Human Rights Day）

3月21日。1960年3月21日，沙佩维尔镇黑人举行和平游行，抗议《通行证法》实施。这部法律要求黑人外出必须携带通行证，否则将会被逮捕。种族主义政府武力镇压游行，导致69人死亡，180人受伤。后来，3月21日被定为"人权日"，也叫"国际消除种族歧视日"。

自由日（Freedom Day）

4月27日，也是南非国庆日。1994年4月27日，南非历史上第一部种族平等的宪法开始生效。

青年日（Youth Day）

6月16日。1976年6月16日，约翰内斯堡市郊黑人聚居区索韦托的黑人学生举行示威，抗议强迫黑人学习African语的《班图教育法》实施。示威遭到镇压，170多人被打死，1000多人受伤。联合国安理会强烈谴责这次暴行，非洲统一组织将这一天定为"索韦托烈士纪念日"，后来被定为南非青年日。

全国妇女节（National Women's Day）

8月9日。1956年8月9日，数百名黑人妇女在比勒陀利亚举行示威游行，抗议当局推行《通行证法》。新政府将这一天定为南非的妇女节，以纪念南非妇女在争取种族平等的斗争中所做的贡献。

76 沙漠里的骆驼之战——西奈半岛南部的骆驼节

Camel racing is an old traditional sport that originated in the desert of the Arabian Peninsula, North Africa, and the Middle East and is a popular sport in Saudi Arabia, Bahrain, Qatar, United Arab Emirates, Australia, and Mongolia. The South Sinai Camel Festival is an annual event that takes place at 3:00 pm on the 1st of May of every year and lasts for the **duration** of the month, thus finishing on the 31st. and over 250 camels take part in this race from 17 different Egyptian tribes. It might sound **bizarre**; camel racing, when we are used to horse racing instead however camels differ just like humans and some are better for racing than others here is how you can tell:

The feet of a racing camel to be small enough to allow for **agility** and quickness, but large enough to support and balance its weight, so the front feet should be as straight as possible, and the **rear** feet are better if they are slightly turned outwards.

The front legs should be close together, straight, and long. Well muscled **elbow**s that are away from the chest pad are ideal.

The rear legs should also be straight and long rather than **bow-legged**. They should muscular as well as the **loins** area.

The thighs of the camel should be thick, full, broad, and muscular.

骆驼比赛是一项古老而传统的体育运动，它发端于阿拉伯半岛、北非、中东的沙漠，在沙特阿拉伯、巴林、卡塔尔、阿拉伯联合酋长国、澳大利亚以及蒙古深受人们喜欢。西奈半岛南部的骆驼节每年举办一次，开始于每年五月一日的下午三点，为期一个月，31日结束。届时，会有来自埃及17个不同部落的250多头骆驼参赛。骆驼比赛，听起来很滑稽，一般我们都说马比赛。然而，骆驼是有区别的，我们将要提到的比赛骆驼比我们通常意义的骆驼要更适合比赛：

用于比赛的骆驼蹄子很小，使得它能够灵活行走，但又足够大，能够支撑整个身体重量，维系身体平衡。因此，该种骆驼的前蹄很直，后蹄能够外翻一点儿更好。

前腿彼此很近，很直，很长。而腿弯肌肉强健，最好远离胸部肌肉。

后退最好又直又长，而不是弓形的。此处肌肉应该像腰部肌肉一样健美。

Muscular forearms, heavy knee **joint**s.

The cannon bone should be flat and clean.

The overall **build** of the racing camel should be long-legged, **slender**, with a strong bone structure.

Even though, camels may look heavy and slow they are in fact incredibly fast; camels can run up to 65 km/h (40 mph) in short bursts and **sustain** speeds of up to 40 km/h (25 mph). So, maybe it's time you know a bit more about these amazing "ships of the desert" and how they are able to stand the heat let alone run and race in it.

The two main types of camels are: **dromedary** or Arabian camel which has one **hump** or the **Bactrian camel** which has two.

The average **life expectancy** of a camel is 40 to 50 years. A fully grown adult camel stands 1.85 m (6 ft 1 in) at the shoulder and 2.15 m (7 ft 1 in) at the hump. The hump rises about 30 inches (75 cm) out of its body. An interesting fact is that when a camel's energy is low from lack of food, the hump shrinks and becomes soft and will actually flop over to one side. Humps, however, are not used to store water as it is generally believed, but rather fatty tissue.

Camels are able to go five to seven days before having to drink but they then make up for it as they can easily drink, up to 21 gallons in about 10 minutes. Their bodies are able to endure changes in body temperature and water content as their temperature ranges from 34 ºC (93 ºF) at night up to 41 ºC (106 ºF) during the day, where their **coat** reflects sunlight, thus shielding them from the intense of the desert sand with their long legs keeping them further away from the hot ground. Also, did you know that Camel milk is richer in fat and protein than cow milk? Bedouin tribes believe that camel milk has great curative powers, but only if the camel's diet consists of certain plants. So, these spectacular creatures deserve all the respect they can get.

Well, now you know a bit about these impressive animals, go attend the festival and have fun.

骆驼的大腿应该肌肉厚实、丰满、宽阔。

小腿应该强壮，骨节坚固。

胫部应该平滑、干净。

比赛体型应该腿长，纤瘦，骨架坚固。

这种骆驼看起来很重，很慢；而实际上却非常迅疾。它们短期内能跑65km/h，能够将速度维持在40km/h。有"沙漠之舟"美誉的骆驼不仅耐热，而且能够赛跑。

骆驼可分为两类：单峰骆驼（阿拉伯骆驼，有一个驼峰）和双峰驼。

骆驼的平均寿命是40岁~50岁。成年骆驼从驼肩算起高1.85m，从驼峰算起高2.15m。驼峰一般高出身体75cm。有趣的是，如果骆驼因为饥饿，缺少能量的话，驼峰会缩小，变软，会耷拉到一边。驼峰并不是我们所认为的那样用来储水，而是组织内富含脂肪。

不喝水的情况下，骆驼能够走5天~7天。它们可以在10分钟之内喝21加仑的水。它们的身体能够抵御体温变化及水质变化。白天，体温一般在34℃~41℃。因为骆驼的毛皮能够反射太阳光，长腿使它的身体能够远离热腾腾的沙漠环境。而且，骆驼奶比牛奶含更多脂肪和蛋白质。贝都因部落认为那些只食草的骆驼，所含的奶水有强大的治病功效。所以，这种神奇的生物真的值得人刮目相看。

有了这些关于骆驼的常识，就好好享受一场骆驼比赛吧。

duration：持续时间，期间	build：体型
bizarre：奇怪的	slender：细长的，纤细的
agility：敏捷	sustain：维持，保持
rear：后面的 elbow：肘部	dromedary：单峰驼 hump：驼峰
bow-legged：罗圈腿的，弓形的	Bactrian camel：双峰驼
loins：腰	life expectancy：期望寿命
joint：关节	coat：（动物的）皮毛

背景知识 PROFILE

印度的比卡内尔骆驼节(Pushkar Camel Festival)

　　每年11月举行。这个节日的主角完全是骆驼，每年的这个时候从印度乡村赶来的人们蜂拥至此参加这个骆驼盛会。节日的前半部分主要是骆驼和牛的交易会，骆驼主人们把自己的骆驼打扮得很漂亮，期望在交易的时候获得一个好价钱。除了牲畜交易，还有宗教庆典以及各种与骆驼有关的项目，比如骆驼赛跑，骆驼舞蹈，骆驼毛修剪等。

77 教徒们的盛典——埃塞俄比亚宗教节之旅

Ethiopia is a land where religion plays such an important part in many people's **lifestyle**s. The Orthodox Tewahedo Church ceremonies are unique and **impressive**; especially Timket and Meskel festivals which provide colorful ceremonies and celebrations. People dress in traditional costume and celebrate festivals across the country. Colorful unique ceremonies such as:

GENNA - (Christmas)

Year after year Christians **recall** the story of the Christ child in a manger. Celebrated on January 7th and preceded by a fast of 40 days, on the eve of Christmas people gather

在埃塞俄比亚，宗教在人们生活方式中起着举足轻重的作用。东正教的Tewahedo教堂仪式是独特而让人印象深刻的，尤其是Timket和Meskel节。在这两个节日上，会举行多姿多彩的仪式和庆典。人们穿上传统服装，庆祝这些日子。非比一般的庆典仪式如下：

热那（圣诞节）

每年人们都会想起耶稣在马槽里诞生的事情。每年的1月7日，人们会以禁食的方式庆祝40

in churches for **mass** that lasts about 3 hours.

The clergy and "Debtera" (scholars versed in liturgy and music of the church) lift their voices in hymns and chant just as it has been for over a thousand years when Ethiopia accepted Christianity. After mass, the fast is broken so the clergy and crowd alike **disperse** to their homes to feast. Food and drink is **plentiful**, with many homes preparing special meals that are characteristic to all big festivities **highlight**ed on the Ethiopian calendar.

TIMKET - (Epiphany)

Timket is the greatest festival of the Ethiopian year, falling just 2 weeks after Ethiopian Christmas. It is actually a 3-day affair preceded by the eve of Timket when the dramatic **procession**s take place through a night of fasting, to the great day itself and the **commemoration** of Christ's baptism in the Jordan River.

Ketera, the Eve of Timket is when the Priests bring out the Tabots - replicas of the 2 tablets of laws received by Moses, which are normally housed inside the altar symbolizing the Ark of the **Covenant**. Priests bless the water of the pool or river where the next day's celebration will take place. Visitors have the unique chance to experience a festival lost to the rest of the world.

FASIKA - (Easter)

Easter is one of the greatest festivals of the Ethiopian people, celebrated after 55 days of fasting. Devout followers of the Ethiopian Orthodox Church offer daily prayers at the Church and do not eat until 3 PM, except Saturday and Sunday when prayers are conducted early in the morning. Easter always takes place in glorious weather and enormous effort is put into making the occasion memorable.

Gifts are prepared for children and most people are **resplendent** in their best clothes, usually the dazzling white traditional dress. Everyone spends Easter Eve at the Church praying until 3 am when it is announced that Christ has risen! This, in dramatic contrast to the brilliant

天，圣诞节前夕，人们会聚在教堂里做弥撒，时间持续三个小时。

牧师们抬高嗓门，高声唱着赞美诗和圣歌。埃塞俄比亚在1000年前接受的基督教。弥撒过后，人们会打破禁食，回家庆祝。饮食非常丰富，很多家庭大摆筵席。

Timket（主显节）

Timket是埃塞俄比亚一年中最大的节日。时间是埃塞俄比亚圣诞节的两周之后。此项庆典为期三天，而在庆典开始的前一天晚上，人们会举行夸张的游行，一晚上禁食。禁食将会持续到庆典开始，然后人们开始庆祝耶稣在约旦河里施洗礼。

庆典前夜叫Ketera，牧师们会从圣坛（象征着约柜）里拿出Tabots（摩西律法石板的拓本），他们会对池塘或溪水祝福，第二天将在此举办庆典。游客可以有机会体验下这个节日，而世界上其他地方已经不庆祝了。

Fasika（复活节）

复活节是埃塞俄比亚人们的重大节日之一，在禁食的55天后庆祝。虔诚的埃塞俄比亚东正教教会的信徒会每天都在教堂中祈祷，并且禁食到每天下午3点，周六日除外。一般，复活节时，天气很好，人们会花心思使得这个节日值得人铭记。

孩子们会收到大人们准备的礼物，大多数人们会穿上新衣，一般都是炫目的传统白色衣服。复活节前夜，人们会一直在教堂中祈祷到早上3点，然后听到耶稣复活了

jewel colors of the ceremonial velvets and satins of the priests' robes and sequined velvet umbrellas, make this festival entirely **splendid**.

的旨意结束。牧师庆典时穿的天鹅绒及缎带上所绽放的绚丽珠宝色，会使得这个节日大放异彩。

背景知识 PROFILE

非洲传统宗教中的神

　　非洲黑人信仰的宗教主要有三种：传统宗教、伊斯兰教和基督教。传统宗教是非洲黑人固有的、有着悠久历史和广泛社会基础的宗教，伊斯兰教和基督教是后来从外界传入非洲的宗教。从表面上看，撒哈拉以南37个黑人国家中，穆斯林和基督徒占全国人口多数的国家有21个（伊斯兰教8个，基督教13个），超过传统宗教信仰者占多数的国家（16个）。实际上，传统宗教在非洲社会生活的各个方面仍有根深蒂固的影响。因为，伊斯兰教和基督教在任何一个黑人国家里都没有能够真正取代传统宗教，而是同传统宗教融为一体。不论是伊斯兰教还是基督教在非洲都有一个吸收传统宗教的因素、走本地化道路的过程。

　　非洲传统宗教有自己的特点，它不同于拥有大量经典著作、众多庙宇和僧侣的世界性宗教，它没有书写的历史和经文。但是，凡是没有文献的地方，人们的记忆力往往较强。直到今天，非洲传统宗教的祭礼上，有的仍使用一种秘密语言，或称其为礼仪语。而这种礼仪语是祭礼发源地的方言。这说明，非洲传统宗教尽管没有经典可查，但是它通过口头方式，师生相承，把礼仪代代相传。非洲黑人传统宗教的基本内容有：自然崇拜、祖先崇拜、图腾崇拜、部落神崇拜和至高神崇拜。它的核心内容是尊天敬祖，所谓天就是自然，祖就是祖先。

　　每个非洲黑人民族往往信奉很多的神祇，例如仅约鲁巴人就传说有1700个神，通常说有401个神。这些神都互有血亲关系，并以一个至高神为首。至高之神被认为是天地万物的创造者，往往与部落起源的神话有关，或被认为是部落祖先的创造者，因此，对神的信奉有时和敬拜部落祖先结合在一起。至高神被非洲黑人认为是万能的神，其特点是：全知全能、无处不在、无时不在，能给人们提供同情、怜悯、友善、保佑和恩惠，它是天地万物的创造者。在至高神之下有一批和人类生产活动密切相关的神，他们专门负责一项人间事务并保护本部落。每个不同的民族各有其最高神，并有其不同的传说。

1、曼代人的至高神——恩盖欧(Ngewo)

塞拉利昂的曼代人信奉的至高神叫做恩盖欧，它是万物的创造者，包括创造有形的天体、人类和无形的灵魂。他们认为，恩盖欧使宇宙充满无形的能力，这种能力有时以雷电、瀑布等鸣响的方式显现，有时也表现在杰出人物身上。所以，曼代人常说："愿恩盖欧赐你长寿"，"愿恩盖欧助佑你"，"恩盖欧是最高裁判者"等等。与他们相邻的科诺人认为，虽然上帝在高高的天上，但他是无所不在的、永存的。人们以祈求上帝主持公道，上帝则用闪电、不孕或难以解释的死亡惩罚恶人。

2、阿散蒂人的至高神——尼阿美(Nyame)

加纳中部的阿散蒂人信奉的至高神叫做尼阿美，基督徒称之为"纳纳·尼扬库蓬"(Nana Nyankupon)，意为"老天爷"。与此相联系的是阿散蒂人的起源神话，有三种说法：尼阿美星期四来到人间；或世界由它创造，星期四完成；或星期四出现在人们面前，接受崇拜。于是星期四就成了它的圣日。阿散蒂人认为，尼阿美是一个大蜘蛛，它织就了一个大世界，包括天国、人间和下界，自己居其中心，是宇宙的创造者和主宰者，无所不在，无时不在。还有一个神话说明了至高神为什么远离苍天："一个老妇人称食物时，秤杆不停地撞天，激怒了至高神，于是它便远离苍天而去。"尼阿美还具有人的特点：时男时女。有几位介绍阿散蒂族的作者认为，尼阿美是女性，是赋予万物生命的圣母。月亮是她的象征。但另一方面太阳却成为至高神的化身，在这一观念中可能存在性别的二元性。基督教论著名的阿格雷博士就谈到过父母神。阿散蒂族神话告诉我们，上帝在宇宙中创造了三界：天堂、人间和地狱，尼阿美统治天堂，生殖女神主宰人间，年老的地母专司地狱，也就是说，专管"埋葬在她口袋里的"死人。

3、约鲁巴人的至高神——奥罗伦(Olorun)

尼日利亚的约鲁巴人称至高神为奥罗伦，每个人都信仰奥罗伦，把它看作是万物的创

造者、全能全知者、生命的给予者和一切人的最后审判者。虽然奥罗伦是伟大的至高神，但是在日常的问候、祷告、谚语中都能听到它的名字。在约鲁巴人的创世神话中，至高神派许多神来管理世界，主要的神得到了鸟和大地，并用它创造了世界。

4. 恩功贝人的至高神——阿匡果(Akongo)

刚果的恩功贝人(Ngombe)信奉至高神阿匡果，他是恩功贝族的主神，也是恩功贝人祖先的主神。阿匡果是宇宙的创造者，是人类的塑造者。人们称他为创始者，是永存的、全能的和不可知的。他与每个人都有密切联系，像守护神一样，既能使人走运也能使人倒霉。虽然他没有寺庙和偶像，但是人们很容易接近他。

5. 巴干达人的至高神——卡通达(Katonda)

乌干达的巴干达人(Baganda)由于已广泛地信奉基督教，以致区分不出哪些是他们的旧信仰、哪些是灌输给他们的新信仰。巴干达人称至高神为卡通达，现在基督教徒已采用这个名字。卡通达是巴干达人信仰的核心，但是在需要时也求援于先知、亡魂等其他能力之源。卡通达是造物者、庇护者和助佑者。在感恩祷告和谚语中经常提及他的名字。他在女人的体内造孩子，据说他把男人和女人身上的水和血搅和在一起，然后模塑成形，就好像用模子做泥人一样。

此外，还有吉库尤人的至高神——木隆古(Murungu)，巴苏陀人的至高神——默里默(Molimo)，祖鲁人的至高神——乌库鲁库鲁(Unkulunkulu)，东非多个民族的至高神——莱扎(Leza)和噶人的至高神——尼欧莫(Nyonmo)等等。

78 电影的大舞台——布基纳法索的泛非影视大展

You are **passionate** about film and you like to travel? FESPACO offers you a package that will **immerse** you into the world of the African cinema. A voyage to the "land of the honest people": Burkina Faso.

Participate at the FESPACO, the most **legendary** film festival known for its offer of movies never seen before!

The 22nd Panafrican Film and Television Festival of Ouagadougou (FESPACO) takes place in Burkina Faso from February 26 - March 5, 2011. Many consider this important weeklong festival to be Africa's Oscars. The **opening and closing ceremonies** are usually very **entertaining** (and a little surreal). The last festival (2009), opened with a

你热爱电影，你喜欢旅游？泛非影视大展将会为你提供一次非常宝贵的非洲电影之旅。赶快去"诚实人的热土"——布基纳法索吧。

泛非影视大展是电影节中非常传奇的一个，因为它会提供你从未看过的电影而闻名于世。

两年举办一次的盛会，第22届电影节在2011年2月26日—3月5日在布基纳法索首都瓦加杜古举行。很多人认为这个持续一周

procession of 10 feet tall **puppet**s and dancing **troupe**s dressed as American cowboys. The closing ceremony starred a group of French **fire fighter**s (in town for a totally different engagement) doing gymnastics in tight red shorts and sweating **profusely** in the 104 degree heat.

While there is some **glitz** and glamor during the ceremonies, the biannual film festival is actually held in eleven dusty cinema halls throughout Ougadougou. Every year there are complaints about the quality of the screenings and the organization of the event, but no one can deny that the atmosphere is fantastic. It's probably more fun to be in the audience though. In 2009, Radio France reported that "filmmakers [were] left **strand**ed without plane tickets and movies playing in cinemas where the lights don't actually go down". But all this makes FESPACO a very accessible film festival for people like us traveling to West Africa during this time.

In 2009, Ethiopia born director Haile Gerima won the coveted Best Film prize for his movie Teza, and received the Golden Yennenga **Stallion**, Fespaco's equivalent of the Oscar statuette.

It is here that a contemporary and dynamic cultural activity can make a difference. To support the African artists contributes powerfully to the strengthening of society, to the opening of the cultural dialogue, the fight against extremism and conflict. Professionalization through training will improve the socio-economic situation. Cinema is the best means of communication in this matter.

We believe that the African artists are the representatives of the people!

的盛典是非洲的奥斯卡。开幕式和闭幕式非常具有观赏性。上届（2009）的开幕式是一队10英尺高的木偶人排队走路以及舞蹈队身穿美国牛仔的衣服入场。而闭幕式是法国消防员穿紧身衣跳体操，在当时的高温度下，他们挥汗如雨。

尽管典礼上星光熠熠，但这个盛典实际上是在瓦加杜古的11个尘土飞扬的电影放映厅举行的。每一年，人们都会抱怨屏幕质量不高，活动组织不力。但无人能够否认气氛简直棒极了。很可能作为观众更棒，因为2009年据报道，"电影工作者们因没有机票而滞留，而放电影的时候，灯光还没有暗下来"。但正是这些因素，使得泛非影视大展能够面向更多的人。

2009年，埃塞俄比亚导演海尔利•杰瑞玛因为电影《泰莎》获得最佳电影奖，拿到了金叶尼佳牡马，这相当于奥斯卡的小金人。

是这里，使得当代流动的文化活动能够产生深远意义，它可以支持非洲艺术家增强社会凝聚力、开通对话交流渠道以及和极端主义、战争做斗争的事业。电影是改善社会和经济状况的最好途径。

我们相信，非洲艺术家是人们的代表。

词汇 VOCABULARY

passionate：有激情的	troupe：歌唱团，剧团
immerse：使沉浸在，使专心于	fire fighter：消防员
legendary：传奇的	profusely：不吝惜地

opening & closing ceremony：开&闭幕式	glitz：闪光，炫目，浮华
entertaining：有趣的，娱乐性的，令人愉快的	strand：（使）搁浅，（使）陷入困境
puppet：木偶	stallion：牡马，种马

背景知识 PROFILE

叶尼佳及种马的由来

故事发生在12世纪初期莫西人统治的达戈姆巴王国，也就是现在加纳的北部地区。达戈姆巴王国的首都是甘巴加，国王名叫内德加。这是一个富有的国家；它的繁荣自然引起了邻国人的注意，尤其是住在遥远南方的马林克人。内德加的士兵勇猛善战，几乎战无不胜。国王的女儿叶尼佳总是为父亲打胜仗助一臂之力。

叶尼佳年轻貌美，每个人都喜爱她。她还是个杰出的骑手，骑术远超过她的兄弟们，甚至比王国的武士还要好。她同样也是一名勇敢的武士，擅长使用投枪、矛和弓。

由于叶尼佳对于她的人民来说太珍贵了，他的父亲因此不许她出嫁。这个决定令叶尼佳非常难过。她觉得自己不能直接向父亲抱怨，所以就种了一块麦田。几个月后，庄稼长成了，但叶尼佳却让它们熟烂在地里，她不愿收割这些庄稼。父亲非常惊讶，向她询问缘由。她说："父亲你看，你正在让我枯萎，就像田里的麦子。"内德加国王非常不高兴，便下令把她关起来。

然而，在国王的守卫中，有一些是叶尼佳的朋友。一天晚上，国王的一名骑士帮助她逃离了监狱。他们两个在漫长的夜路上骑行，后来遭到马林克武士的袭击。叶尼佳和她的恩人一起击退了袭击者，但骑士却为此付出了生命。此时，她独自一人在森林中，离甘巴加很远，很远。

她勇敢地决定继续朝北骑。在路上，有一处她必须要过一条河。她不畏湍急的水流，终于和自己的马一起渡过了这条河。精疲力竭的叶尼佳躺在马背上，这时，她看到了一间房子。这间房是一个有名的猎象人里亚尔的。他与叶尼佳一见倾心，坠入爱河。后来，他们有了一个儿子，取名叫韦德拉奥果(意为公马)，这个名字现在被布基纳法索人普遍使用。布基纳法索最著名的电影制片人之一伊德里萨·韦德拉奥果就是用的这个名字，他凭借影片《蒂莱》获得1991年的叶尼佳奖。

叶尼佳还被认为是莫西人之母。今天，在当今的莫西国王所在的瓦加杜古，人们可以在很多地方看到叶尼佳的雕像。有一个广场和一条大街也是以这位巾帼武士的名字命名的。

79 男人们的选美大赛——尼日尔的Cure Salée节

One of the most important festivals in West Africa is celebration Cure Salée (Salt Cure). It's held annually and each **Nomad** ethnic group has its own celebration. The biggest celebration you can see at Wodaabé (Bororo) tribe, held in September around small town In-Gallu, in North-east Niger. The festival takes about a week, but two days are major. The exact date is not known, it's changing every year and it's announced approximately one month before depending on rains strength.

Wodaabé tribe is part of gibber family called Fulani. Fulani were the originally Nomads and **herdsmen**, but when they **migrate**d from Upper Nile area to West Africa, many of them **convert**ed to Islam and settled down. The rest of them remained Nomads and herdsmen are called Wodaabé. In fact, Wodaabé called themselves "people of the **taboo**s", which is connected to their traditional Fulani law, moral restrictions, honesty and fairness. Some of them are called Bororo which is linked to their life with cattle.

Wodaabé men have often women-like elegant faces. They believe they are very attractive. The beauty is very important for them. The most important for the parents is to have pretty child. In some cases a man who is not so pretty has to share his wife with another more beautiful man, so the **probability** of borning a pretty child is higher. Wodaabé women indeed care about their beauty and surprisingly they have sexual freedom before the marriage.

During the year Wodaabé people spread around almost all West African fields. Because

Cure Salée（撒盐节）是西非重大的节日之一。该节日每年举行一次，每个游牧民族都有自己的庆祝方式，最著名的是博罗罗族的Wodaabé部落。在每年的9月，Wodaabé在尼日尔东北部的小镇In-Gallu举行。该节日持续一周，两天最为主要。确切的日子我们无从知晓，因为每年都变。该部落会根据雨季的势头，提前一个月决定节日的日期。

Wodaabé是富拉尼人的一支。富拉尼人最初是游牧民族，是牧民。后来，他们从尼罗河上游迁徙到西非，很多人停了下来，开始了定居生活。而那些依旧过着游牧人生活的牧民被称为Wodaabé。实际上，Wodaabé自称为"禁忌之民"，这与他们富拉尼人的传统法律、道德限制、诚实与公正是相联系的。他们中一部分人叫博罗罗人，这些人的生活和牲畜联系在一起。

Wodaabé的男人们通常长着一张女人般优雅的面庞。他们自认为很有吸引力。美对于他们来说非常重要。对于父母来说，有个漂亮的宝宝是最重要的事。有时，如果一个男人不够漂亮，他必须和另外一个漂亮的男人共享自己的妻子，这样能够使得孩子漂亮的几率上升。Wodaabé的女人们也很关注自己的相貌。而且她们婚前竟然享有性自由。

平日里，Wodaabé的人民散落在西非广袤的土地上。因为他们的生存要依靠牲畜，他们会每年将牲畜带到In-Gallu地区，一个盐分丰富、有益于牲畜身体健康的地方。而此时正是Cure Salée庆典开始

their living is dependent on cattle, they bring the herds once a year to In-Gallu area, which is rich in the salt and healthy. The area is mostly visited after the raining season when there is enough to eat for the cattle. That's the right time for Cure Salée celebration. The festival is a big social and cultural event. The old friends can meet, men are searching for their wives, and people are chatting about the news.

Wodaabé join the Cure Salee celebration with their own festival Gerewol called after their traditional dance. The right time to attract woman is a **beauty contest**. The main event is Yaake dance. Men are dancing showing their beauty, **charisma**, elegance and charm. Preparation is tough. Men are decorating themselves in front of a small mirror for long hours. The face **make-up** must be perfect. They are carefully selecting bracelets and necklaces. When they are ready, the dance can start. It's a quite strange and different dance we are get used to. Men are dancing in a row, **wobbling**, rolling eyes and showing the teeth. Before the dance they usually take a stimulant drink, so they can dance for hours. It's not rare to see men dancing the whole night. Men beauty is scored according to their dance. Women are watching carefully and quietly select their husbands. If the merry offer is accepted by man, he has to give a calabash of milk to her parents. If they accept it, he has to pay with three cows for the wedding celebration.

的时候。这个庆典是一个大型的社会和文化活动。老朋友们会见面，男人们会找寻自己的另一半，人们会互相交换所知道的新闻。

Wodaabé庆祝Cure Salée的方法是加入他们自己的Gerewol节日，这个节日是因为他们传统的舞蹈而命名的。对于男人们来说，这是一个吸引女性的绝佳时期，他们会通过选美大赛展示自己的美貌。在主要活动Yaake舞蹈上，男人们会通过跳舞来展示他们的美貌、魅力、优雅和迷人的风采。舞蹈前，他们要经历一种非常复杂的准备。他们要在一面小镜子前打扮很长时间。他们的面部妆容必须是完美的。他们会精心挑选手镯和项链。一旦准备就绪，舞蹈马上开始。对于我们来说，他们的舞蹈是有些怪异的。男人们会排成一队，摇头晃脑，转动眼睛以及龇牙咧嘴。舞蹈前，他们通常会喝兴奋性饮料，所以他们能连续跳多个小时。而有些人竟会通宵达旦。而男人们的美会通过他们的舞姿得到评判。女人们会仔细观看，然后默默选择自己的夫婿。如果男人同意，他需要给女方父母一瓢奶。如果女方父母应允，为了庆祝婚礼，他要出三只奶牛。

词汇 VOCABULARY

nomad：游牧民族	probability：可能性
herdsman：牧人	beauty contest：选美大赛
migrate：迁徙	charisma：魅力
convert：皈依	make-up：化妆，装扮
taboo：禁忌	wobble：摇晃，游移不定

世界另类的选美大赛

"变性"靓女选美大赛

2008年10月7日，数位"佳丽"参加了菲律宾举行的一次特殊选美比赛，这次比赛的参加者多为变性者或装扮成女性的人。

巴黎举行"世界上最美丽臀部"决赛

2008年11月12日，"世界上最美丽的臀部"决赛在法国巴黎举行，来自巴西的Nunes Fronckowiak和来自法国的Saiba Bombote分别赢得女子和男子组的冠军。据悉，本次比赛由全球领先的某内衣品牌主办。来自26个国家的45名参赛者参加了这场决赛，冠军除了赢得15000欧元奖金外，还可赢得模特签约合同。

肥女也疯狂 南非举办另类选美赛

2003年11月2日，在南非首都比勒陀利亚以东城镇卡利南举行了"肥女选美"大会。

变性人选美大赛

在墨西哥举行的环球"人妖"皇后(Miss Queen of the Universe transsexual)选美活动中，26岁的泰国经济学家Thanyaporn Anyasiri荣获桂冠。

骆驼选美大赛

阿联酋阿布扎比举行的一年一度的国际骆驼选美大赛（Camel beauty pageant）。每年一次的沙特骆驼选美大赛都选在一年中气温最低的12月举行，比赛持续一个月之久。大赛分为团体赛和个体赛，并按骆驼的毛色分为黑色组、白色组、黄色组和红色组。团体赛分为30峰、50峰、80峰和100峰4个组别进行集体比美。

对于骆驼的美，阿布扎比的评委有一套严格的评判标准，从鼻梁至背脊到尾巴，对每个部位都得明察秋毫。例如，耳朵要坚硬；背部高耸；驼峰大而匀称；臀部不必太大，足够挂上一副骑鞍即可；毛发油光可鉴；头部要长得结实；鼻梁成拱形，与嘴唇斜斜地连成一线。脖子长些更有魅力，腿也是。裁判还得审查两脚的脚趾，这也是评价标准指引中的一项，名曰"分趾长度"。

80 美酒与美食的盛宴——赫曼努斯酒节

Wine Festivals are an experience for all who love **fabulous** wine accompanied by great food. The Hermanus Wine and Food Fair has all the above and located in the beautiful Hemel en Aarde Village, Hermanus. Three days of **indulgence** offering a wide array of world-class **premium** wine and an **assortment** of fresh, local **culinary** creations.

The Wine Village is once again proud to present Hermanus Wine and Food Fair, one of South Africa's Top 10 Wine A true country festival, you will experience an impressive **lineup** of wines that have **garner**ed awards from around the globe.

The Hermanus Wine and Food Festival at the Wine Village is a **gateway** for visitors into the award winning wines of the Overberg. The Overberg wine region produces some of the most sought-after wines in the country and you are invited to browse through the wine show, appreciate, delight in and sense the fruit of the vines, and discover your own favourites.

All the wines will be available for purchase at cellar door prices. This is a unique opportunity to extend your wine collection.

Indulge in your **craving** for fine wine and gourmet food. This event continues to challenge winemakers and foodies to deliver premium quality for the ever discerning **palate**. Not only is this a fantastic wine and food event, but it's a lifestyle that offers one-on-one access to the exciting world of wine craftsmen and renowned foodies.

Experience the wonderful world of our local chefs, cooks and yummy makers in the Food Marquee. Specialities of our region, from lip smacking snackeroos to gourmet meals on the go, a delectable journey in the presence of great music, friends and family.

酒节对于所有爱好美酒和美食的人来说，简直是一次绝美的体验。赫曼努斯酒节就是这样一个美酒与美食荟萃的地方，它位于南非赫曼努斯的Hemel en Aarde村。此活动持续三天，届时，与会人员会喝到一流的美酒并品尝当地的美味佳肴。

酒村的赫曼努斯酒节是南非10大酒节之一。这是一个地地道道的乡村节日，人们将会品尝到各种已经获得世界级美誉的好酒。

赫曼努斯酒节为游客们提供了一种品尝欧弗博格获奖美酒的机会。欧弗博格产酒区生产着这个国家很受追捧的美酒。人们可以看看各种酒展出，可以品尝，可以发现自己的最爱。

所有的酒都可以以最低价出售。所以对于藏酒爱好者们来说，是一个很好的丰富自己收藏的机会。

在这里，不要拒绝那些美酒和美食。对于酒商和食品商来说，能为那些挑剔的味蕾打造出一流品质的商品是一项很大的挑战。这不仅仅是一个美酒与美食出没的地带，还昭示了一种生活品质，通过这项活动，人们能够跟世界一流的酒商和食品商实现一对一交流。

尝尝当地大厨、厨师以及美食家们在美食集市上的美食吧，你

The winemakers, producers and chefs have become our friends and are part of our wine family – come and meet them, taste their magnificent products.

The Hermanus Wine and Food Festival promises to be a vino-experience where you will meet new friends, discover new wines and find that whales are not the only reason for people visiting Hermanus.

As always, children are welcome and we have a special supervised activity centre for them to play and be entertained while you explore the offerings on show.

Please note that you must be 18 years or older to do wine tasting.

一定会流连忘返的。这里有当地的特色美食，有百吃不厌的小吃，总之都是美味。在美妙的音乐、好友、家人相伴的当下，尽情享受吧。

赫曼努斯酒节可以承诺你一次很棒的葡萄酒体验，在这儿，你会认识新朋友，发掘新品种。你会发现，人们来赫曼努斯的理由不仅仅是看鲸鱼。

当局还一如既往地提供儿童活动中心。在你一饱口福之时，不必担心自己的孩子无人照看。

注意，品尝美味，你要满18岁。

词汇 VOCABULARY

fabulous：极好的，巨大的，传说中的	lineup：列
indulgence：放纵	garner：贮藏
premium：高价的，优质的	gateway：入口，通道，途径
assortment：各物品的配合	craving：强烈的欲望
culinary：厨房的，烹调的	palate：味觉

背景知识 PROFILE

世界三大啤酒节

世界最具盛名的三大啤酒节是英国伦敦啤酒节、美国丹佛啤酒节和德国慕尼黑啤酒节，它们在国外家喻户晓，被欧美的啤酒专家们誉为每一个啤酒爱好者都该至少要去一次的狂欢。

英国伦敦啤酒节始于1978年，2005年它再次于伦敦西部的奥林匹亚展览大厅举行。英国是除德国之外的另一个啤酒大国，而伦敦西部则是英国啤酒的中心，所以现在它已被喻为是"世界最大的酒馆"，届时你将会品尝到种类繁多、口味各异的啤酒，甚至别出心裁，比如有加欧石楠的香料啤酒，加蜂蜜、香蕉的风味啤酒。所有酒水都是由小型作坊用手工方法制造，并且多产自英国。单日票分为6英镑、7英镑不等，通票为17.5英镑。

丹佛啤酒节：美国作为一个多民族国家，来到美国的德国移民，自然也把啤酒节的传统带到了美洲，之后其他各族人民，也纷纷以此为借口，参加这个德国的传统节日，大喝啤酒。三天的日票根据活动的不同，在30美元到50美元不等，购买三天通票价格为145美元，比单买日票节省20美元，如果去其官方网站申请会员，还可以在普通票145美元的基础上再获得20美元的额外优惠。

慕尼黑十月啤酒节之所以闻名，不仅因为它是全世界最大的民间狂欢节，而且也因为它完整地保留了巴伐利亚的民间风采和习俗。人们用华丽的马车运送啤酒，在巨大的啤酒帐篷开怀畅饮，欣赏巴伐利亚铜管乐队演奏的民歌乐曲和令人陶醉的情歌雅调。人们在啤酒节上品尝美味佳肴的同时，还举行一系列丰富多彩的娱乐活动，如赛马、射击、杂耍、各种游艺活动及戏剧演出、民族音乐会等。人们在为节日增添喜庆欢乐气氛的同时，也充分表现出自己民族的热情、豪放、充满活力的性格。

节日的第一天上午，来自巴伐利亚、德国其他州以及奥地利、瑞士、法国的游行队伍聚集在一起，人们身穿艳丽多彩的民族服装及传统古装在慕尼黑市长及酒厂老板乘坐的富丽堂皇、花团锦簇的马车引领下，浩浩荡荡、威武雄壮地涌向黛丽丝草场。中午12时，随着礼炮12响，顿时鼓乐齐奏、彩旗飞扬、人声沸腾。市长在做简短致辞后，打开第一桶啤酒，啤酒节便在沸腾的欢呼声中揭开了序幕。这时身穿传统服装的啤酒女郎用单耳大酒杯将新鲜啤酒不断地送到迫不及待的饮客面前。许多身穿鹿皮短裤、背心等民族服装的巴伐利亚人手举啤酒杯穿行在大街上，他们逢人便高喊"干杯"，气氛十分热闹。

慕尼黑啤酒节上只能出售慕尼黑本地生产的啤酒，所以啤酒节的主角一直是当地的几家大型的啤酒屋，如宝莱纳、皇家、欧菲和狮王等几家著名的酒屋。其中最富有传奇色彩的啤酒是以啤酒节命名的OKtoberfest啤酒（音译为：欧菲啤酒），由于该啤酒在每年的三月份酿制，所以在当地又称为Marzen，（德文三月的意思）。经过六个月的低温窖藏，每到九月底的啤酒节上再由慕尼黑的市长亲自敲开第一桶欧菲啤酒，宣布啤酒节开幕。此时酒花四溅，香浓美味，开坛十里香。所以，欧菲啤酒（Oktoberfest）成为慕尼黑啤酒节上最富有代表性、销量最大的啤酒。

10月初的慕尼黑已有微微的秋凉，整个街道被五光十色的灯光装饰得五彩缤纷。节日的广场，数百顶各种各样的大小帐篷鳞次栉比。这里出售的商品琳琅满目，叫卖声此起彼伏。人们背靠背坐在一起，开怀畅饮，并在乐曲的伴奏下，即兴地歌唱跳舞，甚至跳上桌子相互祝贺。

节日期间，规定每晚啤酒供应到10时30分，10时45分乐队演奏流行乐曲，催促人们离去。这时，万千酒兴未尽的游客会齐声抗议，清洁女工不得不把椅子倒置在桌上，对那些久久不肯离去的游客，保安人员也不得不把他们推向出口，强行让其离开。

平日，德国人给人的突出印象是工作态度认真、严谨，服从命令，遵守纪律和原则性强，但似乎缺乏幽默和热情。然而，在慕尼黑啤酒节上，人们可以发现德国人生气勃勃、热情洋溢的另一面。尤其是巴伐利亚人对于自身的文化和传统所表现出的执着与自豪感，给来自世界各地的人们留下深刻印象。

这场被誉为全球最大的节庆活动之一，每年都会吸引超过700万名的观光客，足足喝掉600万公升以上的啤酒！没想到印象中一板一眼的德国人，其实也有如此热情好客的一面。连续16天的啤酒节，每年在特里萨广场上架起可容纳数万个座位的大帐篷，提供游客啤酒、德国美食；帐篷外则竖立着摩天轮之类的游乐设施，会场中不时穿插身着中古世纪服装的游行与民俗活动。

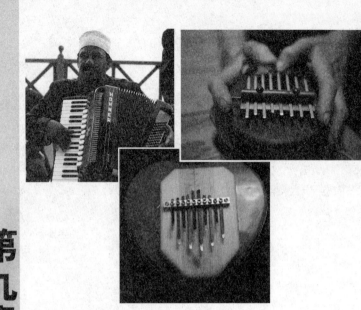

第九章

你不可不知的非洲音乐及乐器

　　非洲的乐器以打击乐为主，本章将为大家介绍几种非洲传统的打击乐器。而南非世界杯上的呜呜祖拉亦曾风靡一时，所以我们也会将关注点放到呜呜祖拉上。

　　最适合形容非洲音乐的词汇，应该是快乐与多元。本章呈现的音乐存活时间或短或长，它们唱出了听众的某些心声，表达出了音乐发起人的观念。

　　除此之外，非洲的音乐很好地和世界流行音乐进行了融合。所以，本章在知识拓展部分，将向各位读者简要介绍一下嘻哈等当代音乐流行趋势。

　　希望在音乐的世界里，我们一起high起来。

81 传统非洲乐器——非洲鼓

The jembe (spelled djembe in French writing) is on the verge of achieving world status as a **percussion instrument**, rivaled in popularity perhaps only by the **conga** and **steel pan**. It first made an impact outside West Africa in the 1950s due to the **world tour**s of Les **Ballet**s Africains led by the Guinean Fodeba Keita. In the few decades **succeed**ing this initial exposure the jembe was known internationally only to a small **coterie** of musicians and **devotee**s of African music and dance. In the U.S. interest in the jembe centered around Ladji Camara, a member of Les Ballets Africains in the 1950s, who since the 1960s has trained a generation of American players. Worldwide, a mere handful of LP recordings were **release**d up to the mid-1980s, most containing just a few **selection**s of jembe playing.

Since the late 1980s international interest in the jembe has taken an **unprecedented** turn. Well over a dozen CD recordings exclusively featuring jembe **ensemble**s have been released in addition to as many recordings featuring the jembe in mixed ensembles. Tours of national ballet troupes from Guinea, Mali, and Senegal, and former drummers from these troupes are playing to swelling crowds. Jembe teachers are **proliferating**, with some of them leading study tours to Africa, and major drum manufacturers have recently found a market for industrially produced jembes.

Mass interest in the jembe has not been accompanied by serious information on its use in its African homeland. **Misconception**s about the instrument abound. Basic questions such as who plays the instrument, on what kinds of occasions, in which countries, and in what kinds of ensembles are ill-understood outside Africa.

作为一种打击乐器，非洲鼓将要取得世界地位了。或许，只有康加鼓和钢鼓能与之抗衡了。20世纪50年代，因为非洲歌舞团的世界巡演，非洲鼓走出西非，获得了一些世界的关注。在随后的几十年当中，世界上知道非洲鼓的仅限于一帮音乐家以及非洲音乐和舞蹈的爱好者们。在美国，对于非洲鼓的兴趣仅限于Ladji Camara，此人是20世纪50年代非洲歌舞团的成员。自从20世纪60年代开始，此人培养了一代美国演奏家。世界范围内，只有20世纪80年代中期，少量的密纹唱片中包涵了一些非洲鼓演奏的片段。

自从20世纪80年代后期，非洲鼓在世界舞台上受到前所未有的关注。有一批专门以非洲鼓合奏组发行的CD诞生，并且有很多音乐录制都混合了非洲鼓的演奏。来自几内亚、马里以及塞舌尔的国家芭蕾舞剧团进行的巡演以及这些剧团曾经的表演者们都在演奏着非洲鼓，以应对人们对此日益增长的热情。教授非洲鼓的老师们不断增多，他们中的一些人还会带领学习小组去非洲。而主要的鼓制造商们也发现了最近制造非洲鼓的商机。

然而，尽管人们对于非洲鼓保持着极大的关注，但人们对于非洲鼓在非洲的用途知之甚少。关于非洲鼓的错误观念大量存在。很多基础性问题，如非洲鼓的演奏者是什么人，在什么场合下演奏，在哪些国家演奏，在何种合奏组演奏等，都在非洲以外

Few non-native jembe players have spent **significant** amounts of time in Africa to see how the jembe functions in the environment in which it **flourish**es. African jembe teachers living abroad try their best to communicate the depth of the instrument to their foreign students, but aside from the classic problem of interpreting a foreign culture, there is another more basic problem: language.

In fact, core jembe traditions come from Mali and Guinea, and appear to be of Maninka/Susu origin. The homeland of the Maninka is called Mande and is located roughly between Kankan, Guinea and Bamako, Mali. Maninka is a local pronunciation of Mande-nka, which means person from Mande. (Mali is a deformation of the word Mande, and Malinke is synonymous with Maninka.) The term Susu can refer in a historical sense to close relatives of the Maninka who originally came from further north in Mali; in this context they are usually called Soso. After their defeat at the hands of Sunjata and his allies in the thirteenth century, Susu groups migrated into Guinea toward the coast absorbing influences from the people among whom they settled; modern usage of Susu usually refers to this later wave settled along the coast. The jembe has also migrated and plays a significant role in the border countries of Senegal, Cote d'Ivoire (Ivory Coast), and Burkina Faso.

的地方受到误解。那些非本民族的非洲鼓演奏者们几乎没有人真正花大量时间去非洲了解非洲鼓在流行的地区起着何种作用。尽管旅居海外的非洲鼓方面的非洲老师们竭尽全力地想要向他们的外国学生深度讲解非洲鼓，无奈两个问题困扰着他们：对外国文化解读方面的问题以及语言障碍。

实际上，核心的非洲鼓传统来自马里及几内亚，来源于玛尼卡/苏苏文化。玛尼卡的家乡叫曼德，大致位于几内亚东部城市康康和马里首都巴马科之间。玛尼卡是Mande-nka的当地发音，意思是曼德来的人。（马里是单词曼德的变体，Malinke和Maninka同义）。而苏苏历史上是指玛尼卡的近亲，他们最初来自马里北部。在这种情况下，人们叫他们索索。13世纪，苏苏人吃了败仗，开始迁徙到几内亚境内，并靠向海岸。他们受到了当地人们的影响。苏苏的现代意义是苏苏人在几内亚境内定居下来之后的事情。非洲鼓也随之迁入，在塞舌尔、科特迪瓦（象牙海岸）、布基纳法索边境上的国家发挥着重要作用。

coterie：小圈子，小集团，志同道合的一伙	significant：相当数量的
devotee：献身者，热爱者	flourish：茂盛，繁荣，兴旺

非洲的打击乐器小常识

非洲有各种各样的乐器，因为非洲音乐是祭典仪式或祖灵的媒介。巫师治病也是以节奏打击乐器为主，打击乐器又以鼓为重心，祭师有时也是鼓手，非洲鼓，在非洲人心中具有神般的崇高地位。细致的弦乐器通常是在声乐、说故事等娱乐活动中出现，弦乐和鼓的合奏齐奏并不常见，这是东、西、中、南非洲音乐的特色。

非洲用于鼓的材料十分多样化，常见的是掏空的圆木、大葫芦、陶土的容器等等。鼓在非洲是最普及的乐器，同样类型的鼓在不同的地区出现，不同类型的鼓也在同一区发现。除了常见的金贝鼓外，还有外型有如漏沙计时的魔力单根双面鼓，我们称之为说话鼓(Talking Drum)。阿希克(Ashikoh)鼓，有以手掌击鼓、鼓棒敲打两种演奏方式。大型的可放地面表演，也有挂在肩上或放在腋下，不一而足。有单面鼓或双面，通常是山羊皮做的，有些鼓皮是钉死的，但大部分是以尼龙绳固定，便于调音。

鼓最能表现充满节奏活力的非洲音乐，巫师借鼓乐咒语仪式的活动，以求得超自然的力量。因此鼓、鼓手、巫术是充满禁忌的，诸如女性不得吹打乐器等，在神秘的巫术仪式中可以感受到。皇家或巫术的鼓手，需要通过层层的考验才足以胜任。因此鼓手的养成是非常严刻的。鼓及鼓手在非洲有特殊地位。

鼓在非洲不仅是巫术、仪式、娱乐、也是生活信息的重要手段。训练有素的鼓手可以用说话鼓模拟任何语言。在17世纪，葡萄牙在非洲到处抓黑人当奴隶，说话鼓是重要的警告利器，同样对洪水猛兽，村庄和村庄的通告也是靠鼓来传达。

探索非洲文化，音乐是最佳的徒径，鼓则是最重要的窗口。对鼓必需以更大的文化范围来认识，才能体认非洲文化的精髓。下面我们来看一下非洲鼓的主要分类。

非洲高脚杯鼓

(说话鼓)African Goblet Drum(Talking Drum)，亦称之为说话鼓，外形如玻璃漏沙计时器，双头鼓上下周边以绳索拉住，击鼓时将鼓夹在手臂腋下同时挤压，以特殊木棒击鼓可发出千奇百怪的鼓声有如说话，相传在数百年前，白人来抓黑人贩卖，村庄的乐师就以此说话鼓来示警及引导逃生方向。

非洲雪克

(沙铃)(African Shakers)，由各种天然果壳，如葫芦或椰子壳挖空，再置入干种子，以手摇动会发出沙沙的音响，因此又称为沙铃。也有比较小的如贡丸大小再以竹棒5个串成一串，作者戏称之为贡丸雪克。

伊波泥可乐弦琴

(Ebony Cora)，鼓身以树干做成，中间挖空，以棍棒击鼓，击不同的位置产生不同的鼓声。

非洲树鼓

(African Tree Drum)，空的树木制成的鼓，又称之为(Jungle wood drum、log drum or Wooden gong)，是用来模仿木头鼓的。

里拉8弦竖琴

(Lyra) 竖琴/共鸣箱由龟壳或其他的材质制成，弓型5弦竖琴(Arched/Bow Harps)/西非鲁特琴(Rebec) 来自阿拉伯弓船型7弦齐特琴。

其他

体鸣乐器：沙沙雪克，木鼓，摩擦筒，木琴(Xylophone)，节拍响板(Castanet)。

膜鸣乐器：乌干达陀型皮鼓，砂型计时鼓，陶瓷鼓，酒桶型木鼓，长型鼓，圆型手鼓等等。

气鸣乐器：牛号角，象牙号界，长喇叭，唢呐，申收笛，直笛等。

Mbira(又称Sanza/Ekende)拇指琴，非洲的旋律钢琴。5到20键。

82 和平与快乐的化身——卡林巴琴

Kalimba comes from Africa, a large and hot continent, and it is a **version** of a magic instrument called Mbira.

Mbira was mentioned for the first time in the ancient African **legend**s. Over thousands of years the story of a tired woman going back home and carrying dry twigs was passed from one person to another. According to this story, when walking past the river this old woman heard a beautiful **tune**. **Magnificent** sounds filled her with peace and she felt better immediately. The bundle she carried on her back seemed to grow lighter and the sun **stoop**ed burning her dark skin, delicately stroking it with its rays. The woman approached the place from which the tune was coming and wanted to see the person who

卡林巴琴来自大而热的非洲大陆，是神奇乐器姆指琴的一种。

人们最初是在非洲传说中听说拇指琴。数千年以前，一个关于疲惫的、手持树枝的女人回家的故事在人们口中传述着。据这个故事所说，当老女人走在河边时，她听到一种优美的旋律。她内心充满了宁静，忽然间觉得没那么累了。她背上的柴捆好像变轻了，那炙烤着她黑皮肤的太阳开始优美地撩拨着她的柴捆。女人逐渐走近发出声音的地方，她想要看到是何方人士演

was playing so beautifully and who changed this hot African afternoon into a magnificent **brisk** day. There was nobody by the river though. The **melody** was still filling the air but one could not see the musician. She went into the water. The cold that reached her feet made her feel even better. She was feeling great when suddenly she tipped over something that was lying at the bottom. It was Mbira—the source of the **incredible** tune.

From that moment onwards the members of an ancient Shona tribe living in Zimbabwe used the magic instrument to contact the spirits of their ancestors. Incredible sounds produced by the inner part of Mbira are so prehistoric and beautiful that they draw spirits that can bear them down to the Earth. Hence this archaic document was used during religious ceremonies. It was forbidden to play it just for fun. It was only used during mystic ceremonies.

Mbira gave birth to many children which turned out to be a large group of instruments called Lamellophones. One of its most joyful daughters is **plump** and charming Kalimba. From the very moment of its birth Kalimba kept wanting to bring people peace and hence its soothing and harmonic sound.

These properties were used by a wanderer who met a hungry lion on his way. The animal started to chase the man. He wanted to save his life, climbed the tree and began to play Kalimba. The king of the jungle curled up and fell asleep, while a happy wanderer, who got out of the whole situation **unscathed**, could continue his journey.

It was the wanderers who most often made use of an incredible strength of the instrument. During their long journeys the magnificent melody gave them strength and helped them to walk large distances.

The soothing character of Kalimba has an impact not only on animals but also on nature. The sailors who witnessed a terrible storm on the sea would definitely agree. Had it not been for the fact that one of the sailors

奏出了如此美妙的音乐，是谁使得非洲这个炙热的午后变得如此清爽。然而，河边没人。旋律仍然在继续，但音乐家却不在女人的视线范围内。她走进水里。凉凉的河水使得女人感觉更好了。然而就在这时，女人被脚底的一个东西绊倒。这就是拇指琴——美妙音乐的来源。

从那时候起，在津巴布韦，古老的修纳部落成员们开始用这种神奇的乐器和祖先的灵魂进行联系。拇指琴那令人难以置信的声音像是来自史前文明，它是如此优美，召唤修纳人祖先的魂灵来到人世。从此，拇指琴只在宗教庆典中使用。人们不能利用拇指琴取乐。它只能用于神秘的典礼。

后来，拇指琴又产生了很多叫做Lamellophone的乐器。其中有一个体积略微宽阔但非常吸引人的便是卡林巴琴。自卡林巴琴诞生之日起，它便带给人和平，它有着能抚慰人心灵的使世界和谐的声音。

它的这些特征曾被一个半路遇上一只饥饿狮子的漫游者发挥得淋漓尽致。狮子开始追这个人。为了保命，他爬上树去，开始演奏卡林巴琴。森林之王听后蜷作一团，竟然进入了梦乡。而这个脱险的漫游者很开心，继续他的旅程。

在漫长的旅途中，漫游者们常常使用卡林巴琴。它美妙的旋律给予他们力量，使得他们奔向更远的地方。

卡林巴琴不仅能抚慰动物的心灵，而且也能安抚自然。对此，经历过海上风暴的水手们肯定赞

started to play Kalimba, their ship would have been destroyed by the dangerous element. Right at the moment when the wind started to carry the magic tune the clouds **dispersed** and the storm faded away. The sun came out and the sailors reached the port, **accompanied** by Kalimba sounds.

Kalimba has a remarkable strength. In difficult situations it comes to people's rescue, bringing them peace and joy.

同。如果不是一名水手在风暴时，开始演奏卡林巴琴，他们的船可能就被海上风浪给毁坏了。在风将卡林巴琴的声音带走后，乌云开始消散，风暴退去。太阳出来了。最终，在卡林巴琴的琴声中，水手们到达了港口。

在当地人心中，卡林巴琴有一种神奇的力量。困难时，它会解救人们，给人们送去和平和快乐。

词汇 VOCABULARY

version：种，类，版本	melo dy：旋律
legend：传说，传奇	incredible：难以置信的
tune：曲调，曲子	plump：丰满的
magnificent：壮丽的，宏伟的，极好的	unscathed：未受损伤的
stoop：弯腰，俯身	disperse：消散
brisk：轻快的，兴隆的，寒冷而清新的	accompany：伴随

背景知识 PROFILE

绍纳石雕（Shona Sculpture）

从严格意义上说，绍纳石雕并不能成为津巴布韦石雕的统称。在殖民主义到来之前"绍纳"这个用来描述现在津巴布韦同种文化族群的词是不存在的，"绍纳"源于恩德贝莱人用语 "abetshona"，意思是那些从那里来的人，这个词在殖民地时代才被广泛应用。那些被统称为绍纳的人并不是起源于一个族群，他们具有不同的文化背景，但因为说着相同的方言而被定义为同一个民族，他们被认为是大津巴布韦缔造者的后裔，但拥有"纯正血统"的"缔造者后裔"在绍纳人里面实际上微乎其微，绍纳是一个由非洲各民族在近代融合成的新民族，如果有人把绍纳称作是津巴布韦最古老的部落，那就错了，他们所谓的绍纳可能是大津巴布韦的建立者，实际上他们中的有些人比恩德贝莱人到达的时间还要晚，所以从民族学的概念上说，称绍纳石雕为津巴布韦石雕应该更贴切。

据说早在两千多年前的大津巴布韦时期，绍纳人的祖先就开始用雕刻表达自己的感情和部落宗教信仰了。绍纳人的宗教非常精神化，他们崇拜祖先留下的精神也信奉善灵和恶灵，恶灵与巫术有关，而善灵则通过医术、音乐和艺术技能来激发个人潜能，绍纳人石雕表现是生活中看得见和看不见的两种向导力之间的关系。雕塑家们相信每一块石头里面包含了一种精神实质，它影响着这块石头在雕刻中以及最后要成什么样的形状，他们的工作就是把石头中的灵魂释放出来，这种信仰就给了艺术家真正创造和表达的能力。很多津巴布韦的艺术家能够自学成才，很大程度上也是赖于原始宗教崇拜在精神上给人的鼓励。

绍纳是一个近代概念，绍纳石雕的崛起也是近几十年的事情。二十世纪六十年代是津巴布韦石雕飞速发展的时期，Frank McEwen和Tom Blomefield两位人物功不可没。McEwen受雇于罗得西亚国立画廊，初衷是要让欧洲艺术在罗德西亚遍地开花。而相比之下，古朴、原始、粗犷的非洲艺术更让他感到稀奇，而且他也发现基本上每一个当地人都可以制作精美的艺术品，把艺术产业化的想法在他的脑海里油然而生，于是，他扮演了一个艺术鼓励者、引导者的角色，经常光顾雕塑家们的"工作室"，挑选、评论、引导他们的创作，一场文化运动就这样在McEwen的带领下悄然展开。McEwen向当地人提供创作材料、工作室，并孜孜不倦地同国际上的文化协会协商，在巴黎、伦敦等地举办了一系列的展览。展览的推出受到欧洲社会的普遍认同，大批的赞美和订单铺天盖地地向他和他的艺术家们涌来。为了避免商业的成功让这种"新生的"艺术形式腐化，McEwen决定成立一个农村艺术公社，他和身边的朋友负责管理公社里的一切事务，这就是被称为Vukutu的艺术公社。当然，McEwen并不单是把非洲的艺术引向欧洲，他也把欧洲的油画技术传授给当地的艺人，在他的影响下，当地涌现出不少出色的油画家。

Tom Blomefield是另外一位在津巴布韦石雕史上举足轻重的人物，和McEwen不同Tom Blomefield非科班出身，他最初是一位经营烟草业的农场主，战争的原因迫使他鼓励自己农场的工人由农业生产向艺术创作转变，后来在McEwen等人的支持下，他组织农场工人在津巴布韦东北部成立了Tengenenge艺术公社，艺术区坐落在一条质地良好适合雕刻的天然矿带上，借助这个条件，在接下来的几十年里，他的工人和他们的作品受到世界各地人们的尊敬和欢迎。Frank McEwen和Tom Blomefield是一种艺术制度的组织者和开创者，早在McEwen到达非洲之前，当地的土著人就已经在打破固有的形式制作石雕向游客出售了，只是土著人的经营方式激发了二人的灵感，他们依靠财力和政府的支持做到了更广泛、更有效的宣传和推广。在Frank McEwen和Tom Blomefield的引导下，津巴布韦出现了几位顶级的石雕大师，像Nicholas Mukomberanwa, Henry Munyaradzi作为第一代石雕艺术家他们的作品深深地影响了第二代和第三代人的作品。

非洲人生来受神的眷顾，他们拥有比其他大洲民族更灵敏的艺术嗅觉，这句话不假，因为很多非洲艺术家即使没有文化，没有受过艺术培训也能雕刻出精美的艺术作品，这是因为他们生活在一个充满神秘、巫术的世界里，如果对其他人来说艺术创造是上帝赋予的奢侈能力的话，对非洲人来说它就像制造工具一样是一种必备的本领。顶级石雕大师Nicholas Mukomberanwa和其他人一样并不是一位饱读诗书的文化人，1940年他生于Buhera的农村，在塞利马教会学校他受到了传统非洲艺术和欧洲宗教艺术的熏陶，但学校的教育非常有限，而且刻板、严厉的教条严重束缚了天赋的发挥。McEwen的到来，他"只要对人天然、潜在的艺术天赋稍加引导，那么这个人就可以成为艺术家"的理念让Nicholas耳目一新。津巴布韦第一代雕刻家很多都不以艺术为谋生的手段，他们有的是农民、有的是工人或者文员，Nicholas最初的职业是警察，还在当警察的时候他就发现自己在雕刻方面非常有天赋，随后在McEwen的帮助下，他开始参加一些国内和国际的展览并广受好评。为了不让早期的成功影响创作，Nicholas对名利非常淡漠，他认为一个艺术家必须明白什么是好的艺术，什么是坏的艺术，这样才能让他的头脑时刻保持清醒状态，他时常用这种方式来激励自己。

近些年，随着中国和津巴布韦经济文化交流的增多，津巴布韦石雕出现在人们的视野中，从2002年至今，中国各地相继举办了很多津巴布韦石雕展，像广东美术馆举办的"非洲的激情"以及上海举办的津巴布韦石雕艺术家展览等，让中国大众的审美得到拓展。北京和深圳的奢侈品市场也出现了非洲艺术品的影子，北京富诺艺术发展有限公司就是中国最早经营非洲艺术品的公司之一，十多年前，公司经营者一个偶然的机会把兴趣变成了毕生致力的事业。对很多人来说欣赏或者拥有一件津巴布韦石雕的机会并不是很多，为了能让津巴的石雕艺术在中国得到更多了解，中国相关的文化部门和津巴布韦驻中国使馆多次邀请当地的石雕艺人在中国参加文化交流活动，使得国内的艺术爱好者能够更直观地了解非洲石雕的制作过程。

现在津巴布韦有越来越多的人从事石雕创作，他们不仅仅是本地人，还有很多人从莫桑比克、安哥拉、南非等地专门赶来加入到艺术公社里面，对于他们来说没有比自由创作更能够让人兴奋的事情了。Raphael是Tengenenge艺术公社的一员，他算是第二代石雕艺术家，目前在南非、津巴布韦等地参加过多个展览，对他来说"艺术像宗教一样，每次敲打都像是深深的祈祷，每完成一件雕塑作品，巨大的满足感充溢着我"。和第一代石雕艺术家的生存环境相比目前津巴布韦艺术公社的条件大大提高，了解和收藏津巴布韦石雕的人也越来越多，面临新的机遇和挑战，Vukutu和Tengenenge艺术公社的艺术家们的心灵依然很平静，他们坚持自己的艺术道路，坚信将来世界各地的人们必定会因为拥有一件津巴布韦的石雕而自豪。

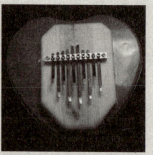

83 奇妙的打击乐——木琴

The xylophone appeared in Southeast Asia about the 14th century. It became highly developed through use in the Indonesian **gamelan**, or percussion orchestra.

The simplest xylophone was a pair of bars that lay across the player's legs. More **complex** instruments were developed that were **mount**ed on a frame.

The use of the xylophone spread throughout the continent of Africa, possibly by being imported through Madagascar. It became a **prominent** instrument in African music. It became **introduce**d to Latin America by African slaves. There it became known as the marimba.

The xylophone received its name from the Greek word xylon, meaning "wood", and the word phone, meaning "sound".

The xylophone arrived in Europe around 1500. It became a widely used folk instrument in central Europe. The Polish and Russian performers had **popularize**d the xylophone in Western Europe by the 19th century. It was first used in the orchestra in 1874.

The xylophone is a musical percussion instrument. It consists of a series of **graduated** wooden or metal bars. The bars are usually mounted on a frame. The bars touch the frame near their end, at the **node**.

Xylophones mounted on a frame may have a **gourd** or tubular **resonator**s suspended under each bar. An alternative is the frame itself. It may form a trough like resonator.

The orchestral xylophone has two rows of bars. They are arranged like piano keys. Tubular resonators are **tune**d to each bar. The range of the instrument is usually four octaves, starting from middle C.

The orchestral marimba has tubular resonators under the bars. It is pitched an octave lower than the xylophone.

14世纪，木琴在东南亚出现。逐渐，它在印度尼西亚木琴乐曲或击弦乐曲中得到了极大发展。

最简单的木琴有两根弦，放置在演奏者的腿上。人们逐渐发展了在一个框架上的更为复杂的乐器。

木琴传入非洲大陆可能是通过马达加斯加。然后，它成为了非洲主要的乐器。非洲奴隶们将它引入了拉丁美洲。当地的人们管它叫马林巴琴。

木琴的得名得益于希腊单词xylon，意思是"木头"；phone的意思是"声音"。

1500年左右，木琴进入欧洲。从此木琴开始作为一种民乐在中欧流行。19世纪，波兰和俄罗斯的表演者使木琴在西欧流传开来。1874年，木琴首次被应用到管弦乐中。

木琴是一种打击乐。它包括一系列的木质或金属制琴弦。人们会将这些琴弦置于支架上。琴弦会直达支架的末端节点处。

安置在支架上的木琴可能在每一个琴弦下面都有一个葫芦或管状的共鸣器。或者支架本身也可以作为一个共鸣器。这就形成了低压槽，发挥着共鸣器的作用。

管弦乐中的木琴有两排琴弦。它们的安排就像钢琴琴键。管状的共鸣器和每个琴弦和谐统

Sound is produced by striking the bars with mallets to produce sound. It can be played with two hard mallets for a dry penetrating sound. It may also be played with multiple pairs of soft rubber mallets for muted chords or a soft passage.

African xylophonists had the widest variety of instruments, including some that were **plucked** instead of hammered and lightweight instruments that were suspended on a rope around the player's neck. They used wooden boxes for resonators as well as clay pots in Nigeria and pits in the ground in Kenya and Central and West Africa. They inserted membranes between the bars and resonators to give the instrument a buzzing sound; these membranes were made of spider cocoons or cigarette papers. In southeastern Africa, the Chopi people play xylophones in groups of as many as six instruments of different sizes and ranges.

一。乐器的音域是4个八度，从中央C(音)开始。

管状的马林巴琴在每个琴弦下面是管状共鸣器。它比木琴低一个八度。

人们手持长柄木槌敲击琴弦，发出声音来。两个质地坚硬的长柄木槌能够敲奏出干净、利落的颇有穿透力的声音。而在舒缓的部分，可以使用软胶皮的槌。

非洲的木琴演奏者们有很多种乐器，其中包括一些弹拨乐器以及一些轻型乐器（可以悬挂在演奏者脖子上的绳子上）。尼日利亚人用木制的盒子或陶罐作为共鸣箱。而在肯尼亚和非洲中、西部地区人们用土罐来做共鸣器。他们在琴弦和共鸣箱之间放入薄膜，这样使乐器有一种嗡嗡的声响。薄膜是用蜘蛛茧或香烟纸做成。在非洲东南部，裘比人将不同大小和音乐的木琴组合来演奏，最多时可达六种。

词汇 VOCABULARY

gamelan：木琴乐器	graduated：刻度的，（税）累进的，分等级的
complex：复杂的	node：节点
mount：将某物置于架上，将某物固定住	gourd：葫芦
prominent：显著的，杰出的，突出的	resonator：共鸣器
introduce：引进	tune：调整（乐器）使合调
popularize：使某物大受欢迎	pluck：弹拨

背景知识 PROFILE

马林巴琴

马林巴传入拉丁美洲大约是在17、18世纪，后来成为印第安人的乐器。而且，演奏马林巴也已成为某些印第安部族仪式的一部分。这些仪式祈求的是宇宙的和谐以及人们的幸福，危地马拉的圣马可斯德古纳地方演奏的马林巴乐曲与非洲加纳的西斯沙拉人的乐曲十分相似。马林巴（marimba）是世界上广泛流行，而且深受人们喜爱的一种旋律型打击乐器。

马林巴是一种木琴。它的结构，音响与一般的欧洲木琴有很大不同。它所采用的琴板比红木的质地软，发音宽厚，音区低，余音较长，每块琴板下面都有用各种果壳、葫芦或罐头盒、长方形木盒等做的共鸣体，这些共鸣体的大小、长短是与对应的琴板相适应的。在每个共鸣体上还开有1-2个小孔，孔上蒙以竹膜、鸡蛋膜、薄纸或动物的尿泡。演奏时声音由琴板传到共鸣体和孔上的薄漠上，听起来嗡嗡作响，产生出一种特殊的共鸣效果。墨西哥国家舞蹈团所用的马林巴琴板下用长方形椎形木管作为共鸣体，在其椎形下端有一孔，孔上贴上了苇膜，说明拉丁美洲的马林巴木琴还保持着非洲的传统。

1894年，危地马拉的音乐家塔多模仿钢琴琴键的排列，为马林巴加上了半音琴板，使之半音齐全，便于演奏新的作品。后来，墨西哥又创造了高音马林巴和大型马林巴。前一种有50块琴板，音域达五个八度，由三人演奏，后一种共78块琴板，音域达六个半八度，由四人演奏。主旋律演奏者左右手都各执两锤，其他人一手执一锤，音色美妙，音响效果很好。

马林巴的制作被认为是乐器制造中最难的一项，它不仅要求制作者有良好的技术和丰富的经验，而且非常了解选材的知识。制作马林巴需要优质红木，在木材的选择上十分苛刻，目前，全世界能够制作马林巴的树木很少，分布范围也很窄。马林巴的普及，使马林巴的制作也成了一些国家的一种产业，并涌现出许多马林巴制作大师。在危地马拉有一个制作马林巴的家族，二十几年间共制作了大小马林巴338台，平均每年制作14~15台，并出口到美、德、法等国家。在当时，危地马拉制作的马林巴很有名望，为其他国家制作马林巴提供了样板。

84 南非球迷们的心曲——呜呜祖拉

World Cup organisers say they will not **ban** vuvuzelas from stadiums in South Africa, despite numerous complaints.

The sound of the plastic horn likes the **drone** of a thousand bees or a herd of **stampeding** elephants.

Portugal winger Cristiano Ronaldo says the noise affects player concentration, while some fans watching on television claim they cannot hear the commentary.

But a World Cup spokesman insisted vuvuzelas are "**ingrained** in the history of South Africa" and will remain.

Rich Mkhondo also said vuvuzelas had worldwide **appeal**.

"Let us not make this a South Africa instrument alone," he said. "A vuvuzela is now an international instrument. People buy them and **stuff** them in their suitcase to go home."

"Only a minority are against vuvuzelas. You either love them or hate. We in South Africa love them."

England **defender** Jamie Carragher said the noise did not bother him when he came on as a half-time **substitute** during the 1-1 draw with the United States and he said he had already bought two to take home to his children in Liverpool.

"When I came on I didn't notice it too much. I think you notice it more when you are watching on TV," he said.

"But my kids have been on the phone and asked for two so I'll have to take two home for them. I've got two in my bag already.

"Anyone who watches me play at Anfield will know that I am louder than the vuvuzelas!"

世界杯举办方说,尽管抱怨声不断,他们也不会禁止南非的球场上出现呜呜祖拉。

那个塑料管发出的声音就像一千只蜜蜂的嗡嗡声或是惊慌逃窜中的大象发出来的声音。

葡萄牙边锋球员克里斯蒂亚诺•罗纳尔多说呜呜祖拉的噪声使得球员们不能集中精力,而电视机旁的球迷们也抱怨他们听不见评论的声音。

但是世界杯的一位发言人坚持说,呜呜祖拉在"南非的历史中是根深蒂固的",而且将来也会如此。

组委会主席里奇•姆洪多说,呜呜祖拉已经引起了世界的兴趣。

"我们不应该仅仅把它当做一种南非乐器,"他说。"如今,呜呜祖拉已经是一种世界性的乐器了。人们会买它,然后塞满旅行箱里带回家。"

"只有一小部分人不喜欢它。对于一项事物,你可能喜欢或是讨厌它。我们在南非,我们爱它。"

英国后卫杰米•卡拉格说,当英国和美国1:1平时,他在中场作为替补队员上场,这声音对他没影响。他还买了两个,准备带回利物浦,给孩子们玩。

他说,"我打比赛时,并没有注意它。不过,我想看电视的话可能会有影响。"

"但是我的孩子们打电话给我,叫我带两个给他们。我已经买了两个放在包里了。"

FIFA president Sepp Blatter also **weigh**ed into the debate and believes vuvuzelas are part and parcel of football in South Africa.

"I have always said that Africa has a different rhythm, a different sound," he commented on social networking site Twitter.

"I don't see banning the music traditions of fans in their own country. Would you want to see a ban on the fan traditions in your country?"

A recent survey found that the sound **emit**ted by a vuvuzela was the equivalent to 127 **decibel**s—louder than a drum's 122 decibels or a **referee**'s whistle at 121.8 decibels.

"It is difficult for anyone on the **pitch** to concentrate," said the Real Madrid forward. "A lot of players don't like them but they are going to have to get used to them."

France captain Patrice Evra blamed the noise generated by the vuvuzelas for his side's poor showing in their opening group game against Uruguay, which finished goalless.

He added: "We can't sleep at night because of the vuvuzelas. People start playing them from 6am." "We can't hear one another out on the pitch because of them."

Backing for the under-fire vuvuzela has come from the England Supporters' Band, which has not missed an England game—home or away—since 1996.

Trumpeter John Hemmingham, who is leading an eight-man team in South Africa, said the plastic instruments were part of the local culture and should not be banned from stadiums.

"It's the way the South Africans express their joy and pleasure at the tournament being here," said Hemmingham. "It's certainly a challenge for us but there's no point whinging about it."

Some people have complained the noise from

"如果有人看我在安菲尔德球场比赛的话，就会知道我要比呜呜祖拉的声音大得多。"

国际足联主席赛普·布拉特也仔细考虑了这个争论，他认为呜呜祖拉是南非世界杯的一部分。

布拉特在Twitter上评论说，"我一直说非洲有种不同的旋律，不同的声音。"

"我认为没有必要禁止球迷们在自己的国度里实现自己的音乐传统。如果是你，你愿意吗？"

一项最近的调查显示，呜呜祖拉的声音相当于127分贝，高于鼓的122分贝或裁判员121.8的哨声分贝。

皇家马德里队说，"这使得球员们很难在赛场上集中精力。很多球员不喜欢它，但他们得逐渐适应。"

法国队队长帕特里斯·埃弗拉将自己球队对抗乌拉圭时的糟糕表现归因于呜呜祖拉。那场，他们一分未得。

他补充说："因为呜呜祖拉，我们睡不好觉。早上六点人们就开始吹呜呜祖拉了。而在赛场上，因为呜呜祖拉，我们听不见彼此的声音。"

虽然呜呜祖拉倍受抨击，但England Supporters乐队支持，自从1996年开始，他们从未错过任何一场有英国队参加的比赛，无论是在国内还是国外。

鼓手John Hemmingham在南非是一个八人组的领队，他说，这个塑料的乐器是当地文化的一部分，赛场上不应该禁止。

"这是南非人民对世界杯在自己的国家举办，表达喜欢和高兴的一种方式。" John Hemmingham说。

"对于我们来说这是一种挑战，但是

the vuvuzelas has stopped fans from generating chants around the ground.

But Hemmingham, who was at Saturday's game between England and the United States in Rustenburg, revealed: "We didn't have any problem."

"The fans around us were all singing along and a lot of our fans were joining in with us using their vuvuzelas. It all added to the atmosphere."

"There was definitely a different vibe about the place—the South Africans are loving it—and when in Rome, you just have to go along with it. I bet there is not a single South African player complaining about the vuvuzela. They see it as more than just a noise, it's about the whole spirit of the thing."

没有理由抱怨。"

一些人抱怨呜呜祖拉的噪声使得球迷们在地面上不能唱歌。

但周六那场美国队对阵英国队的比赛时，John Hemmingham也在现场，他说，"我们没问题"。

"我们身边的球迷都随着我们一起唱，并用呜呜祖拉的声音加入我们。它使得气氛非常棒。"

"南非确实有一种不同的旋律——南非人们喜欢这个——我们应该入乡随俗。我相信没有南非的队员会抱怨呜呜祖拉。他们只是将它看成精神。"

词汇 VOCABULARY

ban：禁止	defender：后卫
like：像	substitute：替补
drone：嗡嗡声	weigh：仔细考虑
stampede：（指动物或人）惊逃，乱窜	emit：释放，发出
ingrained：根深蒂固的	decibel：分贝
appeal：兴趣	referee：裁判
stuff：塞满，填满	pitch：球场，沥青，音调

背景知识 PROFILE

呜呜祖拉的起源

关于呜呜祖拉的起源有两种说法，一是据说这种喇叭是南非凯萨酋长俱乐部的著名球迷弗雷迪·马克的发明。早在1965年他就将自己的铝制自行车喇叭略加改装，成了可以用嘴巴吹的球迷喇叭，后来发现长度不够，特意加了一根管子。上世纪七八十年代他就带着自己心爱的呼呼祖拉出现在南非的球场上，而1992、1996以及1998年世界杯的球迷看台上，我们都能发现吹着呜呜祖拉的马克。可是之后国际足联认为这个铝制喇叭是一件"危险的武器"而禁止他携带入场，马克不得不找到一家塑料制品公司，从此便有了现代版的呜呜祖拉。

　　另外一种说法和上面的完全不同，据称呜呜祖拉最早是由非洲大羚羊的角制成的，人们用它来驱赶狒狒，这种喇叭发出的呼呼声甚至可以杀死一头狒狒，也难怪南非球迷都喜欢这个家伙，认为它是"杀死对手"的武器。国际听力组织对呜呜祖拉进行了分贝测试，发现其声响超过100分贝，足以对人听力产生伤害。

　　呜呜祖拉甚至成功入驻《牛津英语词典》。

85 最自然的声音——椰铃

The shekere is a **handmade rattle**. It consists of a hollow gourd or **calabash**, covered on the outside with a net of seeds, beads, shells, or any available material. Although its origins are West African, today it is found in the Americas and Caribbean as well.

The calabash or gourd (as it's commonly known in the United States) is a functional creation of nature with a wide variety of uses and traditions in cultures around the world. A fruit of varied shape and size, it commonly grows on a vine not unlike the squash, but there are also varieties that grow on bushes and trees. In so-called "third world" countries the calabash was historically used as a **container** for water, and still is an essential **utensil** in many parts of the world. In rural areas of the U.S., they are often used as birdhouses. Throughout Asia, Africa, the Pacific Islands, the Caribbean and the Americas, gourds are used as resonators for musical instruments.

"Shekere" is a general name to describe the beaded

椰铃是一种手工制作的乐器。它是由一个空的葫芦制成，葫芦外面有一层网状物，这层网状物可能是种子、珠子、贝壳或任何可用的材料。尽管椰铃的发源地是西非，但人们也可以在美洲以及加勒比海看到椰铃。

葫芦的用法是利用自然的一种创作性发挥，在世界上不同的文化下，葫芦的作用是不同的。葫芦的大小不一，像南瓜一样长在藤上。当然也有长在灌木丛里或树上的。在所谓的"第三世界"里，人们用葫芦盛水。在美国的乡村，人们用葫芦来做鸟笼。但不论是亚洲、非洲、太平洋沿岸各岛，还是加勒比海、美洲地区，人们都会用葫芦来做乐器的共鸣器。

gourd rattle. It comes in many shapes and sizes, is played in a variety of styles, and has many different names. In Africa it is found primarily, but not exclusively, in the countries of Nigeria, Togo, Ghana, Benin, Sierra Leone and Côte d'Ivoire (there are many parts of Africa where you will not hear this instrument). Different language groups in each country often have their own names, styles, techniques, and traditions associated with the shekere.

In Nigeria, the very large beaded calabash is called an "agbe", and traditionally is owned and played only by professional musicians (Olatunji, Music in African Life). It is a personal instrument and never loaned or shared, even with family members. However, a son who is a professional musician may inherit his father's agbe. Shekeres among the Yeruba of Nigeria are often connected with religion, given great respect, and play a very important role in certain traditional musical forms.

Throughout West Africa you will also a smaller gourd, covered with a **woven** net which is tied off at the bottom, leaving a tail of loose strings. In Ghana and Togo among the Ewe language group it is known as the "axatse" and is often used to accompany a drum or bell orchestra on important **occasion**s. In Sierra Leone you will find a similar type of shekere with a very loose net and long tail, often called a "shake-shake" or "shaburay".

When African slaves were taken to the "New World", they carried with them many of these rich musical traditions, which took root in **vary**ing degrees in different parts of the Americas and the Caribbean.

椰铃是一个统称，它有很多大小不一、形状不同的变体，也有很多名称。最初，人们在尼日利亚、多哥、加纳、贝宁、塞拉利昂以及科特迪瓦发现了椰铃。不同国家，椰铃会有不同的名称、风格、技巧和传统。

在尼日利亚，那个非常大的、串了珠子的葫芦叫"agbe"，一般是由专业的音乐人所有以及演奏。这是一种私人乐器，人们通常不借出，不分享。即便是家人也是如此。然而，一个专业的音乐人子嗣可能会继承父亲的agbe。而尼日利亚约鲁巴人中，椰铃是和宗教相关的，它们受到尊重，并在一些传统的音乐形式中举足轻重。

而西非，葫芦会更小一些，外面的网子会一直到达葫芦底部，并且会不收尾。在加纳和多哥的埃维人中，椰铃叫"axatse"。在重大节日时，它经常会伴随鼓或铃一起演奏。在塞拉利昂，和椰铃比较相似的就是"shake-shake"或"shaburay"。

当非洲奴隶被贩卖到"新大陆"时，他们带去了很多非洲的音乐传统，这在美洲的不同地区，有不同表现。

词汇 VOCABULARY

handmade：手工制作的	utensil：用具，器皿
rattle：发出声音的东西	woven：编织的
calabash：葫芦	occasion：场合
container：容器	vary：改变，变化，使多样化

教你做椰铃

材料：

葫芦（你也可以用塑料瓶子）；

线（最好是尼龙线，线要细，能够穿过珠子）；

珠子（也可以是种子、贝壳、纽扣等，只要能制造出咯咯声）。

需要的工具：

具有摩擦作用的刷子以及洗涤剂；

钢锯；

衣架或长棍；

打火机或蜡烛；

油或虫漆（如果想要保存的话）。

准备葫芦：

葫芦要是干的葫芦。将葫芦中用肥皂水洗净，然后用刷子彻底清洁表面。

用钢锯将葫芦顶端锯掉，当然留一部分以便手持。用衣架或长棍将葫芦内的纤维和种子戳松，然后将它们摇出来。一定要手轻——葫芦很容易裂。

葫芦内壁越干净、越光滑，葫芦越能发生共鸣。

你可以在上面涂油或漆加深葫芦颜色，然后将它放起来。

葫芦乐器：

现在你的葫芦就是一个乐器了，用手掌根部敲击葫芦的底部，听听声音。

椰铃外的网：

有很多方式做那个椰铃的这个"裙子"，最常见的做法是：

在葫芦嘴处围一圈绳子，作为它的"衣领"。然后将绳头系起来。绳头不要太短，最好系完之后还有余，可以垂下来。

截15根~30根长绳，每根绳子应该是网的长度的6倍~8倍。用打火机断开，不要用剪刀。

将绳子拴在葫芦嘴上的绳子上。

穿珠子（穿珠子有很多做法，你可以随心所欲）。

收线尾。

86 社会的良心——非洲强音（Afrobeat）

Afrobeat is the **hard-driving** African funk sound pioneered in the 1970s by the late Nigerian **bandleader** Fela Anikulapo Kuti—and few genres are as identified with one artist as Afrobeat is with Fela.

The **scion** of an **influential** Yoruba family, Kuti began his musical career while studying medicine in England in the early 1960s. Seduced by London's fertile African jazz scene, Kuti eventually abandoned his studies and returned to Nigeria to form his own band. But it wasn't until a brief, 1969 stay in Los Angeles that Afrobeat began to take shape. While recording there with his band Kuti was inspired by the radical politics of the Black Panther movement and the **emerging** funk sounds of the era—esepcially those of James Brown. Upon his return to his hometown of Lagos, Kuti **disband**ed his group Koola Lobitos and formed Afrika 70, the band that would translate his new **Afrocentric** vision into reality. Collaborating with drummer and **arranger** Tony Allen, Kuti fused the brash horn charts, spiky guitar licks and muscular bass lines of American funk with freeform jazz improvisation and dazzlingly complex Yoruba rhythms. The result was an African answer to American funk that was the equal of anything recorded **Stateside**.

Kuti also **infuse**d the music with pointed social and political messages. Singing in pidgin to avoid tribalism and appeal to the widest audience possible, Fela **appropriate**d the language of black power, socialist critique and Nigerian proverb to poke fun and level criticism at the military **dictatorship** running Nigeria in the 1970s. His angry **broadside**s against the government won Kuti the love of the common man and the wrath of the authorities, and it

Afrobeat是20世纪70年代产生的极富动感的非洲放克音乐，其先驱是已故的乐队指挥库提。

作为约鲁巴人中一个有名望的家庭的后裔，库提早在20世纪60年代在英国学医期间就已经开始了他的音乐生涯。在伦敦，非洲爵士乐大受欢迎，这使得库提受到诱惑，他最终决定放弃学业，去尼日利亚组建自己的乐队。但Afrobeat直到1969年才成形，此时，库提在洛杉矶做了短暂停留。与乐队一起录音时，库提受到黑豹运动时狂热的政治热潮影响，受到当代日益兴起的放克声音——尤其是灵魂乐教父詹姆斯·布朗的启发。他一回到家乡拉各斯，就解散了之前的乐队，新成立了Afrika 70乐队。这个乐队将他新型的非洲主义中心论变为现实。他和鼓手、编曲者托尼·阿伦合作，在音乐中融合了粗鲁的喇叭声，欢快的吉他声，美国放克的男低音的曲子，爵士乐中的即兴演奏以及复杂的约鲁巴旋律。这样就形成了能与美国放克媲美的非洲放克。

库提还在音乐中加入了尖锐的社会及政治信息。他以混杂语演唱，以避免部落主义和吸引尽可能多的观众。库提将黑人权力语言，社会评论、尼日利亚谚语纳为己用。这在70年代尼日利亚军事独裁的环境中制造乐趣，也引起了批评。库提愤怒地抨击政府引起了普通民众的喜爱，引发了官方的愤怒。这也使得Afrobeat作

cemented Afrobeat as a form of protest music.

Kuti disbanded Afrika 70 at the end of the decade, forming a new band, Egypt 80, in 1980. But despite growing international fame, the 80s were a difficult decade for Kuti and he was jailed more than once by the Nigerian authorities. The 1990s weren't much easier, and by the time of his death in 1997, Fela was almost as well known for causing controversy as he was for his prodigious musical output.

Luckily, Kuti's musical legacy lives on. Tony Allen and other former bandmembers such as Bukky Leo continue to push the original sound forward, while Kuti's sons Femi and Seun carry on the family **franchise**. In the new **millennium**, Afrobeat has become a truly global sound. Its social **consciousness** tailor made for such outfits as Brooklyn ensemble Antibalas, whose success helped pave the way for homegrown Afrobeat bands around the world.

为一种抗议音乐确定下来。

70年代末，库提解散Afrika 70，他在1980年重新成立了一个新的乐队Egypt 80。尽管拥有日益壮大的国际声誉，80年代对于库提来说仍很是艰难。在此期间，他不止一次被尼日利亚当局逮捕并坐牢。90年代也不轻松。到1997年库提逝世为止，他因为倍受争议以及庞大的音乐作品数量而闻名于世。

值得庆幸的是，库提的音乐并未消失。托尼•阿伦和其他之前的乐队成员继续推动这种音乐的发展。而库提的孩子们继承了家族的经销权。在新千年，Afrobeat真正成为了一种国际音乐。布鲁克林合唱组Antibalas的成功有助于非洲这种本土音乐走向世界。

![词汇 VOCABULARY]

hard-driving：富于野心的，充满活力的	Stateside：美国国内的
bandleader：乐队指挥	infuse：注入
scion：子孙，后裔	appropriate：将……纳为己用
influential：有影响的，有权势的	dictatorship：独裁
emerging：新兴的	broadside：猛烈抨击
disband：解散乐队	franchise：特许经营权
Afrocentric：非洲中心主义的	millennium：千禧年
arranger：编曲者，组织者	consciousness：良心

美国灵魂音乐的教父——詹姆斯·布朗

詹姆斯·布朗（James Brown）是无可争议的美国灵魂乐的教父（Godfather of Soul），是一位传奇的R&B歌星、作词家，他是"放克"（Funk）音乐的缔造者，在饶舌、嘻哈、迪斯科等领域也独树一帜。詹姆斯·布朗一生录制了逾50张专辑，单曲超过119支，20世纪60至70年代是他的黄金时期，每张唱片都跻身百强榜单，一曲《大声说"我是黑人，我为此骄傲"》更是在1968年种族权利运动中具有里程碑意义。詹姆斯·布朗曾于1965年和1987年获得格莱美两项大奖，并于1992年加冕格莱美终身成就奖，他还是1986年首批入选摇滚名人堂的大师之一。

詹姆斯·布朗的舞蹈也很有名，影响了从米克·贾格尔（"滚石"乐队主唱）到迈克尔·杰克逊（Michael Jackson）等很多人的表演。也有人说："詹姆斯·布朗在现场演出中的古怪行为和舞蹈场面，成了他艺术的主要部分"。詹姆斯·布朗的演唱变得更加原始、粗犷，强调"呼喊"，而音乐却变得十分简单，常常在二三个和弦的衬托下，依靠即兴重复音型，即所谓"连复"手法，使情绪热烈和激动起来。

1986年，詹姆斯·布朗的名字被写进摇滚名人堂。最近几年里可圈可点的说唱明星，几乎全部用"取样"的数字技术，借鉴了他的歌唱素材。他的许多作品，后来被"胖男孩"、Ice-T、"公敌"和其他说唱歌手重新演唱过。

詹姆斯·布朗1989年在接受《滚石》杂志的采访时曾经开玩笑说："现在音乐的水平，和我的最后一张唱片差不多。"

1992年，詹姆斯·布朗获格莱美终身成就奖。此前的1965年和1987年，他还分别以《爸爸有个新袋子》（Papa's Got a Brand New Bag）和《生活在美国》（Living in America），夺得格莱美的最佳R&B唱片奖、最佳R&B男歌手表演奖。1986年，他和猫王普莱斯利、Chuck Berry以及其他新音乐流派开创者一道，第一批走进摇滚名人堂。

2003年，詹姆斯·布朗对于自己取得的成就也是心知肚明，感到自豪。他曾颇为得意地告诉美联社记者："迪斯科就是詹姆斯·布朗，嘻哈音乐也是詹姆斯·布朗，说唱音乐还是詹姆斯·布朗，你知道我说的什么意思吗？我所听到的说唱艺人的歌，90%的内容都是我的。"

小布什曾评价说，"劳拉和我对詹姆斯·布朗的逝世深感悲痛。半个世纪以来，'灵魂音乐教父'革新的天才丰富了我们的文化，影响了一代又一代的音乐人。作为一个独创式美国天才，他的歌迷来自各行各业，来自不同的社会背景。在这个圣诞节里，我们向詹姆斯·布朗的家人和朋友送去祝福和祈祷。"

詹姆斯·布朗是最富于改革精神的一位艺人，爆炸式的演唱风格、饱含深情的嗓音。

詹姆斯·布朗是易于辨认的，没有了詹姆斯·布朗，Funk的历史演变必定会不同，詹姆斯·布朗在舞台上的爆炸力和他的嗓音是天生的，也是可以复制的。但他对Funk的改革并使其成为一门独立的音乐流派，却是无人能及。就此点而论，詹姆斯·布朗对现代音乐史的贡献要远大于许多大师级人物，他创造了属于自己的世界，却极少获得好的名誉。

就像"猫王"阿尔维斯·普莱斯利（Elvis Presley），鲍勃·迪伦（Bob Dylan）一样，詹姆斯·布朗也是过去的50年当中最具影响力的音乐人之一。至少有一代人都曾经崇拜过、并时常公开地模仿过他。包括摇滚变色龙大卫·鲍伊（David Bowie）的《Fame》，王子（Prince）的《Kiss》，乔治·克林顿（George Clinton）的《Atomic Dog》以及Sly and the Family Stone乐队的《Sing a Simple Song》等歌曲都明显是基于詹姆斯·布朗式的节奏与演唱技巧之上创作出的。詹姆斯·布朗之于节奏与舞曲音乐就如同鲍勃·迪伦之于歌词，他是那个领域中毫无争议的最伟大的革新者。

事实上，后来的音乐人想超越布朗几乎是不可能完成的任务。1964年，滚石乐队在参加一次音乐会时被安排在布朗前面上场，结果尽管他们使出浑身解数，布朗上台后，之前所有艺人的表演还是被乐迷忘到了脑后。布朗对于自己的乐队十分严厉，如果哪个成员缺席合练就会被罚款。

迈克尔·杰克逊曾在访谈中说过："我认为詹姆斯·布朗是天才，他的能力完全被人们低估了。"

87 和声与节奏的完美合一——强节奏爵士舞曲

Highlife is a distinctive **genre** of popular dance music that originated in Anglophone West Africa in the early 1900s. Pan-ethnic and pan-national in approach, highlife music **blend**s African musical principles with Western concepts of harmony and the polyphonic musical **innovation** from African Diaspora. It draws inspiration from African American jazz, Caribbean calypso, and West African dance orchestra.

Vibrant exchanges and collaborations across the African Diaspora took place among early black highlife **artiste**s. On the political front, Kwame

强节奏爵士舞曲是一种流行舞曲，在20世纪初源于讲英语的西非。强节奏爵士舞曲在方法上属于多种族及多国家。它将非洲音乐的原则同西方国家关于乐曲和声的观念、源于非洲民族离散多音调音乐创新性地融合起来。它的灵感来源于非洲裔美国人的爵士乐，加勒比海地区的卡利普索小调、西非的伴舞乐队。

早期黑人强节奏爵士舞曲的艺人们在非洲民族离散中进行着有活力

Nkrumah, the first president of independent Ghana, and a **Pan-Africanist**, adopted highlife as the national music under his Africanization policy. Highlife music reached its peak in the 1950s and 1960s, spreading to different parts of the continent and beyond. However by 1975, the popularity of the music had declined, giving way to new musical **trend**s.

A highlife orchestra typically consists of African percussive instruments (idiophones, membranophones) and European wind and string instruments (aerophones, chordophones), which give it its distinctive sounds and cosmopolitan **ambience**. The music **retrain**s the pronounced **syncopated** polyrhythm characteristic of African music, which is ingeniously reproduced on the pattern of the European brass and **marching band**s.

Highlife bands were first introduced to colonial-centered institutions such as schools, police, and military forces. Unable to comprehend the principles of African music, especially its complicated rhythm and **call-and-response** style, European arrogantly dismissed it as undisciplined and mere noise. In its place they introduced Western-style music, especially the marching and brass bands that were considered critical in instilling discipline among African recruits in colonial institutions. To the Africans, European music was all harmony and no rhythm, so to satisfy their musical aesthetics, the African in the marching bands explored ways of blending the two. The result was a brass pop band with lively tunes and rhythms.

There is no doubt that highlife **cater**ed to the needs of the emerging African elites who occupies the new urban spaces and who, in spite of their excellent Western qualifications, were not especially welcome at clubs and other entertainment venues reserved for colonial officials. However, the new social space also needed the services of semiphrofessionals, traders, artisans, and other workers for its maintenance.

的交换和合作。政治方面，加纳独立后的第一任总统恩克鲁玛实行非洲化的政策，将强节奏爵士舞曲进行全国推广。20世纪50年代和60年代，强节奏爵士舞曲达到顶峰。它传遍了非洲大陆的很多地方，甚至是非洲大陆以外的地方。然而，到1975年，强节奏爵士舞曲的受欢迎程度慢慢降低，取而代之的是新的音乐趋势。

强节奏爵士舞曲管弦乐主要包括非洲打击乐器（体膜乐器，膜质乐器），欧洲管弦乐器（管乐器、弦鸣乐器）。这种组合赋予了强节奏爵士舞曲独特的音质以及都市氛围。它重新培育了非洲音乐的多旋律特点。这在欧洲铜管乐器以及军乐中得到了再现。

最初，强节奏爵士舞曲被引入殖民地机构，如学校、警察局及武装部队。欧洲人不懂非洲音乐的原则，尤其对它复杂的节奏以及启应方式一窍不通，他们骄傲自大地将它视为一种无规则的噪音。取而代之，他们引入西方风格的音乐，尤其是军乐以及铜管乐器。他们认为在非洲殖民地机构融入纪律是非常重要的。而对于非洲人来说，欧洲音乐只是和声，没有节奏。所以为了满足非洲人的音乐审美，军乐中的非洲人进一步探索，将和声与节奏合二为一。结果就产生了轻快乐曲与节奏的铜管乐队流行音乐。

毫无疑问，强节奏爵士舞曲迎合了非洲新型精英们的需求，他们占有着新型的城市地域。尽管他们有着接触西方文化的资历，但是他们在殖民地官员独有的俱乐部以及其他娱乐

Predictably, migrants from the rural interior flocked to these urban centers to perform the required services and to partake of the new highlife. For their own entertainment needs, they brought with them their ethnic-flavored brand of African music. Although they did not have the financial resources to equip their orchestra with expensive, imported Western instruments, they did not lack the creativity to adapt indigenous wind and string instruments to produce more contemporary, cosmopolitan tunes and rhythms. Kakraba Lobi, a former laborer at the Waterworks in Ghana, exemplified such adaptations: in between playing on the streets of Ghana and Nigeria, he was invited to join the Institute of African Studies at the University of Ghana in Legon as a master xylophonist.

场所并不是很受欢迎。不出所料地，从乡下内地的移民蜂拥至市中心，他们提供需要的服务以及参与到强节奏爵士舞曲当中。对于他们自己的娱乐需求，他们带来了自己非洲音乐的民族风味乐队。尽管他们自己不具备财力置办昂贵的西方乐器，他们并不缺少创造性。他们将当地的管弦乐器融入新的文化当中，制作出了更多现代的都市曲调以及节奏。加纳的之前的一个工人曾举例说明这些改变：他曾经在加纳和尼日利亚的街上演奏，如今，他却当做一个木琴师被邀请加入在莱贡的加纳大学非洲学研究所。

词汇 VOCABULARY

genre：种类，类型	ambience：环境，气氛
blend：融合，混合	retrain：重新培育
innovation：创新	syncopated：切分音节的
artiste：艺人	marching band：军乐
Pan-Africanist：泛非主义者	call-and-response：启应（独奏紧跟合奏的方式）
trend：趋势	cater：迎合

背景知识 PROFILE

爵士乐简介

爵士乐(Jazz)，一种起源于非洲的音乐形式，由民歌发展而来。爵士乐以多种形式呈现出繁荣景象，其乐曲风格极其耀眼，节奏一般以鲜明、强烈为主。

爵士乐相较于其他音乐，其自身有很多独特之处：

1. 即兴演奏或者是演唱

2. 运用布鲁斯音阶

3. 爵士乐节奏的极其复杂性

4.独有的爵士和弦

5.独特的音色运用

爵士乐的主要分类：

蓝调(Blues)

蓝调音乐的产生是为了抒发演唱者的个人情感，顾名思义，这种音乐听起来十分忧郁(Blue)。这种以歌曲直接陈述内心想法的表现方式，与当时白人社会的音乐截然不同。蓝调音乐最重要的作曲家即是W. C. Handy，这位1873年出生于美国的"蓝调之父"，创作了许多知名的蓝调音乐，例如：St. Louis Blues、Yellow Dog Blues、Aunt Hagars' Blues、The Memphis Blues、Beale Street Blues。

繁音拍子(Ragtime)

这是一种采用黑人旋律，依切分音法(Syncopation)循环主题与变形乐句等法则，结合而成的早期爵士乐，盛行于第一次世界大战前后。其发源与圣路易斯与新奥尔良，而后美国的南方和中西部开始流行，它影响了新奥尔良传统爵士乐的独奏与即兴演奏风格。繁音拍子后来发展成结合流行音乐、进行曲、华尔兹与其他流行舞蹈的形式，因此繁音拍子的歌曲、乐器管弦乐队编制的曲目陆续出现，它不但在黑人乐手与乐迷间流行，也被美国白人中产阶级所接受。

新奥尔良传统爵士乐(New Orleans Traditional Jazz)

这种乐风的组成元素，就如同美国是一个民族文化大融炉那般复杂、多元化，它包括：蓝调、舞曲、进行曲、流行歌曲、赞美诗与碎乐句(Rags)等音乐元素，以对位法(Countpoint)与繁音拍子的切分音法等主体性音乐创作为动力元素，结合大量独奏、即兴装饰性演奏与改写旋律核心为要件所展现出来的音乐体系。新奥尔良传统爵士乐队以小型团体为主，演奏主旋律的乐器是：短号、黑笛、萨克斯风与伸缩喇叭；伴奏乐器则有：大号、班卓琴、贝斯(常以拨奏为主)、小提琴、鼓和钢琴。它们经常多部同时进行对位吹奏，制造出一种热闹、欢乐气氛。

狄西兰爵士乐(Dixieland)

1917年~1923年间，在新奥尔良与芝加哥等地的爵士好手发展出来的早期爵士乐风，它也是新奥尔良传统爵士乐的一个分支。Dixieland的英文原意是军队露营之地"Dixie's Land"，可想而知它与进行曲等音乐有关。这种风格的取材大都来自蓝调、进行曲，与当时的流行音乐，甚至某乐曲的某一小乐段，都可以拿来加以延伸、推展，这便是即兴演奏的滥觞。有的爵士乐历史学者将"白人"乐手演奏的"New Orleans Traditional Jazz"称为狄西兰爵士乐；而黑人演奏的"New Orleans Traditional Jazz"则称为新奥尔良传统爵士乐。

大乐团(Big Band)

大乐团时代大约是起源于20年代中后期，以艾灵顿公爵(Duke Ellington)、贝西伯爵(Count Basie)、班尼·固德曼(Benny Goodman)等人为主的爵士乐风格，它不只兴盛于30年代中期的摇摆乐时期，40年代中期的咆哮乐、50年代的酷派爵士乐及改良咆哮乐、60年代的自由爵士乐、70年代的爵士/摇滚融合乐，乃至80年代的新咆哮乐中，都找得到它的踪迹。大乐团的编制一般在10人以上，涵盖3支以上的小喇叭、2支以上的伸缩喇叭、4支以上的萨克斯风及贝斯、吉他、鼓和钢琴等伴奏乐器，透过这个大型组织，演奏各种爵士乐风的曲目。

摇摆乐(Swing)

最早起源于1930年前后，在1935-1946年间达到巅峰，其中最能代表这个乐风的则是"摇摆乐之王"班尼·固德曼所领军的六重奏（Benny Goodman Sextet）。20年代中后期，爵士大乐队在美国各主要都市的夜总会、舞厅等场所大受欢迎，许多年轻乐迷都被吸引到此地玩乐，因此需要更多适合跳舞的音乐，来满足蜂拥而至的年轻人与中产阶级。摇摆乐后来随着艾灵顿公爵大乐团的脚步，演变成为歌舞表演的伴奏乐队和演奏会音乐(如：艾灵顿公爵每年定期在卡内基音乐厅演出)；摇摆乐因适合于跳舞，每小节有四拍，因此又被称为"四拍子爵士乐"。

自由爵士乐(Free Jazz)

此乐风是以创始人Ornette Coleman在1960年灌录的专辑《Free Jazz》为名，同期的代表人物包括Cecil Taylor和Albert Ayler等人，后期的倡导人则是约翰·柯川(John Coltrane)。自由爵士乐是舍弃在它之前的爵士乐和弦结构，重新建立自己一套松散、自由的集体即兴演奏方式的音乐形态。它不照本宣科，不重覆叠句和变化不定的进行速度，如此展现出的音乐风格常夹杂着人声的哭号、小喇叭或萨克斯风的乐器悲鸣。自由爵士乐的诞生有其政治上与种族上的背景因素，因为它曾是黑人争取人权与自觉运动的战歌，因此与60年代初期黑人民权运动息息相关。

88 刚果伦巴的产物——索克斯

Ask young people in Congo about soukous and you might be told that it's a soccer move in which a player **feint**s and **dribble**s the ball around an **opponent**. Your informants, who probably speak French as well as several Bantu languages, may explain that the word derives from the French verb secouer, "to shake". Ask middle-aged Congolese men and women, and they will tell you that soukous is the name of a dance that was popular in the late 1960s. Don't bother asking elderly folk about it; the word hadn't yet been **coin**ed when they were playing soccer or keeping up with dance **craze**s. Outside of Africa, however, around the same time that the concept of "world music" took hold in the late 1980s, soukous was adopted as the **generic term** for contemporary Congolese music—or at least the sound being made by Congolese and Zairean musicians in Paris. This artfully produced, **indefatigably** upbeat music, with its **genial** voices and **mesmerizing** guitars, filled **dancefloor**s around the globe for much of the following decade.

Whether defined as a particular dance or a musical genre, soukous is an outgrowth of Congolese rumba. One characteristic of rumba Congo that is germane to soukous—both the dance and the music—is the sebene. The Congolese guitarist Henri Bowane is **reputed** to have invented the sebene in the 1940s, but this kind of instrumental bridge, on which one or two musicians develop **arpeggios** in circular progressions while another improvises around them, has forever been common to music for Congolese harps, lutes, thumb pianos and xylophones. Bowane and his peers adapted traditional structures to two or three guitars

如果问刚果的年轻人，索克斯是什么，也许你得到的答案是它是一种足球步法，指的是一名球员围着对手佯攻和带球的行为。而如果你问的对象会说法语和一些班图语，他们可能告诉你，这个词来源于法语的secouer，意为"摇晃"。如果你问刚果的中年人，他们会告诉你，这是20世纪60年代非常流行的舞蹈的名称。别去问那些上了年纪的人，因为他们踢足球或是跳舞的时候，还没有这个词。然而在非洲大陆以外，就在20世纪80年代末"世界音乐"诞生之时，索克斯作为了一条专业术语，指的是刚果的当代音乐——或者至少指由刚果和扎伊尔音乐家在巴黎制作的音乐作品。在随后的十年中，伴着迷人的吉他之声，这种富于艺术性、富有不屈不挠乐观精神的音乐在世界各地的舞会上大显身手。

不管是定义为某种舞蹈或是一种音乐形式，索克斯都是刚果伦巴的产物。伦巴的特点之一——包括音乐和舞蹈——是sebene，即一种典型的电吉他上执行的器乐桥。一般认为，刚果吉他手Henri Bowane在20世纪40年代发明了sebene。然而，这种器乐桥区在刚果竖琴、笛子、拇指琴以及木琴中大为推广。Henri Bowane和他的同行们将传统结构改成两到三把吉他，并从西班牙吉他和古巴音乐的相互作用中，借鉴一些想法。

他们的跟随者们又选择了电吉

and borrowed some ideas from the interplay of the Spanish guitar and the trés in Cuban sones and guajiras.

Their disciples—guitarists such as Franco, Papa Noel, Nico Kassanda and Nico's brother Dechaud—picked up electric guitars and a few tricks from rock 'n' roll, Western swing and Hawaiian music, and heated up and stretched out their sebenes. The typical rumba congo of the 1960s and 1970s tended to start at a moderate tempo, shift up for the chorus and then hit cruising speed for the sebene.

Soukous musicians made most of their music in Paris studios. Their albums became elaborate productions involving synthesizers, programmed drum machines and the top session players and audio-technicians in the city. The best soukous records achieved a sophisticated balance between craft and hedonism, but too many sounded sensationalistic or formulaic. Most of them failed to win over the public back in Congo, where rougher sounds and greater spontaneity were preferred. And in due time soukous fell out of favor with followers of world-music trends. However, instead of ending the careers of talented musicians, the demise of soukous has propelled such artists as Sam Mangwana, Mose Fan Fan, Samba Mapangala and the former members of 4 Étoiles to revive Congolese rumba and create the best music of their lives. Somewhere in the world at this very moment a band is playing a fantastic sebene.

他，借鉴了一些摇滚乐、西方摇摆乐、夏威夷音乐的技巧，发展了sebene。20世纪六七十年代，刚果最典型的伦巴开始趋向于适度的节奏，合唱时会加速，而sebene部分速度最快。

索克斯音乐家们在巴黎的录音棚里制作了大部分音乐。他们的专辑里包含了合成器、处理的鼓声以及融合了巴黎顶尖的演奏者和录音技术人员。如此包装之后，他们的专辑非常精致。最好的索克斯是在技术和享乐主义之间取得了平衡。而实际上很多的作品听起来不是哗众取宠就是刻板模式化。他们的很多作品已经赢不了刚果当地人的心，因为那里更喜欢粗糙点儿、即时性强点儿的音乐。索克斯终将会被那些追逐世界音乐潮流的弄潮儿们所厌弃。不过，这并不会结束那些有天赋的音乐人的职业生涯，索克斯的终结促使一些音乐家们复兴了刚果伦巴音乐，并且创造了他们人生中最好的音乐。就在现在，在世界的某个角落，一支乐队可能演奏着非常棒的sebene。

词汇 VOCABULARY

feint：佯攻	indefatigably：不厌倦地，不屈不挠地
dribble：带球	genial：友好的，（气候）温暖的
opponent：对手	mesmerizing：迷人的
coin：创造（新词）	dancefloor：舞池
craze：狂热，风尚，裂纹	reputed：说是……的，被认为……的
generic term：专业术语	arpeggios：和音急速弹奏；琵音

伦巴简介

伦巴（Rumba）英文Rumba的音译，用R表示，也被称为爱情之舞，拉丁舞项目之一。源自十六世纪非洲的黑人歌舞的民间舞蹈，流行于拉丁美洲，后在古巴得到发展，所以又叫古巴伦巴，舞曲节奏为4/4拍。它的特点是较为浪漫，舞姿迷人，性感与热情；步伐曼妙、缠绵，讲究身体姿态，舞态柔媚，步法婀娜款摆，若即若离的挑逗，是表达男女爱慕情感的一种舞蹈。伦巴是拉丁音乐和舞蹈的精髓和灵魂，引人入胜的节奏和身体表现使得伦巴成为了舞厅中最为普遍的舞蹈之一。

伦巴（rumba）名字可能是来自"rumbosoorquestra"，该词是1807年一支舞蹈队的名字，在西班牙"rumbo"是通道的意思，"rumba"是堆积的意思，在加勒比海地区"rhum"是一种非常受欢迎的酒精饮料的名字，当跳这种舞蹈的时候，有可能有饮用该饮品。也有人认为伦巴的名字是起源于西班牙语的单词——喧闹的酒会。伦巴的节奏为4/4拍，每分钟27~29小节。每小节四拍。乐曲旋律的特点是强拍落在每小节的第四拍。舞步从第4拍起跳，由一个慢步和两个快步组成。四拍走三步，慢步占二拍（第4拍和下一小节的第一拍），快步各占一拍（第二拍和第三拍）。胯部摆动三次。胯部动作是由控制重心的一脚向另一脚移动而形成向两侧作"∞"型摆动。具有舒展优美，婀娜多姿，柔媚抒情的风格。

在古巴，乡村伦巴被认为是一种家禽的哑剧表演，其观赏性超过了大众的参与性。当跳舞的时候，需保持肩膀的平稳，这可是来源背着沉重物品而移动的奴隶的肩膀特点。

伦巴舞的风格和律动特点，可以归纳为稳中摆、柔中韧、快合慢。

稳中摆：伦巴舞的动律产生于劳动，劳动的黑人头顶大筐搬运香蕉等水果时，要求上身平稳，走起来上压、下顶，形成臀部的摇摆。因此跳伦巴舞时，要求保持脊椎直和两肩平，臀部的摇摆则是由于重心的转移自然形成的，而不是故意摆动臀部。当脚出步时，脚掌用力踩地，膝部稍屈，这时另一条腿的膝部是直的，当重心移到出步的脚，脚后跟放下，胯部随之向侧后方摆动；另一条则放松稍屈。整体感觉是提气，平稳地控制住上身，而臀部则不停地自如摆动。

柔中韧：出步后，膝部使劲顶直，臀部的摆动看起来轻快柔和，而实则内部用力，有一股内存的韧劲，因此跳伦巴舞时间长了会有臀部的酸涨感。

快合慢：伦巴舞用四拍走三步，节奏为快快慢，快步一拍一步，慢步两拍一步。臀部是走三步摆三下。它的出脚动作迅捷，无论快步或慢步都是半拍到位，而臀部的摆动则是快步占一拍，慢步占两拍。实际上是四拍三步中，每步都是半拍脚步到位，而臀部则是连绵不断的左、右摆动。这种上、下、慢、快矛盾统一的运动，形成了伦巴舞有特色的动律。

89 性感、欢快的音乐之声——塔拉波

In Kenya, The taarab ensembles and orchestras of Swahili-speaking East Africa offer one of the more **unexpected** sounds in African pop—elegant, sensual **composition**s filled with poetic nuance and musical **virtuosity**.

Centered in the coastal cities of Tanzania and Kenya, taarab's fusion of Indian, Arabian and African elements has spread beyond local communities to become popular from Mozambique to the Arabian Gulf. The root word of taarab, tariba, means "to be moved or **agitated**". Like much of Swahili culture, taarab began in the Kenyan port of Lamu.

Swahili ngoma or drum song styles like vugo, kumbwaya and the driving chakacha with its sexual **overtone**s—animate most forms of taarab. Egypt's firquah film orchestras provided an important model in the 1950s, and more recently, Egyptian and Lebanese pop and especially Hindi film pop have influenced taarab melodies and vocal stylings. Taarab groups range from small "parties" to orchestras that can include African drums, tablas, dumbek (**hourglass** drum), rika (tambourine), oud (fretless lute), qanun (trapeziform plucked zither), taishokoto (a banjo-like instrument of Japanese origin with a typewriter-like keyboard used to pluck the strings), as well as **organ** and **accordion**. Guitar and bass typically play, but often get overwhelmed by clusters of violins and cellos. Right up front in the sound, male and female **vocalist**s use high, clear-toned voices, Islamic in flavor, but cooler and less **wail**ing than the Muslim singers of North and West Africa.

Taarab songs explore romance and marriage, though their stylized Swahili poetry can suggest political interpretations. During the wedding season in Mombasa,

在肯尼亚，非洲东部操斯瓦希里语的塔拉波合奏组和管弦乐队伟人们提供了无与伦比的非洲流行音乐节奏——优雅、性感的作曲加上诗意般的精妙之处以及音乐演奏的高超技巧。

塔拉波主要集中在坦桑尼亚及肯尼亚的沿海城市，融合了印度、阿拉伯非洲的音乐元素。它不仅仅在这些地区有名，而且从莫桑比克远播到阿拉伯湾。塔拉波的词根是"感动的或激动不安的"。像很多斯瓦希里语的文化一样，塔拉波开始于肯尼亚的拉姆港口。

斯瓦希里语恩戈麦鼓或鼓乐的歌曲风格很像vugo，kumbwaya和chakacha，带着一种性感的余味。1950年，埃及的firquah电影管弦乐提供了一种重要的模式，最近，埃及和黎巴嫩的流行音乐以及印地的电影流行音乐影响了塔拉波的旋律以及发声的方式。演奏塔拉波的组合大小不一，乐器一般包括非洲鼓类，印度鼓，沙漏鼓，铃鼓，笛子，齐特琴以及管风琴和手风琴。一般人们也会和着吉他和铜管乐器，但这些声音会被小提琴和大提琴的声音所淹没。在如此的声音之下，男、女歌唱家用高音、清晰的曲调演唱，并带着些许伊斯兰的风格。比起西非的穆斯林歌者，这些人更加冷酷而且不那么悲伤。

尽管斯瓦西里语的诗歌带着

Kenya, people flood the streets coming and going to and from men's and especially women's taarab parties where musicians play styles of music especially suited to each day of the week-long wedding ritual. Kenyan star Zein L'Abdin, specializes in the old Lamu style of Swahili taarab. His languid rhythms and floating, world-weary vocals revolve around virtuoso oud flights. But Maulidi & Musical Party dominate the Mombasa scene. Formed in 1972 by singer/composer Maulidi Juma Iha, this group plays both Hindi pop-oriented tunes and the older Swahili styles.

政治阐释的暗示，但塔拉波歌曲的主题是浪漫和婚姻。在肯尼亚蒙巴萨的结婚季，人们从街上到女方的家庭中，会有音乐家演奏适合每天结婚电子的音乐风格。肯尼亚歌星Zein L'Abdin的风格是慵懒、浮夸的，他那厌世的嗓音会配上笛子大师的演奏。而成立于1972年的音乐团体既演奏印地流行风格主导的曲调，也演奏旧式斯瓦西里的风格。该音乐团体是由歌手/作曲者Maulidi Juma Iha发起的。

词汇 Vocabulary

unexpected：意想不到的	hourglass：沙漏
composition：作曲	organ：管风琴
virtuosity：精湛技巧，高超	accordion：手风琴
agitated：激动不安的	vocalist：流行歌手，声乐家
overtone：寓意；眩外音；暗示	wail：悲叹，哀诉

背景知识 Profile

斯瓦希里语简介

斯瓦希里语属于班图语族，是非洲语言当中使用人口最多的一种（5500万多人），是坦桑尼亚的唯一官方语言，肯尼亚和刚果民主共和国的国家语言之一，和赞比亚、马拉维、布隆迪、卢旺达、乌干达、莫桑比克等国家的重要交际语。

斯瓦希里语（简称斯语）属班图语系东班图语族，为非洲一主要通用语言。目前使用斯语者约有五千万人，分布在东非各国和地区，包括坦桑尼亚、肯尼亚、乌干达、马拉维、布隆迪、刚果、赞比亚、津巴布韦、莫桑比克、索马里等国。坦桑尼亚和肯尼亚已定斯语为国语。其他如乌干达等国居民大都使用这一语言。据东非权威性的《语言研究学报》报导，不少语言学家根据语言发展趋势推测，认为斯语极有可能成为整个非洲地区的通用语言。

近年我国人民和东非各国人民之间的友好往来日益频繁，从事斯语研究及翻译工作的人逐渐增多。在援外工作中，我国派往坦桑尼亚工作、学习或考察的人先后已有数十万人次之多。无论在国内学习或出国工作，对于学好斯语，均感觉有迫切需要。斯语作为专业学习在我国自一九六零年开始，北京广播学院、北京外国语学院先后设置斯语专业，次年中央广播电台增设斯语播音节目。一九六四年《人民画报》创刊斯语版，外文出版社也开始出版斯语书籍。由北京外国语学院斯语专修班译编的《斯汉辞典》，亦经外文局编辑出版问世。但有关斯语语法方面的书籍，依然不多。多年以来，从事斯语工作或学习的人，只能参考英国出版的《自学斯瓦希里语》（Teach Yourself Swahili）一书的中译油印稿。该书编于三十年代。

90 近一百年的音乐传奇——祖祖

For many years the most popular style in Nigeria, juju music evolved from Yoruba **folklore** and a variety of international elements. Early in the 20th century, Lagos was a place where local peoples encountered freed slaves from the New World. Together they created a **recreational** music that came to be known as **palm wine** music, as it usually accompanied drinking. Banjos, guitars, shakers and hand drums supported **lilting** topical songs and produced local celebrities, notably "Baba" Tunde King, apparently the first to call his music juju.

Tunde Nightingale established the core **repertoire** that would shape this fast-evolving style. Electricity and the ability to **amplify** voices and strings created the possibility of bringing in heavier percussion, in particular the Yoruba taking drum, or gangan. Starting in the late 1950s, I.K. Dairo became the first juju singer to exploit these possibilities adding electric guitars and an accordion, which he played himself, to the mix. Dairo was followed in the 1960s by Chief Commander Ebenezer Obey, and in the 1970s, by King Sunny Ade and his African Beats.

The competition between Obey and KSA, as

祖祖一直以来是尼日利亚最流行的音乐风格。它是从约鲁巴民谣和很多国际元素演变过来的。在20世纪初，当地人在拉各斯可以遇到来自新大陆的自由奴隶。当地人和这些自由奴隶就创作出了这种娱乐的音乐，那会儿人们叫它棕榈酒乐，这是因为这种音乐是伴随着饮酒的。那些热带地区轻快的歌曲的伴奏乐器是班卓琴、吉他、拨浪鼓以及手鼓，"Baba"便是玩这些乐器的名人。他是第一个叫自己音乐为祖祖的人。

Tunde Nightingale建立了核心曲目，这些曲子塑造了这种演变很快的风格。电吉他和扩大声音及琴弦声的能力使得重重的打击乐加入成为可能，尤其是说话鼓。20世纪50年代末期，I.K. Dairo成为了第一个将这些可能性进行探索的歌手，他加入了电吉他和手风琴。然后出现了60年代的Ebenezer Obey以及70年代的King Sunny Ade（KSA）。

Obey和KSA的竞争吸引了公众的

Nigerians know Ade, engaged the public and **fuel**ed rapid evolution of the juju sound as **trap drum**s, **pedal steel guitar**, synthesizers, and more and more percussion instruments joined the lineup. By the time KSA first toured internationally in the early 1980s, juju could compete with that era's best rock music for its force of expression, theatricality and **visceral** impact. With some 20 musicians on stage, Ade quickly won a loyal audience and effectively launched the international Afropop phenomenon. Other African artists, like Miriam Makeba and Manu Dibango, had made a splash, but after KSA began touring, a larger awareness of African music began to dawn. As such, juju holds a unique position in the history of all African pop.

Meanwhile back in Nigeria, after the long, virtually unchallenged reign of KSA and Ebenezer Obey, master showman "Sir" Shina Peters opened the door to a new generation of juju musicians. He and singer Segun Adewale started out backing juju veteran Prince Adekunle, but in 1977, Shina and Segun formed Shina Adewale and the Superstars International. In 1980, the two young rebels went different ways, Segun promoting a fusion style he called yo-pop, and Shina emerging in the late 1980s with his Afro-juju style, a more percussion-heavy take on the juju sound. Shina's music nods to Fela Kuti's funky afrobeat and to the percussion frenzy of fuji music, but it remains essentially juju. With songs stressing moral themes, Shina has won awards in Nigeria in 1989 and 1990. Around the same time, Dele Taiwo **made hay with** a punchy, keyboard-rich sound he called funky juju.

In the 1990s, percussive fuji music and local **reggae** became very popular with Nigerian listeners, ending juju's long-held dominance. These days, as elsewhere in Africa, hip-hop aesthetics are popular with young musicians and fans, and new variations on juju are emerging as the style changes its shape to suit the times.

眼球，为祖祖音乐又加入了架子鼓、踏板电子吉他、合成器以及越来越多的打击乐器。到80年代，KSA第一次开始国际巡回演出。在表达力、戏剧效果以及震人心弦方面，此时的祖祖可以与那个时代最好的摇滚乐一决高下。巡演时，舞台上有20位歌者。Ade赢得了一批忠实粉丝，有效地形成了非洲流行音乐的国际效应。其他的非洲艺术家也是倍受关注。KSA巡演之后，人们对于非洲音乐有了更深的认识。因此，祖祖在非洲流行音乐史上地位独特。

与此同时，尼日利亚见证了KSA和Obey在乐坛叱咤风云的时期。后来有Shina Peters出现，他是祖祖音乐人新一代的代表。1977年，他和歌手Segun Adewale成立了Shina Adewale以及国际巨星。1980年，两个年轻的反叛者分道扬镳。Segun开始了yo-pop，一种混合风格；Shina的zuzu打击乐的声音更为浓重。Shina的音乐像库提的放克Afrobeat，有很重的打击乐风格，但本质上是祖祖。Shina的音乐主题是道德，他曾经在1989和1990年间在尼日利亚获奖。几乎同时，Dele Taiwo创作出了放克祖祖。

90年代，尼日利亚的人们喜欢上了雷盖摇摆乐，这才结束了祖祖的长期统治地位。如今，就像非洲其他地方一样，年轻的音乐人和粉丝们喜欢嘻哈的风格，而祖祖亦产生了很多新的变种，以追赶当今的潮流。

folklore：民谣	fuel：加燃料(油)；刺激
recreational：娱乐的，消遣的	trap drum：架子鼓
palm wine：棕榈酒	pedal steel guitar：踏板电子吉他
lilting：轻快的	visceral：发自肺腑的
repertoire：全部曲目	make hay with...：搞垮……；使……陷於混乱
amplify：扩大，放大	reggae：雷盖摇摆乐（一种牙买加流行音乐）

背景知识 PROFILE

嘻哈

　　Hip-hop是20多年前始于美国街头的一种黑人文化，也泛指rap（说唱乐）。Hip-hop文化的四种表现方式包括rap（有节奏、押韵地说话）、b-boying（街舞）、dj-ing（玩唱片及唱盘技巧）、raffiti writing（涂鸦艺术）。因此rap（说唱乐）只是hip-hop文化中的一种元素，要加上其他舞蹈、服饰、生活态度等才构成完整的hip-hop文化。

　　说唱起源于60年代，而作为音乐理解的hip-hop则起源于70年代初，它的前身是rap(有时候会加一点R&B)。这是一种完全自由式即兴式的音乐。这种音乐不带有任何程式化，拘束的成分。在任何时间，任何地点你都可以炫hip-hop只要你high。

　　Hip-hop从字面上来看，hip是臀部，hop是摇摆，加在一起就是轻扭摆臀，是以前美国的蹦迪。原先指的是雏形阶段的街舞(也就是我们以前说的霹雳舞)，后来才逐渐发展成一种巨大的概念——我们现在说的hip-hop文化还包括了那些宽大的衣服、沉甸甸的纯金饰品、平时说话来就"YoYo? what's up? men！"的口语习惯——总之就是那种美国贫民街区里黑人的生活方式以及他们的"范儿"。

　　我们可以分成New York Style与L.A Style两种。这个两个地区的东西呈现两极化的风格。例如New York Style它就是我们一般所看到的身体扭曲变形，各种街舞大串联的风格。或许New York是HENRY的大本营，所以自然而然的这个地区的hip-hop风格也较偏向HENRY的风格，原地性的舞蹈加上身体奇怪的扭曲与LOCKING（锁舞）popping（机械舞），WAVE（电流）这些东西的大会串，我们不难想象它正是一种黑人的随性作风。

　　而L.A Style的hip-hop，它承袭延续了MC HAMMER及巴比布朗时期所流行的街舞。大动作及脚步的变化性，也保有了其劲爆的特性。只是在动作的变化上增加了许多新的花样。也因为hip-hop分成了这两大派系，所以许多舞者或杂志媒体上就不再统称他们为hip-hop DANCE。他们称New York Style的hip-hop为NEW SCHOOL。而称 L.A Style 的hip-hop为STREET DANCE。

具体风格如下：

西海岸说唱乐(West Coast Rap)

在hip-hop 世界里，这不仅是一个地理的分割。东西海岸说唱的区别在于它们不同的风格和内容。尽管也受 Hip-Hop 前辈如 Grandmaster Flash 和 Afrika Bambatta 的影响，西海岸说唱比起东海岸说唱，进一步从老派说唱游离开去。他们使用更 funky 的独特节奏，支持着流畅的、有旋律的曲调。西海岸说唱手还率先把"黑帮"文化良莠不分地带入hip-hop 文化的前沿。尽管在说唱乐继续演变的过程中，东西海岸说唱的界限正在慢慢淡化，但仍有一个明显的西海岸体系，包括从精髓的说唱乐队 N.W.A. 到 Snoop Dogg 和 Vallejo，以及加州的E-40 等。

南部说唱乐(Southern Rap)

所有的种类中，南部说唱包括的艺人和风格是最宽泛的。从歌词上讲，南部说唱乐人的共同特点是带有浓重的地方口音。然而音乐上，在不同地区的乐队间的区别各不相同。亚特兰大的 Organized Noize Productions的创新器乐，就很大程度地区别于新奥尔良的 Cash Money 和 No Limit 的粗犷的合成跳跃风味。而 Underground Kingz（来自德克萨斯州的休斯顿）和Eightball & MJG（来自田纳西州的孟菲斯）这些乐队则以慷慨深情的、用吉他点缀的动感，进一步扩展了此风格的范围。

流行说唱乐 (Pop Rap)

流行说唱是适合电台广播的说唱，主要特点是吸引人的旋律与节奏、干净利落的制作，以及噱头的推广，这种风格也称"干净说唱"。艺术家包括Will Smith , MC Hammer 和 Young M.C 等，尽管常受硬核说唱者嘲弄，但因注意年轻人的市场而不断掀起强力热潮。

老派说唱乐 (Old School)

老派说唱指的是说唱的初创时期，在 1979~1984 期间，当时的节拍更直接，重点在于娱乐，而不是对社会的诠释或讲述堕落的故事。老派说唱的全盛期是由Sugarhill Gang 的劲曲 "Rapper's Delight" 开始的，随后走红的分别是一些其他单曲，而非某一位艺人。U.T.F.O 的 "Roxanne Roxanne"，Whodini 的 "Freaks Come Out at Night" 和 Kurtis Blow的 "Basketball" 在此期间尽享成功，但是被流行主流所记住的主要是热门单曲，而没有包括他们广泛的其他作品。几个现代乐队如 the Arsonists 和 Jurassic 5 有着明显的老派说唱音调，为新一代听众介绍 B-boy 的精髓，如高能量的合成音韵以及 DJ 的重要性。

中西部说唱乐 (Midwest Rap)

尽管他们的制作技术也同样代表了他们的音乐，美国中西部的说唱乐手主要还是通过其人声部的革新而使自己独树一帜。Emcees Twista 和 Bone Thugs 通过人声旋律的实验给中西部说唱找到了应有的位置，其中 Emcees Twista 则更加快了旋律的速度。芝加哥的 Do or Die 与克里夫兰（Cleveland）的 BoneThugs N-Harmony 之间的良性竞争又更巩固了中西部说唱乐在说唱界中的地位。双方竞相宣传，吸引了不少听众。

拉丁说唱 (Latin Rap)

自从说唱一开始，就有来自拉丁圈子的说唱。但是它直到很晚才闯入流行主流。Mellow Man Ace 的"Mentirosa"和 Kid Frost 的"La Raza"的双重成功标志着拉丁说唱——用多种语言（尤其是西班牙语）的说唱，拉丁韵律和拉丁裔人的都市生活形象——在流行乐坛的成功。Mellow Man Ace 的兄弟，Sen Dog 是最著名的拉丁说唱行动 Cypress Hill 的创建成员之一。

硬核说唱 (Hardcore Rap)

当说唱已经以更直接的态度叙述城市挣扎主题的时候，于 20 世纪 80 年代末冒出了更具挑衅性的一种表现形式，称为"硬核"。它是说唱中一种更具有力量感的音乐形式，打破以往说唱及舞曲的形式，具有更强的破坏力和煽动力，其背景总是伴以不断弱化的鼓点，而歌词也大都反映与社会背道而驰或与一般人相异的思维方式。艺术家如 Ice-T, PublicEnemy, Eminem, Geto Boys 和 Mobb Deep 等，他们用辛辣的歌词与粗糙的制作工艺创造音乐。

黑帮说唱 (Gangsta Rap)

黑帮说唱叙述街头生活的故事，主题常是暴力暗杀或女人祸水，成为一种乐风的同时更是一种暴力型的形象。N.W.A 在 1989 年的成名专集 Straight Outta Compton 首次开创了这种 hip-hop 中最具争议性的说唱，其中Fuck The Police 和 Crooked Officer 控诉了执法者的暴行。政客和宗教权益者的抗议和恐吓一下子充斥于市，压倒多数的负面报导使媒介巨头为了躲避审查而不得不放弃许多极有潜力的音乐家和唱片公司。尽管如此，精良录制并熟谙媒介的Notorious B.I.G. 及其同道们的音乐录影还是在 20 世纪 90 年代末让黑帮文化靠近了主流。

外来说唱乐 (Foreign Rap)

所有非英语国家对 hip-hop 的贡献，总称为外来说唱/Hip-hop，它取用说唱的基本信条并加入多种文化鞣制而成。法国说唱乐队 MC Solaar 和日本艺人 DJ Kensei合并其他类型，包括舞曲和酸性爵士，把其他文化的风味注入日常的hip-hop 血脉。

东海岸说唱乐 (East Coast Rap)

东海岸说唱总的来说比其西海岸说唱保留了更多的老派风格。Public Enemy, Boogie Down Productions, Run-D.M.C. 和其他精华的东海岸艺术家直接引鉴他们的前辈的简朴与直接性，与西海岸的华丽风格形成对比。由此产生了更有棱角的节奏和严谨而又有力的韵律。随着东西海岸的融合，说唱成为两岸文化的合金，清晰明快的东海岸之声继续蓬勃发展，涌现了一批如Nas, Mobb Deep 和Juru the Damaj a 之流的年轻有为的创新艺人。

第十章

你不可不知的中非关系要点

　　中非友谊源远流长，最早可追溯到公元前2世纪。1956年，埃及成为第一个与新中国建交的非洲国家。由此便开启了中非交往的新篇章。

　　本章只是截取了中非关系中的极小一部分实例，力求达到窥一斑而知全貌的效果。

　　对于中非关系，国际上的微词颇多，多集中在"中国危险论"、"中国殖民论"上。对此，编者借用温总理在第四届部长级会议中答记者问时的一句话——"路遥知马力，日久见人心"。让我们把希望寄托于中非友谊更加美好的明天。

91 非洲境内中国第一人——杜环

Du Huan was a Chinese travel writer born in Chang'an during the Tang Dynasty (AD 618—907). He was one of a few Chinese **capture**d in the Battle of Talas along with **artisan**s Fan Shu and Liu Ci and fabric **weaver**s Le Wei and Lv Li, as mentioned in his writings. After a long journey through Arab countries, he returned by ship to Guangzhou in 762. There he wrote his Jingxingji, a work which was almost completely lost. A few **extract**s survived in Tongdian under volume 192 and 193, an **encyclopaedia compile**d in 801 by one of his relatives, Du You. In the 8th century, Du You's encyclopaedia quoted Du Huan himself on Molin (North or East Africa):

"We also went to Molin, southwest of Jerusalem. One could reach this country after having crossed the great desert of **Sinai** and having travelled 2,000 li (approx. 1500 km). The people there are black, and their customs are **bold**. There is little rice and cereals, with no grass and trees on this land. The horses are fed with dried fish, and the people eat Gumang. Gumang is a **Persian date**. Subtropical diseases (Malaria) are widespread. After crossing into the inland countries there is a mountainous country, which gathered a lot of **confession**s here. They have three confessions, the Arab (Islam), Byzantine (Christianity) and Zimzim (Judaism). The Zimzim practise **incest**, and in this respect are worst of all the barbarians. The followers under the confession of Arab have a means to **denote** in law, while not entangling the defendant's families or **kin**s. They don't eat the meat of pigs, dogs, donkeys and horses; they don't respect either the king of the country, nor their parents; they don't believe in supernatural powers, perform only sacrifice to heaven (Allah) and to no one else. According to their customs, every seventh day is a holiday (Jumu'ah), on which no trade and no currency transactions are done, whereas when they drink alcohol, and behave in a ridiculous and undisciplined way during the whole day.

杜环是一位中国游记作家，生于唐朝长安（今陕西西安）。怛罗斯战役中，杜环是一万余唐军俘虏中的一员，其他还包括杜环在其书中提到的匠人樊淑、刘泚，织工吕礼等。762年，长期旅居于阿拉伯国家之后，杜环乘船回到广州。在此，他撰写下《经行记》，可惜已失传。唯杜佑《通典》卷192、193中引用此书一些片段，因此得以留存后世。《通典》是一部百科全书，编者杜佑，801年成书。8世纪，杜佑的百科全书引用了杜环关于摩邻国（非洲北部或东部）的叙述：

"摩邻国，在秧萨罗国（耶路撒冷）西南，渡大碛（西奈半岛沙漠）行二千里至其国。其人黑，其俗犷，少米麦，无草木，马食干鱼，人餐鹘莽。鹘莽，即波斯枣也。瘴疠特甚。诸国陆行之所经也，山胡则一种，法有数般（多数宗教并存）。有大食法（伊斯兰教），有大秦法（基督教），有寻寻法（原始拜物教）。其寻寻蒸报，于诸夷狄中最甚，当食不语。其大食法者，以弟子亲戚而作判典，纵有微过，不至相累。不食猪、狗、驴、马等肉，不拜国王、

Within the confession of the Byzantines, there are **beneficent** medical doctors who know **diarrhea**; they could either recognize the disease before its outbreak, or could remove the worms by opening the brain."

父母之尊，不信鬼神，祀天而已。其俗每七日一假（伊斯兰教礼拜制度）；不买卖，不出纳，唯饮酒谑浪终日。其大秦善医眼及痢（基督徒医生医术高明），或未病先见，或开脑出虫。”

背景知识 PROFILE

怛罗斯战役

　　怛罗斯战役又称怛逻斯之役或但逻斯之役，是中国唐朝玄宗时唐朝的势力与来自现在阿拉伯、新兴和信奉伊斯兰教什叶派的新兴阿拔斯王朝（即黑衣大食）的势力在包含昭武九姓国、大小勃律、吐火罗在内的中亚诸国相遇而导致的战役。怛罗斯战役是一场当时历史上最强大的东西方帝国间的碰撞。

　　据中国史书记载唐安西节度使高仙芝领兵征讨，石国请求投降，高仙芝允诺和好；但是不久高仙芝即违背承诺，攻占并血洗石国城池，掠走男丁、屠杀老人、妇女和儿童，抢夺财物，并俘虏石国国王并献于阙下斩首。侥幸逃脱的石国王子向阿拔斯王朝求救。高仙芝得到消息后，决定采取先发制人之策，主动进攻大食。鉴于当时唐帝国在西域的影响，有许多葛逻禄及拔汗那国的军卒参加大唐的军队，组成的大唐联军有三万多人（另有说法为七万多人），其中唐兵占三分之二。高仙芝率领大唐联军长途奔袭，深入七百余里，最后在怛罗斯与大食军队遭遇。怛罗斯的所在地还未完全确定，但应在吉尔吉斯斯坦与哈萨克斯坦的边境，接近哈萨克斯坦的塔拉兹（曾称江布尔）的地区。

根据现在历史研究，怛罗斯战役是东西方两大帝国势力扩张的必然后果。早在公元七世纪后半叶，被阿拉伯人称为"列王之父"的阿布杜勒·马利克（685—705年在位）的任命之下，哈查只·伊本·优素福被任命为掌管东方的最高权利者，在他的领导下，阿拉伯帝国的疆域向东方获得了极大的扩张，由于垂涎中国的富庶，他应许他的两个大将：穆罕默德·伊本·卡西木和古太白·本·穆斯林·巴西里，谁最先踏上中国的领土，就任命谁做中国的长官。于是古太白征服了塔立甘、舒曼、塔哈斯坦、布哈拉等大片中亚地区，而穆罕默德征服了印度的边疆地区，当阿拉伯帝国的势力在和唐王朝经营的安西四镇接壤后，战争无法避免。在开元三年（715年）和开元五年（717年），阿拉伯帝国倭马亚王朝对唐代所属的安西四镇的入侵战争均遭到失败之后，阿拉伯帝国仍旧执着地向中亚进行扩张。750年，阿拉伯帝国发生革命，阿拔斯王朝建立，继续执行东扩的计划。在此情况下，唐王朝经营西域的四镇都知兵马使高仙芝以石国（昭武九姓之一，阿拉伯帝国的附属国）无蕃臣礼节为由，发动了对石国的战争，借机打击阿拔斯王朝在中亚的势力，战争由此爆发。

　　史载战斗持续了五日。初期战斗唐王朝的精锐步兵占上风，但是兵力悬殊战争变成僵局，其间大唐联军的葛逻禄部见势不妙，倒向大食。唐军步兵因此与唐军主力失去联络。阿拔斯王朝联军乘唐军士兵发生暂时混乱的机会，出动重骑兵主力对唐朝步兵猛攻。高仙芝受到大食与葛逻禄部两面夹击，无力支撑而溃不成军。势危之时，副将李嗣业劝高仙芝弃军逃跑，于是高仙芝、副将李嗣业和别将段秀实收拢残部向安西逃遁，途中恰逢大唐联军的拔汗那兵也溃逃至此，兵马车辆拥挤堵塞道路。李嗣业惟恐大食追兵将及，杀死百余名拔汗那军士才得以率先通过。别将段秀实责备李嗣业说："惮敌而奔，非勇也；免己陷众，非仁也。"李嗣业甚感惭愧。最后高仙芝等和数千名唐兵逃至安西。此役以大食军完胜奔袭问罪的大唐联军为结局，唐三万余士卒近乎全没，只有少数逃脱。

　　尽管怛罗斯战役战败，唐王朝的整体实力，以及在西域的影响力并未受到动摇；战后，唐王朝仍在中亚继续扩张，而于755年达到了西域经略的鼎盛。尽管阿拔斯王朝取得了怛罗斯战役的胜利，但是慑于唐军强大的战斗力，打消了东进扩展领土的打算，而默许了葛逻禄在阿姆河与锡尔河流域附近的扩张；他们自立了一国家，并一直维持至九世纪末被后来建立黑汗王朝的入侵者消灭。

　　也有一种说法指出，发源于中国的造纸术因为唐军战俘中的造纸工匠被带到由阿拔斯王朝第一任哈里发阿布·阿拔斯-萨法赫在撒马尔罕新建的造纸坊里工作，而传到中亚和中东；但考古证据显示，造纸术在此役之前就已流传于中亚，只是通过日后伊斯兰政权对中亚的征服，才终于传布到了伊斯兰世界及西方。

92 永载史册的明朝航海家——郑和

Viewed from the **rocky outcropping** of Dondra Head at the **southernmost** tip of Sri Lanka, the first sighting of the Ming fleet is a **massive** shadow on the horizon. As the shadow rises, it breaks into a cloud of **tautly ribbed** sail, **aflame** in the tropical sun. With relentless determination, the cloud draws ever closer, and in its fiery embrace an **enormous** city appears. A floating city, like nothing the world has ever seen before. No warning could have prepared officials, soldiers, or the **thunderstruck** peasants who stand atop Dondra Head for the scene that **unfold**s below them. Stretched across miles of the Indian Ocean in terrifying majesty is the armada of Zheng He, **admiral** of the imperial Ming navy.

Exactly 608 years ago in July the great Ming **armada** weighed anchor in Nanjing, on the first of seven epic voyages as far west as Africa—almost a century before Christopher Columbus's arrival in the Americas and Vasco da Gama's in India. Even then the European **expedition**s would seem **paltry** by comparison: All the ships of Columbus and da Gama combined could have been stored on a single deck of a single **vessel** in the **fleet** that set sail under Zheng He.

Its commander was, without question, the most **towering** maritime figure in the 4,000-year annals of China, a **visionary** who imagined a new world and set out consciously to **fashion** it. He was also a profoundly unlikely candidate for admiral in anyone's navy, much less that of the Dragon Throne.

The greatest **seafarer** in China's history was raised in the mountainous heart of Asia, several weeks' travel from the closest port. More improbable yet, Zheng was not even Chinese—he was by origin a Central Asian Muslim. Born Ma He, the son of a rural official in the Mongol province of

从斯里兰卡最南端的露出岩石的栋德勒角来看，明朝舰队在远处的海平面上形成一个巨大的阴影。接着，阴影逐渐升起，此时，人们能完成看清那是风帆组成的云，这些帆在热带太阳的照射下，一片火红。那片云朵逐渐靠近。在它火红色的拥抱下，一个大型的城市出现在人们面前。这是一座人们前所未见的浮游城市。官员、士兵以及吓坏了的农民们停下来，看这个在他们面前展开的景象。在印度洋上绵延数里的是郑和的舰队，郑和是明朝海军的舰队司令。

608年前的7月，伟大的明朝舰队在南京起锚，迈出了七次下西洋的第一步，郑和舰队最远已达非洲——其壮举比哥伦布达到美洲新大陆和达伽马达到印度早近一个世纪。欧洲的远征相形见绌：哥伦布和达伽马所有的船加起来只能装下郑和舰队一条船的一层甲板。

毫无疑问，舰队司令是中国4000年年鉴中最为杰出的航海人物，他富于远见卓识，他按照想象的新世界的样子，去有意识地探索世界，使想象变成现实。

最伟大的航海家在中国诞生，他从最近的港口出发。郑和不是汉人，而是中亚穆斯林。郑和原名马三宝，其父是云南的一名乡下官员。1382年，明朝军队进攻云南。马三宝10岁，被掳入明营，

Yunnan, he had been taken captive as an invading Chinese army **overthrew** the Mongols in 1382. Ritually castrated, he was trained as an imperial **eunuch**21 and assigned to the court of Zhu Di, the bellicose Prince of Yan.

Within 20 years the boy w had become one of the prince's chief aides, a key strategist in the rebellion that made Zhu Di the Yongle (Eternal Happiness) emperor in 1402. Renamed Zheng after his exploits at the battle of Zhenglunba, near Beijing, he was chosen to lead one of the most powerful naval forces ever **assemble**d22.

Zheng He's legacy, a 10,000-mile (16,093-kilometer) journey would carry us from Yunnan to Africa's Swahili coast.

被阉割成太监，之后进入朱棣的燕王府。

在随后的20年中，郑和成了朱棣的主要心腹之一，在1402年的朱棣称帝中，是主要的战略家。后因在战争中的英勇行为，改姓为郑。明成祖任命他为最为强大的舰队司令。

郑和出使里程达16093公里，范围是从云南到非洲的斯瓦西里海岸。

背景知识 PROFILE

郑和七下西洋

郑和第一次下西洋

永乐三年六月十五日（1405年7月11日）从南京龙江港启航，经太仓出海，永乐五年九月初二（1407年10月2日）回国。第一次下西洋人数据记载有27 800人。

郑和第二次下西洋

永乐五年九月十三日（1407年10月13日）出发，到达文莱、泰国、柬埔寨、印度等地，在锡兰山迎请佛牙，随船带回，永乐七年夏（1409年）回国。第二次下西洋人数据载有27 000人。

郑和第三次下西洋

永乐七年九月（1409年10月）从太仓刘家港启航，姚广孝、费信、马欢等人会同前往，到达越南、马来西亚、印度等地，回国途中访锡兰山，永乐九年六月十六（1411年7月6日）回国。

郑和第四次下西洋

永乐十一年十一月（1413年11月）出发，随行有通译马欢，绕过阿拉伯半岛，首次航行东非麻林迪，永乐十三年七月初八（1415年8月12日）回国。同年11月，麻林迪特（肯尼亚）使来中国进献"麒麟"（即长颈鹿）。第四次下西洋人数据载有27 670人。

郑和第五次下西洋

永乐十五年五月（1417年6月）出发，随行有蒲寿庚的后代蒲日和，途经泉州，到占城、爪哇，最远到达东非木骨都束、卜喇哇、麻林等国家，永乐十七年七月十七（1419年8月8日）回国。

郑和第六次下西洋

永乐十九年正月三十日（1421年3月3日）出发，往榜葛剌（孟加拉），史载"于镇东洋中，官舟遭大风，掀翻欲溺，舟中喧泣，急叩神求佑，言未毕，……风恬浪静"，中道返回，永乐二十年八月十八（1422年9月2日）回国。永乐二十二年，明成祖去世，仁宗朱高炽即位，因经济空虚，下令停止下西洋的行动。

郑和第七次下西洋

宣德五年闰十二月初六（1431年1月）从龙江关（今南京下关）启航，返航后，郑和因劳累过度于宣德八年（1433年）四月初在印度西海岸古里去世，船队由太监王景弘率领返航，宣德八年七月初六（1433年7月22日）返回南京。第七次下西洋人数据载有27550人。

93 中非关系第一步——盘点中埃关系要点

The Egyptian and Chinese civilizations are the oldest known to mankind. They each go back 5000 years in history. There were trade routes between the two nations since 2000 years ago. Hence the **long-enduring** friendship between their peoples.

The First Stage (1954—1970):

Cairo recognized the People's Republic of China on May 30, being the first African country to do so. Egypt also supported China's efforts to regain its seat at the United Nations and expressed surprise at Washington's **stance** of **cold-shoulder**ing China.

On August 15, 1965, the Chinese government of Zhou Enlai issued a statement declaring China's support of Egypt's decision to **nationalize** the **Suez Canal**; in September the Zhou Enlai government **reiterate**d its support of the nationalization decision and rejected the Tripartite aggression launched by Britain, France and Israel in a statement delivered to the Egyptian government. Over three days in November 1956 millions of Chinese took to the streets in demonstrations **denouncing** the aggression and expressing support for the Egyptian people.

In the mid-1960s, China denounced the Israeli aggression and expressed full support of Egypt.

The Second Stage (1970—1981):

In the early years of President Anwar al-Sadat's rule, a precious part of Egypt's territory was still under occupation.

In China, the **fallout**s of the Cultural Revolution were still being felt at all levels. Beijing **withdrew** all ambassadors from the Middle East, but not from Egypt, which indicates the high standing the country holds in China's foreign policy.

The Third Stage (1981—2011):

Under incumbent of the former President Hosni Mubarak, Egyptian-Chinese relations entered a new phase.

埃及和中国的文明历史悠久。他们分别都有5000年的历史。自2000年以前，他们已经有贸易往来。从此，中埃友谊绵延不绝。

第一阶段（1954—1970）

1956年5月30日，埃及成为第一个承认新中国的非洲国家。埃及也曾支持中国恢复在联合国的合法席位，曾对美国怠慢中国的态度表示不满。

1965年8月15日，周恩来代表中国政府发表声明，支持埃及将苏伊士运河国有化。9月，周恩来总理重申支持埃及将苏伊士国有化的决定，排斥英、法及以色列三国在给埃及政府的声明中所提出的三国侵略。1956年11月，中国人们上街游行示威，谴责侵略行为，支持埃及人民，游行持续三天。

60年代中期，中国谴责以色列的侵略行径，全面支持埃及。

第二阶段（1970—1981）：

埃及总统沙达执政前期，埃及的一块宝贵领土仍在殖民之下。

而中国，文化大革命在各个方面全面展开，北京政府决定撤出所有非洲中部地区的大使，但埃及除外。这暗示出在中国外

Political, economic and cultural exchanges greatly **intensified**. Traveling and tourist visits also multiplied. A relationship of strategic partnership was finally established during President Mubarak's visit to China in 1999.

After talks, Mubarak and Chinese President Jiang Zemin signed a joint statement establishing strategic cooperation relations. The statement underlined the need:

To create a new political and economic world order that is fair and reasonable.

To **solidify** cooperation and solidarity between developing countries and to bridge the gap between the world's rich and poor.

To achieve a comprehensive and durable peace in the Middle East by totally committing to and fully abiding by the agreements signed between the Palestinian Authority and Israel.

The international community to **entrench** the concept of disarming particularly in respect of weapons of mass destruction so that no country or region would be excepted.

To condemn terrorism in all its forms and to cooperate in the international war on terror.

The many visits exchanged in addition to the increased volume of trade and joint ventures have created a solid foundation.

The strategic cooperation agreement signed in 1999 also represented a turning point. Visits exchanged between officials from both countries have doubled.

In addition, a meeting of the foreign ministers of Egypt and China takes place on the sidelines of the UN General Assembly meetings in September every year.

Economic relations have further taken a turn to the non-conventional. Besides imports and exports, a number of joint ventures have been established.

交政策中埃及所处的重要位置。

第三阶段（1981—2011）

前总统穆巴拉克在任时，中埃关系进入崭新阶段。政治、经济以及文化交流大大加深。旅游也大大扩展。1999年，穆巴拉克访华时，中埃最终确定战略合作伙伴关系。

会谈会，穆巴拉克与中国时任主席江泽民签署联合声明，确定战略合作关系。声明着重强调以下几点：

建立公正、合理的新政治、经济秩序；

巩固发展中国家间的合作和团结，缩小贫富差距；

实现中东地区全面、长久的和平，为此，完全遵守与履行巴以协议；

国际社会应确保非武装观念，尤其在大规模杀伤性武器，任何一个国家都不例外；

谴责任何形式的恐怖主义，实行全球合作。

两国除逐渐增长的贸易和合资总量之外，多次访问也巩固了中埃关系。

1999年签署的战略合作协议代表了一种转折点。两国官员互访加倍。

另外，每年九月，在联合国大会的框架下，中埃都会召开双方外交部长会议。

经济关系进一步转向非常规化。除进出口以外，很多合资企业成立。

long-enduring：持久的	denounce：谴责，指责；告发
stance：立场	fallout：（政治）余波，附带结果
cold-shoulder：冷漠，怠慢	withdraw：撤消，撤退
nationalize：使……国有化	intensify：加强
Suez Canal：苏伊士运河	solidify：使巩固
reiterate：重申	entrench：确保

94 沟通让生活更美好——坦赞铁路

The TAZARA railway line between Kapiri Mposhi in Zambia and the port of Dar-es-Salaam in Tanzania is a **vital** link which really needs **a new lease of life**. The standards of service for the railway firm have **plummet**ed over the years, while **infrastructure** has suffered **tremendous wear and tear** and requires a **facelift**. Cargo has been **maroon**ed while passengers have not been spared when a **derailment** occurs on the network.

Apart from wearing out, the facility, which was constructed between 1970 and 1975 has been **vandalise**d, rendering operations difficult. Thus, the $39 million interest-free loan from the Chinese government, is one feat which would facilitate the redemption of this vital firm, operating about 1,860 kilometre railway line.

Though the railway line was constructed as an alternative route to address the disturbances in the then Rhodesia, Angola, and Mozambique, the facility is still useful because the port of Dar-es-salaam is just as convenient as other points on the continent and in

连接赞比亚卡皮里姆波希与坦桑尼亚达累斯萨拉姆的坦赞铁路是一条非常重要的交通线，急需修缮。铁路公司近年来的服务标准每况愈下，这使得很多基础设施存在很大问题，需要整修。脱轨事件发生时，货物陷入困境，人员也难免遇难。

1970年~1975年修建的这条铁路线除了年久失修外，还遭到恣意破坏，这使得正常运营变得很困难。因此，中国政府免息提供的3900万贷款可谓是雪中送炭，这会挽救这家经营着1860千米铁路线的公司。

尽管这条铁路线是连接罗得西亚（正式名称津巴布韦共和国）、安哥拉、莫桑比克的一条替代线路，但这条线路亦非常有用，因为达累斯萨拉姆港是非常便捷的。

中国政府一直是雪中送炭的朋友，尤其是在坦赞铁路方面。这个"亚洲巨龙"曾出资5亿，用以在这块

fact better than some of them.

The Chinese government has always been an **all-weather** friend and particularly for TAZARA, the Asian giant **spearhead**ed the $500 million project in one of Africa's most rugged terrain.

Communications and Transport Minister Geoffrey Lungwangwa outlined that the money would be used to procure new **locomotive** engines, new wagons and repairing of 120 wagons. The money would also be used to rehabilitate the rail track and acquire equipment for the mechanical workshop. It is also important that security is tightened to safeguard equipment such as communication facilities along the stretch and the rail sleepers, which some **unscrupulous** people have **uproot**ed for sale.

Modern technology should be introduced while more training programmes must be initiated among employees to enhance capacity. Once new equipment has been acquired and the infrastructure **rehabilitate**d, there will be efficiency in service delivery and ultimately improve profit levels because clients would be attracted as a result of quality service.

Employees' salaries and conditions of service will also improve and the firm will have a motivated workforce.

TAZARA should therefore, be redeemed in earnest so that the country can reap the benefits and ensure that loan repayment is on course.

非洲极为坎坷的路上修建铁路。

信息与交通部长Geoffrey Lungwangwa指出钱会用在购买新机车发动机、新火车以及维修现有120辆火车、修复铁轨以及为机械车间添置设备上。当然，安全非常重要，要重视设施的安全，以防一些不道德的人偷窃。

另外，还要引入现代化的科学技术，在员工中间启动更多的培训项目，以提高他们的能力。一旦设施被购买，基础设施得到修缮，运力将会大大提供，公司利润也会上升。因为人们会被高质量的服务所吸引。公司会提高员工待遇以及服务质量，实行激励制度。

因此，坦赞铁路需要认真对待，这样国家才能获得利润，确保贷款的顺利偿还。

wear and tear：（正常使用造成的）损坏，损耗，用坏	unscrupulous：不道德的
rehabilitate改造，修复，恢复……的名誉	uproot：连根拔起，根除
facelift：整修，整容	vandalise：肆意破坏

95 中非合作及交流全面展开——中非合作论坛

The Creation of FOCAC:

In the 21st century, maintaining peace, seeking stability and promoting development have become a shared **aspiration** of people of all countries. In order to further strengthen the friendly cooperation between China and Africa under the new **circumstance**s, to jointly meet the challenge of economic **globalization** and to promote common development, and in light of suggestions of some African countries, the Chinese Government made the **proposal** on the **convocation** of the Forum on China-Africa Cooperation—**Ministerial Conference** Beijing 2000, which was positively responded to by the vast number of African countries.

Logo:

Red part of the LOGO is "C", standing for China; the whole LOGO is a letter "a", standing for Africa. Red colour stands for **vigorousness** and prosperity; Green colour stands for peace and development. The FOCAC LOGO represents unity and cooperation between China and Africa.

Characteristics of FOCAC:

The Forum on China-Africa Co-operation is a **platform** established by China and friendly African countries for collective consultation and dialogue and a cooperation mechanism between the developing countries, which falls into the category of South-South cooperation. The characteristics of the Forum are as follows:

Pragmatic Cooperation: Its purpose is to strengthen

论坛产生

进入21世纪，维护和平、谋求稳定、促进发展成为各国人民的共同愿望。为进一步加强中非在新形势下的友好合作，共同应对经济全球化挑战，促进共同发展，根据部分非洲国家的建议，中国政府倡议召开中非合作论坛北京2000年部长级会议，得到了广大非洲国家的积极响应。

会徽：

会徽左翼红色"C"代表中国，整个标志是字母"a"代表非洲，会徽寓意中非团结与合作，绿色象征和平与发展，红色表示活力与繁荣。

论坛特点：

中非合作论坛是中国与非洲友好国家建立的集体磋商与对话平台，是"南南合作"范畴内发展中国家之间的合作机制。其特点是：

务实合作：以加强磋商、扩大合作为宗旨，重在合作。

平等互利：政治对话与经贸合作并举，目的是彼此促

consultation and expand cooperation and its focus is on cooperation.

Equality and Mutual Benefit: It promotes both political dialogue and economic cooperation and trade, with a view to seeking mutual **reinforcement** and common development.

The First Ministerial Conference of FOCAC

It was held in Beijing from 10 to 12 October 2000.

China's top officials and African top officials attended the opening ceremony and the closing ceremony respectively and **deliver**ed important speeches.

More than 80 ministers from China and 44 African countries, representatives of 17 regional and international organizations, people from the business communities of China and Africa were invited to the conference. The conference **chart**ed the direction for the development of a new, stable and long-term partnership featuring equality and mutual benefit between China and African countries.

The Second Ministerial Conference of FOCAC

From 15 to 16 December 2003, it was **convene**d in Addis Ababa, capital of Ethiopia.

Chinese Premier Wen Jiabao, Ethiopian Prime Minister Meles Zenawi, six African presidents, three vice presidents, two other **prime minister**s, and one president of the senate as well as President Alpha Oumar Konare of the Commission of African Union and the representative of the UN Secretary General attended the opening ceremony and delivered speeches.

More than 70 ministers from China and 44 African countries responsible for foreign affairs and international economic cooperation and the representatives of some international and African regional organizations attended the conference.

The Third Ministerial Conference of FOCAC

It was held in Beijing from November 3 to 5, 2006. Hu Jintao, President of China, and heads of state or heads of government from African countries attended this Summit.

The Fourth Ministerial Conference of FOCAC

进，共同发展。

第一届

2000年10月10日至12日，中非合作论坛第一届部长级会议在北京举行。

中非双方领导人及高级官员分别出席开幕式和闭幕式，并发表重要讲话。

中国和44个非洲国家的80余名部长、17个国际和地区组织的代表，以及中非企业界人士应邀与会。会议为中国与非洲发展长期稳定、平等互利的新型伙伴关系确定了方向。

第二届：

2003年12月15－16日，中非合作论坛第二届部长级会议在埃塞俄比亚首都亚的斯亚贝巴举行。

时任中国国务院总理温家宝和埃塞俄比亚总理梅莱斯·泽纳维以及其他非洲国家的6位总统、3位副总统、2位总理、1位议长，以及非盟委员会主席阿尔法·乌马尔·科纳雷、联合国秘书长代表出席开幕式，并发表讲话。

中国和44个非洲国家负责外交和国际经济合作事务的70名部长及部分国际和非洲地区组织的代表参加会议。

第三届：

第三届部长级会议于2006年11月3日~5日在中国北京举行，时任中华人民共和国主席胡锦涛及非洲国家的元首、政府首脑或代表出席。

第四届：

The 4th Ministerial Conference of the China-Africa Cooperation Forum (FOCAC) wrapped up in the Egyptian Red Sea resort of Sharm el-Sheikh on Monday, with the adoption of the Declaration of Sharm el-Sheikh and Sharm el-Sheikh Action Plan, defining new programs of cooperation between the two sides in the next three years.

为期两天的中非合作论坛第四届部长级会议星期一在埃及海滨城市沙姆沙伊赫落下帷幕，会议通过了《中非合作论坛沙姆沙伊赫宣言》和《中非合作论坛－沙姆沙伊赫行动计划（2010年至2012年）》两份成果文件，明确了未来3年的中非合作方向。

aspiration：强烈的愿望，志向，抱负	platform：平台
circumstance：环境，情形，情况	pragmatic：实用主义的，实际的
globalization：全球化	reinforcement：增强，加固，增援力量
proposal：提议，建议，求婚	deliver：投递交，发表，接生，给予，解救
convocation：会议，召集	chart：制成图表，绘制地图，规划
Ministerial Conference：部长级会议	convene：开会，集合，召集
vigorousness：朝气蓬勃	prime minister：总理，首相

96 非洲和亚洲：发展伙伴——非行理事会年会

The 42nd Annual Meetings of the **Board of Governors** of the African Development Bank (AfDB) and the 33rd Annual Meetings of the Board of Governors of the African Development **Fund** (ADF), opened on May 15, 2007 in Shanghai, China, with calls for wider and mutually beneficial cooperation between Africa and China on the one hand and Africa and Asia on the other hand.

Chinese Premier, Wen Jiabao **preside**d over the o**pening session attend**ed by Presidents Pedro Pires of Cape Verde, Marc Ravalomanana of Madagascar and Paul Kagame of Rwanda, alongside with the Chair of the Board of Governors, Zhou

第42届非洲发展银行理事会年会和第33届非洲发展基金会理事会年会于2007年5月15日在中国上海隆重开幕。会议旨在扩大中非互利共赢合作以及更大范围的亚非合作。

国务院总理温家宝出席开幕式并致辞。佛得角总统皮雷斯、马达加斯加总统拉瓦卢马纳纳、卢旺达总统卡加梅、非洲开发银行行长卡贝鲁卡等出

Xiaochuan and Bank Group President Donald Kaberuka.

Mr. Wen **review**ed the **long-standing** relationship between China and Africa, noting that the annual meetings would surely boost relations between Africa and Asia as well as increase the Bank Group's global influence and its capacity to **leverage** partnerships for the development of Africa.

He underscored challenges Africa was facing as a result of globalization and assured that the Chinese government and people were committed to helping African countries **tackle** some of the challenges.

He said the country applied zero-**tariff** regime to exports of some least developed African countries to China and provided greater market access to African products. The Premier said his country would further expand market access in line with agreements reached by both sides during the Beijing Summit on China-Africa Cooperation in November last year.

"China will fully **deliver on** the commitments and is working with the African countries to **implement** the measures," he said, calling for the expansion of cooperation between the two sides for their mutual benefit.

China, he said, attached high importance to its cooperation with the AfDB and sub-regional development organizations in Africa, adding that the Chinese government was most willing to strengthen cooperation with other countries and international financial institutions.

Also speaking at the session, the governor of the People's (Central) Bank of China, Zhou Xiaochuan, described the gathering as "a fresh starting point for all parties to intensify cooperation and promote development in both Asia and Africa."

Two members of the Bank Group's high level panel, former President Joachim Chissano of Mozambique and former Canadian Prime Minister, Paul Martin also attended the meetings along with four former Bank Group Presidents – Messrs. Omar Kabbaj, Babacar Ndiaye, Wila Mung'Omba and Kwame Fordwor.

席会议。

温总理回顾了中非深厚的传统友谊。他认为，此次年会必将会促进亚非关系，增强非洲发展银行的国际影响力，提高非行平衡非洲发展合作方面的能力。

他强调了非洲国家因为全球化所面临的挑战，明确指出，中国政府和人民仍会致力于帮助非洲国家处理其中的一些挑战。

他说，中国已经对非洲一些欠发达国家实施零关税政策，并且提高了非洲商品进入中国市场的机会。温总理还说，中国还会根据中非合作论坛北京峰会中所达成的协议继续扩大非洲商品的市场准入。

"中国会全心全意实现承诺，将与非洲国家一道实现这些措施"，温总理说，他呼吁在双方互利的基础上进一步扩大合作。

他说，中国非常重视与非行及非洲次级区域发展机构的合作，中国政府非常愿意加强同其他国家以及国际金融机构的合作。

另外，会上发言的还有中央人民银行行长周小川。他称此次集会"对于所有与会方来说，都是加强合作，促进亚非发展的一个崭新起点。"

非行最高理事会两名成员，莫桑比克前总统若阿金·希萨诺，加拿大前首相保罗·马丁等也参加了此次会议。同时与会的还有四位前非行集团主席——Messrs. Omar Kabbaj, Babacar Ndiaye, Wila Mung'Omba and Kwame Fordwor.

board of governors：理事会	long-standing：长久的，经久不衰的
fund：基金会	leverage：力量，影响；杠杆作用
preside：主持	tackle：处理
opening session：开幕式	tariff：关税
review：回顾	implement：执行
attend：参加	deliver (on)：不负所望，履行承诺

背景知识 PROFILE

主要全球区域型国际合作金融机构

非洲发展银行(African Development Bank；AFDB)成立于1964年11月，总部原设于科特迪瓦经济中心Abidjan，但由于2002年政局不稳搬迁至突尼斯。非洲开发银行为非洲最大区域型国际合作开发机构。

1963年7月31日，在喀土穆举行的非洲国家财政会议通过协定，决定成立非洲发展银行。1964年9月正式成立。1966年7月开始营业。原规定只吸收非洲独立国家为成员国，1979年作修改，美、日、西德、加、法等21个非本地区国家加入。1985年5月有成员国75个(其中非洲国家54个)。其宗旨是"帮助非洲大陆制定总体战略"，"协调各国的发展计划"，为成员国的经济和社会 发展提供资金，以便达到"非洲经济的一体化"。与非洲发展基金等4个金融机构组成"非洲发展银行集团"。1980年为止已为非洲国家提供贷款达25亿美元。

宗旨：非洲发展银行宗旨为提供非洲机构贷款、加强非洲人力资源利用与促进成员国经济发展，优先对有利于地区经济合作与扩大成员国贸易项目提供资金与技术援助，并协助成员国研究、制定与执行经济发展计划。

欧洲复兴开发银行(European Bank for Reconstructionand Development, EBRD)是"二战"后由美国、日本及欧洲一些国家政府发起成立的银行，于1991年4月14日正式开业，总部设在伦敦。主要任务是帮助欧洲战后重建和复兴。该行的作用是帮助和支持东欧、中欧国家向市场经济转化。

建立欧洲复兴开发银行的设想是由法国总统密特朗于1989年10月首先提出来的，而后得到欧洲共同体各国和其他一些国家的积极响应。1991年，该银行拥有100亿欧洲货币单位（约合120亿美元）的资本。欧盟委员会（前欧洲共同体委员会）、欧洲投资银行和39个国家在银行中拥有股权。最大股份拥有者是美国，占10%，其次是法国、德国、意大利、日本和英国各占8.5%，东欧国家总共拥有股份11.9%，其中前苏联占有6%。

董事会主席任银行行长，行长任期4年。截至2000年5月，该银行共拥有61个成员（包括59个成员国和2个国际机构：欧洲联盟和欧洲投资银行。）

宗旨：在考虑加强民主、尊重人权、保护环境等因素下，帮助和支持东欧、中欧国家向市场经济转化，以调动上述国家中个人及企业的积极性，促使他们向民主政体和市场经济过渡。

欧洲投资银行（European Investment Bank, EIB）是欧洲经济共同体成员国合资经营的金融机构。根据1957年《建立欧洲经济共同体条约》（《罗马条约》）的规定，于1958年1月1日成立，1959年正式开业。总行设在卢森堡。

宗旨：利用国际资本市场和共同体内部资金，促进共同体的平衡和稳定发展。

国际清算银行（Bank for International Settlements, BIS）是英、法、德、意、比、日等国的中央银行与代表美国银行界利益的摩根银行、纽约和芝加哥的花旗银行组成的银团，根据海牙国际协定于1930年5月共同组建的，总部设在瑞士巴塞尔。刚建立时只有7个成员国，现成员国已发展至45个。

此外还有亚洲开发银行、泛美开发银行与加勒比开发银行等。

97 非营利性社会机构——中非国家贸易促进会

China-Africa Countries Trade Promotion Association is a **non-profit** social organization which is established under the approval of the **State Council** and the **Ministry of Civil Affairs**. Its **mission** is to promote China-Africa trade and cooperation, to strengthen the mutual understanding and friendship between Sino-African enterprises, to expand the products exportation and **contribute** to the **undertaking** by China in building a **well-off** and harmonious society in an all-around way.

China-Africa Countries Trade Promotion Association strives to develop foreign trade, to make good use of foreign capital, import foreign **advanced technology** as well as carry out all kinds of economic and technical cooperation home and abroad. Meanwhile we are responsible for promoting trade and economic relationship with African countries and regions thus to enhance the friendship and understanding

中国—非洲国家贸易促进会是在国务院和民政部批准下成立的社会团体，其宗旨是本着互利共赢原则，推动中非贸易交流与合作，增强中国—非洲国家企业之间的相互了解和友谊，扩大产品出口，繁荣社会主义经济，为我国全面建设小康社会和构建社会和谐做贡献。

中非贸促会积极开展对外贸易、利用外资、引进外国先进技术及开展各种形式的中外经济技术合作等活动，促进中国同非洲各国、各地区之间的贸易和经济关系的发展，

between China and African trade and economic sectors.

The aim of China-Africa Countries Trade Promotion Association is to serve economic and trade enterprises of China and Africa, to promote economic and trade development between China and Africa, to carry forward the cooperation spirit of FOCAC, to make great efforts to compose a new chapter of china-Africa cooperation in order to build the bridge for China-Africa cooperation and communication to further share the results of FOCAC in 2006. We seek to expand new cooperation areas between China and Africa, to provide trade platform for Chinese companies to invest in Africa also to offer African enterprises and relevant units a chance to get familiar with the Chinese social customs and culture and to seek commercial opportunities.

China-Africa Countries Trade Promotion Association takes the tasks listed below as its core mission, that is, to conduct market investigation and analysis, to help member enterprises to find the development opportunities to tap the potential market in African continent and neighboring countries; to provide the information and data on economic, political, management and trade, to enlarge member enterprises' perception in expanding their business and development; to hold **forum** and training session on expertise and professional knowledge under various form to sharpen member enterprises' **competitive edge**; to organize business trips and to set up exposition, promotion marketing saloon and business and industry cooperation discussion, to serve as a business and trade plat-form for member enterprises; to propagate member enterprises' operation performance and achievements to uplift their reputation and social image. Our association expect to joint hands with entrepreneurs and friends from all walks of African countries to make efforts for the friendship and cooperation between China and Africa.

China-Africa Countries Trade Promotion Association will achieve one success after another and play ever growing important role in Sino-Africa trade and cooperation.

增进中非经贸界之间的友谊与了解。

中非贸促会的宗旨是：服务中非经贸企业，促进中非经贸发展，发扬2006中非论坛的合作精神，努力开创中非经贸合作的新篇章，进一步加强中非之间沟通合作的桥梁，进一步发展2006中非论坛的成果，寻求并扩展中非之间新领域合作，给中国企业提供到非洲投资的贸易平台，给非洲企业和相关单位了解中国民俗文化以及寻找商机的平台。

本会的任务是：开展市场调研和市场分析，帮助会员企业寻找发展机遇，开辟非洲各国及周边国家市场；为会员企业提供经济、政策、科技、管理和贸易信息，拓宽会员企业发展思路；举办各种形式的论坛和专业知识培训，提高会员企业竞争力；组织商务考察和举办展览、展销和商务洽谈会，为会员企业搭建商贸平台；开展法律咨询服务，维护会员企业合法权益；宣传会员企业经营业绩，扩大会员企业影响，提高会员企业知名度。促进会期望与非洲各国企业家，各界朋友携手，为中非友谊与合作而努力。

促进会一定会越办越好，在中非贸易中发挥越来越大的作用！

non-profit：非营利性的	well-off：小康的
State Council：国务院	advanced technology：先进技术
Ministry of Civil Affairs：民政部	forum：论坛
mission：使命，任务	competitive edge：竞争优势
converge：捐款，贡献，有助于	undertaking：事业

背景知识 **P**ROFILE

中非贸易现状

近年来，随着中非经贸关系的不断深化，中国内地自非进口额不断扩大，2004年至2008年保持着年均35%以上的增长率。2010年一季度中非双边贸易额达到278亿美元，为历年同期最高，同比增长76%。其中，中国内地自非进口152亿美元，同比增长167%。2009年，中非贸易额为910.7亿美元，中国成为非洲第一大贸易伙伴国。

98 非洲展示独特魅力——非洲亮相世博会

Africa is a unique continent which is rich in civilization, culture and colorful social life and its **participation** in the Shanghai World **Expo** is **inseparable** to the success of such a big event, Chinese Ambassador to Kenya Deng Hongbo said on Wednesday.

In an interview with Xinhua, Deng Hongbo said that the Shanghai World Expo is a golden opportunity not only for China to **display** itself as a country with long history in civilization but also serves as an important **platform** for China to **strengthen** exchanges and **promote** understanding with the rest of the world.

"This is a very good and important stage for the countries to learn from each other. The participation of the African countries in the World Expo will provide

"非洲国家拥有丰富、独特的人文文化和多彩的社会生活，非洲国家的积极参与是上海世博会不可或缺的重要组成部分"，中国驻肯尼亚大使邓洪波24日在接受新华社记者专访时说。

邓洪波说，上海世博会不仅对于中国来说是一个展示自己的机会，而且也为中国提供了一个重要的平台，在此与世界其他国家加强交流，增进理解。

"对于各国来说，上海世博会提供了一个可以互相学习的平台。非洲国家积极参与世博会为

the Chinese people with a very good chance to better understand Africa and the African people's **achievement**s in their economic, social, cultural and technological development."

The ambassador **stress**ed that Africa has played a very positive and active role in participating in the Shanghai World Expo by **register**ing a record high number of 50 African nations which are ready to attend the event. "So far the preparation for Africa's participation in the World Expo is under way and going smoothly."

With regard to China's assistance to African nations' participation, Deng said the Chinese government has attached special attention to the facilitation of African countries' participation through various formalities including visa, information provision, logistics and financial support.

Meanwhile, Deng also termed the Shanghai World Expo as a good opportunity for China and Africa to further promote **bilateral** relations and mutual beneficial cooperation, which, according to him, is not just in the economic and technological fields but also in the cultural, social and people to people exchange sectors.

The ambassador said he strongly believes that after the Shanghai World Expo there will be better understanding between China and Africa and the exchanges and cooperation between the two sides will be further **expand**ed and intensified.

"Further substantial, mutual and beneficial cooperation between China and Africa in the years ahead will benefit the interests of our two peoples."

The Shanghai World Expo is an international exposition that will take place from May 1 to October 31 this year and cover a surface of more than 5 square km in Shanghai, under its main theme of "Better City, Better Life".

It is expected to attract 70 million people from the public and private sectors, civil society, international organizations and others. As far as now, 242 participants have confirmed their presence.

中国人们提供了一个绝佳的机会，借此机会，中国人们可以更好地了解非洲，了解非洲人民在经济、社会、文化和科技发展中的进程。"

邓洪波强调，非洲高达50个国家准备好参展，他们起到了非常正面、积极的作用。"到目前为止，非洲各国都在筹备当中，工作进展顺利。"

邓洪波说，中国方面同时为非洲国家参展提供了各种方面措施，如护照，提供信息，物流以及资金支持。

同时，邓洪波称上海世博会为进一步提升中非关系，增强互利合作提供了契机。这不仅仅指的是经济、科技领域，也涵盖文化、社会及人员交流方面。

邓洪波坚信，上海世博会后，中非之间将增进理解，加深交流和合作。

"中非进一步实质性、互利共赢的合作将符合双方人民的共同利益。"

世博会是一场国际盛会，于2010年5月1日至10月31日在中国上海举行，占地5平方公里，主题是"城市，让生活更美好"。

预计，将有7000万人来华观世博。目前，全球已有242个国家和国际机构或组织确认参展。

——摘自中国驻肯尼亚大使世博会展前讲话

participation：参加，参与	promote：提升，促销
exposition (expo)：展览	achievement：成就
inseparable：分不开的，不可分离的	stress：强调
display：展示	register：注册
platform：平台	bilateral：双边的
strengthen：加强，强化	expand：扩展

背景知识 **P**ROFILE

阿尔及利亚民族院议长世博会访谈（摘录）

记者：阿尔及利亚方面积极参加了此次上海世博会，在参观了非洲联合馆和阿尔及利亚馆之后，请您谈谈观感。

议长："每一个国家的场馆都反映了这个国家所取得成就，尤其是非洲联合馆，不仅反映了非洲各国的发展，更反映了非洲大陆的古老文化和对明天美好生活的向往，以及把光辉灿烂的过去在未来重现的雄心壮志。当然，由于时间的限制，我不能把所有的场馆都一一参观完毕，毫无疑问所有的场馆都非常精彩。本次世博会的主题是关于城市的，关于现在的城市和未来的城市，我们注意到，在阿尔及利亚馆中所展示的这个生活的场景，正是紧紧地与这届世博会的主题联系在一起。"

记者：阁下此次代表总统先生出席开幕式，表示阿尔及利亚方面对发展两国友好关系的高度重视，请您谈谈两国关系的发展前景。

议长："总统先生对与中国的关系特别关注，因为他知道两国的关系十分重要，非常清楚中方发展两国关系的诚意，无论是高层的还是民间的。阿中两国的友好关系有着非常悠久的历史，它产生于两国为了自由和独立的共同斗争。我们非常清楚地记得中国对阿尔及利亚的支持，我们对此表示崇高敬意。在过去的几年里，两国关系有了质的飞跃。总统先生曾多次访问中国，参加一些在中国举行的重大国际活动。同时，胡锦涛主席和其它一些中国领导人也多次访问了阿尔及利亚。阿中两国的战略合作水平不断提高，两国间的项目涉及诸多领域，如阿境内的高速路、塔玛拉石输水管工程等等以及其它的一些项目。这些都体现了阿尔及利亚要把阿中关系发展成为国与国关系的典范的良好意愿。毫无疑问两国合作的前景将更为广阔，我们希望不断发展两国关系，为两国、两国人民带来更大利益。"

99 世界的汉语热潮——汉语文化节

In the evening of November 4, 2010, cheerful chatting and **laughter** filled in the teaching building of the Modern Language Department of University of Ghana. Chinese Ambassador to Ghana Gong Jianzhong with wife, University President Mr. Aidy and **faculty** members gathered with nearly 200 students and fans of Chinese language on and off campus to appreciate the performances of the Second Chinese Cultural Festival with great interest. Well-**rehearse**d comedies and dances and clear and fluent speeches in Chinese won warm applause time and again. The performers **interact**ed with the audience in dialogues as if the whole **auditorium** had turned into a happy classroom of Chinese language.

After the performance, Ambassador Gong presented the Best Performance prize to the students and gave a warm speech. He thanked the students for their full devotion to the performance, and praised the results that they achieved in learning. Gong introduced China's development to the students, highlighting the remarkable achievements China had made in development. But he pointed out that China was still a developing country like Ghana, and was faced with a **daunting** task in development. Gong spoke highly of the traditional friendship between China and Ghana, saying that China was willing to work together with Ghana in mutual support to seek common development and create a better future for the peoples of both countries.

Gong fully acknowledged the achievements in cultural exchanges between the two countries, noting that the increasingly close bilateral relationship had raised new requirements on bilateral cultural and educational exchanges. As a tool of communication and carrier of culture, language plays an increasingly prominent role

2010年11月4日晚，加纳大学现代语言系教学楼内欢声笑语不断，驻加纳大使龚建忠夫妇和加纳大学校长阿依蒂先生以及全校各院系负责人和教师，与该系近200名汉语专业学生和校内外的中文爱好者欢聚一堂，兴趣盎然地欣赏加纳大学第二届汉语文化节汇报演出。同学们精心排演的中文小品和歌舞、清楚流利的汉语演讲等节目，不时赢得观众们的热烈掌声。台上表演者与台下观看者交流互动，有问有答，一唱一和，俨然将整个演出现场变成了快乐的汉语教室。

表演结束后，龚大使向获得最佳表演奖的学生颁发了奖品，并发表了热情洋溢的演讲。他感谢同学们精彩投入的演出，称赞他们在汉语学习中取得的好成绩。龚大使向同学们介绍了中国的发展现状，强调中国发展取得了举世瞩目的成就，但中国与加纳一样仍是发展中国家，面临着艰巨的发展任务。龚大使高度评价中加传统友谊，表示中国愿与加纳携手努力，相互支持，共同发展，为两国人民创造更加美好的未来。

龚大使充分肯定两国文化交流取得的成绩，指出日益密切的中加关系对双边文化教育交流提出了新的要求。语言作为交流的工具和文化的载体，在两国交往中的作用日渐突出。他殷切期望有更多的加

in the exchanges between the two countries. He earnestly hoped that more young people would learn Chinese language in Ghana and become a bridge between the two peoples. He hoped the younger generation could take over the torch of China-Ghana friendship, strengthen exchanges and mutual learning and **shoulder** the responsibility of promoting in-depth development of China-Ghana relations.

President Aidy welcomed Gong to the University of Ghana and watched the performance. He **recall**ed the experiences of setting up Chinese language learning program in University of Ghana, and thanked the Chinese embassy for its great support to the campus education activities. He was very satisfied with the achievements the students had made. Aidy said that the excellent performance of the students had proved the establishment of Chinese language learning was a right decision of strategic vision. He encouraged the teachers and students to continue to keep their leading position in Chinese language teaching in Ghana.

Since the Chinese Culture Festival in University of Ghana was **launch**ed for the first time last year, it has become an important platform for promoting Chinese language and culture in Ghana. Spanning across three days, the Second Chinese Cultural Festival is divided into several parts such as speech contest, short play, music and dance performances, and making and displaying of traditional handicrafts in Chinese language. Under the guidance and organization of the teachers of Chinese from China, the students worked out a wonderful program by virtue of their passion for learning Chinese. It makes the festival an effective test of the achievements of the Chinese language teaching and touches off a "China **whirlwind**" on the campus.

纳青年学习汉语，成为促进两国人民沟通的桥梁。他希望两国年轻一代接过中加友谊的火炬，加强交流互鉴，肩负起推动中加关系深入发展的重任。

阿依蒂校长欢迎龚大使光临加纳大学并观看演出。他回顾了加纳大学开设汉语专业的历程，感谢使馆对该校开展汉语教育提供的大力支持，为同学们取得的成绩感到高兴。他表示，同学们的精彩表演证明，成立汉语专业是一个有战略眼光的正确决定，他鼓励师生们再接再厉，继续保持该校在加纳汉语教学领域的领先地位。

加纳大学汉语文化节自去年首次举办以来，已成为在加纳推广汉语、宣传中国文化的重要平台。本届汉语文化节为期3天，分为汉语演讲比赛、中文小品、歌舞表演、用汉语对中国传统手工艺品制作和展示等几个单元。学生们在中国公派中文教师的带领和组织下，凭借对汉语的热情创作了精彩的节目，使文化节成为对加纳大学汉语教学成果的有效检验，在加纳大学校园内掀起一阵"中国风"。

laughter：笑声	daunting：令人畏惧的
faculty：全体教员	shoulder：承担
rehearse：排练	recall：回忆
interact：互动	launch：发起，推出（新产品），发射
auditorium：观众席，听众席	whirlwind：旋风

背景知识 PROFILE

孔子学院简介

为发展中国与世界各国的友好关系，增进世界各国人民对中国语言文化的理解，为各国汉语学习者提供方便、优良的学习条件，中国国家对外汉语教学领导小组办公室将在世界上有需求、有条件的若干国家建设以开展汉语教学为主要活动内容的"孔子学院"，并在中国北京设立"孔子学院总部"。

孔子的学说传到西方，是从400多年前意大利传教士把记录孔子言行的《论语》一书译成拉丁文带到欧洲开始的。而今，孔子学说已走向了五大洲，各国孔子学院的建立，正是孔子"四海之内皆兄弟""和而不同"以及"君子以文会友，以友辅仁"思想的现实实践。

孔子学院，即孔子学堂（Confucius Institute），它并非一般意义上的大学，而是推广汉语和传播中国文化与国学的教育和文化交流机构，是一个非营利性的社会公益机构，一般都是下设在国外的大学和研究院之类的教育机构里。孔子学院最重要的一项工作就是给世界各地的汉语学习者提供规范、权威的现代汉语教材；提供最正规、最主要的汉语教学渠道。孔子学院总部（Confucius Institute Headquarters）设在北京，2007年4月9日挂牌。境外的孔子学院都是其分支机构，主要采用中外合作的形式开办。孔子是中国传统文化的代表人物，选择孔子作为汉语教学品牌是中国传统文化复兴的标志。为推广汉语文化，中国政府在1987年成立了"国家对外汉语教学领导小组"，简称为"汉办"，孔子学院就是由"汉办"承办的。它秉承孔子"和为贵"、"和而不同"的理念，推动中国文化与世界各国文化的交流与融合，以建设一个持久和平、共同繁荣的和谐世界为宗旨。不列颠哥伦比亚大学中文教授、加拿大中文协会会长陈山木先生是本计划的最早倡议者。中国国家领导人非常重视孔子学院的建设发展，许多孔子学院的授牌挂牌仪式都有国家相关领导人参加，2009年习近平副主席亲自参与挂牌仪式的就有3个，未来中国向世界出口的最有影响力的产品不是衣服等有形物，而是中国文化及国学。自2004年11月全球首家孔子学院在韩国成立以来，已有超过300家孔子学院遍布全球近百个国家和地区（美国及欧洲最多），成为推广汉语教学、传播中国文化及国学的全球品牌和平台。

目前，孔子学院各大洲都有，其中截至2009年10月，非洲有15国家开办了21所孔子学院。

100 非洲国家庆祝中国传统节日——塞舌尔龙舟节

Accompanying Senegalese National Assembly Speaker Mamaduke Seck (transliteration), Gong Yuanxing, Chinese Ambassador to Senegal, attended the opening ceremony of First M' bao International Dragon Boat and Canoe Race in Senegal on March 4, 2011. Some **senior** local officials and embassy staff were also present, including Bly Sawyer, Senegalese Minister of Culture and **Entertainment**, Baba Farrar, Vice Governor of Biji Na (transliteration), and She Mingyuan, cultural **counselor** of the embassy. President of the International Dragon Boat Federation, Ambassador Gong and Speaker Seck delivered warm speeches at the opening ceremony **respectively**.

Gong expressed his happiness to see M' bao town of the Dakar region to hold the International Dragon Boat and Canoe Race, and sincere wish for the event to succeed. He pointed out that Dragon Boat Race has a long history in China and is widely popular among the Chinese people as a cultural and sports activity. Having strong national characteristics, it reflects the spirit of working together in the same boat and racing forward with courage. It has become a major international event loved by peoples all over the world. He believed the event would play a positive role in promoting tourism, environmental protection, cultural and **socio-economic** development at M' bao.

Speaker Seck expressed his sincere thanks in his speech for the Chinese Embassy's valuable support and the athletes from different countries for actively participating in the race. He noted that it was the first time for an African country to host an international dragon boat and canoe race and it had a long-lasting and **far-reaching** significance. Seck said M' bao is an under-developed region facing pollution and destruction of the local forests and water sources. The race would raise the awareness for environmental protection,

2011年3月4日，驻塞内加尔大使龚元兴陪同塞国民议会议长马马杜·塞克出席"首届姆巴奥国际龙舟和独木舟赛"开幕式。塞文化和娱乐部长布莱·索耶、比基纳省副省长巴巴·法勒、使馆文化参赞佘明远等陪同。国际龙舟联合会主席以及龚元兴大使、塞克议长在开幕式上发表了热情讲话。

龚大使对达喀尔大区姆巴奥镇举办国际龙舟和独木舟赛表示非常高兴，由衷祝愿本届比赛取得圆满成功。龚大使指出，"龙舟赛"是中华民族历史悠久、流传广泛、深受中国人民喜爱的一项文化和体育运动，具有浓厚的民族特色，体现了同舟共济、勇往直前的拼搏精神，并已成为一项深受世界各国人民喜爱的重要国际赛事。他相信，此次赛事对促进姆巴奥的旅游、环保、文化和社会经济的发展将产生积极的推动作用。

塞国民议会议长塞克在讲话中对中国大使馆的宝贵支持和各国健儿踊跃参赛表示衷心感谢，并指出这是黑非洲首次举办国际龙舟和独木舟赛，影响深远。塞克表示，姆巴奥地区发展滞后，森林、水系面临

push the fishermen to work in unity and help each other out, and advance the local economic development, said Seck.

The opening ceremony drew in a large crowd of **spectator**s, bustling with noises and excitement. Athletes from different countries wore red headbands **embroider**ed with Chinese-style dragon, looking smart. The performance of traditional dances and drumming by the locals pushed the atmosphere to a height. The national flags of China and Senegal **flutter**ing in the wind appeared brilliant against the background of beautiful sunlight and white beach, like spectacular **sparkle**s created in the encounter of different cultures.

This year's Dragon Boat Race is co-sponsored by the M' baoregional government, sailing clubs, Senegalese Rowing Federation and International Dragon Boat Federation. The International Dragon Boat Association sent a number of teams including those from France, Germany and Britain, to take part in the event. The Chinese Embassy provided materials such as themed T-shirts, scarves, and accessories to the race.

污染破坏，本届比赛将提高人们环保意识，促进渔民团结互助，带动当地经济发展。

开幕式现场人山人海，热闹非凡。各国健儿头戴绣有中国龙的红色头巾，煞是好看。颇具黑人特色的传统舞蹈和击鼓奏乐更是将现场气氛推向高潮。迎风飘扬的中塞两国国旗在明媚的阳光和白色的沙滩映衬下愈加鲜艳，仿佛各国文化交融碰撞产生的美丽火花。

该届龙舟赛由姆巴奥地区政府、航海俱乐部、塞赛艇联合会、国际龙舟联合会共同举办，国际龙舟协会派出了法国、德国、英国等多支队伍参赛。我国使馆为比赛提供了文化衫、头巾、饰品等物资。

词汇 VOCABULARY

senior：高级的	far-reaching：深远的，伸至远处的，广大的
entertainment：娱乐	spectator：观众
counselor：顾问；参赞；律师	embroider：刺绣，修饰
respectively：分别地	flutter：飞舞
socio-economic：社会经济的	sparkle：闪光，闪烁，活力

背景知识 PROFILE

中国节日在世界

　　曾在数千年历史中极大影响过东亚地区的中国传统节日，如今在世界上的影响更加广泛。据媒体报道，虎年春节，世界各地许多地方的"中国年"都过得红红火火，热闹非凡。除了旅居这些国家的华人华侨外，很多外籍人士也起劲地过起中国新年来。那些被随机采访的老外小外、男外女外们，对着电视镜头都能说出中国春节的不少道道来。他们知道中国人过年要放鞭炮、吃饺子、回家团圆。他们也知道中国的每一年都有一种Animal（动物）与之相应。毋论东亚东南亚，欧美许多地方都办起了"春节庙会"，荷兰的海牙市甚至喊出了"春节是中荷两国民众共同的节日"的口号。看到这样的场景，心里自然是高兴的：在前若干年咱"哈"完这家"哈"那家后，终于，别人家也如此这般地"哈"起咱们国家来了！

于是，中国人应该如何向世人推广自己的传统节日，被提到议事日程上来了。

当然，海外的中国春节，并不是从虎年开始的。荷兰海牙"中国春节庙会"已搞了十来年，日本名古屋的"中国春节祭"，也已举办数届了。甚而至于前几年美国还冒出过一个博士，呼吁"抵制中国新年"的。可是不但没能抵制得住，反而更加红火起来了。春节在纽约已经被规定为法定假日，不管是不是华人华侨，这一天都可以休假。这说明，中国春节今在海外，已然走出了"唐人街"，向更广泛的社会范畴、社会群体蔓延。有人说，现在全球至少有40亿人过春节。